Acclaim for Chris Mackey a

THE INTERRO___

Task Force 500 and America's Secret War against Al Qaeda

"Fascinating. . . . If you've ever found yourself wondering what it's like behind the scenes in the new war against terrorism, here's your answer: a game of cat and mouse in which a player's wit is his only weapon. . . . These are real men and women struggling with difficult moral issues — and most often taking the high road, rather than the one that leads to naked human pyramids and vicious dog bites. . . . A riveting read."
— Patti Thorn, *Rocky Mountain News*

"Watching Mackey agonize over the ethics of his techniques provides rare insight into a process that, in the wake of Abu Ghraib, we urgently need to understand." — Lev Grossman, *Time*

"Only the handful of Americans who participate directly in the interrogations of prisoners can describe these battles of psychology and intellect, of will instead of weaponry — battles that the public never sees. . . . Mackey and Miller offer an illuminating examination of the psychology and physiology of lying and determining whether someone is telling the truth." — Forbes.com

"This fascinating memoir reports from one of the most crucial and controversial fronts in the war on terror. . . . Full of the engrossing lore and procedure of interrogation, the thrust and parry of baited queries and cagey half-truths, and the occasional dramatic breakthrough when a prisoner cracks. . . . A vivid, gritty look at the pressures and compromises attendant on this unconventional war." — *Publishers Weekly* (starred review)

"A close-up view of a number of terrorists is provided by *The Interrogators,* a fascinating insider's account by the supervisor of U.S. military interrogations in Afghanistan during the pre–Abu Ghraib period. The book discusses a range of interrogation techniques, from the well-known 'Good Cop, Bad Cop' to less obvious approaches such as one termed 'the Befuddled Interrogator.'"

— Peter Bergen, *Washington Post*

"A nicely balanced, insightful work."

— Justin Marozzi, *Evening Standard*

"Highly readable. . . . *The Interrogators* weaves scenes of Army life with accounts of the different personalities encountered within the confines of the interrogation booth, including the self-possessed teenager who is recruited as a spy and Taliban fighters claiming to be farmers to an evasive member of Al Qaeda. . . . Mackey describes the techniques and wiles used by interrogators in a grueling war of wits in the fight against terrorism, a nontraditional war where knowledge is the chief weapon."

— Eva Ciabatoni, *Los Altos Town Crier*

"Working round the clock, Mackey and his team had to discard outmoded Cold War interrogation techniques and evolve breakthrough psychological strategies and complex mind games. But the interrogators too were under immense pressure; relentlessly matching their wits against suspected fanatics, ever fearful that their prisoners might know of another 9/11, but constrained from unleashing their tempers by the Geneva Conventions, it was not always just the prisoners who cracked. . . . Mackey's compelling picture of the exhausting interrogations and pressure-cooker atmosphere which built up under the relentless Afghan sun gives a troubling insight into the temptations and obstacles in the path of sound military judgment. But it is also a testament to the strength of character of those many interrogators who remained professional, rational, and played by the rules." — *Eye Spy*

THE
INTERROGATORS

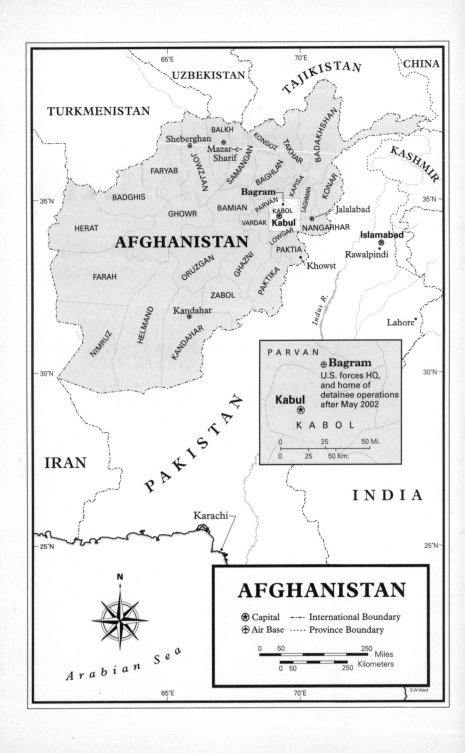

THE INTERROGATORS

TASK FORCE 500 AND AMERICA'S SECRET WAR AGAINST AL QAEDA

CHRIS MACKEY
and GREG MILLER

BACK BAY BOOKS
Little, Brown and Company
NEW YORK   BOSTON

Back Bay Books/Little, Brown and Company
Time Warner Book Group
1271 Avenue of the Americas, New York, NY 10020
Visit our Web site at www.twbookmark.com

Originally published in hardcover
by Little, Brown and Company, July 2004
First Back Bay paperback edition, May 2005

Library of Congress Cataloging-in-Publication Data

Mackey, Chris.
  The interrogators : Task Force 500 and America's secret war
against Al Qaeda / Chris Mackey and Greg Miller. — 1st ed.
    p. cm.
  ISBN 0-316-87112-5 (hc) / 0-316-01153-3 (pb)
  1. Afghan War, 2001– — Prisoners and prisons, American.
2. Afghan War, 2001– — Military intelligence. 3. Afghan War,
2001– — Personal narratives, American. 4. Military interrogation —
Afghanistan. 5. Military interrogation — United States. 6. Mackey,
Chris. I. Miller, Greg. II. Title.

DS371.414.M33 2004
958.104'7 — dc22

                                                    2004011892

            10 9 8 7 6 5 4 3 2 1

                        Q-MART

        Printed in the United States of America

To the memory of Sgt. David Travis Friedrich,
who fell fighting for his country in Iraq and never failed to
Put New England First

And to Kerri Miller, for her patience and unwavering support

CONTENTS

PART III

PART IV

CAST OF CHARACTERS

Aier, Hafiz   British prisoner who spoke flawless Arabic.

Atley, Tim   Specialist, 500th MI Battalion (Fort Gordon, Georgia). Mackey translated for Atley (a Spanish linguist) the first time he confronted a prisoner. Later played opposite Singhal during the interrogation of the brothers with a "missile" in their basement.

Berrara, Jim   Specialist, interrogator (Russian linguist), 325th MI Battalion (Reserves). A member of Mackey's reserve unit and part of the relief unit sent to replace Task Force 500 in August.

Booker, Luke   Major, Colorado national guardsman who joined Task Force 500 in February as an Uzbek linguist. His mature appearance made him a successful character actor — he became an "FBI agent" whenever an approach called for such a prop.

Carlson, Jamie   Specialist, analyst, 500th MI Battalion. Part of the original Task Force 500 element in Afghanistan and responsible (at age nineteen) for analysis and research related to interrogations.

Cassidy, Evan   Staff sergeant, interrogator (German linguist), L.A. National Guard. Cassidy was left at Kandahar after major interrogation operations were concluded; he eventually rejoined what was left of the main body of the task force when Kandahar was completely closed in July.

Cathcart, David   Sergeant, interrogator (Russian linguist), 103rd MI Battalion. Cathcart was part of the Serial 93 element that originally deployed to Kandahar.

Cavanaugh, Tom   Sergeant, interrogator (Russian linguist), 519th MI Battalion (Airborne). Fitzgerald dubbed him the Celtic Warrior Reborn, and this tall Philadelphian used his imposing size — coupled with a booming voice — to great advantage. Although critics called his technique one-dimensional, his energetic tactics were almost the sole source of success in the earliest days of the deployment.

Corcoran, Dan   Specialist, interrogator (Arabic linguist), 519th MI Battalion (Airborne).

Dawson, Kim   Warrant officer class 2 ("sergeant major"), serving with the intelligence corps of one of our coalition allies. Leading his country's interrogation section, Kim spent most of his time in the U.S. Facility. His experience was broad and included service in counterterrorism operations in East Timor.

Davis, Ben   Sergeant, interrogator (Arabic), 103rd MI Battalion. The quiet Cape Codder was one of the finest interrogators and a top Arabic linguist, noted for his unnervingly careful delivery during questioning. Prisoners could not know his most potent weapon was his capacity for forensic research.

Eamon   Civilian, FBI.

Ellis, Bill   Warrant officer class 2 ("sergeant major"), member of one of our major coalition allies' military intelligence teams and their senior interrogator in Bagram. Ellis literally wrote the book on his country's interrogation techniques. His vast experience and good nature made him an invaluable asset to the U.S. interrogators.

Fields, Specialist   Specialist, interrogator, Arabic linguist, 500th MI Battation. Fields led the interrogation of Ghul Jan while he was still in Bagram; when he "got too close" to the prisoner, both Fields and Ghul Jan came to Kandahar, where Fitzgerald took over — before being replaced himself by Lillian, an agent from OGA.

Finch, Lt.   Executive officer of "C" Company, 500th MI Battalion. Took over as company commander when Rawles left the theater due to illness.

Fitzgerald, Geoff Sergeant, interrogator (Arabic linguist), 325th MI Battalion (Reserves). A highly talented interrogator, Fitzgerald was friends with Mackey from Fordham University. His larger-than-life personality and renowned humor made him a major personality among the interrogators.

Gibbs, Kate Major, engineers, unit affiliation unknown. Replaced Vaughn and Hartmann as the liaison between the interrogators and the Joint Working Group.

Grenauld, Jamie Staff sergeant, interrogator (Russian linguist), 323rd MI Battalion (Reserves). Day-shift senior interrogator at Kandahar.

Guilford, First Sergeant Most senior sergeant in "A" Company, 500th MI Battalion. In charge of "beans and bullets" (day-to-day operations) in Bagram.

Harper, Paul Sergeant, counterintelligence agent, 500th MI Battalion. Assigned to detainee operations as a "high side" (top secret–level clearance) analyst. At Bagram he also questioned detainees connected with suspected acts of espionage. Fiancé to Walker.

Hartmann, Major Major, Judge Advocate General Corps, V Corps. A reservist from New York, Hartmann was the main liaison between the Joint Working Group and the Facility's interrogators.

Hasegawa, Henry Ritsuo ("Haas") Sergeant, interrogator (Spanish linguist), 519th MI Battalion (Airborne). Because of lack of Arabic, Hasegawa started his deployment as the clerk in the ICE. He eventually teamed up with Davis (and then later Kampf) to become perhaps the most talented interrogator in the task force. His stamina, ruthless questioning style, and relentless desire to support combat operations were unparalleled.

Heaney, Gary Sergeant, interrogator (Arabic linguist), 323rd MI Battalion (Reserves). Heaney took over prisoner in-processing when the great Shami left and developed his own trademarks of fear-inspiring screening. He was the first interrogator new prisoners would encounter.

Hedder, Paul Staff sergeant, interrogator (Russian linguist), 519th MI Battalion (Airborne). Replaced the author as senior interrogator in August 2002.

Holmes, Mark Major, 519th MI Battalion (Airborne). Leader of the advance party that paved the way for Task Force 500's replacements in August 2002.

Howe, John Warrant officer 4. The liaison officer between signals intelligence and the interrogators.

Irvine, Chris Warrant officer 2, 519th MI Battalion (Airborne). Daytime shift officer-in-charge of the ICE in Kandahar. Known to Fitzgerald as "the ratmaster."

John Civilian, FBI.

Kampf, Ethan Sergeant, interrogator (Arabic linguist), 519th MI Battalion (Airborne). One of the top interrogators and best linguists, Kampf was among the team that pioneered new interrogation techniques to break the toughest prisoners.

Kane, Jim Major, counterintelligence agent, USMC. Appointed the liaison between Joint Task Force 180 (XVIII Airborne Corps), which ran the war on the ground, and Task Force 500, the unit responsible for questioning detainees.

Kavalesk, Victor Sergeant, interrogator (Russian linguist), 500th MI Battalion. Reinforced Task Force 500 from its parent unit, the 500th MI Battalion, in June 2002.

Kelleher, Jimmy Sergeant, interrogator (Russian linguist), 325th MI Battalion (Reserves). Deployed with Mackey as a reservist when the unit was called up; spent most of the war at Fort Bragg, but was among the unit who replaced Mackey's when Task Force 500 was relieved.

Laughton, Dawn Specialist, analyst, 500th MI Battalion. Reinforced Task Force 500 from its parent unit, the 500th MI Battalion, in June 2002.

Lawson, Dan   Specialist, interrogator (Arabic linguist), Second Armored Cavalry Regiment. Capable of keeping up with Fitzgerald's fast wit, Lawson was a central character of the day shift.

Lee, Jonathan   Sergeant, interrogator (Arabic), 103rd MI Battalion. A member of the original Serial 93 reinforcements sent to Afghanistan in December 2001.

Lewis, Michael   Lieutenant colonel, MI. Commander of Task Force 500.

Lopez, Eric   Warrant officer 2, 500th MI Battalion. Officer-in-charge of the Ops Section at Kandahar.

McGinty, Sean   Sergeant first class, interrogator (German linguist), 325th MI Battalion (Reserves). Childhood friend of the author and senior interrogator in Cuba.

McGovern, Sean   Sergeant, interrogator (Arabic linguist), 325th MI Battalion (Reserves). Deployed with Mackey as a reservist when the unit was called up; spent most of the war at Fort Bragg, but was among the unit who replaced Mackey's when Task Force 500 was relieved.

Pearson, Lynn   Sergeant, interrogator (Arabic linguist), 103rd MI Battalion. Solid Arabic-speaking interrogator who eventually became head of document exploitation at the Facility at Bagram.

Rabinowicz, David   Affiliation unknown. Fort Huachuca classmate of the author.

Rawles, Tim   Captain, military intelligence, 500th MI Battalion. The officer-in-charge of "C" Company, 500th MI Battalion, which was responsible for most interrogation and counterintelligence operations in Afghanistan.

Roberts, Edward   Staff sergeant, interrogator (Arabic linguist), 323rd MI Battalion (Reserves). Although his family name suggests differently, Roberts was a native Arabic linguist whose talents were always in demand. His intolerable demeanor eventually gave rise to a crisis and his departure.

Rodriguez, Joe   Warrant officer 2, interrogation technician and officer-in-charge of the detachment, 325th MI Battalion (Reserves). Chief Rodriguez was the head of interrogation operations at Bagram after various leadership roles in Kandahar. He was tireless, and his commitment and leadership were always in evidence.

Santos, David   Sergeant, interrogator (Spanish and Persian Farsi linguist), 500th MI Battalion. Originally deployed as part of the 500th MI Battalion's mobile interrogation team, Santos took part in the massive screening operations at Sheberghan Prison early in the war. Back at Kandahar and later at Bagram, he was the reports editor at the ops (company) level.

Shami, George   Warrant officer 4, interrogation technician, affiliation unknown. The thunderous in-processing chief whose voice was known to drive prisoners to lose control of their bladders. Replaced by Heaney.

Simon   Civilian, working for one of our coalition allies' civilian intelligence services.

Singhal, Jason   Specialist, Virginia Nation Guard. Urdu linguist of Pakistani heritage. A key player in the interrogation of the two brothers with the "missile" in the basement.

Sutter, Kevin   Major and the executive officer of the 500th MI Battalion. Among Sutter's responsibilities was the coordination of intelligence gathered through interrogation within the community.

Stowe, Mark   Staff sergeant, interrogator (German linguist), 323rd MI Battalion (Reserves). Stowe was the night-shift senior interrogator before being replaced by Mackey.

Tafford, James   Warrant officer 2 "promotable," 500th MI Battalion.

Talbot, Brian   Specialist, interrogator (Russian linguist), 519th MI Battalion (Airborne). Fitzgerald's good-humored pal on the day shift, Talbot was an example of the precocious and affable composition of the interrogator ranks.

Turner, Doug   Sergeant, interrogator (Russian linguist), 325th MI Battalion (Reserves). Eager but ultimately miscast interrogator, Doug was ineffective in the "booth." He eventually found an important niche in the administrative apparatus of the team.

Tyler, Keith Warrant officer 1, 103rd MI Battalion (Third Infantry Division, Fort Stewart, Georgia). Night-shift officer-in-charge of the ICE in Kandahar.

Vaughn, Tom Major, Armor, V Corps. One of two liaison officers working in the Joint Working Group when Task Force 500 replaced the mobile interrogation team operating in Bagram.

Walker, Anne-Marie Sergeant, interrogator (Persian Farsi linguist), 500th MI Battalion. This young Michigan soldier surprised prisoners by her youthful appearance and icy tone; she lured unsuspecting detainees into letting their guard down and pounced when the moment was right.

Weikmann, Frank North Carolina National Guard MP and senior MP sergeant in the Facility at Bagram; earlier served as the night-shift senior MP at Kandahar.

KEY TO ABBREVIATIONS AND TERMS

————

Beretta — A 9 millimeter pistol and common sidearm for officers, machine gunners, and rear-echelon troops.

Booth — A cell or tent where an interrogation is conducted.

CFLCC — Combined Forces Land Component Command;
name for the overall command in charge of operations in
Afghanistan prior to May 2002.

Chinook — A large, two-rotor-blade helicopter used for troop
and equipment transport.

Colt M-16 — A shortened version of the 5.56 millimeter
M-16A2 service rifle.

Echo — Slang for interrogator.

Facility — Euphemism for the interrogation apparatus at a prison
camp.

GTMO — Short for Guantánamo Bay, the U.S. naval garrison
on Cuba.

High side — Top secret.

HUMINT — Human intelligence.

ICE — Interrogation control element; the oversight body that
organizes and tasks interrogators.

IIR — Intelligence information report; highly structured template
to report intelligence collected during an interrogation.

IMINT — Imagery intelligence.

IRP — Instructor role-player; a schoolhouse term for an interrogation instructor playing a source for training purposes.

JIF — Joint interrogation facility; the part of a POW compound used for questioning prisoners.

Joint Working Group — Oversight committee in charge of the search for "high value" fugitives like Osama bin Laden and Mullah Omar.

JTF 180 — Joint Task Force 180; name of the overall command in charge of operations in Afghanistan from May 2002 onward.

KP — Kitchen patrol; additional duty working in the field kitchen assisting the cooks with menial chores.

LBE — Load-bearing equipment; the name for the belt and harness used to carry ammunition pouches, canteen, bayonet, and other individual fighting equipment.

MI — Military Intelligence Corps.

MIT — Mobile interrogation team; a small group (four to six) of interrogators, usually led by a warrant officer assisted by a sergeant.

MP — Military police.

N-7 — Another name for strategic debriefer (see below).

NCOIC — Noncommissioned officer-in-charge (senior sergeant).

OGA — "Other Government Agency," the name used to obscure our civilian intelligence agency counterparts' presence in a combat theater.

OIC — Officer-in-charge.

Ops — Operations section; the overall leadership element for the interrogation element, encompassing collection, management, and dissemination (tasking interrogators and getting their reports out).

SAW — Squad automatic weapon; a 5.56 millimeter machine gun with a high rate of fire, usually issued as the heaviest weapon in a squad (nine soldiers).

Senior echo — The most senior interrogator in the ICE.

Serial 93 — The group of reinforcements, of which Mackey was one, that fleshed out the Task Force 500 complement of interrogators.

Serial 99 — A second wave of interrogator assets that arrived in February to bolster Task Force 500's capacity.

SIGINT — Signals intelligence.

SIR — Summary interrogation report; a structured record of
an interrogation, featuring interrogators' observations, non-
reportable information useful for further questioning at a later
date, and ideas for further exploitation in the event the writer
is not the next person to question a source.

SPOT report — An abbreviated IIR meant for critical information
that must get the field commander's attention immediately.

Strategic debriefer — An interrogator trained at the army's senior
interrogation school specifically to conduct sophisticated
questioning of senior-level, willing sources.

Task Force 500 — The group of composite intelligence personnel
responsible for detainee operations; formed principally from
the 500th MI Battalion out of Fort Gordon, Georgia.

Task Force Mountain — The expeditionary force that invaded
Afghanistan in October 2001; composed mainly of the Tenth
Mountain Division.

Terp — Slang for interpreter.

TOC — Tactical operations center; the physical establishment of
a headquarters element of a military unit.

Twenty-sixth Marine Expeditionary Unit (MEU) — Name of the
marine unit — roughly brigade size — that conducted
operations in the south of Afghanistan.

Waziristan — Region straddling the frontier of Pakistan and
Afghanistan in the north, populated by lawless and fiercely
tribal peoples.

INTRODUCTION TO THE
PAPERBACK EDITION

This is a story about the war in the shadows, of battles the public never sees. Most of the time, they take place inside a dusty tent or a dank cell, furnished with little more than a table and a couple of chairs. There are no bullets flying or bombs dropping. They are battles of psychology and intellect, of will instead of weaponry. And yet they are as dramatic and important as any in the war on terrorism because of the nature of the threat we face. The might of the United States military has been on frequent display since the September 11 attacks, with stealth aircraft dropping precision-guided bombs, unmanned planes firing Hellfire missiles, columns of tanks racing across deserts, and Special Forces soldiers slithering up to unsuspecting targets. But in the post–9/11 world, success doesn't hinge on seizing territory or even having superior firepower. The hijackers were armed with simple box cutters. Rather, success depends on discovering the enemy's intentions before it is too late. And in this new war, the most crucial weapon in the American arsenal may be the ability of a relative handful of "soldier spies" to get enemy prisoners to talk.

We interrogators who deployed in the fall of 2001 have always regarded ourselves as part of something unique. We were mobilized in direct response to the attacks on our country's capital and on one of its great cities. There was great honor in that, and there still is, but it has become increasingly difficult to cling to those feelings of pride because of the spreading stain of the prison abuses at Abu Ghraib. Before that scandal came to public light in the spring of 2004, I would have thought it impossible that American troops could engage in such sadistic behavior. But the months since have brought an unrelenting tide of disturbing disclosures. Eight soldiers were initially charged with the abuses at Abu Ghraib in Iraq, but the number continues to grow as the scandal spreads to other facilities, including those in Afghanistan. Military investigations have already documented at least three dozen cases in which prisoners died in American custody, and these investigations keep turning up new cases of abuse. Much of the blame has fallen on lowly enlisted soldiers, though it is increasingly clear that senior military commanders not only failed to set clear guidelines but in some cases effectively sanctioned harsh treatment of prisoners. As of this writing, leaked government memos show that while we soldiers were still setting up prisons in Afghanistan and at Guantánamo Bay, Cuba, top Bush administration lawyers were making the morally suspect case that America wasn't bound by antitorture statutes. Even a year after the abuses at Abu Ghraib, Red Cross reports continue to cite a litany of violations, and the headlines in the newspapers land like body blows almost every day.

My unit, which was among the first to arrive in Afghanistan, has not been implicated in these abuses. Not because we were perfect or particularly altruistic. Readers will see that we embraced increasingly harsh interrogation methods over time. And you can judge for yourself whether we did the right thing. But if we bent the rules, we did not break them, in part because we didn't think it necessary or likely to be effective, but largely because we feared the consequences. None of us was eager to go from running a prison to serving in one. But we have all been touched by the scandal. Two prisoners died at our facility in Afghanistan just months after my unit left. Several soldiers in the unit went on to serve in Iraq and were at Abu Ghraib when the abuses occurred, although none has been accused of being directly involved. Even those of us who left the army before the scandal erupted will always be angered by the damage to our corps, our cause, and our country. Interrogation is critical to winning the war on terrorism, but the scandal at Abu Ghraib showed that there is more than one way to lose.

Since the September 11 attacks, the United States has detained thousands of prisoners captured in Afghanistan and dozens of other countries around the world. The most senior Al Qaeda operatives captured have been taken to facilities whose locations have not been disclosed. Hundreds more have been sent for long-term detention at a specially built prison at Guantánamo Bay, Cuba. The war in Iraq added more facilities to this constellation, including the now-infamous Abu Ghraib prison on the outskirts of Baghdad. But for most of the Al Qaeda prisoners captured in the war on terrorism, the first stop was one of two U.S. prisons on the parched plains of Afghanistan. The interrogators with whom I served were the first people to greet them there.

The facility at Kandahar was open for a relatively brief period, from the early weeks of the war in Afghanistan until the following spring. The second prison, at Bagram Air Base north of Kabul, will probably be operational for years to come, as the United States continues to scoop up Afghans and Arabs and sift them for ties to terrorism. It is a squat, windowless warehouse, boarded up and ringed with barbed wire. From the outside, it would appear lifeless if it weren't for a steady plume of smoke from behind the building, where barrels of waste are dragged out to be burned. A sign with the spray-painted words NO ACCESS hangs over a nondescript entrance.

Most of the interrogation work was performed not by the CIA or the FBI, but by a relatively small cadre of U.S. Army interrogators. Some were active-duty troops just a few years out of high school. Others, like me, were reservists called away from civilian careers as accountants, teachers, computer experts, and the like. Our training generally included boot camp, at least a year at the military's language academy in Monterey, California, and then several months studying interrogation techniques at the U.S. Army's intelligence school at Fort Huachuca, Arizona.

When the war in Afghanistan started, the army had just 510 interrogators, including 108 of us who spoke Arabic — a tiny number for a nation about to embark on a massive effort to dismantle Al Qaeda, set up a string of new bases around the Persian Gulf, and, within a year and a half, invade Iraq. The numbers reflected years of neglect of human intelligence, or HUMINT, as it's called in military and intelligence circles. Indeed, there were deep cuts throughout the 1990s, a time when the terrorist threat to the United States was escalating. The basement bombing of the World Trade Center in 1993 was followed by the bombing of the Khobar Towers barracks in Saudi Arabia in 1996, the bombing of American embassies in East Africa in 1998, and the bombing of the USS Cole warship in Yemen in 2000. When hijacked airplanes struck the World Trade Center and the Pentagon in the fall of the following year, shortcomings in specialties like mine were dramatically evident.

To succeed, interrogators have to know what they're doing. The wrong approach can squander a potentially valuable source — and, in the war on terror, one missed clue could result in unnecessary deaths. These were not nickel-and-dime stakes. We have seen how clues that might have prevented the September 11 hijackings were mishandled or ignored. We know what happened and can count the cost.

Often the first task for interrogators is sorting out who's been caught, distinguishing the fighters from the farmers, the terrorists from the townspeople — to some, evil from good. Prisoners might be captured at gunpoint on the field of battle, rounded up in predawn raids on safe houses, or turned over by warlords or foreign intelligence services with agendas of their own. The intermittent release of prisoners from Guantánamo Bay underscores the extent to which this aspect of the mission is still a work in progress.

But the main objective of interrogation, as the army's field manual on the subject states, "is to obtain the maximum amount of usable information possible in the least amount of time." That imperative meant one thing before September 11. It has taken on another meaning since.

Al Qaeda trained tens of thousands of fighters at its camps in Afghanistan, and only a tiny fraction of them are pictured on Washington's most-wanted lists. For every Khalid Sheikh Mohammed, the September 11 mastermind captured in Pakistan in 2003, there are hundreds of lower-level Al Qaeda alumni who are all but anonymous. Some may be harmless, others not. If you're an interrogator, your job is to determine which is which, and to get them to tell you what they know.

How far to go in that pursuit was a difficult enough question when an interrogator's fellow soldiers might be threatened, when the objective was to spare a troop from walking into a minefield or an ambush. Of course, those possibilities were always in play for us in Afghanistan. But beyond those immediate concerns, what if a prisoner sitting across the table knew about a plot in the United States, a planned attack that might claim your sister or brother or parents? What if a prisoner could provide a scrap of information that might lead to bin Laden or members of his inner circle? We encountered dozens of prisoners who had been close to bin Laden in the days and weeks before their own capture. How far should we go to get that information?

There are rules to this game. The Geneva Conventions try to be explicit. Article 3 forbids "violence to life and person, in particular murder of all kinds, mutilation, cruel treatment, and torture." It also bars "outrages upon personal dignity, in particular, humiliating and degrading treatment."

The army's interrogation training focuses on sixteen basic

"approaches" to making people talk. The manual is explicit on the subject of torture. "The use of force, mental torture, threats, insults, or exposure to unpleasant and inhumane treatment of any kind is prohibited by law and is neither authorized nor condoned by the U.S. government." Every interrogator learns that by rote. But the manual carefully tiptoes around what is allowed, saying the prohibition on the use of force should not be confused "with psychological ploys, verbal trickery, or other nonviolent and noncoercive ruses."

There is no ambiguity, and yet there is ambiguity. What is humane and what isn't? Certainly the disgusting abuse at Abu Ghraib was inhumane. It was also counterproductive: any experienced interrogator will tell you that degrading prisoners does nothing to help the collection of intelligence. But is keeping a prisoner from getting a good night's sleep inhumane? And if the interrogator himself has gotten even less sleep, does that change the equation? The Geneva Conventions are clear, but they cannot possibly offer specific answers for every situation. As readers will see, there were numerous times when our jobs and the Geneva Conventions collided.

The tension between doing what is right and doing what is expedient is fundamental to the work of interrogation. The pressure to get a prisoner to talk is often acute, life and death. And prison conditions breed contempt — people who were out to kill one another were suddenly cooped up together in one big cage, with one group in complete command and the other at their utter mercy. We don't risk our lives like soldiers in the infantry, but we confront the enemy in the closest possible quarters. We smell their breath while they look us in the eye and lie.

The military investigations of Abu Ghraib and other prison abuses have produced tens of thousands of pages of sworn statements, factual findings, and officer reports. But the item that comes closest to capturing the morally corrupting forces at work in the facility is a six-page document buried among the annexes to the so-called Taguba report. It is a psychological assessment of the abuses at Abu Ghraib by an air force psychiatrist.

He cited the main ingredients of the breakdown — the cultural frictions between largely Christian soldiers and Muslim detainees, the woefully inadequate supervision at the facility, and the frayed nerves at a compound that was coming under mortar attack almost daily. In such a cauldron, "the worst human qualities and behavior came to the fore," the psychiatrist wrote. Indeed, one American guard had such hatred of Iraqis that he was sure his canines had come to share his racist opinions. Military guard dogs "came not to like the Iraqi detainees," the guard said. "They didn't like the Iraqi culture, smell, sound, skin tone, hair color, or anything about them."

Then the psychiatrist offered an unsettling observation about my profession: "Inadequate and immoral men and women desiring dominance may be drawn to fields such as corrections and interrogation, where they can be in absolute control over others."

Inadequate and *immoral* are the last words I would choose to describe the men and women with whom I served in Afghanistan. But all of us came to know the debilitating and often psychologically unhealthy aspects of our work. Guarding against abuse in such an environment requires more than intense supervision and vigilance. It requires a broad and deep understanding of the psychological forces at work and the consequences of immoral behavior.

The abuses at Abu Ghraib are unforgivable not just because they were cruel, but because they set us back. The more a prisoner hates America, the harder he will be to break. The more a population hates America, the less likely its citizens will be to lead us to a suspect. One of our biggest successes in Afghanistan came when a valuable prisoner decided to cooperate not because he had been abused (he had not been), but precisely because he realized he would not be tortured. He had heard so many horror stories that when he was treated decently, his prior worldview snapped, and suddenly we had an ally.

The early story of the war in Afghanistan was one of frustration and failure for us. Many Al Qaeda prisoners had been trained to resist, and our schoolhouse methods were woefully out-of-date. But by the end of the period covered in this book, our small group of "soldier spies" had engineered a breakthrough in interrogation strategy, rewriting techniques and tactics grounded in the Cold War. By the time of our departure from the baking, arid plains of Afghanistan, we could boast that virtually no prisoner went unbroken. And we didn't do it by pretending to wire a prisoner up or using the MPs to humiliate them.

Broken does not mean that we uncovered all that there was to know. In the movies, one evil genius knows all and conveniently spills the pertinent information in a quick two-minute stretch. Real espionage doesn't work that way. Interrogators find tiny bits of the truth, fragments of information, slivers of data. We enter a vast desert, hundreds of miles across, in which a few thousand puzzle pieces have been scattered. We spend weeks on a single prisoner, to extract only a single piece. We collect, and then we pass the pieces on, hoping that someone above us can assemble them. Of course, sometimes we did some assembling ourselves; by figuring out bigger pictures we could better question the prisoners in our custody. We could only hope that those who got our information used it wisely.

Sometimes we had our doubts. We were hampered again and again by a lack of cooperation between agencies. The civilian intelligence agencies almost never shared information with us; the FBI was willing, but seldom had relevant information to share. We would often find the truth the hard way — by ourselves. But we would, and did, find it.

This book is a collaborative effort that involved numerous people. My coauthor, Greg Miller, spent hundreds of hours interviewing other members of the unit, double-checking my memories, and adding details that I could not have known at the time.

Our aim was to produce a complete and accurate account. Because of the sensitive nature of the subject, certain details had to be obscured. As a member of the Military Intelligence Corps, I was obligated to submit the manuscript of this book to the army for a security review. The purpose of the review was to determine whether the manuscript contained classified information. As part of that process, the army asked me to refrain from naming certain U.S. intelligence agencies, military units, classified documents, coalition partners, and intelligence collection platforms. In most cases, we simply refer to these subjects in more generic terms. We have complied with the army's request and changed the names of virtually all of the interrogators and of the prisoners, to protect their safety. It is possible that Al Qaeda might be interested in the real identities of soldiers who interrogated its members, or of prisoners who betrayed the cause. In certain instances, we have changed the locations of events because saying where something happened would expose individuals or operations. This applies in particular to a story about a young prisoner we call Hadi. The events in his life are exactly as described, but the setting of the story that brought him into our custody was altered. At the army's request, we also altered the names or numeric designations of certain military units to prevent disclosing their classified assignments and locations. Often, the specific entities will seem obvious. Finally, at the army's insistence, I do not use my real name; Chris Mackey is a pseudonym.

Though some material was removed and certain details obscured, the army did not censor my account of events, and the changes made at their behest did not materially alter the book.

To understand the secret war against Al Qaeda, one absolutely must understand what went on in the cages, in the booths, and in the prisons. One must understand not only who was being questioned but also who was doing the questioning. We were in a desperate race, hoping to foil another 9/11. Every interrogation held the promise of saving lives if we did it well, and costing lives if we did not. Right now, as you read this, interrogators are trying to find yet another piece of the puzzle before it is too late. This is our story.

THE
INTERROGATORS

PROLOGUE:
THE ABATTOIR

As always, it happened at night. A cargo plane touched down in darkness, its lights doused to avoid attack, and lumbered across the rutted runway toward what had once been the passenger terminal of the Kandahar airport. Its rear ramp lowered, revealing a ragged train of enemy fighters in bare feet and rags, emerging like aliens in the red-hued light of the cargo hold. Their heads were covered in burlap sacks, but their breath was still visible in the frigid air. Some were wounded, others had relieved themselves, and all stank. They were bound together in long chains. As they were spirited down the ramp, if one were to stumble, he would pull the others down with him.

On the tarmac, MPs swarmed in from all sides, shining flashlights in the prisoners' concealed faces and screaming a stream of commands and obscenities audible even over the roar of the plane as it pulled away and made its escape into the Afghanistan sky. They led the prisoners toward a barbed-wire enclosure that only the U.S. Army could call a "reception area." Unlike the rest of the cantonment, it was illuminated by stanchions of lights that gave it the feel of a high school football stadium. It was accessed through a long, rickety door made of sheet metal and topped with concertina wire. The prisoners ambled through under the gaze of MPs in towers above, who kept their weapons at the ready.

With a mighty *thud* the prisoners were hurled, one by one, into a three-sided sandbag "pin-down." Rubber-gloved MPs armed with surgical scissors made them lie on their stomachs and began cutting away the rags. At the first snip of the scissors, the prisoners howled and wailed and struggled to roll over, fearing there could only be one purpose for being held face-down and stripped. The screaming stirred the line of prisoners still waiting in the reception area to states of supreme agitation.

The pin-down was the entry point to an abattoir-like tent tunnel through which the prisoners would pass as they were processed into U.S. custody. This is where it began.

Once they had gone through a quick intelligence screening, the prisoners were examined by a doctor. He scanned the prisoners' torsos, arms, and legs, moving a gloved hand quickly across their skin, searching for scars and fresh wounds that might need dressing. He checked their mouths with a gloved finger, and searched their eyes with a flashlight, looking for any sign of disease. Then an MP would shout one of the few phrases he had mastered in Arabic: *"Wa' all'an lill act el emptihan!"* — "And now for the ass inspection!" One MP would put his knee into the back of one of the prisoners' knees while the other put his hand on the prisoner's neck and pushed it down until the prisoner was properly positioned. The doctor's probe always prompted new shrieks from prisoners convinced they were about to be raped.

From there the prisoners were forced down on a dusty, stained mat at the end of the tent, always good for another round of wailing, but usually a bit more restrained, the facedown routine having been established. The MPs would remove the shackles and coat the prisoners with lice powder. At about this point the prisoners would be photographed and fingerprinted by FBI agents trying vainly to match the frequently misspelled or made-up names of new arrivals to terrorist watch lists.

Then the MPs would start pulling prison garb over their

heads and limbs. Struggling, each MP looked like a parent dressing a two-year-old. They'd yank on thermal underwear, then pull the prisoners' hands and feet through holes in light blue jumpsuits that sat piled in the corner of the tent. There was another pile of rubber shoes, like the kind you might buy out of some airline catalog for gardening. The MPs would stand each prisoner up in his ill-fitting outfit and scrawl a number across his chest in black marker — the prisoner's new identity. An MP at the end of the tent gave each prisoner two giant blankets and a second pair of long johns. Then the bag went back on the prisoner's head and he was taken to the main prison compound. Half the time, the prisoner would wet himself again within minutes, soiling his fresh, clean outfit and inducing the whole process to start again from the beginning.

The scene would sometimes go on for hours, as prisoner after prisoner was led through the in-processing tent. By the end, chunks of earth would be missing from the tent entrance, as MPs scooped up urine-soaked sections of dirt with spades and tossed them out of the way. Soiled latex gloves littered the floor around the doctor's station. The clothes that marines cut off the prisoners in the pin-down were collected in a pile and burned in a barrel.

On a night like this, three months after the United States began dropping bombs on Afghanistan, a marine knocked politely on the pole of a tent not far from the reception area. Poking his head inside the flap, he said, to no one in particular, "Sir, a transport has arrived with prisoners."

Inside, a dimly lit assemblage of army interrogators, analysts, and counterintelligence agents barely stirred. Each was a bundle of military and nonmilitary winter clothing, looking like a collection of suburban, white gangsta rappers. We were still new to the mission, numbed by the cold, and not particularly eager to move. Some were clicking away at laptops, trying to catch up on the endless reports their work required. But as the senior interrogator glanced around the tent considering whom to select for the night's assignment, the clicking — and any other activity that might draw attention — stopped.

The marine said the incoming prisoners were Arabs, but there weren't many Arabic speakers left in the tent. The others were already in interrogations. The "senior E," as the lead interrogator was known, picked a three-man team. One spoke Russian, one Spanish, and the other Arabic. They quickly packed laptops, dictionaries, files, and forms needed for in-processing. As reports editor, I wasn't supposed to leave my post in front of my laptop. But I spoke Arabic and was always eager for any action that might pull me away from a job that mainly entailed combing through our interrogation reports for format errors. I decided to tag along. The stars were so bright that we left our red-lensed flashlights in our cargo pockets as we walked toward the reception area, whose smoldering waste barrels and makeshift shelters gave it the silhouette of a Calcutta ghetto.

The pin-down area was like a theater in miniature, and already, off-duty MPs who had no particular business in the reception area were gathering for what qualified in Kandahar as a diversion. MPs new to the garrison pressed against one another, crowding in to see a live version of the nocturnal, badge-versus-bad guy confrontations they grew up watching on reality television shows like *Cops*. Indeed, nearly all who witnessed the drama in the pin-down couldn't help but sing or hum the show's reggae theme song: "Bad boys, bad boys, Whatcha gonna do? Whatcha gonna do when they come for you?"

I thought the Oz-like spectacle in the adjoining tent was more intriguing. Inside, an imperious, Lebanese-born chief warrant officer — who had mysterious above-the-law status in the interrogation unit — functioned as a one-man screening team. He had been a translator for Gen. Norman Schwarzkopf in the Persian Gulf War and was sent by Central Command to "assist" in the handling of prisoners in Afghanistan. He had a thick cap of white hair, a huge push-broom mustache, the eyebrows of a Russian party chairman, and a voice like a cannon. Prisoners before him sometimes collapsed with fright, falling limp to the ground until they were hoisted up again by two MPs.

Like a temperamental diva, Chief Shami often had to be coaxed into taking the stage. But he was a master at his task. His job was to make an instant assessment of a prisoner's intelligence value, an inexact art in which he relied to a large extent on his own gut instincts. He examined their "pocket litter" — papers found in prisoners' pockets at the time of capture and bagged for the screener's use — and paid close attention to their accents, their countenance. He also bombarded prisoners with a barrage of questions designed to provoke as much as to elicit practical intelligence.

"When was the last time you saw Osama bin Laden?" he would boom, always first in English to test the prisoners' language abilities. "Never," or "You're crazy," was the inevitable reply, usually in Arabic or Pashtu. "When was the last time you saw Mullah Omar?" And so on.

As I watched this particular night's performance, I heard something odd outside in the pin-down. A prisoner was being searched before his turn in front of the Chief, making the usual noisy protest. His pleas were guttural in tone, but weren't in Arabic or Pashtu. I moved toward the door of the tent, over to the pin-down, and saw the aged frame of a prisoner whom I correctly assessed to be speaking German. He was older, perhaps in his fifties, slightly wounded in the side and one hand, and trembling to the point of convulsions from the terrible cold.

As this prisoner was brought before the Chief, naked but for the burlap sack on his head, the master attacked in English and then in Arabic. But the German came first in every attempt the prisoner made to respond. The Chief turned redder and redder, convinced the prisoner was being evasive, pretending not to understand Arabic. As the Chief bore in, the prisoner began to cry beneath his sack. He shook so violently that the MPs struggled to keep his torso straight. They suspended him from his armpits, but he dropped his head and pulled his knees up toward his abdomen, curling into a suspended, fetal ball. After watching this pathetic display awhile, I did something few dared, and interrupted the Chief. Summoning my deepest, most authoritative voice, I said, *"Woher kommst du?"*

The prisoner's legs uncurled and skimmed the ground. He whimpered: *"Aus Hamburg."*

How interesting.

Perturbed at having the stage stolen, the Chief dismissed the prisoner, sending him forth into the abattoir. I followed the prisoner to the doctor's station and tried to explain what was about to happen. The prisoner assured me he had nothing hidden in his orifices. "Routine," I replied in German, and the examination commenced. After the prisoner's wounds were dressed, he was dusted with anti-lice powder and washed perfunctorily under the arms, between his legs, and on his backside. The FBI agents rolled out his fingerprints and removed his burlap bag for a picture. The flash caught him off guard and he blinked repeatedly. *Off guard,* I thought, *if only prisoners could be kept that way.* Finally, the prisoner was given two thick blankets, a wool watch cap, long underwear that was too small, and rubber shoes that were too big. As he was dressed, the MPs dragged a thick marker across the front and back of his wrinkled, baby blue jumpsuit, assigning him his new identity: Prisoner 140.

Prisoner 140 was shackled with bright chrome leg and wrist irons. As he stood unhooded in front of me, he got his first long, hard look at an American soldier. He seemed terrified. Fear is often an interrogator's best ally, but it doesn't have a long shelf life.

Prisoner 140 was taken to the main holding area, a giant,

mud-walled field that had once, before the droughts, been a lush apple orchard. Inside were eight large tents, each with its sides permanently rolled up, and ringed by three coils of concertina wire. There were twenty prisoners in each tent, all of them clumped in piles of blankets, and all evenly spaced by the vigilant guards.

Back in the interrogators' control tent, I couldn't push the curious prisoner out of my mind. In the abattoir, 140 said he had come to Afghanistan "to lead a more pure Islamic life," a quote so ubiquitous among the prisoners that interrogators had actually begun to believe it, as yet unaware of the global network conveying radical Muslims from Europe to Afghanistan. My German was better than my Arabic, and I saw 140 as a chance to conduct an interrogation without letting language limit my selection of interrogation tools.

I asked the MPs to bring 140 to the JIF, the joint interrogation facility, a set of six small, round canvas tents surrounded by a wall of barbed wire. It had been an hour since 140 had entered the main holding area, and it took the MPs about ten minutes to fetch him. As he was ushered into one of the canvas interrogation booths, 140 suddenly looked remarkably well composed, sturdier than I had thought. The harrowing trip through the screening tunnel had already begun to wear off.

Prisoner 140 was ordered to sit down on a metal folding chair. As the MP peeled his wool cap from over his eyes, 140 barely glanced at the giant guard standing beside him with a homemade walking stick that might double as a truncheon. Instead, he offered a polite bow, effected while still seated, with a flat hand pressed against his chest. Speaking in German, I opened the conversation with a tone that was authoritative, measured, and clear. I wished to convey competence and hopefully an unsettling capacity for forensic analysis. In the opening stages of an interrogation, it's important to remain neutral in order to preserve as many options as possible. It's also important to open by focusing on rather mundane material. Pressing for meaningful information too early only exposes your intelligence gaps.

"Where did you enter Pakistan?" I began.

"Through Lahore."

"Why did you enter Pakistan through Lahore?"

"It was where my tickets took me."

"Who told the airline representative that your arrival city should be Lahore?"

"Me."

"Why did you want to go to Lahore?"

"I was told to."

Already the questioning of 140 was settling into a dismayingly unproductive and familiar pattern. I pressed on.

"By whom were you told to go through Lahore?"

"By the Imam at my mosque."

"Why did the Imam at the mosque tell you to enter Pakistan through Lahore?"

"There was a hotel there that catered to immigrants."

"What was the name of the hotel?"

"I don't remember."

"Describe the look of the hotel."

"It was big."

"When you say the hotel was big, exactly how big was the hotel?"

"Very big."

"When I say to tell me 'exactly' in any case referring to anything, I mean for you to describe in detail the dimensions or features of the object or place."

"Okay."

"Exactly how big was the hotel in which you stayed on the instructions of the Imam?"

"Very, very big."

For hours this nonsense continued. Prisoner 140 claimed

he couldn't remember the name of the hotel, the names of friends in his native Algeria, the name of his landlady in Hamburg, or even the name of his Imam at the mosque. It was incredible, and it was infuriating, but it was virtually all that we had encountered since the first batch of interrogators had stepped off their transport plane into the cold air three weeks earlier. When prisoners were questioned, everyone's name had been "lost" to fragile memory. There were no identifying features, no addresses, no telephone numbers. In the recesses of our minds where logic ruled, we knew it was impossible for so many prisoners to have forgotten so much. But we were confounded by the utter directness of the lies. It wasn't a kind of cocktail party fib, easily seen through, easily peeled away. It was the mindless refutation of the obvious. And forbidden from punishing anyone for noncooperation, we couldn't do a damned thing about it. We could only gaze back in disbelief and do our best to follow the school mantra: interrogators feign emotions, we never betray them.

"Who were you to meet at the hotel?"

"A man."

"Who told you to meet a man at the hotel?"

"The Imam."

"What was the name of the man you met at the hotel in Lahore on the advice of the Imam?"

"I don't remember."

"How were you to know the man at the hotel whom you met on the advice of the Imam?"

"I don't know."

"Describe the man you met at the hotel on the advice of the Imam."

"He was a man."

On and on, the session dragged through the night. Here and there, Prisoner 140 disclosed some details of his life. He said he was a petty thief who had spent time in a German prison before coming to Afghanistan to build a new life. He had stayed in a house in Jalalabad. He wanted to pursue a purer Islamic existence, away from the temptations of the West. He had been told he would be able to find a Muslim bride. Alas, Afghanistan wasn't the Islamic paradise others had made it out to be, and 140 had wanted to go home almost as soon as he had arrived. But he couldn't get out.

The story was nearly identical to every other prisoner's. Nobody came to wage jihad. And certainly nobody came to join Al Qaeda. Everyone's motives were pure, if utterly implausible. I knew this as well as anybody. I had seen the pattern in dozens of other interrogators' reports I had edited and sent along since the war started. But sitting in front of one of these wretched prisoners, and watching the night waste away, had a way of eroding one's incredulity. Against my instinct, I began almost to want the man's tale to be true. It would be easier if it were.

An hour later, I noticed I was no longer squinting at my notebook. A ray of light from the morning's sunrise had found the open seam in the tent. I had spent more than six hours with 140. We were both fatigued and frozen. The night had been a waste, and I, a senior sergeant in the unit, was risking a rebuke from the leadership for squandering so much time. I closed out the session, told the guard to return the prisoner to the cages, and stood up to leave.

As I gathered my belongings, I noticed a scrap of paper on the table with the word "owner" scribbled on it. I had written the note to myself while 140 was pattering on about some other subject. It was a reminder to ask 140 who had owned the house where he'd stayed in Jalalabad.

The prisoner had already stood up from the metal chair, had had his cap pulled down over his eyes by the MP, and was being led away. I stepped around the table, pulled up the rim of the prisoner's cap, and asked, "Who owns the house in Jalalabad?"

Without any hesitation, Prisoner 140 replied, "Al-Jezari."

Then 140 raised his head with a jerk that might have been caused by an electric shock. The prisoner had yielded a name. He had slipped. It was a tiny slip, to be sure, but it was, for me, the first evidence that the code of silence in Afghanistan could be broken.

Perhaps it was the exhaustion of the all-night interrogation. Maybe it was because the prisoner, being led away from the booth, had let his guard down. Or the fact that I, in a slip of my own, had posed the question in Arabic rather than German, the language in which we had been speaking all night. Whatever it was, it had caused a momentary short in the elaborate, evasive circuitry of Prisoner 140's mind.

In time, 140 would provide critical intelligence about the Hamburg Al Qaeda cell, betray many other enemy fighters, and expose a never-before-understood connection between Al Qaeda and Islamic groups across North Africa. All of that lay ahead. But for now, all that mattered was that 140 had cracked. And if he did, others might too.

PART

I

TRAINING

Most students slipped quite naturally out of their school uniforms at Immaculate High School in Danbury, Connecticut, and into the country's better universities. I slipped out of my uniform and into army fatigues. I was seventeen when I enlisted in 1989, and it came as a surprise to all of my friends but one, Sean McGinty, who enlisted with me. We suffered from a debilitating condition: too many siblings. Our working-class parents — my father was a telephone line repairman, McGinty's an accountant — had made it clear some time earlier that we were going to have to pay our own way through college. And so we decided to enlist together, jokingly trying to be the first to complete the army oath so as to be "senior" to the other in our new military lives. McGinty skipped a phrase or two, arriving at the "so help me God" line first. I would argue for years that he had invalidated his oath by jumping ahead, but that was a debate I would never win.

Originally we thought the infantry would be good. The army brochures made it all look fairly glamorous, with lots of pictures of armored personnel carriers rolling through German landscapes and Teutonic villagers smiling at passing Americans. But my father had been an artilleryman who was called up from the Connecticut National Guard during Korea, and he wanted me to pursue a military field far away from cannons and endless gunnery drills. The Saturday morning after McGinty and I signed up, I found myself waiting in a parking lot with my father, while a parade of distinctly unmilitary people walked into a vaguely industrial-looking building surrounded by a chain-link fence. A yellow fifties hot rod pulled into the lot and a tall man stepped out and stooped to pick up a knapsack from the rumble seat. My father, taller still, stretched out his big hand and the two men smiled at each other and exchanged greetings. "So this is your boy," the man said, pausing to conduct a quick inspection. I was inspecting him, too. He sported an outrageous pompadour haircut that looked about as military as a ponytail. His wrinkled battle dress uniform was practically white with wear. An absurd unit patch on his shoulder depicted a pilgrim with a blunderbuss.

The first few minutes reinforced every stereotype about the reserves and national guard. The man, First Sergeant Staib, excused himself to tend to the business of his office, which appeared to consist of drinking Dunkin' Donuts coffee and kidding around with his colleagues. My father and I stood in the vestibule looking at plaques honoring Soldier of the Year for 1975 and the winning platoon in the 1969 handball competition. Only the posters exhorting soldiers to "protect classified documents" and "Beware the Bear" indicated there might be something here of interest. All the while, overweight soldiers with gray hair and outdated uniforms pushed by to join a gaggle in the center of a gymlike open area.

After his doughnut, Staib came out of the adjoining office, stood at the top of the open area, and bellowed, *"Fall in!"* His Hollywood-quality command voice startled me. The resulting movement wasn't exactly a scramble, more of a high-speed shuffling, but the suddenness of the soldiers' motion, and their final arrangement in neat little squares of troops, was more than a little impressive. Suddenly Staib's uniform didn't look so wrinkled after all.

After the formation, Staib brought my father and me into

an office. The unit's commander was there, a Major Gregoire, and a very old female officer who looked so much like a nun I nearly called her "sister." They asked me if I knew what the unit did, and I said something like "only that you are linguists." They smiled and said that was more or less correct, but that there was more to the story. In fact, they were an interrogation unit, responsible for questioning prisoners of war, refugees, border crossers, and other sources of intelligence information. *Interrogators,* I thought.

After a chat with Staib, the commander, and the nun, I was taken around the dirty facility and introduced to the various groups. Sizing them up, I was a little concerned that they were the grown-up versions of the nerds and dweebs I had tried so hard to steer clear of in school — maybe a little conscious that I was too close to them on the social ladder for comfort. The last thing we did was sit in on a practice interrogation. A large group of reservists stood or sat around a little wooden table. A man about thirty with a very big nose and mustache sat in one chair, while a slightly older, balding man sat opposite. Sitting behind the big-nosed man was a particularly old fellow with white hair, glasses, and a crooked front tooth. If there had been a few banjos, it might have been a scene from a Louisiana bayou.

The balding man was the interrogator. He posed questions to the big-nosed fellow in English. The crooked-toothed guy translated the English into German, whereupon Big Nose answered in German. The German was translated back into English, and the balding interrogator scribbled in his notebook. After the first few questions passed through this circuit, there developed a kind of disjointed conversation. "How did you come to be captured, Mah-yohr Schmidt?" Big Nose said something about conducting reconnaissance on the river Elbe for his unit. The balding guy asked questions about the prisoner's men: why hadn't they helped him avoid capture as they had done? He began to suggest that Schmidt was a coward.

Soon the balding man was screaming at Schmidt, who in response began to look more and more dejected. This went on for some time.

The script was well written. The prisoner was overcome by his ordeal. The violence of his capture had affected him deeply, and he was unprepared for the flurry of insults and baiting his interrogator offered. He was reduced nearly to tears by the grilling. Then the tenor of their conversation changed. The bald interrogator produced a cigarette. The prisoner declined, too distressed to accept. But he began to talk, yielding information about his unit as if he were unburdening himself of personal secrets he no longer wished to keep.

When the show was over, I found my father in the motor pool speaking with Staib. We parted company with our uniformed hosts, making promises of speaking again soon and various nonbinding expressions of interest. My father asked for my impressions on the way home, and I told him I thought it was interesting but not exactly very military. Not being "military" was the point, my father said. "It's the intelligence corps, after all."

That comment began to sink in. I started to realize there might be advantages to the new route, not least of which was the opportunity to study a foreign language as part of the initial training.

I spoke with McGinty about all this. We debated the merits of the infantry and the intelligence corps in the bleachers of the school gym. McGinty visited the reserve unit a few weeks later and was impressed enough to at least consider a change. With some reluctance (and lots of lobbying by parents who thought the intelligence corps sounded significantly less dangerous than being an infantry grunt), we revisited our recruiter. The big sergeant seemed to accept our change of heart pretty well — almost as if he'd expected it, really. Although he tried to get us to join the intelligence corps as active-duty troops, the six-year commitment was a little too much. The training even for the reserves was long and would give us a good flavor of life in the army. If we liked it we could always switch to active duty, but going the other way — from active duty to the reserves — wasn't possible. Sean and I signed our contracts alongside the signatures of our parents, a requirement for enlisting under the age of eighteen. We were in the army now, and achieved some minor celebrity at school because of it.

We spent the rest of our senior year going to the reserve center once a month for training. We were paid, given uniforms, and because of our high school Spanish, were attached to the unit's Latin America section. We sat spellbound weekend after weekend as Chief Warrant Officer Edward Archer, an Argentinian with a voice reminiscent of Ricardo Montalban's, described the various techniques and methods for persuading enemy prisoners to talk. He stressed the importance of basic skills, of leveraging one's own personality strengths, and of having a broad knowledge of military structure, tactics, and equipment. When summer arrived and high school graduation came, the other members of the reserve unit gave McGinty and me a farewell party as we prepared to depart for boot camp. The unit even gave us going-away presents: army ID cards showing our ages to be twenty-one rather than seventeen.

DLI

Among army intelligence recruits, the Defense Language Institute, or DLI, was often referred to as the Defense Lust Institute. The reputation was one of an idyllic existence among the palms, studying after class on the beach, and wild parties with beautiful California girls. As McGinty and I rode a bus from the San Francisco airport south toward Monterey, we were struck by the wide highways, the stucco houses, the palm trees, and the dizzying array of fast-food places. Even the little reflectors embedded in the highway constituted a curiosity for two kids from the Northeast. Then there were the girls. Right away, I wished I had picked a language with a longer course of instruction than German, still a priority tongue in those waning Cold War days.

Our new barracks looked like high-rent condominiums. McGinty and I were billeted together and discovered a private bathroom, a television, and a refrigerator. After twelve weeks of basic in Missouri, at Fort Leonard Wood, this was paradise. There were thirty students in the German class, divided into three sections of ten each. There were two navy pilots, two West Point Rhodes scholars, an army sergeant MP, a Louisiana National Guard officer learning German because the French course had filled up, and a large group of young, green soldiers like McGinty and me. The vast majority were going into the forces as intelligence professionals, but there were some non-service personnel, mainly State Department types, and then there were spouses and assorted dependents when class space permitted. Classes at the DLI become very close. There are always a few weddings in a class (we had four), usually followed by divorces when the pressure of the school is over.

Sometimes it seemed like the DLI was a repository for every ethnic stereotype. The Italian instructors always seemed to be having picnics. Russians were socialist technocrats, forever organizing sports days and parades. The Arabs were always accusing their students of conspiracies. And the Germans were obsessed with structure and order. My instructors were twelve grandmotherly, but exceedingly strict, native Germans. Under their instruction, we didn't learn just to conjugate verbs, but to sit up straight, enunciate, and be timely in all things.

"PAZZ IN YER HOMEVERK ALFA-BETIKLY!"

Class went from 8 a.m. to 3:30 p.m., with an hour break for lunch. The first hour was always *Nachrichten*, whereby students would take turns summarizing news stories in German. This was followed by quizzes, language labs, reading hours, and audio-visual sessions in which students watched German TV programs recorded twenty-four hours a day by satellite dishes all over the post. The last hour was my favorite, and by far the most valuable. The class broke up into groups, two or three students to an instructor, and they picked topics to discuss, the more controversial the better. The ground rules were simple: speak only in German. Sometimes we'd go to the kitchen and chat while we cooked German food. Sometimes we'd go for walks on the shore a short distance away, the locals tolerating a daily inundation of budding linguists. It was a fantastic language workout and great fun.

The culminating event of the DLI is the Defense Language Proficiency Test, a three-day ordeal that is a sort of bar exam for soldiers who must prove they've learned a foreign language to begin their careers in intelligence. About half those who passed were headed to Fort Huachuca, the army's intelligence center and school in southeastern Arizona, the other half to the signal intercept school at Goodfellow Air Force Base in San Angelo, Texas. Either way, it meant back to life as army trainees, back to drill sergeants.

We took the DLPT in a set of low-lying, Polynesian-looking exam buildings on the edge of the post. There were several who didn't make the cut and others who were surprised by their poor performance. I did okay; smack in the middle of the pack, and along with McGinty, headed for the desert.

HUACHUCA

Interrogation is as old as war, but interrogators — that is, soldiers specially trained to question prisoners — are a relatively recent addition to military ranks. Through most of military history, when prisoners were captured, they were questioned by whoever was on hand. There's even a scene in the *Iliad* in which Ulysses and Diomed capture a Trojan spy and question him themselves, extracting information on the strength and disposition of Trojan troops. (In the end, they cut his throat, leaving his head "rolling in the dust while he was yet speaking," but that's another matter.) They didn't cuff him and take him to the rear to turn him over to clean-uniformed intelligence troops. There was no instruction on interrogation in the Achaean army, no doctrine to follow, no choreographed "approaches" to use to get prisoners to talk. And there wasn't any of that in any other army either until well into the twentieth century.

The U.S. Army was no exception. Prisoners were always considered important sources of information. Indeed, senior commanders, including George Washington and Ulysses S. Grant, were known to sometimes take it upon themselves to question high-value captives. But in general, interrogation was regarded as low-skilled labor, a tedious task that commanders tended to assign to troops who couldn't be put to more productive use doing something else. Capturing prisoners was the hard part, asking them questions was barely worth mentioning alongside more daring categories of intelligence collection. In his account of intelligence methods in the Civil War, University of Nebraska historian Peter Maslowski wrote that interrogation "was less romantic than spying, less dangerous than scouting and cavalry reconnaissance, and as mundane as reading the enemy's newspapers."

The first troops that had anything in common with today's interrogators were created in World War I. American units took their places alongside British and French forces that had already been fighting for several years, were far better organized, and had developed significantly more expertise in gathering intelligence. Warfare was changing, fueled by new technologies — including tanks, airplanes, and radios — that required armies to evolve from masses of men to collections of specialized components. The infantry obviously played the predominant role in the trench warfare of World War I, but militaries needed men to operate their new machines, and better-trained intelligence personnel not only to decrypt codes and analyze aerial photos, but to ask the right questions of captured prisoners. Assessing the enemy was no longer just about tracking soldiers, it required understanding the enemy's weapons systems, supply lines, operational tactics, and organization in enough detail that even small bits of information from a detainee could help piece together a larger intelligence puzzle. American forces were so unprepared for these new requirements that at first they had to rely on their European counterparts even for the most rudimentary training. U.S. soldiers assigned to intelligence duties including interrogation were sent to the British Army Intelligence School at Harrow, England, for weeks of instruction. By July 1918, the U.S. Army had set up its own tiny intelligence school in Langres, France. (Interrogator trainees even practiced on actual German prisoners before being assigned to field units.) But at the end of the war, the troops went home, the U.S. Army shrank back to its peacetime dimensions, and whatever expertise these interrogators acquired on the job was institutionally forgotten. Two decades later, the army's intelligence apparatus had to be entirely rebuilt.

Whatever intelligence assets it had squandered, the U.S. military didn't waste time mobilizing for World War II. In July 1940, a month after German troops entered Paris, the army issued its first field manual on interrogation, or more specifically, on the "examination of enemy personnel, repatriates, documents and material." The twenty-eight-page manual described in detail how prisoners were to be evacuated from the front lines, discussed the use of carrier pigeons to transmit time-sensitive information, and warned interrogators to observe the Geneva Conventions' ban on coercion. It devoted pages to listing what sort of information to seek from prisoners from various kinds of enemy units. But there was no mention of anything resembling the sixteen distinct approaches outlined in today's interrogation manuals. Indeed, about the only guidance it offered on method was that "a cigarette or a cup of coffee will frequently elicit more accurate and important information than threats."

The manual was part of a flurry of field guides that the War Department published that year. In June 1942, the army opened its first centralized intelligence training center, at Camp Ritchie, Maryland, a former national guard armory a few hours north of Washington, D.C. Its first priority was to train interrogators, but the army found itself so ill equipped to teach the subject that it had to bring a British colonel over from the School for Interrogators of Prisoners of War at Cambridge to help get the program off the ground.

The interrogator trainees were mainly soldiers who grew up in German- or Italian-speaking households. (Japanese linguists were schooled at other facilities in California and, later, Minnesota, but there were so few Japanese POWs that the emphasis was on document exploitation, not interrogation.) The students at Ritchie learned "methods of interviewing, personality analysis, ways of influencing people and making friends (the Dale Carnegie approach applied to prisoners of war)," according to an internal army history of Camp Ritchie. They practiced interrogating instructors who spoke in German and wore German uniforms supplied by the Brits. The program ended with a massive eight-day exercise in which all of the troops from various disciplines staged mock exercises under conditions the army tried to make realistic by blasting battle-field sounds over base loudspeakers. The first class was "long on theory and short on experience," the army study said. But within months Camp Ritchie was producing a stream of trained, foreign-language-fluent interrogators for the front, and within three years, the program had trained 2,641 interrogators who spoke German and 326 who spoke Italian. Each division got two prisoner-interrogation teams, and each team consisted of two officers and four enlisted men. Camp Ritchie was no accomplishment on the order of the Manhattan Project, but it was considered a major success in the army, and one army review after another praised the contributions of interrogators in the war. A report by the Twelfth Army Group, dated July 1, 1945, was typically appreciative: "All Corps agreed that prisoners of war constituted by far the most fruitful source of information."

Camp Ritchie shut down after the war, but the army didn't make the same mistake it had after World War I. Interrogation units became permanent parts of the active-duty and reserve forces. The interrogation manual swelled from twenty-eight pages to ninety-plus, as the army's training and doctrine staffs incorporated techniques borrowed from allies and law enforcement experts, gradually delineating the cookie-cutter inter-rogation approaches in use today. Immediately after World War II, intelligence schools were set up in Georgia and Kansas before the army consolidated much of its intelligence training at Fort Holabird, near Baltimore, in the mid-1950s. When that space became too cramped the Army Intelligence Corps set its sights on a location with seemingly nothing but room to grow: a nearly forgotten fort in the Huachuca Mountains in southern Arizona. The dusty, rustic encampment had been established in 1877, serving as the army's headquarters in its campaign against Geronimo and the Apache tribe. In 1971 Fort Huachuca became the home for the U.S. Army Intelligence Center and School, and the training ground for hundreds of interrogators every year.

We crossed Arizona in a tiny airplane that seemed to fly sideways through a lightning storm that illuminated the desert and clouds below like the surface of some gaseous moon. "Moon" was the word that sprang to mind when we landed, too: the horizon was seabed flat save for what appeared to be colossal gray gravel heaps in the farthest distance. The tiny airport was almost exclusively for military transients, with their PX-purchased T-shirts bearing mottos like "3rd Signal Battalion: The Signal Dogs" and luggage made of fake camouflage embossed with a gold U.S. Army seal. Nine months at the DLI had allowed my hair to grow out to prearmy levels, and Tom's was longer still. We got into a taxi with two fare options: to the post, and out of the post. Sensibly, it cost the same: two dollars for either direction.

Reilly Barracks, where the interrogators were billeted, stretched three city blocks, with apertures and nooks and platforms making it look like a battleship. The trees outside were staked into place as if they had to be tied down to keep from fleeing this arid climate. There were dozens of concrete slabs in front of the building, each separated by a bed of white landscaping rocks, carefully raked and evenly distributed. On the slabs were hundreds of outlines of boot soles, which formed the unmistakable forty-five-degree angle of the position of attention. *They must really start at the basics here,* I thought. *The drill sergeants have even painted the proper spacing for one's feet.*

Next morning, all of Reilly Barracks was ordered to turn out in battle dress uniforms on those concrete slabs and the reason for the boot prints was revealed. It wasn't to guide soldiers in the spacing of their feet; the marks were from boot soles and polish melting onto the concrete in the scorching Arizona sun.

The main instructional facility was a converted World War II barracks. Half of the ground floor was a classroom. The other half was office space for the instructors and the latrine. Above, on the second floor, was a single long hallway with twelve doors. Each door led to a small room with just a table and three chairs. A camera poked out from the ceiling in each space. There were tiles on the wall to absorb noise and thick shades on the windows to keep out even a sliver of natural light.

Class started with an overview of what lay ahead. As each section was introduced, I was struck by how cool the job I had enlisted for sounded. An ominous-sounding course called Air-Land Battle was scheduled for more than two weeks. Warsaw Pact Battle Doctrine also sounded very manly. Intelligence Collection in Unconventional War made us feel like we were going to be part of something from Wild Bill Donovan's Office of Strategic Services, the OSS. And on the syllabus horizon was the most tantalizing material of all: the black arts, the approaches, the techniques for "breaking" prisoners.

But before we could get near any of those subjects, we had to pass a section on the Geneva and Hague Conventions. These were the bibles for interrogators, documents we had to know inside and out, and treat with a reverence that was sometimes hard for a group of hormonal young soldiers to muster. The Geneva Conventions cobble together a series of international agreements that date back to 1864, when Henry Dunant, the Red Cross founder who had been horrified by the abandonment of wounded soldiers at the Battle of Solferino, led an effort to get nations to agree to protect the sick and wounded in wartime. In 1929 two more conventions were added, requiring belligerents to treat prisoners humanely, provide information about them, and permit visits to prison camps by neutral representatives. After the carnage of World War II, still more conventions were added, spelling out the rules regarding treatment of prisoners that are the basis for the enforcements in effect today. They ban torture, coercion, and punishment for prisoners who refuse to provide more than basic identification. We spent days reading the conventions aloud in class, passage by passage, and were tested on even the most obscure points. Even so, it was clear after only a single reading which passages mattered most to future interrogators. The language practically jumped out at you: the prohibitions on "violence to life and person, in particular murder of all kinds, mutilation, cruel treatment and torture," and on "outrages upon personal dignity, in particular, humiliating and degrading treatment"; the Article 13 stipulation that "prisoners of war must at all times be protected, particularly against acts of violence or intimidation and against insults and public curiosity"; and the simple requirement that "prisoners of war must at all times be humanely treated."

The instructors, who typically had a knack for making even the most fascinating material dull as dirt, were remarkably creative in the ways that they impressed upon students why these laws had to be obeyed without exception. Of course, the first and often most effective motivation for enforcement was self-interest. Anyone caught violating the conventions could expect to spend a good chunk of time at the military prison at Fort Leavenworth, Kansas. Those grim prospects were repeated so often that by the end of our time at Huachuca the three syllables "Lea-ven-worth" were ringing in our ears.

Then there was the slightly more nuanced argument that the conventions ought to be observed because failing to do so only produced bad intelligence. Staff Sergeant Casey, our senior instructor, hammered home the idea that prisoners being tortured or mentally coerced will say anything, absolutely anything, to stop the pain. All of the instructors told us stories of the experiences of army interrogators working in Vietnam alongside South Vietnamese units that would do the most unspeakable things to prisoners — take two of them up in a helicopter and shove one out the door, torture one of the prisoner's relatives right in front of him — and the squeals of anguish and false information that would flow. The goal of interrogation isn't just to get prisoners to talk, our instructors stressed, it's to get them to tell the truth.

The final and most compelling argument was the human argument. The Geneva Conventions are codifications of basic tenets of humanity. There is no way to violate them and "win." It was while making this case that one of the instructors set down a stack of photocopies and told the students to pass them around. When we got the pages and flipped them over we saw the famous photo of a South Vietnamese officer firing a pistol point-blank into the temple of a Vietcong prisoner on a street corner in Saigon. What was our reaction to seeing this picture? we were asked. How did this make us feel? Well, it made us feel the same way a generation of Americans felt when they saw that searing image for the first time in 1968. Horrified. Disgusted. Perhaps even moved to hatred of the figure pulling the trigger. "This only makes the enemy hardened against you," the instructor said. "This isn't the way Americans do business." The Genevas, Casey said, were our Hippocratic oath. There would always be pressure to choose expediency over principle, he said, but interrogators have to be the ones to resist, because they are the ones who are educated in the code, they are the ones who need to know there is only one right answer.

This doesn't mean that American interrogators are supposed to go into the booth with their hands clasped just hoping their genuine niceness will move the prisoner to talk. After learning what you can't do, we spent a good chunk of class time delving into the murky depths of what you can do. Even the army's interrogation field manual says that the prohibition on the use of coercion "is not to be confused with psychological ploys, verbal trickery, or other non-violent and non-coercive ruses used by the interrogator in questioning hesitant or uncooperative sources." Those are all fair game.

The instructors loved to toss out scenarios and get the students talking. "You are on a mission with the infantry, who capture an enemy soldier. You question him as directed. When you've acquired what information you need, the infantry officer decides there's no way for the patrol to survive with a prisoner in tow. You know you and the squad will never get caught if the prisoner is killed. What do you do?"

Later on, as we got farther along and started practicing interrogations in the booths, instructors loved to bait us to step over the line. Even students overheard by an instructor expressing macho admiration for this or that torture technique were given a failing mark for the day. If there was any suspicion on the instructors' part about the restraint of a student, the offender was dismissed from the program.

But we were also coached in how to walk the Geneva Conventions tightrope without falling off, how to make a prisoner feel threatened without issuing an explicit threat. One scenario involved telling Soviet prisoners they were going to be turned back over to their country, which had a history of executing or imprisoning troops it suspected of betrayal. You could tell the prisoner something like: "Do you know how many of your own people were killed at the end of World War II when the German prisons opened?" But you couldn't take that extra step and say, "If we send you back, you know they're going to kill you." It was a thin line. As the Huachuca instructors said constantly, "You can't put a dagger on the table."

Even when I was training at Huachuca in 1991, the instruction seemed entirely built around a single scenario: a gargantuan clash of Soviet and NATO forces across central Europe, with tens of thousands of soldiers captured, carrying in their heads precious, perishable information that would need to be extracted almost instantly.

The map-reading course focused exclusively on the terrain of Eisenach Hunfeld, a 25-kilometer-square part of central Germany. Any interrogator who went through the school during the Cold War knows it by heart: the villages, the bridges, the church steeples; defensive positions, slow and no-go terrain. We studied driving times for the Soviets' ZIL trucks and BMP infantry fighting vehicles between two points. We examined the weight ratios for bridges to see what types of Soviet equipment could traverse which roads, and which would be restricted to the major highways. We learned how the Russians and their allies tactically deployed for action and the reasons behind their movements. Even today I can explain where a field bakery unit would be in a Soviet line of march, and how that differs from where it would be found in a retrograde movement. We were also shown a video of Russian army basic training that made Fort Leonard Wood look like kindergarten.

Finally, after four weeks, Introduction to Battlefield Interrogation started with a film from Vietnam. The footage was shot by a camera from a corner of a room, overlooking an interrogation. The interrogator's back was to the camera, and you could see the back of his shaved head and the edges of his big Buddy Holly glasses. The prisoner, facing the camera from across an army field table, had black hair in a bowl cut and was dressed in a civilian shirt with large checks. The interrogator was asking questions through a third man, a Vietnamese interpreter wearing green fatigues and a pistol belt.

"Did you see the Vietcong move through the village?" the interrogator asked in English. Then the interpreter posed the question in Vietnamese, his words scrawled along the bottom of the screen in subtitles. Except the question he asked was different.

"Was it raining when you were captured?"

The prisoner said no.

Satisfied, the American followed up with another question: "Do the Vietcong use your village to acquire foodstuffs and other supplies?"

Again, the question was changed in translation: "Do you have twenty-three brothers?"

The prisoner said no.

And so it went. We wondered how anyone could be that stupid, that unobservant? And yet, we suspected, this sort of thing happened more often than our side would like to admit.

The next day my fellow students and I entered our classroom to a surprise: in walked a dozen members of the interrogation school faculty dressed up in Red Army uniforms that made them look like a reunion of some suburban Fidel Castro fan club. These were the IRPs, the instructor role-players. They were going to play enemy prisoners, and we were going to interrogate them.

The instructors started by having us pair up in buddy teams. I drew Victor Rabinowicz, a Russian Jew from Brooklyn whose accent was so stereotypical that it almost had to be an act. We were each given a sheet of paper with details of a fictitious prisoner. It listed how he was captured: where, when, by whom, and some basic facts about the circumstances. We were instructed to spend the next twenty minutes preparing to interrogate this prisoner.

Staff Sgt. Casey sent half the students upstairs into the booths to sit as observers as their partners went first. As we filed upstairs, we caught a glimpse of a huge room filled with television sets and monitoring devices that would record our performances. I went into my assigned booth and sat on the chair

along the wall. One of the IRPs came in and took his place behind the table. He told me to watch, learn, and not to say a word.

A few minutes later Rabinowicz's head peeped into the
room through a little window in the wooden door to the booth.
He smiled, steadied himself, then threw open the door with
such force that it banged against the inner wall of the room and
slammed shut in his face before he could walk in. The IRP
looked through the window and tried not to laugh. Rabinowicz
tried again. He opened the door, walked in, pounded his books
and notepad on the table, and said in a deep, rehearsed voice:
"My name is" — he paused to look at me — "Chris Mackey.
I'm wit' da CIA!"

The IRP went bananas. "The CIA! The CIA! Oh my GOD,
you kill people! Save me! Help me! The CIA!" This raised a
fury in the other booths, and before long all of the pretend prisoners were howling, "The CIA!" up and down the corridor.
Rabinowicz just stood there, paralyzed. He moved a pencil
through his fingers like he was threading a needle. He hadn't
even taken his seat in the booth yet and his expression had "defeated" written all over it.

The IRP took Rabinowicz out into the hall and dropped him
for a set of push-ups that had the New Yorker sweating through
his battle dress top. Then he told him there was no place in interrogation for those who couldn't mask their frustration. If Rabinowicz couldn't mask his emotions himself, the instructor said
he would help him mask them with push-up fatigue.

Before Rabinowicz had collected himself for another pass, a
bell like the one that used to signal the end of a class period in
high school sounded, and the second group was told to go to
the main classroom while the first group got feedback on their
performance. I was just glad to get out of the vicinity of Rabinowicz and his visibly irate instructor.

We in the second group were to interrogate a "Major Victor
Rubenski," an artillery officer in the Sixty-fourth Guards Divi-

sion. "You will be the first interrogators to question him," the instructor said. "His capture occurred as you see it on your capture sheets. Does anyone have any questions?"

No one answered.

"Very well then," the instructor said. "You will have fifteen minutes to run an approach to persuade the major to cooperate. We are looking for you to develop the approach, not necessarily to run it successfully. Good luck."

This time it was Rabinowicz's turn to sit against the wall. Mindful of his disastrous entry, I opened the door calmly. "I'm Private Mackey," I said. "I'm here to ask you some questions, and I expect you to be helpful. I want —"

The prisoner interrupted: "How old are you, Private?"

For a second I didn't know whether the question came from the IRP or the prisoner he was playing. "I'll ask the questions here," I said. "Now, I want —"

Again an interruption: "I just want to know because you have such soft skin." Soft skin? What was this guy on about?

"Yes, well, that will do, Major. You have —"

"And fresh, tanned skin it is, too," the IRP said.

Totally confused, I asked, "Are you the prisoner now or the IRP?"

"Well, my dear little boy," the prisoner said, "I don't know what an IRP is, but if you would come here and sit on my lap and explain it to me, I would be happy to learn."

What the fuck is this about? I thought.

Suddenly there was a ruckus in the corridor, and Corporal Kennedy — a macho classmate particularly ill equipped to handle even a fictional homosexual advance — stormed out of his booth while a flurry of papers and an upended chair settled on the floor. The nature of the game suddenly dawned on me. I sat down in my chair and the prisoner looked at me and smiled.

"Where are you from, little handsome one?" he asked with a

Russian accent. "Are there more like you there, all tanned and lovely?"

I tried to ask a couple of questions, but the prisoner only became more and more amorous. Then, with both of us leaning on the table, the prisoner reached out to stroke my hand. I jerked it back but in so doing sent my pen rolling across the table. The prisoner picked it up and clutched it close to his chest.

"You really must come and get it from me," he said, his accent becoming more Greenwich Village hairdresser than Kiev-born guards artillery officer. Several times I ordered him to give it back, each more firm than the last. But still he refused. Then I snapped.

"Give me that pen back or it will be the last time you hold something with all your fingers!" I bellowed in genuine rage.

"That," began the IRP, his voice suddenly flat, and his demeanor clearly signaling that prisoner had given way to instructor, "is the *last* word you will speak as an interrogator if you don't reform yourself when we start for real."

He got up and threw my pen back at me. "Why don't you write that lesson down?" And with that he walked out of the booth, leaving Rabinowicz and me as prisoners to our ignorance.

"Damn, bro, he totally dogged yo' ass, bro!" Rabinowicz said.

"My name is . . . Chris Mackey . . . and I'm wit' da CIA," I said, mocking my partner's performance. The bell rang, and the class was directed back downstairs. The first lesson had nothing to do with the art of interrogation or even the mechanics of it. It was a fundamental building block of the job: interrogators must *never* be victims of their emotions. Interrogators prey on the emotions of the enemy.

* * *

Over the next several weeks, the instructors at Fort Huachuca dove directly into the art of breaking prisoners. These "black arts" were divided into sixteen methods, or approaches, that were basic psychological ploys for getting prisoners to talk. (The appendix of this book describes each of them in detail.) There was Love of Comrades and Hate of Comrades. There was Love of Family and Incentive, Pride and Ego Up and Pride and Ego Down. And then there was the one with the most provocative name: Fear Up.

Some made more sense than others. Love of Comrades required convincing the prisoner to betray his cause and provide precise information about the location and strength of his fellow Soviet forces so as to allow U.S. forces to swiftly defeat them with fewer casualties. To me this sounded absurd — a captured enemy soldier would betray his friends because he wanted to save their lives? Any fool would be smart enough to know that providing precise locations would only bring a devastating barrage of artillery or air attacks on his comrades' heads. But still the interrogators were obliged to run these approaches with a straight face and were graded on persuasiveness and convincingness.

I had the most trouble with Fear Down, a strategy particularly suited to a prisoner on the verge of panic. The idea is to comfort and reassure, and hopefully coax him into replacing the bond he had with his former comrades with a new bond with his sympathetic captors. I couldn't do it convincingly, according to my instructors. It wasn't that I couldn't see the usefulness of such an approach or couldn't understand the mechanics — the reassuring tones of voice, the gentle gestures, and the soothing words. It was that communicating those feelings wasn't easy for me.

One of the most profound lessons of interrogation is this: your weaknesses in the booth are a reflection of your weaknesses as a person. The approaches that trip you up with a prisoner tend to center on emotions or feelings that trip you up in life. My interrogation booth attempts to console a prisoner came off as strained, transparent, manufactured, fake. Over time I would learn that the best interrogators, perhaps like the best actors, become the person they need to portray in the booth. They tell lies with the conviction of truth. And yet even the best have weaknesses.

Everyone in class was initially undone at one point or another by the weak link in his or her personality or intellect. Jamie Jorgenson, the gentle Mormon, stumbled when he had to be assertive. Rabinowicz couldn't sell "incentive" approaches because he always made the deals too complex by half. Certain women reverted almost instinctually to the coy gestures that had been effective for them in bars and clubs. True intellectuals — the sorts of geniuses whose presence in the enlisted ranks never ceased to amaze me — fell apart when pure logic could not persuade.

The corollary, of course, is that an interrogator's best approach tends to leverage his best traits as a person. My best approach, my favorite to run, was Establish Your Identity. It calls for the interrogator to assert falsities against his prisoner, so the prisoner feels compelled to tell the truth to escape the consequences of the more sinister interpretation of events. It is one of the most elaborate approaches, requiring keen attention to detail. I would listen for things the prisoner would say and then attempt to twist them into incriminating evidence. It is a bold strategy that entails significant risk.

During one practice session, I was given a prisoner who was clearly very scared. The capture tag — a note fastened to the prisoner's uniform by the soldiers who captured him — indicated that he had been separated from, if not abandoned by, his unit. The objective was to get him to talk about a series of mines he and his unit were suspected of laying near a river ford-ing point. All of the indications were that this prisoner should be the focus of a Fear Down, orchestrated with Hate of Comrades (since his brother soldiers had left him to be captured). But I loathed Hate of Comrades because I thought it would be impossible in a real-life environment to convince someone that their best bet was to rat out their own side in an act of revenge. I was determined to run the Establish Your Identity approach — to assert falsities against him in the hope that it would prompt him to tell the truth.

The conversation opened well enough, with the prisoner saying he was captured the night before while he was "working" with his unit. "What is the full unit designation of the unit you refer to as 'my unit'?" I asked, only to get the inevitable reply: "I can't tell you that." The interplay that followed felt like a thumb wrestle, with one of the two parties pinned, only to free himself and resume the standoff. In interrogation there can be no long pauses, and once doors are opened, either in a retreat or an attack, they cannot be closed easily.

I lobbed questions about the night of the prisoner's capture, and he appeared only to answer the ones he wanted to. Some of his initial fear was tinged with a barely apparent smugness that I interpreted as the IRP's own feelings seeping into his character. My instinct was to turn up the heat.

"You know, Lieutenant Gremyenko, the reason I am so interested in your case is because of the atrocity."

"What do you mean? What atrocity?"

"Your attempt to deny even knowing about it is admirable, but we know so much already," I said matter-of-factly.

The IRP sensed immediately what I was trying to do and tried to get me back on the track.

"You are lying to put me on the defensive," he said.

Thinking for just a moment, I replied: "Not at all, we have no reason to lie, no reason to accuse you of anything which isn't a genuine suspicion."

The prisoner wouldn't budge. "I know this trick. You cannot win." Now this was definitely the IRP speaking, and any sensible person would have taken the hint. Clearly, I was not among the sensible.

I continued to pepper the prisoner with accusations, on the fly developing a wild but complex story about an orphanage in the town of Griesbach (the map of Eisenach Hunfeld so clear in my mind I could have recited the intersection). I asserted that the prisoner was part of a group of Russian reconnaissance troops who had broken into the cellar of this clearly marked building and had taken advantage of two of the nurses and "my God man, one of the adolescent girls in residence there! Have you no shame?"

The prisoner asked for more details, to prove there really was such an incident. I supplied them in excruciating exactitude. With each sentence my voice raised and took on tones of disgust. I culminated with a two-minute diatribe about what the West Germans could do to him when they caught him.

The prisoner, who had seemed quite moved by this monologue, rapidly lost his pasty-white look of fear just as I finished. Quite calmly, he asked, "How many people were raped?"

"Four," I told him.

To which he replied: "A moment ago you said two plus an adolescent girl."

It was my turn to know what was coming next: a hail of specific questions about what I had said. I could hardly remember one thing precisely as I had said it. When the bell rang, the prisoner was still reciting this catalog of failures to me.

Afterward, the prisoner-turned-IRP made me watch my entire performance in the monitoring room, well past the time the rest of the class had left on the bus for the other side of the post. The IRP told me to walk back to think about my arrogance. The whole stroll home I fumed about the school, the system, and instructors.

When final exams came, I entered the booth with confidence, left in shambles, but passed. My prisoner "broke" as if on cue. His story was that of a downed pilot captured in civilian clothes — a perfect candidate for Establish Your Identity. I accused him of spying and reminded him that prisoners who shed their uniforms lose the protections of the Geneva Conventions, navigating around the fact that the prisoner had his Soviet identification and Komsomol card, walking a thin line exactly as I had been taught. Some classmates weren't so lucky. Even McGinty, who had done well in class, had to retake his final exam on a second-chance policy. At least two in the class were required to start the interrogation course over again, from the beginning.

By the time of the exam, I had been in active-duty service for just over a year and was aching to be done with the army. At the graduation parade, a colonel gave a speech about how intelligence had helped achieve a speedy victory in the Gulf War. He spoke of continued vigilance in the face of the Soviet collapse, and he exhorted us to keep the motto of the Military Intelligence Corps — Always Out Front — uppermost in our minds. The whole time, all I could think about was getting to college and getting to know all those girls, real ones, who didn't know how to fire rifles and don chemical warfare gear in nine seconds.

McGinty and I, "real" soldiers now, gathered our bags and dashed for the airport. As I boarded the plane, I felt like a fugitive, as if my drill sergeant and the company commander were going to grab me by the collar and yank me back to fill out some forgotten form, perform some duty left undone. When we got to La Guardia Airport, McGinty's parents were there to pick him up. I found a bathroom, changed out of my uniform, and took a cab to Fordham University.

BRITISH SCHOOL

Reservists always do their most intense training in the summers. Infantry or artillery part-time soldiers generally pack off for weeks of war games in some sweltering spot in the United States. The destinations in the intelligence corps were a bit more appealing. I spent my first summer working as an interrogation instructor at the army's Sixth Reserve Forces Training School on Treasure Island in the middle of San Francisco Bay. A summer later, McGinty and I were part of a contingent sent to Germany to take part in an elaborate intelligence exercise called Bavarian Inquisitor. The exercise was useful, with lots of practice interrogating "prisoners" in Cold War scenarios and writing up lengthy "intelligence reports" that would never be read by any analysts. The most valuable part of the experience, however, came by chance.

Shortly after the conclusion of Bavarian Inquisitor, I spotted some British soldiers making preparations for some event to follow the army's. McGinty cornered a Brit in a bar and discovered they were offering their interrogation course to some of their U.S. counterparts. We managed to get ourselves enrolled.

From the start, it was obvious that the British model of interrogation was different from ours. American training was clinical, performed almost in the abstract. Even the Gulf War was rarely mentioned, though some of the instructors had just returned from that campaign. We trainees were taught how to break prisoners . . . and typically given all of twenty or so minutes to accomplish the task before it was on to the next thing. The thinking at Huachuca was that 95 percent of prisoners would break on the direct approach, and if one wouldn't, there would be a thousand other Iron Curtain comrades behind him with essentially the same information. So instead of working on approaches, far more time was spent rehearsing clunky Cold War questions to ask an already cooperating prisoner. The principal American objective was to get the prisoner to reveal his "full unit designation," meaning the division/brigade/battalion/company/platoon label that would show his unit's precise place in his home country's larger military hierarchy. With his FUD, analysts could pinpoint his unit on a map and enable the interrogator to come back at the prisoner with detailed questions about his unit's plans, recent movements, its stocks of fuel and other supplies. It was as if the battlefield were a chessboard and this prisoner had just helped the United States learn the position of another enemy piece. If an interrogator could get the full unit designation, the Huachuca instructors said, the prisoner could be considered broken.

To my mind, the British concentrated on other, more subtle aspects of the job. They made constant references to combat experience in Malaya, the Falklands, the Persian Gulf, and, above all, Northern Ireland. The latter had taught the British a great deal about insurgency warfare and counterterrorism interrogation.

To Huachuca grads, the British training was incredibly disorienting. One of the first exercises was set in a police substation in the jungle. (Where was the enemy order of battle? Where was the Eisenach Hunfeld map of central Germany?) The "prisoner" came in shackled and "bleeding," wearing a wig of wild hair and a fake beard. Two banana republic policemen simply threw him into the chair and stomped off.

I was looking for a capture tag or a screening sheet — those essentials to the U.S. model of interrogation. When I stepped outside the booth to ask for these materials, the British warrant officer in charge of the exercise only grinned and said, "Get back in there! You have all the 'background data' yer gonner get!"

Back in the cell, I discovered the prisoner in the corner taking a leak. "Hey, you asshole!" I screamed. "You're going to clean that up — not me." The wild-eyed, bearded prisoner just laughed a crazy laugh and hopped and skipped around the room. It wasn't so much an interrogation as a scene from an asylum. I got nowhere.

The British had their students conduct interrogations in cars, in the dark, with madmen in corners of cells — even "friendly debriefings" over drinks. The stories were unlike anything we Huachuca alums had trained for. I didn't interrogate a single tank commander or radio operator. I did, however, interrogate prostitutes, a medicine man, drug runners, a lookout from a foiled car bombing, a handful of murderers already in custody, and several guerrilla fighters.

In Huachuca training, scripts called for prisoners to do one of three things: just start talking, refuse to talk but leave clues as to what formula would overcome their reluctance, or employ some sort of elementary cover story to thinly disguise their real purpose (for example, a Russian prisoner wearing farmer's clothes picked up along the road near a pile of Russian uniforms and an empty farmhouse clothesline). Now, for the first time, we were confronted with "layered lying," with one cover story embedded in another and another and another. For example, a prisoner suspected of knowing where an arms cache was hidden violently denied anything to do with the assault rifles but eventually dropped some clues about a small-time thief who had broken into a television appliance store. *Ah-ha!* I thought. Under intense questioning the prisoner admitted that he was, indeed, the thief. Having cracked the case, I called it a day. My report included the trenchant observation that "the prisoner appears to have sympathies with the insurgency."

There were howls of laughter as the class watched my performance on video that afternoon. I had gotten to the second layer of deception. Had I been smarter I might have discovered a third layer: the prisoner was part of a criminal gang; or maybe the fourth, that he was actually the leader of the criminal gang. If I had been an expert interrogator, I might have uncovered the ultimate truth: the prisoner was the weapons officer in the terrorist cell using the arms cache. (At least I got to the thief part. One of my colleagues made out his report to say the man was innocent and should be released.)

My final interrogation exercise at the British school was with a deaf-mute who could not read or write. After an hour and ten minutes of studying and questioning this prisoner, I still didn't have a clue whether he was faking. Taking a cue from Humphrey Bogart in *The Caine Mutiny*, I found some marbles in a desk drawer and rolled them around in my palm. Suddenly I dropped them and bent to pick them up. Down on my knees, I looked at the prisoner and said, "Simon, there's one right by your feet," using the role-player's real name. Simon obligingly reached for it. When he looked up I was staring back with a huge smile. Gotcha.

In the analysis that followed, others thought I should have stomped on his foot and made him yelp, until a British instructor pointed out that "a jail sentence for physically abusing a prisoner is a tough place to learn even deaf-mutes can yelp."

Back in Connecticut, McGinty and I wrote a long review of the British course, urging that every interrogator in our reserve unit be sent. The unit commander instead ordered his eager charges to request the British training materials, which they very sportingly did. In a trunk of scripts and course documents the Brits sent was a sports water bottle. Taped on the outside was a single instruction: "For use in the Jungle script with crazy prisoner who takes a leak in the corner."

SEPTEMBER 11

Over the next few years, while other students at Fordham were partying every weekend, I was traipsing off to Connecticut, doing recruiting for my reserve unit and lining up volunteers to serve as role-players in increasingly elaborate exercises. McGinty and I were selected for the army's Strategic Debriefing School, the pinnacle of military interrogation training. We both did numerous stints as instructors at Huachuca and elsewhere, and took over the planning of major interrogation exercises in the Northeast, spending hundreds of hours plotting new scenarios to replace the irrelevant old Cold War texts on which we had been taught.

In one case, we spent weeks drafting "prisoner" scripts based on a fictional United Nations intervention in Mozambique. When we requested maps from the Defense Mapping Agency, Pentagon officials got wind of the plans and went apoplectic. "Do you knuckleheads have any idea what Mozambique might think if it learned the U.S. Army was conducting war games against it in Connecticut?" The maps showed up a few days later anyway.

For more than a decade, the army, the reserve unit, and a growing expertise in interrogation, were a central part of my life, helping define who I was. But gradually the adventure of it started to feel more like an obligation. After Fordham, I had gotten hired at a big accounting firm in Manhattan and increasingly devoted my energies to mastering the tax code and striving to make manager. I took a leave from the firm in 1996 to return to DLI, this time to learn Arabic. (The 1990s brought a major change in language emphasis at DLI, a shift later accelerated by the September 11 attacks: the number of students studying Arabic was 740 in 2003, double what it had been in 1990; the number studying Russian had tumbled to 474, less than half of what it had been thirteen years earlier.) But my experience at DLI the second time didn't live up to the gloss of my memories of the first. I even reconsidered my participation in the reserves when a particularly massive exercise McGinty and I had spent months planning was unceremoniously canceled by the army. I put in my paperwork to leave my unit and transfer to the ready reserves, a kind of emergency temp pool status in which you are still part of the military but unlikely to get called up and no longer obligated to take part in regular weekend training. My uniforms and army equipment were shoved farther and farther back into the closet and eventually disappeared into my sister's cellar.

In the summer of 2001, I accepted a position with my accounting firm's office in London. I found an apartment in Covent Garden, a trendy Greenwich Village sort of neighborhood with cobblestone streets, ancient pubs, and expensive restaurants. That fall, Geoff Fitzgerald, a Fordham friend whom I had talked into joining the reserves, traveled to London to visit. Fitzgerald had gone through DLI with me the second time I was there, learned Arabic, and then moved to Dubai for the better part of a year to lock in all those lessons. On September 8, over dinner, we talked about the army and the reserve unit, strictly in the past tense. That part of our lives was over, I said. Fitzgerald, who unlike me had no fondness for life in the armed forces, feared we wouldn't get off that easy.

"They're not done with us yet, Mackey," he said. "This world is too crazy."

I was at my computer when my officemate from Spain swiveled her chair around and announced that an airplane had "slam-ed into the Two Towers." It took me a moment to figure out what she meant. I remembered my father's story about the Army Air Force plane that had hit the Empire State Building in 1946.

Then the second tower was hit.

Everyone in the office felt obligated to bring the American in the office updates or offer him condolences. The lead partner came down. "Do go home if you need to, we will of course understand." I found someone whose computer was on CNN before the attack and who therefore had one of the few connections the server didn't boot off. I watched the horrible images and grew angry. "Chris, I'm so sorry. I hope you don't have friends there," said another partner.

"Don't feel sorry for me," I replied. "Feel sorry for the ones who did this."

As I left the office, the streets were already dark, fall having chased nightfall to early evening. I turned down my street, put the key in the front door, and heard "The Star-Spangled Banner" playing through a window in the building next door. It was coming from the flat of an elderly gay couple with whom I had had a cup of coffee now and again. Eugene was in the window, waving a sad sort of wave, while Karl held the speaker of their stereo on the windowsill. I didn't know whether I should look upset or come to attention and salute. It was a little embarrassing, really. I waved politely and went inside.

A month later, the official e-mails started to arrive. Many of them were subject-lined "Raging Bull," the Cold War–era "secret" notification for mobilization. I arranged to transfer out of the ready reserves and be reattached to my unit, the 325th Military Intelligence Battalion. On October 25 I was given three days to report to Fort Bragg, North Carolina, where I could expect immediate orders to proceed overseas. I sat back at my desk in the office and breathed a massive sigh of relief. It was here. When the Gulf War had happened, I had been in Monterey, and stuck there when my unit was called up. The same thing had happened with Kosovo. But now I was finally going to be in a war. I arrived in New York in the middle of the night, and, going through customs, got my first exposure to the cresting wave of patriotism in the country. "Welcome back to America the beautiful, sir," the passport clerk said. I rented a sedan and, en route to Connecticut, craned my neck over the Triboro Bridge to try to glimpse the empty space in the city's fog-shrouded skyline.

FORT BRAGG

The four-lane highway entrance to Fort Bragg bore all the signs of the new post–September 11 reality in the United States. Military police with machine guns and grenade launchers sat under every overpass along the road. The queue for vehicle inspections at the gate stretched out half a mile. Military IDs were inspected as if they were high-value banknotes. MPs with stern faces looked under each car with mirrors and checked every bag in every vehicle. When we were at last waved through, we had been in line for almost an hour.

We pulled into a section of the garrison known as the personnel holding area, a portion of Fort Bragg used to isolate troops before major deployments so they don't interact with any other units — and don't compromise the mission. Around the Humvee parked in front of Building 5451, I saw a rogues' gallery of familiar faces from my reserve unit.

Among them was Chief Warrant Officer Joe Rodriguez, my first squad leader in Connecticut and now an experienced and crucial personality within the group. He was the only real veteran in the outfit, having dropped into combat as a paratrooper in Grenada, switched to the intelligence corps, and then served as an interrogator in the Gulf War. There was also Doug Turner, a thirty-two-year-old sergeant who had joined the reserve unit when he was twenty-nine. He loved the military and the sense of structure and belonging it gave him, but had no experience with interrogation beyond his tutelage at Huachuca.

There were also a large number of troops whom I had personally recruited, including college friends I had persuaded to join the army over one too many beers. Geoff Fitzgerald, whose September 8 prediction now seemed uncanny, greeted me with a bear hug and the affected patois of a Civil War general: "Why good mownin', suh, good mownin', it is truly a delight to see you, suh!" Five foot nine with a shock of black hair, Fitzgerald was built like a fire hydrant. He had a colossal head, which he used to great effect on the rugby pitches of Fordham and which also housed an oversized brain.

After Fordham, Fitzgerald had taken a job in Manhattan at a public relations firm, work his larger-than-life personality suited. But in the summer of 2001, he surprised everyone by bagging his rocketing career as a big-city publicist to move back home to Buffalo and sell real estate in his old neighborhood. On September 11 he was a couple of hours into his first real estate class when someone came in to whisper a message to the teacher. The students gathered around a television and saw the smoldering first tower. Then they saw the second tower get hit.

Fuck, Fitzgerald thought. *I'm going to be in the army.*

That night Fitzgerald went to his parents' home, walked down the steps into their basement, and moved items around until he had uncovered his military kit. He pulled it into the middle of the room and unpacked his uniform and gear. Then he washed it, folded it, and repacked it. It would be another month and a half before he would actually get the call-up. But he knew it was coming.

The command at Fort Bragg had decided that the reservists wouldn't be deployed until they had been "validated" by the 525th MI Brigade, the active-duty military intelligence brigade that supports the XVIII Airborne Corps. The 525th was our new parent unit, and their validation requirement meant that we weekend warriors were going to take a remedial course in soldiering.

This meant passing an array of basic tests, from requalifying on weapons to retaking army drivers' license tests to refreshing our skills at donning chemical weapons suits. When all that was done, we would have to set up a POW compound from scratch and interrogate enemy "prisoners" in a massive prewar exercise. A good deal of it seemed more useful in preparing us for the illogic of army thinking than for the war ahead.

One of the physical fitness tests was a four-mile run that all 2,100 members of the airborne brigade, both active duty and their new reserve sister unit, were required to finish in less than thirty-eight minutes. On the morning of the big run the troops assembled at the brigade's parade field at Bragg in the cold North Carolina dawn. The commander of the 525th Brigade stood up to announce that today would be a "great day . . . because today we will have joining us on this brigade run the commander of the XVIII Airborne Corps." This prompted a round of "hoo-ah"s followed by frantic scurrying of battalion and company commanders, checking and rechecking to make sure that everything was perfect for the arrival of this semiroyal personage.

Fifteen minutes later, as the sun crawled up above the water tower near the parade ground, a column of three minivans rolled in carrying the XVIII Airborne's commander, the deputy commander, a host of underlings with assorted hangers-on, and a group of noncommissioned officers dedicated to making sure the cadences were clean of foul language.

"Brigade, atten-*shun!*" There was a thud of 4,200 running-shoe-clad feet coming to attention on soft damp grass. Lieutenant Gen. Dan McNeill, who six months later would be put in charge of all ground military operations in Afghanistan, seemed to pause for a moment and scan the assembly.

"I understand that today is the first day that the 325th Military Intelligence Battalion is joining us," he said, prompting an outbreak of jeers, hoots, and whistles, except within our reserve unit itself, which stood mute. "I know the 3-2-5 will carry on the fine traditions of this brigade. All the way, Airborne!"

As the run got under way, the general trotted up alongside my battalion commander to make some idle chitchat. I was a few steps behind, straining to carry the battalion colors. Feeling the weight of being alongside such an august personality, our lieutenant colonel began to grope for topics. In one of those painful, measuring glimpses, her eyes fell upon me.

"General, I'd like to introduce you to one of our soldiers, Sergeant First Class Mackey."

The general turned slightly, nodded, and looked back to the front. Unsatisfied with this, the battalion commander offered a little more information: "Sergeant Mackey came to us all the way from London."

This time the general turned farther around and gazed at me a bit longer. Quiet seconds passed as I too groped for something to say. It occurred to me that perhaps the general didn't quite understand the battalion commander. Maybe he thought she meant that I had come from New London, Connecticut. We were a Connecticut reserve unit, after all. So I thought some elaboration might be in order.

"It's in England," I blurted.

The battalion commander buried her face into her hands as McNeill took a third, harder look at me before picking up his pace and pulling away.

Next up was a test of the unit's ability to form a convoy of Humvees, navigate a thirteen-mile course, and handle a series of obstacles along the way. Sitting in the lead vehicle with a clipboard was Lieutenant Snow, a cantankerous but able woman who would grade every maneuver. I sat in the backseat, filling in the *New York Times* crossword puzzle. Not long after leaving the starting point, my driver, Specialist Gonzalez, announced in his Filipino-Bronx accent that there was an injured man in the road ahead.

I peered around the front seat and observed a man in civilian clothes, his arm in a sling with a red blood splotch, standing in the middle of the dirt road. Behind him and to the left was a pickup truck that had run off the road into a shallow ditch. Gonzalez had by this time slowed down to a crawl, but I instructed him to "drive past him and we'll radio for help when we're down the road." As we passed what was obviously an exercise participant attempting to lure us into some trap, Lieutenant Snow leaned over and told me that we needed to go back.

"Back? Why on earth would we want to go back?" I said.

"Because, Sergeant Mackey, that was the ambush exercise and we need to test your ability to react to it."

I squinted down at my paper and then back at the lieutenant. "Seems to me if that was the ambush this team has passed with flying colors."

She was adamant we return to be evaluated in a more conventional manner. I reluctantly assented, but insisted there was no way we were going to simply back up, "literally stumbling into the ambush ass first." The map indicated another small road that would take us back to the ambush entry point. As we reached the junction we stopped, and I saw, two hundred or so yards in the distance, four or five men in civilian clothes with their backs to us.

I motioned for the team to gather around and explained the plan. Leaving one soldier to look after the vehicles, we walked up to the main road, where we took cover and set our rifles' sights on the brightly clothed but heavily armed role-players. I walked straight down the road, still undetected, with my rifle slung over my shoulder until I reached a point about sixty yards from where they were standing.

"YOU THERE!" I shouted, startling them. "Put down your weapons or my men will shoot!" From behind me, a female voice corrected me. ". . . And women!"

"Ahem, yes," I said. "Put down your weapons or my men *and* women will shoot."

Back in the Humvee, Lieutenant Snow was not at all impressed.

All of the interrogators were reading as many books on the Taliban and their fight with the Northern Alliance as we could lay our hands on. It was difficult to find any information that would help lay out a meaningful order of battle for the opposing force. Indeed, it was nearly impossible to lay our hands on any good maps of Afghanistan. But we were also concerned that we might never need a map, good or bad.

By mid-December, much of Afghanistan was already under U.S. or allied control. Mazar-e-Sharif had fallen November 9. Three days later the Northern Alliance had punched into the largely abandoned capital city of Kabul. Kandahar, the Taliban's last major stronghold, was taken December 6. We had been at Fort Bragg since October 22, and it was starting to look as if we interrogators were going to miss the war.

Then one evening after dinner, a runner from the battalion HQ appeared and requested that the interrogators report to company headquarters at once. Once we were inside, the doors were locked and the battalion staff officers placed big manila envelopes — all marked "secret" — on a table. The seals on the envelopes were broken and sets of orders were produced, each perhaps twenty or twenty-five pages long, and stapled in the corner.

"Gentlemen, for you the war is about to begin," said Major

Michnowitz, the battalion executive officer and one of our most impressive leaders. Every time the army responds to a request for reinforcements and mobilizes troops for that mission, a new serial number is generated. We would be known as Serial 93.

The orders instructed part of the 325th to join Task Force 500 "somewhere in the Combined Forces Land Component Command (CFLCC) area of operations." The interrogators were assured that this meant either Uzbekistan or Mazar-e-Sharif. The orders called for five interrogation teams, each consisting of four soldiers. The requirement was for Arabic speakers, Russian speakers (anticipating perhaps significant numbers of Chechens), and Persian Farsi speakers.

With twenty slots to fill, it seemed a good-sized chunk of my Connecticut interrogation unit would be going. But later the 525th Brigade commander indicated that his active-duty units would be taking up the majority of the slots. The reserve unit, my unit, would account for only one of the teams. Thus the composition of the "tasker" would be: one team from my reserve battalion (325th Military Intelligence Battalion), one team from Fort Stewart (from the Third Infantry Division), and one team from Fort Bragg (drawn from the same battalion that had hosted the reserves during the validation process). The remaining teams were to stay behind until some future and unknown date whereupon they would receive instructions to join the rest. That meant that of the three hundred–odd reservists who had spent the past ten weeks at Fort Bragg, only four would be deployed: Geoff Fitzgerald, Doug Turner, Joe Rodriguez, and me. We four were chosen by our company commander, Major Landau, based on the requirements of the tasker, which called for an Arabic speaker (Fitzgerald), a Russian speaker (Turner), and two noncommissioned officers.

Those of us on the list were rushed through a deployment center, where we renewed all our shots and got some we had never heard of before. We were issued new equipment, including desert parkas, boots, fatigues, giant rucksacks, sleeping bags, and flak vests. We were also given auto-injectors for atrophine and 2-PAM chloride, antidotes to exposure to nerve gas. Inevitably, the departure was postponed three times before it was, at last, scheduled for December 26. The unit celebrated Christmas in Fort Bragg, attending a mass with a happy congregation of military families.

The next day, MPs from a national guard unit in Kentucky helped us take our bags and equipment to waiting rental vans with envy: at least somebody was getting to go to the front. Each soldier carried three duffel bags full of uniforms and specialized gear, as well as $850 worth of civilian winter clothes we had purchased and were told would be paid for by the army. (Of course, we were never reimbursed.) Solemnly the interrogators piled into the vans at dawn and stopped only once — at a Hooters in Virginia to buy some wings — on our way to the Baltimore airport.

We were ushered to a small corner of the departures terminal. A 1970s-era sign told us we would be traveling aboard World Airlines, a little-known government charter service that Fitzgerald jokingly called Airline Airways. For all intents and purposes, it was a regular commercial passenger plane with reclining seats and flight attendants and meal service — though there was no alcohol. We flew seven hours to Rhein-Mein Air Force Base in Germany, then another six to Incirlik, Turkey, where we stayed several nights before boarding a cargo plane that took us to the doorstep of Afghanistan, a former Soviet air base in Uzbekistan called Karshi Khanabad. The troops there just called it K-2.

An enormous Uzbek soldier with a preposterous hat boarded the C-141 plane and ordered us to form a line some two hundred meters behind the open cargo bay door. Our names had been written phonetically in the Russian alphabet on a manifest he gripped in his hands. We had to help him sound out many of the names as he called them off, one by one. When at last he was finished checking them off, we were freezing and eager to find some shelter from the biting wind. We took showers, ate American food in the giant chow tent, and slept in borrowed billets.

Two days later we were ordered to prepare to depart for Kandahar, a city in southern Afghanistan that was founded by Alexander the Great, overrun by invaders from Ghengis Khan to the Soviets, and most recently had served as the last stronghold of the Taliban, the fundamentalist Islamic faction that had taken control of most of the country in 1998. The U.S. Marines had added their name to the list of Kandahar conquerors just a few weeks earlier, on December 14, and the first elements of Task Force 500 had flown in just five days later to establish a prisoner of war camp. But the environment was still considered dangerous enough that we MI troops, who had stowed our weapons in safe boxes for the first two legs of the trip, would now be ordered to carry our rifles, pistols, and ammunition on our laps.

As we opened the gun safes, took the rifles out of their bubble wrap, and began unpacking the crates of ammunition, Sergeant Cavanaugh, a big, red-haired Philadelphian, asked me where the M-16 magazines for my reserve troops were. I said they were in one of the boxes. No, Cavanaugh said, all the boxes had been emptied. There were no more magazines.

Underneath dead vines that had once shaded the commander of a forward Soviet air base, I stood wondering where the hell I was going to lay my hands on eighteen assault rifle magazines in the half hour before the airplane was to take us to the combat zone. I ran back into the bermed firebase and searched like a man possessed for a supply or armorer's office.

At last I found the supply sergeant's tent for the Tenth Mountain Division Heavy Engineer Battalion. Inside, in various stages of undress, were half a dozen crusty-looking sergeants smoking pipes or cigarettes or spitting huge quantities of tobacco saliva into empty Snapple bottles.

"Gentlemen, I need eighteen M-16 magazines. Can any of you help me?"

"If you don't mind my asking, sir, who the fuck are you?"

"My name is Chris Mackey, I'm with military intelligence, and I need eighteen M-16 magazines as quickly as I can lay my hands on them. Can any of you help me?"

"M-16 magazines are a controlled item; we don't just have them lying around here, Mr. Mackey."

I pulled out my wallet and slapped a hundred dollars in twenties on the field desk. The sergeants dug into their own equipment, pulled out every bullet in their magazines, and handed the empties to me. When I had eighteen, I plopped another twenty on the table and ran back for the Russian Air Force villa. I distributed the magazines and boarded the C-141 like it was the last chopper out of Saigon.

Once we were airborne, Rodriguez ordered everyone to strip their uniforms of rank insignia, standard procedure for interrogators, who don't want prisoners sizing up their officer patches, or lack thereof. A group of Special Forces soldiers had also boarded the plane, like upperclassmen on a school bus. They had taped their loaded magazines to the stocks of their rifles. Dan Corcoran, a nineteen-year-old active-duty trooper from Fort Bragg, was impressed by the look of this and taped one of his magazines to his rifle, too. He laid the tape on so thick I asked him how he would get the thing off the rifle stock and into the magazine well to fire.

"I'd use my knife," he said, brandishing a PX-purchased bowie knife and a queer little smile.

I told him to untape the magazine and put it in his ammunition pouch on his belt like the rest of us, and as regulation dictated.

As we entered Afghan air space, the air force crew peered out of tiny portholes in the fuselage of the plane, scanning the night sky for "launch signatures." I couldn't help thinking about all the Stinger missiles the CIA had circulated to help the Afghans and jihad Arabs oust the Soviets, and how some of those might now be aimed at our plane.

Most everyone was a study in nervousness, checking their bags, gripping their guns, or just staring blankly ahead. Conscious of my position as the senior noncommissioned officer, I closed my eyes and dozed, supposing that to be the ultimate expression of quiet confidence. Suddenly I was jolted awake. Everyone was shifting gear at their feet and looking like dogs alerted to a suspicious noise. The plane rose and then fell, banked left and right. The air force crew put on flak vests — they looked like lead aprons at a dentist's office — and took up positions with their rifles at the back cargo entrance. I realized I had slept most of the three-hour flight, and we were now descending rapidly, indeed practically dropping into Kandahar.

The lights inside went from dim white to a menacing red and the plane shook violently as it touched down and came to what seemed like an aircraft carrier halt. The cargo door lowered the whole measure of its gape, and the armed air force crew dashed to the runway and knelt down with rifles at the ready. A mini swarm of vehicles with no headlights raced toward the plane from the distance. A goggled airman shouted, *"Move!"* and the troops scrambled down the cargo door just in time to avoid being skewered by a forklift retrieving the pallets of equipment on board.

The stars were staggeringly bright. Despite the midnight hour, the sky had a baby-blue hue that draped on every feature — landscape, mountain line, rooftop, and, closer in the foreground, a white minaret. The Special Forces troops set off for a large terminal building in the distance without a guide. But we interrogators knelt on one knee at the side of the airfield for ten minutes before someone approached and asked who we were.

"We're with Task Force 500," said Chief Irvine.

The female sargeant motioned that we should follow her. The plane over our shoulders revved its massive props, swung around, and climbed back up into the sky. As we drew closer to the terminal, the fresh air turned putrid and sickly, ashy sweet: the unmistakable smell of burning shit. Blown-out glass crunched underfoot as we passed between closely spaced railings, designed to prevent luggage carts from being taken out to the tarmac. The Kandahar airport terminal had a Planet of the Apes look about it. The blown-up snack bar, the burned-out luggage reclaim area, the ticket counters — it was all postapocalyptic. Here and there, tucked into the odd corner, marines were curled up in sleeping bags, boots by their sides, rifles close at hand.

A tall, long-faced man beckoned us over and introduced himself as Lieutenant Colonel Lewis, commander of the 500th MI Battalion out of Fort Gordon, Georgia. He wore a black wool watch cap, an army-issue Gore-Tex jacket, and a pistol on his hip.

"We've got a mission of the most critical importance here," he squeaked in a high-pitched voice. "I know I needn't tell you that." A miniature cloud of condensed breath rose above the heads of the assemblage.

"You can tell there aren't many amenities here, and the weather leaves a little to be desired. But the eyes of a vengeful and hurt nation are on you, and will remain on you, until your duty here — and justice — is done." The marine sentries who heard Lewis's speech were mildly groaning in the eaves. I thought it was a touch dramatic but overall pretty appropriate.

Lewis turned us over to a still taller officer named Captain

Rawles, who was much quicker to the point, giving the no-frills particulars of the new command. He rattled off our new designation — Task Force 500 — names of several key people, and something about the spot on the fledgling firebase we were responsible for holding in the event of an enemy assault. It was the bombed-out baggage claim area. I looked at a few of the nearby airport signs and made a mental note to look up the Arabic words for "baggage claim" as soon as I had a free minute.

Rawles led us outside to a tent situated in a courtyard, protected on three sides by the walls of the terminal building. It was cold and windy, and the tent flaps blew and snapped while wind crept beneath the framed tent walls and puffed up the whole thing like a garbage bag caught in the wind. Inside, sitting on crates of MREs (meals ready to eat) around a single potbellied stove, were a handful of interrogators who had arrived some days earlier, none of whom was familiar to me. They were wearing civilian winter clothes over their service uniforms. Most had army brown T-shirts on their heads as makeshift babushkas.

Rawles directed us out of the tent and continued his tour. The next stop was a broad, shallow hole the marines had dug in the middle of a rose garden that had been something of a landmark at the airport. The hole was the garrison "piss pit," and there was a chemlight at the bottom to help you find it in the night. There were no special accommodations for women. Lynn Pearson, one of the females in our group, squirmed a little at this thought. Next, Rawles took us to a halved fifty-gallon drum, upon which sat a square piece of wood with a hole cut in the middle. "That's the shitter," he said, adding that it was an improvement over the "spade" method employed until recently. He then began a brief lecture on the chemical properties of human waste, explaining that the barrels of shit wouldn't burn properly if they contained urine. "The shitter is for shitting," he said. "The piss pit is for pissing."

We skirted a crop of marine pup tents and weaved in and out of half-unpacked pallets to a point where we could see a ramshackle cluster of adobe rooftops surrounded by metal, wood, and mud walls topped with barbed wire.

"That," Rawles said, "is the detention compound."

Then Rawles stopped and faced the group, turning more businesslike. "Now, you should know the rules of engagement," he said. "You will have one thirty-round magazine in your rifle at all times. You will have the safety on, and you will *not* have a round in the chamber." There was a cacophony of clicking and jamming. "You will never leave your rifle more than an arm's distance away. You will engage any target that threatens you. Remember, this is a combat zone."

Another sergeant who had shadowed our tour then showed us to our sleeping tent. The only light came from the moon, shining into the open flap on one end. The sergeant went off to fetch a drop light. Everyone was fumbling in the darkness, trying to find items in their duffels, when Rodriguez sidled up to say there was about to be a second, VIP tour: Chief Lopez, Task Force 500's operations officer, would take us into the prison compound.

Lopez led Rodriguez, myself, and a few others past a ramshackle collection of buildings to a large, iron, two-sided gate. It was topped with barbed wire and marked with a spray-painted sign that said No Entry. There were guard towers on either end of the fence line, flat-roofed boxes, each with two marines clutching rifles or squad automatic weapons (SAWs), a light machine gun. The area behind the checkpoint was illuminated by massive stands of stadium lighting. It looked like something out of *Mad Max*.

Lopez pulled aside a marine and gave some instructions. After a pause, one half of the gate creaked opened and a marine jailer, straight out of central casting with a slightly hunched back and a long scar down his cheek, waved us in. The jailer was evidently very cold, stomping his feet into the baby powder–fine sand, causing a small cloud of dust to rise from the ground. Once the group was inside, he wrestled the gate shut and fitted a huge metal bar across the width of both doors as they closed. "Welcome to the Rock," he said with unsophisticated drama.

We were in a corridor of sorts, a long, narrow space between an outer wall of tin and concertina wire erected by the marines and engineers, and an inner, fifteen-foot-high mud wall built by some previous generation of Afghans. The mud wall at one point had guarded a fruit tree orchard from the elements and, probably, from thieves. The trees were gone now, but a number of sheds and barnlike structures remained.

We followed Chief Lopez into the largest of the barns, which was covered with corrugated tin. Inside were five cells, with sides of concertina wire and pitched tent roofs. Both ends of the barn had a large open doorway. But blocking these openings were rolling staircases used to board airplanes from the tarmac. On the sides of these vertical gangways was the Afghan national airways symbol and the word "Ariana," the name of the defunct service. Perched atop each set of stairs was a single marine guard.

Of the five cubes, only two were occupied, with a prisoner in each. They were wearing blue jumpsuits and knit wool caps, and both were smothered in thick blankets. One was asleep, the other seriously agitated — indeed, he was practically hyperventilating, emitting a steady plume of frosty breath. When he saw us, he shed his blankets, sprang up on his feet, and began shouting in Pashtu, spitting through the wired enclosure and grabbing his crotch. The marines on the rolling stairways turned guard towers shouted at the prisoner, and one tossed a rotten apple near him. Surprisingly, this appeared to act as a calming agent. The prisoner recovered the warmth of his blankets and, sitting up, began to rock back and forth methodically. I noticed there were numerous rotten apples near his cube.

"He's not all there," Lopez said, twirling his finger at the side of his head. The barn was for isolation of key prisoners, he told us. There was really only one — the sleeping one — who qualified, but the crazy one had been eating his own shit earlier that day and had been threatened by other prisoners, so the marines put him in the barn, too.

The tour continued around the barn and into the main, mud-walled prison compound. It was a wide area, under open sky, with ten tents set up in neat rows. Each row was encircled by barbed wire. All of the tents had their sides uniformly rolled up, exposing the occupants to the gaze of the marine guards — as well as to the bitter cold wind. The prisoners, perhaps forty in total, were divided into two tents. They were shapeless heaps of blankets, only the occasional knit hat indicating a head here or there. One prisoner was rising and falling, using his blanket as a kind of shawl, and praying. Whatever spiritual benefit was derived from his routine of stand up, kneel, prostrate, stand up, it also helped keep him warm.

We turned around and headed out of the mud-walled compound. Lopez led us down the dusty exterior corridor to a place where the tin fence jutted out sharply to the right, creating a squared-off fortification thirty yards deep and eighteen yards wide. High coils of concertina wire indicated that this was a place of maximum security. Lopez directed our attention to six conical tents, in rows of three with a pathway down the center. These were the interrogation booths. Each had a small scrap of cardboard affixed above its entrance with an assigned number, 1 to 6.

At the far end of this space, framed between the two rows of tents, was a fire burning in a halved fifty-gallon drum. Around it sat three marines and two interrogators. The two interrogators motioned for us to look into the tent nearest them. Therein we spied a plump interrogator, hat off (exposing a completely bald head), questioning a prisoner. There was a propane tank inside the tent, just like the ones people hook up to their gas-powered barbecues, but this one had a coil attached to the top that spurted a wide flame for warmth.

"That's Prisoner 17," said Lopez, nodding at the prisoner. "He's a real motherfucker — the real deal."

I stared into the dimly lit olive drab opening. There it was. The first POW interrogation I had ever seen. *God-damn,* I thought, *I can't wait to get in there and do this. I cannot possibly wait.*

When we got back to our tent, most everyone was asleep. Specialist Brian Talbot, a member of our newly arrived group, informed Rodriguez and me that everyone was to report to the Task Force 500 HQ area at 0530 hours. Rodriguez and I stumbled around, kicking our shins into obstacles positioned for maximum pain, trying to get settled and thinking about what we had seen. Just before I went to sleep, I pulled out my flashlight and looked in my Arabic dictionary for the words "baggage claim."

PART

II

REPORTS EDITOR

At 0445 hours, the sun was already inching its way up, and a magnificent purple and blue horizon cast the mountains in silhouette. The dusty earth extended forever in all directions and looked dead — even decayed. There were a few miserable, leafless trees and some clumps of long-dead grass, a variety whose healthier cousins one sees on sand dunes at the seashore. As I brushed my teeth, I noticed that the tin screen bulging out from the main prison compound — the enclosure for the interrogation booths — was just twenty yards in back of the sleeping tent. My commute wouldn't be long.

In front of the tent was the main Kandahar terminal, some seventy-five yards away, a surprisingly graceful piece of architecture built in the 1950s. It had handsome archways, curving hallways, a sandstone facade, and light blue accents of color.

Chief Lopez and Captain Rawles were waiting outside the operations tent, the headquarters for intelligence operations at the prison. Its official name was the interrogation control element. Everyone called it the ICE.

"Who here has combat interrogation experience?" Lopez asked. A smattering of hands went up, including those belonging to Talbot, Specialist Henry Hasegawa, Sgt. Tom Cavanaugh, and Chief Rodriguez. "I do not count Bosnia or Kosovo as combat interrogations," he added. Only Rodriguez's hand stayed up, his Gulf War service still singling him out.

"How many here have strategic debriefer training?" Lopez asked, referring to the advanced army course to teach intelligence soldiers more sophisticated techniques for interrogating prisoners or debriefing defectors. *Oh, thank God — I won't be the last kid picked in gym class,* I thought, and raised my hand. Only Rodriguez, Chief Irvine, and I had been to that program, known as N-7 school. I was positive this would mean a high position, maybe even senior echo, which would mean running the entire interrogation operation for either the day or night shift. But in this crowd it was hard to tell who had senior rank. Everyone had stripped the insignia from his uniform.

"Okay, here's the deal," Lopez continued. "We're going to create two shifts: day and night. This is Staff Sergeant Jamie Grenauld; he is the day-shift senior echo. Chief Irvine, you will be the officer-in-charge." That meant he would be over the senior echo, but serving more as a general manager than a coach. The officer-in-charge (OIC) is the liaison to the command, briefing them on major developments and making sure their priorities are communicated to the interrogators. The OIC works in the interrogation control element and makes the big calls but leaves the day-to-day planning to the senior E.

Then Rawles, flipping through his clipboard, located the list for the night shift. "This is Staff Sergeant Mark Stowe; he's going to be the night-shift senior echo. Chief Tyler — you're the night-shift OIC."

Rawles read off the names of the soldiers on the day shift, then the night. Rodriguez interrupted: "Sir, you didn't mention Sergeant First Class Mackey or myself" — and I thanked God again, this time that Rodriguez had said my full rank so that the captain could see the error of appointing a staff sergeant over a sergeant first class.

"Right . . . sorry to miss you, Chief. You and Sergeant Mackey are the day- and night-shift reports officers, respectively."

My heart sank. Night-shift reports officer? What kind of a punishment was this? "You two are the only ones available who have strategic debriefer," Rawles said, "and we need qualified N-7s to do frontline reports editing."

Fitzgerald, the other night-shift interrogators, and I walked back to the tent, with twelve hours to kill before our first shift would start. Fitzgerald tried to console me, but it was no use. The prospect of being a reports editor for the war on terror was worse than not going to the fight at all. How could I ever explain this? "I spent the war on terror correcting format and grammar on the government's standardized intelligence-reporting system." No interrogations, no confrontations with the enemy, no nothing. Just summaries of other people's work and a click of the spell-check option.

After seizing the Kandahar airport from a small contingent of dug-in Taliban fighters, the marines had spent the intervening period detonating caches of rifles, rocket-propelled grenades, and other ordnance, clearing hundreds of land mines, and disposing of at least twenty Taliban corpses from the bomb-cratered landscape. All told, there were fewer than a thousand marines holding the airport, and many of them were still digging bunkers on either side of those sections of runway that could be used.

The marines and navy Seabees had also built the prison, using concertina wire and other materials they brought as well as scrap parts found at the airport. It was designed to hold up to three hundred detainees — with the expectation that at least that many might be taken in the wake of mid-December fighting in Tora Bora, where bin Laden and hundreds of Al Qaeda fighters had holed up in crevices and caves after the rout of the Taliban. But that fighting was largely over by December 16, two days after the airport had been taken, and the would-be prisoners had melted away.

For the time being, the prison was little more than a holding pen, with about forty prisoners, almost all of them Arabs and all of them hard-core. Some had been shipped down from Sheberghan, a Northern Alliance prison where American Taliban John Walker Lindh had been found and CIA paramilitary officer Mike Spann had been killed. Others had been taken in fighting around Mosul. And a few had been captured nearby in Kandahar. For the moment — with seventeen members of my unit reinforcing a nine-member team of interrogators already in place — the number of interrogators rivaled the number of prisoners.

The first shift change came at 2100 hours, and all the members of the night and day crews filed into a dark green tent that served as the ICE, twenty yards outside the prison compound. Inside there were laptops on field desks, a dry-erase board, a coffeemaker on its last legs, and a table with all kinds of dictionaries. Everything was filthy, coated in the baby-powder-fine dust that settled on every surface. In the center of the room, a stove running on jet fuel burned hot enough to boil water, though it barely kept the corners of the tent above freezing.

The day-shift senior echo, Jamie Grenauld, rattled off some statistics: how many interrogations had been completed during the day shift, how many reports had been written and submitted, and how many prisoners were expected to arrive that night. Grenauld then turned it over to Captain Rawles, who capped his brief remarks with a vague warning that the marines had reported suspicious activity on the perimeter of the camp and that other intelligence indicated the enemy was regrouping in small numbers near Kandahar and planning attacks on the new U.S. base in its midst.

And, to my surprise, that was it. No discussion of how the day-shift interrogations had gone. No mention of the latest intelligence priorities in Washington or the chief intelligence concerns among the leaders in the local command. We were in the middle of a war — the war on terrorism, no less — and our first real meeting had all the purpose and substance of a cash-register count at the end of the day at some shopping mall.

I made my way to a row of laptops at the back of the tent. As I settled in, the night-shift interrogators were making their first trips into the booths. Most were more nervous than the prisoners they faced. Fitzgerald's first screening was typical: an awkward blur, a forty-minute session in which his observations of the prisoner were overwhelmed by observations of himself, a bout of acute self-awareness brought on by booth-performance anxiety. He fumbled for Arabic words that should have come easily. He became distracted by what he took to be the sensation of adrenaline coursing through his veins. He later said that it was as if his eyes had left his head to watch the proceedings from the back of the tent.

Fitzgerald had tried to adhere to the Huachuca script, even prompting the sullen Arab in front of him for his "full unit designation." But the prisoner had just stared back blankly. Then Fitzgerald had tried a less formal tack and got replies but not answers.

What do you do?

I do lots of things.

Who do you work for?

I work for Ali.

Who is Ali?

Ali is the boss.

What does he look like?

Dark skin, curly hair, brown eyes.

When Fitzgerald got back to the ICE, I asked him how it went.

"Not too bad," Fitzgerald said. "He told me how much he hates the Taliban, referred to me as 'my dear one,' and then asked whether or not he's in America." If this was how we were going to fight the secret war on terror, we were in a lot of trouble.

*   *   *

A new shipment of prisoners arrived later that night, and the command began to buzz when they heard that three were Pakistanis from England. Any detainee with ties to the West went immediately to the top of the priority list because it was assumed they were more likely to have information on terrorist cells in Europe and the United States.

I was still chafing at my assignment. As reports editor, I wasn't supposed to spend any time in the booth. When the Brits showed up, I saw a possible way in.

"Mark, I've been living in London and practicing my Arabic in the coffee shops on Edgware Road; let me take these three, " I said, pleading with the night-shift senior echo whom I otherwise outranked.

Stowe refused, noting that there was already a backlog of reports that needed editing. A while later, sensing my disappointment, Stowe relented, sort of. He still wouldn't let me interrogate the Brits but did tap me to translate for a non-Arabic-speaking interrogator heading into the booth.

Tim Atley, a cocky, twenty-three-year-old specialist from Arizona, ordered me to get my gear in a tone too abundant with self-assurance, and we stepped outside the ICE and into the biting cold. The Marine Corps infantry who served as the military police force were dressed like Sta-Puft marshmallow men, attempting to warm themselves on the embers of a drum fire built from the dense cardboard boxes that rations came in. There were two other interrogators already waiting for their prisoners to be retrieved: Gary Heaney, the bald-headed Marylander I had seen the first night, and Jon Lee, a quiet active-duty interrogator from Fort Stewart.

The group shivered for half an hour before two tiny men in jumpsuits were hauled in by gigantic marines, one MP on each prisoner's arm. The prisoners were in handcuffs and leg irons. They raced along in short baby steps, struggling to keep up with the marines' long strides. The prisoners' heads were covered with sandbags, and puffs of steam rose out of the two pointy ends on top, making them look like devils.

The marines put the prisoners in separate booths, sitting them down on folding metal chairs covered with beige bedspreads. The prisoners were then wrapped in rust-colored leopard-print blankets that the marines said had been purchased in bulk from Pakistan. The marines wore surgical gloves with rubber bands around the wrists and cocked their heads to the side as they handled the prisoners, straining to distance their faces from the intense body odor.

One of the marines asked Heaney if he wanted the sandbag taken off the prisoner's head. "Yeah, why not," Heaney said, as if he were opting for an order of fries with a burger.

"And the cuffs?" the marine asked.

"Better leave them on; he's an unknown quantity," Heaney said.

After watching Heaney place his order, Lee said, "Can I have mine the same?" and stepped into his tent, too.

After another thirty-minute wait, the marines dragged out a third prisoner in the same fashion, and Atley and I followed him into the booth. Atley faced the prisoner across a folding army table. I sat behind the detainee, out of range of his peripheral vision and slightly to his right, just as the instructors at Huachuca had taught.

Atley took off a glove and lit a cigarette. "I'm going to ask you some questions," he said.

That was easy enough, and I translated my first Arabic sentence in a combat environment with a fairly good Saudi accent. Just as the Huachuca instructors said would happen, the prisoner turned to look at the Arabic speaker — me — behind him. And just as the teachers instructed, Atley demanded in a loud voice that the prisoner turn and face him. There was ten years between my 97E training at Huachuca and Atley's, but this exchange showed how little the playbook had changed. In an interrogation, the interrogator and the prisoner are always to face each other, behaving as if the translator isn't even in the room.

Prisoner 44 proceeded to explain how he had been forced to fight for the Taliban even though he was just an Arab who had come to look for the body of his dead brother, a victim of the Taliban who had come to Afghanistan for a "pure Islamic life."

The prisoner said he and his brother hated the Taliban with their living and dead souls, respectively. But for him, it was either fight for the Taliban or end up like the brother whose body he had come to reclaim. Out of practice, I missed a lot of words but managed to piece this story together through context and pass it on to Atley, who took notes on the screening sheet in front of him.

But as Atley delved deeper into the prisoner's story, the translation got harder. At one point Atley asked the prisoner about his affiliation with an Islamic group.

"I don't know how to say 'affiliation,'" I said.

"Okay, how about 'connection,'" Atley offered.

"I don't know how to say 'connection,' either" I said.

"How about 'relationship'?"

Nope. I couldn't do it.

Atley tried backing up and coming at the subject from a different direction, but my Arabic kept breaking down. No matter what Atley tried, he kept wending his way back to the same dead end. Frustrated, Atley asked me to step outside and asked why I was having so much trouble.

"Listen, I've been out of the army for almost two years," I said, "so my Arabic's a little rusty." As Atley shook his head in disgust, I blurted out that I didn't know why the hell Atley was asking the questions he was asking anyway.

This set Atley back. It was the first time my voice and body language suggested there was a serious disparity in rank. Atley reminded me that — rank aside — *he* was the interrogator and that *he* would pose the questions *he* saw fit.

"This is *not* an interrogation. This is a *screening*," I replied. "We are not here to interrogate this man unless you hit upon priority intelligence information. This exercise should take no more than five minutes."

"It's going to take a hell of a lot longer than five minutes with you translating," Atley shot back, and with that he turned on his heel and reentered the tent.

We finished up and asked the marines to take the prisoner back to the main compound. Atley had gathered enough information to fill out the screening report. He organized his notes, and I made a list of words to look up.

Lee and Heaney had long since finished their screenings, and a new group of interrogators surrounded the hobo fire. Atley and I left the joint interrogation facility (JIF) and picked our way across the short expanse between the prison entryway and the ICE. Atley was quiet, frustrated with me but unsure how far he could go in correcting me without actually knowing my rank.

I was relieved to be back in the ICE, back in the precinct of the potbelly stove, but as my body thawed I realized how badly I needed to relieve myself in another sense. I grabbed my red-lens flashlight and rifle — which took some time to find among the two dozen other M-16s hanging from the hooks on the tent frame near the door.

I was a few paces away from the tent, admiring the canopy of stars, when I remembered that I was in a combat zone at night, alone. I took my rifle off my shoulder and held it in a slightly absurd position around hip level. A voice from ten yards away startled me.

"You one of those MI fellas?" it said in an immediately identifiable Boston accent.

"Who's asking?" I said, stopping to adjust the position of the rifle just enough to be ready but not so much as to be construed as aggressive.

"Just that you don't find many marines walking around the inside of a fire base with their M-16 held like Rambo," he said.

I wasn't exactly sure how to answer. "You can never be too careful," I said, quickly adding, "You from Boston?" as a means of changing the subject quickly.

"Nah, Foxboro," he said.

"Ah, home of the Pats. Go, Pats!" I said. Incident forgotten.

I followed the voice to the edge of the piss pit, which was about ten feet wide, ten feet long, three feet deep, and lined with stones. As I got closer, I could begin to make out the moonlit face of the Patriots fan pissing away and targeting a chemlight in the center of the pit with his stream. I placed my rifle near a tree stump and set to the business at hand. The marine buttoned up, unslung his own rifle from his shoulder, and said, "Take cahre."

As the marine left, the stump I had placed my rifle near stood up and walked away, too, spooking me so badly that I nearly leaped into the steamy rock-lined hole. Smirking, the stump-turned-marine sauntered off with a familiar quote: "You can never be too careful."

Back in the ICE, I returned to my seat and another report on a laptop so clogged with Afghan dust that pressing the keys practically required leaning into every stroke. The keys didn't click so much as crunch when I pressed them. There were field desks lining the side of the tent, on top of which were scattered work papers, notes from interrogations and dozens of one-liter bottles of water that froze solid at night if they were left too close to the edge of the tent.

Mark Stowe sauntered up and asked how the screening had gone.

"Started off okay, but it's amazing what happens to your Arabic when you've been out of the army for two years," I said.

"It'll come back," Stowe said charitably. Atley rolled his eyes.

The one advantage of being a reports editor was that you got to see what the other interrogators were collecting, how they were doing in the booth, what the prisoners were saying. After just a few days on the job, I could see that the prisoners were generally falling into two categories: a small group of ideologically committed Al Qaeda types, and a second, far larger group who claimed to be noncombatants or to have been coerced or tricked into fighting for the Taliban.

The trouble was, it was sometimes very difficult to distinguish between the two. Both sets of stories usually started out the same way. The prisoners all professed to hate the Taliban. If they were Arab, they would generally describe how they had arrived in Afghanistan two or three years before, taken up residence in one of the larger cities, married a local bride, worked occasionally at some in-law's "shop," and spent their recreational time reading the Koran.

If the prisoner admitted to any military service, it was only to have attended a mandatory two- or three-day camp to learn how to use the "Klash," the Arabic bastardization of *Kalashnikov*, the Soviet assault rifle. The interrogators would get the prisoners to describe the camps from memory, then attempt to diagram them in PowerPoint in their reports. But there were no facts or names, and the diagrams were about as precise as a football play drawn in the schoolyard dirt.

Nobody was having much success in the early going. The one who got off to the fastest start was Tom Cavanaugh, the active-duty sergeant out of Fort Bragg. He was big, at least six foot two, and the most physically intimidating interrogator in the unit. Because of his size and red hair, Fitzgerald called Tom

the Celtic Warrior Reborn. Cavanaugh was a former infantryman, and sometimes that background seemed to define his approach in the booth. As an interrogator, he was tough and
indefatigable, if somewhat one-dimensional. He didn't go for
trickery or any of the "softer" approaches. His favorite tactic in
the booth was to step into the tent, stare menacingly at the prisoner, and say, "You're fucked."

Quite often it worked. Within a week of his arrival, Cavanaugh was getting through three interrogations a day. And he
was setting that pace as a Russian linguist with no Arabic or
Pashtu in his repertoire. That meant every session took twice as
long, because each sentence had to be spoken twice — once by
the interrogator or prisoner and a second time by the interpreter. Cavanaugh wasn't finding anything earth-shattering,
but he was getting good stuff. He reported on backdoor routes
of travel into Afghanistan, which in the long run were not of
huge intelligence value but very edifying to interrogators. From
prisoners captured in Jalalabad, he pieced together an interesting account of the police force there and how it had attempted
to enlist local men in an ad hoc army to face the advancing
Americans and Northern Alliance. He wrote a report on how
medical supplies were being brought in from Pakistan to hospitals in Kabul, where enemy fighters were being treated. He
wasn't on bin Laden's trail by any stretch, but in the under-
stated jargon of military intelligence, he was "collecting," and
that's more than could be said of most of the others.

Cavanaugh had the advantage of having done some interrogation work in Bosnia, as well as a fearless personality. Doug
Turner had neither of those arrows in his quiver. He was a Connecticut reservist, thirty-two years old, but had been in the
army only three years, and his entire experience in interrogation had come from his stint at Fort Huachuca.

Facing a prisoner across a small table in a field tent in the
middle of a war isn't easy business. There's a huge mental

component, obviously. Keeping track of all the intelligence requirements, directing a fast-moving conversation, and doing it all in Arabic or Farsi or Pashtu can be like three-dimensional chess. It also takes nerve. Prisoners who are adamant, whose convictions are steeled, whose posture is aggressive, can unnerve even good interrogators. But Turner was having trouble with pussycats. Old Afghans and farmers appeared to be confusing him.

For example, when an interrogator hears a prisoner mention a weapon, a hundred follow-up questions should leap to mind. Huachuca practically tattooed these onto your brain. But when a prisoner would mention to Turner that he'd gone to a camp to learn how to operate the Klash or a ZSU antiaircraft system, Turner would draw a blank. He had no memory of entire scripts and questioning courses that should have been second nature. So Turner started bringing his big three-ring binder from Huachuca into the booth with him, which is a no-no. It doesn't exactly inspire awe when a detainee looks across the table and sees his interrogator flipping through a three-ring cheat sheet. And besides, follow-up questions are supposed to come quickly, almost rapid-fire. If you give a prisoner time to think, you lose. But Turner would be thumbing through his book for the section on weapons systems as if he were looking up names in a phone book. A minute of silence would pass. Then another. Unlike Cavanaugh, who was getting scraps of information from almost every prisoner he faced, Turner and others like him were coming back to the ICE saying the same thing over and over again: "Nothing to report. He's a low-level fighter. He didn't have anything."

If nobody was too alarmed by such troubles in the early going, it was largely because nobody was terribly sure about the mission. We knew we were there to question prisoners. And we knew our first priority, as interrogators working in the combat zone, was to press detainees for any information they had about enemy plans or weapons or people posing an immediate threat to U.S. forces. But Kandahar was what was known as a "brigade cage," which meant that it was designed to take in prisoners from the front, question them quickly, and hold them for several days before moving them to the "rear" for longer-term questioning and custody.

The "rear" in this case was some seven thousand miles away on the eastern tip of Cuba, on a patch of land the United States had occupied since first leasing it from the then-friendly Cuban government in 1901. When we arrived at Kandahar, we weren't even aware of the Pentagon's plans to transfer prisoners to Guantánamo Bay, Cuba. (The plans had been announced by Defense Secretary Donald Rumsfeld while we were en route to Afghanistan from Fort Bragg.) Guantánamo offered some obvious advantages. It was isolated, far from the Arab world, and secure enough to hold prisoners that the United States saw as terrorists, "unlawful combatants," not conventional prisoners of any conventional war. Guantánamo was also a safe remove from U.S. territory, where prisoners might have successfully sought access to the American legal system. The United States would have plenty of latitude to decide what to do with these worst of the worst, in the words of more than one Bush administration official, and plenty of time to interrogate them in more detail.

When we interrogators at Kandahar learned about the plans for Guantánamo, we were elated. To us, that meant our mission was likely to be a short one. We would stick around long enough to process Arabs and other "high-value" detainees being picked up by U.S. forces or culled from the thousands of prisoners being held by the Northern Alliance. Then we would be done. How long would that take? A couple of months maybe, no longer. This wasn't just wishful thinking by the troops, this was the signal coming straight from Rawles and the other members of Task Force 500's leadership, who, within weeks of their arrival at Kandahar, were already talking about when they would begin "winding things down." Kandahar, they said, was strictly a short-term operation that would shrink quickly.

Our job was twofold. First, we were to interrogate prisoners for "tactical" intelligence, meaning information that could help the commanders in charge of running the war. We weren't supposed to play detective or pursue big-picture questions on the organization of Al Qaeda. If we tried to get too fancy in our reports, we'd get scolded by the colonels at Camp Doha, Kuwait: "We'll do the analysis." We were supposed to function like a M★A★S★H unit, performing intelligence triage on the prisoners who came through and then sending them off to Guantánamo for detailed debriefings. And that brought up the second part of our job: sorting who was to be sent to Cuba. The criteria were worked out at the highest levels of the Pentagon and were spelled out for us in guidelines issued by Central Command: "U.S. forces are required to detain the following categories of individuals: (1) all Al Qaeda personnel; (2) all Taliban leaders; (3) non-Afghan Taliban/foreign fighters; and any others who may pose a threat to U.S. interests, may have intelligence value, or may be of interest for U.S. prosecution." Strictly speaking, that meant every Arab we encountered was in for a long-term stay and an eventual trip to Cuba. Only Afghans with considerable intelligence value were supposed to be sent.

Of course, we only put prisoners into these categories; the actual decisions on who was transferred to Cuba and when were made at Camp Doha by something of a review board with high-ranking officials representing four constituencies: army intelligence, the military police, the various civilian intelligence organizations, and the FBI. Each had its own interests. Civilian intelligence and the FBI might want a certain prisoner sent on to Guantánamo because it looked as though he might have

information on Al Qaeda cells in Europe and the operation at
Cuba was better equipped to do that kind of detailed drilling.
The army representative was looking out for the troops in the
field. If he thought certain prisoners had intelligence about a
planned attack on the base at Kandahar or some other threat to
forces in the field, he might make a pitch for the prisoners to
stay put. The MP representative was mainly accountable to his
crew at the prison. He might want to move out a detainee because the prisoner had diarrhea and was taking too much of the
guards' time cleaning him up every day. The board would con-
vene once a week or so, put together a list of prisoners to be
shipped out, and then send the list to Kandahar. The Task
Force 500 command could raise objections if they saw a problem — say, a prisoner due for transfer who had just been broken and whose interrogation shouldn't be interrupted. But as
we would learn later, once a prisoner's name was on a manifest
for Cuba, it was next to impossible to get the name off.

The first batch of twenty prisoners was shipped off to
Guantánamo on January 10 aboard a C-17 Globemaster on
which the MPs outnumbered the prisoners, two to one. Other
similar-size shipments were off in quick succession. Within two
weeks, 138 other prisoners had been sent off. Airplanes loaded
with prisoners seemed to depart every other night, weather and
the lurking enemy at the end of the runway permitting.

But anyone who was paying any attention at the shift-
change meetings also knew that the flow out to GTMO, as it
was known, wasn't keeping up with the flow in. Which meant
the brigade cage was holding prisoners for a lot longer than a
couple of days. And nobody had any idea that in a little over a
month, the flow out would stop altogether.

MEET THE BEATLES

The three Brits in custody had quickly acquired the nickname "the Beatles" from the guards. Screening them had established little besides the fact that all three were from London. The handwritten notes in their manila folders alluded to travel to Pakistan and crossing the border near Kandahar.

Mark Stowe, the night-shift senior echo, had tapped an interrogator named Cassidy to question the Beatles. Cassidy, in his late thirties, was from Virginia but lived in New Orleans with his wife, who attended medical school there. He was one of the original interrogators at Kandahar, having arrived two weeks before the rest of the unit. Already he looked exhausted.

Still chafing at Stowe's refusal to let me question the Beatles, I approached Cassidy and offered some unsolicited help. I said I bet the Beatles had come from one of several radical mosques in London, probably one near Finsbury Park. I pulled Cassidy over to one of the nonclassified Internet terminals, where I started clicking around and digging up information on the prominent mosques in London and the firebrand Imams. I urged Cassidy to get himself assigned to all three Brits so that he could compare their stories, play them off against one another. This was basic, television-cop-show stuff, but it was the sort of thing that was being neglected every day by the interrogators in the ICE, who were concentrating on keeping up with the flow of detainees rather than on refining their technique.

The screening report said the Brits were "outraged" that they were being held and were refusing to answer any questions until they saw a representative of the British government. It was as if they'd been busted for shoplifting and were demanding to speak with an attorney. Again I saw an opportunity to get myself into the booth. Maybe I could pose as a British officer, I said. I had spent enough time in London to pick up a passable upper-crust accent. I could introduce Cassidy, turn the interrogation over to him and leave the tent.

Cassidy thought it was worth a shot. But to pull it off would require a costume — a British army uniform. I half asked, half told Mark Stowe that I would be assisting Cassidy, grabbed my rifle, and asked one of the marines to direct me to the cluster of tents on base where a small group of soldiers from New Zealand had recently arrived. Being a Commonwealth country, their uniforms were the same ones the Brits used.

The Kiwi camp was near the airport mosque and was guarded by a corporal who directed me to speak with the senior sergeant inside.

"I'm an interrogator from the intelligence unit around the corner, and it would be useful if I could borrow a battle dress top from one of your soldiers," I said. This kind of a request would have occasioned major interservice inquiry in the American military. But the New Zealand NCO just pointed to a camouflage jacket hanging from a nail nearby and asked me to bring it back when I was done.

Meanwhile, Cassidy had been thrown into another interrogation, leaving me to handle the Brits by myself. Showtime. Just before going in, I put on my maroon airborne beret to go with the Kiwi jacket.

"Hello. My name is Burke," I said, using the accent of my boss in London and the name of a college pal who was among the Cantor Fitzgerald employees killed in the World Trade Center attack. The detainee moved to the edge of his seat and sat up straight and turned his burlap-bagged head toward the British voice. I situated a stack of papers printed off the Internet with the symbol of the Foreign Office clearly visible on top.

"Private, would you be kind enough to take that bag off the prisoner's head," I said to the marine. A dirty hand grabbed a tuft of the burlap sack and pulled it off, revealing the face of a distinctly Western-looking young man about the age of twenty.

"I understand you're from London," I said. "So am I — originally anyway. I suppose we are both a very long way from home. . . . Of course, the difference is, I can explain why I'm here and you, on the other hand, have had some difficulty with that."

Well, there it was. The prisoner was going to either tell "Matt Burke" to go to hell for pretending to be British or start talking.

"When am I going to go home?" he asked.

Thank God, I thought. *It worked.*

"Well, that depends on a lot of things," I said in a low, measured voice. "Not least how cooperative you are with my investigation and the investigation of our American friends."

I proceeded to explain, with admirable British detachment, that the Americans were in a foul mood, not distinguishing between young British troublemakers and committed terrorists. The young man had two choices: he could either work with a sympathetic European or try his luck with the Yanks. With that, the first Beatle started talking.

His story was so outrageous, it was almost comical. He said he had left England for Karachi to marry a Pakistani woman as part of a long-standing marriage contract. He and his companions got bored waiting for the wedding date and, with the help of a Pakistani, arranged a sort of adventure holiday to Afghanistan to see a "real war" between the Taliban and the Northern

Alliance. Along the way they were grabbed by Taliban thugs and taken to a prison cave near Mazar-e-Sharif. The sixty or so prisoners were allowed out to the edge of the cave, where they could see puffs of smoke from the daily skirmishes between the Taliban and Northern Alliance. Then after several weeks they heard a noise they had never heard before. An American jet "ripped the sky open" as it flew overhead, the first Beatle said.

That, number 79 claimed, was the first inkling any of them had that American forces had come to Afghanistan. No one in the cave had even heard of the September 11 attacks until sometime later, when a group of newcomers delivered the news. Not long after that, the number of guards at the cave's entrance began to dwindle, until there were so few that the prisoners easily overpowered their elderly keepers and made for the city.

The Beatles' experience from there was like a wartime farce. First they were captured by a Northern Alliance patrol. Then that patrol was captured by Taliban forces. Then those forces were overrun by another Northern Alliance unit. Finally, the latter turned the three Brits over to U.S. forces, which, after a stay at the Northern Alliance prison at Sheberghan, is how they arrived in Kandahar.

I sat in front of Prisoner 79 and listened as he described everyone he had encountered on his travels exactly the same way: 170 centimeters tall, black hair, beard, mustache, no scars, no glasses, no distinguishing features of any kind. By the time we had finished, the sun had started to creep up, warming the tent enough that the ink in my pen started to flow more freely and I could take the glove off my writing hand.

Back at the ICE, I had to turn my attention to a pile of reports that had accumulated while I had been questioning number 79. I was practically asleep at the keys when I finished and left.

I made my way back to the tent and was amazed to see my night-shift mates still up and about. Fitzgerald was lying out on some sandbags, reading the *National Review*. God knows where he got it. Dan Corcoran, the plump and distracted Fort Bragg trooper, was thumping away on his Game Boy. Pearson, one of the Serial 93 troops who arrived with me, was listening to "Learn Pashtu" tapes and cleaning her rifle. Except for the weapons, it might have been a scene from a college dorm.

The army is, of course, a melting pot, but military intelligence tends to be a distinct breed. Mostly, but not entirely, white. Better educated than most. Considerably more liberal than their combat peers. Indeed, Fitzgerald was an exception to the rule of thumb, having grown up with a William F. Buckley poster on his bedroom wall. At the DLI and now again in Kandahar, he complained that he was surrounded by "NPR people," and he wasn't that far off. When Fitzgerald and I were at the DLI, it wasn't unusual to see soldiers with LEGALIZE POT T-shirts and bumper stickers supporting Clinton.

At Kandahar, the backgrounds of the interrogators, particularly the reservists, were striking. Scott Aiken was a Skidmore grad who had studied history. Kerri Debolt finished Penn State as a drama major. Even the active-duty troops in MI came from fairly unbeaten paths. Brian Talbot had a degree in sculpture and fine arts from the University of Dallas. Dan Lawson had studied English literature at Whittier College in Southern California and was eager to finish up his army tour so he could start on a master's degree at NYU. David Cathcart also had an English literature degree, from Sarah Lawrence. Anne-Marie Walker, a twenty-one-year-old from Michigan, had moved to Iceland after high school to spend a year learning Icelandic. Then she joined the army to learn Farsi. This group might just as easily have joined the Peace Corps.

Ethan Kampf, who had to leave Texas A&M because he ran out of money, loved to goad everyone by declaring that the war in Afghanistan was just the first adventure in a new American imperialism. Everybody knew Iraq would be next, and there was all manner of hand-wringing over whether it was right for the United States to open a "war of aggression." The group would argue fiercely. Fitzgerald would shake his head as if he couldn't believe what nincompoops he was surrounded by. "Of course the United States has embarked on a new imperialism," he would say, "but it's an enlightened imperialism!" I dismissed the uncommitted, too, calling them neo-Chamberlainites. Everyone got the reference.

The only one in the tent who generally went straight for the sleeping bag was Turner, always with a set of giant earphones strapped on his head. Turner had brought an enormous CD collection, all movie scores — and not movies particularly known for their soundtracks: stuff like *Weekend at Bernie's,* and *Point of No Return,* some Bridget Fonda spy flick. Of course, he also had every *Star Wars* soundtrack, and as he squirmed into his bag and cupped the phones to his ears, you could hear the *bom bom bom, bom-pa-bom, bom-pa-bom* that cued up every time Darth Vader approached.

I agreed with Turner on one thing: it was smart to catch some sleep when you could. The temperature swings on the high desert of Kandahar were extreme, and the tent only made it worse, barely containing any heat at night but trapping every spent calorie and soaking up the sun's rays during the day. It was about thirty degrees when the shift ended, the sun just a glimmer on the horizon. That wasn't any colder than a typical winter day in Connecticut, but it had a way of wearing on you when you basically lived outside in the elements twenty-four hours a day. I would emerge from the ICE in long underwear, three pairs of socks, two sweaters, my battle dress jacket, and a Gore-Tex parka. It was still so cold in the sleeping tent that I could afford to take off just one layer — the Gore-Tex — before getting into the sleeping bag.

Then the temperature would start to climb, so quickly that you had to peel off other layers every half hour. By midday it might be seventy degrees outside, but a tiny thermometer hanging inside the tent would register in the mid-nineties. The air was so suffocating that everyone was in boxers and a T-shirt, lying on top of his bag in a pool of perspiration.

Then, as the sun made its early, winter descent, the cold crept back and the rerobing began. What a pain in the ass. And even when I managed to doze off, I had to get up at least three times a "night" to go to the piss pit, which was always an olfactory treat in the warmth of the Afghan day.

The second member of the Beatles trio was a knucklehead. He was originally from Manchester, third-generation British — more British than I was American. Prisoner 83 was tall and lanky. His hair, for whatever it may have been when he left London six months previously, was absurdly long now, making him look like a wild man. His goofy working-class accent was ridiculous. The first thing he said after the marine guard took off his knit hat was "Y'got a fag, mate?"

My plan was simple: force the Brits to tell their stories in excruciating detail and prey on any inconsistencies. I had Prisoner 83 start at the point in the story when he arrived at the cave. Skipping to the middle, I hoped, might throw him off if he had rehearsed his story from the beginning. It didn't work. Prisoner 83 told the same story as his compatriot had. There was nothing so different that it couldn't be explained by a simple variation of recollection. There were also the same maddening vagaries. He couldn't even remember what airlines he had flown on.

The prisoner went out of his way to characterize himself as a crappy Muslim, going on and in vulgar detail about his assorted U.K. girlfriends and the clubs he frequented. Maybe this was his strategy — to portray himself as so lackluster a Muslim that I would conclude there was no way he had come to sign up for Al Qaeda. After a couple of hours I dismissed 83 and sat for about thirty minutes in the booth, rubbing my temples. After a while, the marine guard came back in and asked why a Brit was wearing an American field jacket. Jesus, I had forgotten to put on the Kiwi top. Oh well, maybe 83 would prove as inattentive.

I went back to the tent more tired than the day before. Talbot had erected a small sign that said DEPARTMENT OF VIRTUE AND THE PREVENTION OF VICE, a dig at the Taliban religious police. I admired it while I washed a uniform and some boxers in pails of Arctic-cold water.

Inside the tent, Henry Hasegawa, Dan Corcoran, and Ben Davis were all talking shop. Davis was usually so sullen and quiet that it was rare to hear him speak. But now his voice was rising, and he was complaining that the prisoners were making fools of the interrogators. One of his prisoners had disclosed some interesting details about a training camp — raising the possibility that some of the Al Qaeda instructors had been Syrian, but at the next shift the prisoner completely changed his story, refusing to admit any of his previous statements.

Needless to say, they never taught this one at Huachuca. Once a prisoner was broken, you weren't supposed to have to break him again. You weren't supposed to have to fight for the same ground twice. This prisoner hadn't even tried to segue into a new story. No "you know that stuff I told you yesterday? Well, I was exaggerating a little bit. Here's how it really happened." This prisoner stared straight at Davis and said, in effect, there was no yesterday. Never happened.

How to explain it? Well, Davis had a pretty good guess. The prisoner's first story came fresh after his capture, when the shock of it all was still in effect and his mind was still swimming with anxiety over what was about to happen to him. Then he spent a night — or in his case, a day — in the cages with the rest of the prisoners. And he found out what was about to happen to him: nothing. At least nothing bad. He'd be questioned for a couple of days. He'd get three square meals a day. He'd sleep in a cage. And that was about it. Well, if that's the case, why bother to come clean? In fact, why not withdraw everything already said?

"Think about these prisoners," Hasegawa said. "The Arabs come from countries where prisoners are tortured all the time, especially if they are caught taking part in some terrorist enterprise trying to topple the government. And the Afghans, well, until a few weeks ago they were living in a country where people who fucked up in some way were routinely dismembered in front of packed crowds at Olympic Stadium in Kabul on Fridays. They must think Americans are complete pussies." To Davis and Hasegawa, the solution was clear: they were both slamming their fists and saying things like "Just two minutes. Give me just two minutes alone with him." Of course, it's always easy to talk tough like that when you know it's not going to happen. If there's one thing you learned at Huachuca, it's that if you take your two minutes with a prisoner, you'll get twenty years in a cage yourself.

Still, their fist pounding wasn't just hollow posturing. The question was the subject of frequent debate among the interrogators. How far could you go? How far *should* you go? The Geneva Conventions bars "violence to life and person . . . cruel treatment and torture." But there are methods of applying pressure that stop short of "violence" or "cruel treatment" or "torture." What about sleep deprivation? What about "stress positions," uncomfortable poses such as kneeling or being forced to hold something over your head until your arms turn to rubber? What about just forcing the prisoner to stand? Was that "cruel"? Was that wrong? Some didn't think so.

Early on at Kandahar, Cavanaugh was down in one of the booths with a real prick of a prisoner. You could hear him bellowing at him all the way in the ICE. Then it got quiet and one of the other interrogators returned to the ICE and said, almost with a chuckle, that Cavanaugh was down there with his prisoner in a stress position. He was making his prisoner kneel on the ground and hold his arms out straight in front of him. Chief Irvine, the officer in charge of the day shift, whipped his head around when he heard this. He grabbed the radio and called down to the JIF. "Put Cav on," he said. When Cavanaugh got on the line, Irvine asked sternly, "What the hell are you doing?"

Cavanaugh said his prisoner was being a "cocky fuck," so he put him in a stress position. Irvine told him to get the prisoner out of the stress position. Cavanaugh protested, saying he had put his prisoner in the same exact position that army drill sergeants put young troops in when somebody screws up in boot camp. The same position drill sergeants had put *him* in. "You're telling me it's wrong to do to a prisoner what the army does to its own soldiers?" Cavanaugh asked.

"Cavanaugh, you *volunteered* for basic training!" Irvine said.

And that was the end of that. We got the message but continued to talk about it. Davis and Hasegawa were just the latest to carry on the debate.

I proceeded with my bedtime ritual of baby wipes and teeth brushing and climbed into my bag for a day's sleep. At 6:00 p.m. my wristwatch beeped its modern reveille. I shivered while applying the baby wipes that served as my morning shower, and roused the troops. Somebody tried to turn on the lightbulb hanging in the middle of the tent, but it didn't work — again — so we broke a chemlight and got on with it.

Prisoner 84, the third Beatle, was certainly clever. He, too, tried to paint himself as a fallen Muslim, a hedonist by hard-core Islamic standards. Mustafa, as he called himself, just kept saying that he and his friends had made a big mistake. He said they were after adventure, and that was it. They had done a stupid thing but were not guilty of joining up to fight anybody. He just wanted to go home.

I abandoned trying to find some crack in their ludicrous cover story and started looking for other sources of leverage. "What trouble have you or your friends been in with the law in England?" I asked.

The prisoner's ankles crossed under the table and his cuffed hands touched his mouth — both very common gestures for someone about to lie. "Nofing. . . . We was nefer in any trouble."

"You know the Americans took your fingerprints when you came in."

"Yeah."

"You know we will check with the police?"

"Yeah."

"Do you want to change your answer, Mustafa?"

"Nah. I told you dat eye waz nefer been in trouble wid'da law."

I was pretty sure I was onto something with the "trouble with the law" bit. The prisoner's body language said so. I decided to throw a second curveball I'd been working on.

"I don't imagine you get an awful lot of news from home in here," I said, producing a sheet of paper with an official seal at the top of the page. I had pulled it off the Internet and pasted it onto the top of a document I had written myself on the crusty laptop in the ICE. It was a memorandum in "transmission" format with lots of carets — <<FOR OFFICAL USE ONLY>> — and Teletype-looking gibberish code. The message looked real. It said that the government had passed a new law allowing the authorities to deport from the country any immigrant family whose sons had gone to Afghanistan to train with "any known or suspected terrorist organization." There were lots of official-looking footnotes and legal turns of phrase, but the message was eminently clear: if this kid was labeled anything remotely smelling like a terrorist or terrorist trainee, his family would be booted back to Pakistan.

I hoped the point about expelling a suspect's family would grab 84 by the balls, since his family members were more recent immigrants from Pakistan; he himself had come to England as a baby. I wanted to make this personal for him and to have a real stick to use before he presented the carrot. He put the memo down on the table when he finished reading it, and I held my breath, waiting for a reaction.

"You see, this is serious business," I said. Then I tossed out a detail I'd gotten from one of his comrades. "Your sister is at Exeter University, isn't she?"

"Yes."

"Well, then, perhaps you ought to have kept your adventure holiday to white-water rafting, eh?" This was it. If he went for the bait, his first sentence would be the tip-off. He dawdled, then picked up the sheet of paper and looked at it again.

"They can't do this," he said miserably.

Sweet Jesus, he bought it.

I told him there were "a lot" of Brits just like him in American hands "up and down the length" of the country. "You may be able to depend on your two pals, but every Brit the Americans have will be shown a photo of you. Not all of them will have seen you, but some will have. Your family's future will be very different if just one of those prisoners says he saw you in Afghanistan engaged in something more than just a holiday to 'see what war is like.'"

He sulked. I got nervous again and caught myself before my body language said so. At last the prisoner looked up and replied: "Eye've been telling you the truf. We'f all been telling you the truf."

Damn. Maybe he was.

UNDER ATTACK

———————

Several days later, during a shift change, Captain Rawles announced that the base was under attack. Rawles, who had previously served as a rifleman in a Ranger battalion, made this announcement almost the way one might say, "I think we're out of milk."

"Go back to your tents, get your combat gear, and report back to the defensive perimeter," he said. He paused, remembering that he was dealing with MI soldiers, not Rangers. "Does everyone know where the defensive perimeter is?"

Awkward pause. Fitzgerald fumbled for his cigar, and Mark Stowe, whispering, asked whether anyone had seen the incendiary grenade used to destroy files if the base were overrun.

Quickly, the captain broke the silence: "Okay, let's *move!*" and suddenly there was a scattering of shadows into the darkness.

We ran with rifles to our tents, where the rest of our combat equipment lay, neatly stacked on our cots. Already it was clear this was no drill. There was the clack-clacking of machine-gun fire and some flashes in the darkness, though certainly at some distance. Then explosions.

Everyone was dashing here and there, cursing and swearing while he put on his gear. Some grabbed their stuff and ran with it in a big unwieldy armload, back toward the airport. I counted the seventeen troops in my tent and grabbed a medical kit. We scurried back into the airport so quickly that Turner got caught in some concertina wire. Of course, there were a handful of marines with a squad machine gun on hand to watch. Another interrogator and I ripped Turner out, ruining his uniform. Running past the giggling marines, I said, "Yeah, but you don't speak Arabic, dumbasses." Neither did Turner, but never mind.

The airport was never brightly lit in the best of times, but now it was *really* dark. The Turner madness had delayed our arrival on the scene. Rodriguez was looking for me, practically feeling faces to find me. All the MI guys were standing around as though they were waiting for a bus. David Cathcart, one of the Serial 93 interrogators from Fort Stewart, pointed out some very wide support columns that were suitable for cover. The chosen troops scampered to the assigned positions.

Wild rumors sprang up from positively nowhere: there were enemy troops in the wire; there was a suicide bomber at the main gates; there was a Stinger missile attack on a Blackhawk chopper. We were isolated in the baggage claim area of the airport terminal, far from the perimeter of the base, but still the smell of spent munitions crept to our corner of the war. Then there was a crash of outgoing mortar fire, not at all the *thump* in the movies.

Gradually, the fire grew more sporadic, the rumor mill slowed down, and the adrenaline wore off. Captain Rawles put his pistol in its holster. The only lingering activity was among a late-arriving group of soldiers taking up position in front of us. These newcomers kept running back and asking the interrogators what unit we were with. Somebody would tell them MI, and they would blink and run off.

A quartet of these confused creatures took up position very near the baggage claim area, and at last I saw — in the flash of a camera, of all things — the patch of the 101st Airborne Division, the Screaming Eagles. Their arrival, to replace the Twenty-sixth Marine Expeditionary Unit, had been rumored since

December. Now a handful, who had arrived on a plane earlier that day, were preparing their machine-gun position just a few feet away.

Captain Rawles motioned for me to step forward. "Go tell those numb-nuts that there is a platoon of marines just over there," Rawles said, motioning toward silhouettes in the darkness a dozen or so yards in front of the rattled Airborne troopers and their machine-gun post. I jogged over to the soldiers and told them to mind where they pointed that gun.

"It's okay," a junior officer said, "we don't have any ammo."

When I relayed this exchange to Rawles, the captain smiled for the first time since we had met.

The next day we discovered that the photo flash had come from the marines, who made a poster out of the resulting photograph, which they plastered all over the garrison with the following prominently featured beneath the Xeroxed image:

1. Kevlar helmets: $200
2. 5.56 millimeter squad automatic weapon: $2,200
3. Night vision goggles: $3,700
4. The look of a 101st Airborne lieutenant when he realizes the brigade landed in combat with no ammo: *Priceless*

SOMALI BOB

———◆———

Before U.S. forces launched the large assault on Tora Bora in December, there had been a serious push for new intelligence on the area. We undertook a massive effort to identify any prisoner in custody who had so much as mentioned the region at any stage in his questioning. One of these prisoners was a gaunt African with dark skin and a hollow expression. The guards called him Somali Bob.

Prisoners who had cooperated in their initial interrogation didn't always do so a second time around. Some of them stewed about succumbing, felt humiliated or disloyal, and pledged to themselves that their next encounter would be different. When the MP pulled the knit cap off Somali Bob, I could tell by his smug, gangland expression that he had changed since his last interrogator wrote, "Anxious about his future; broke on fear of long-term incarceration," in his report.

My job, I explained, was to review prisoners' stories for accuracy and help determine which prisoners were terrorists and which were foreign fighters supporting the Taliban. "You want to be in the second group," I told him. "We are basing our evaluations on your willingness to clarify some of your statements made to your case officer during your conversations last week. It is essential for your future and eventual release that you give me no reason to doubt where you stand."

Somali Bob just sat there giving me a hateful, voodoo stare.

Even before I went in with him, word had already circulated in the cages that our new round of questioning was focused on Tora Bora, and Somali Bob clearly knew this. Because ours was to be a fairly straightforward session on order-of-battle questions, I trusted my Arabic to get me through and went without a translator. I opened with a circuit of rather unimaginative questions on other topics, and his short, flat replies demonstrated extreme uninterest. But when we got to the four weeks he spent trying to get across the border to Pakistan, his posture improved and the volume of his voice increased. He started to use his shackled hands to emphasize his points.

My guess was that Bob was going to be defiant and uncooperative, trying to restore the honor he had lost in his previous interrogation. But I was wrong.

"Where in the Paktia Province were you hiding?" I asked him.

"In the mountains," he said. "In Tora Bora."

It came too fast. He said, "Tora Bora," before I had uttered those words. He knew that's what I wanted to hear.

"Why were you hiding in the mountains in Tora Bora?"

"There are excellent places to hide there. There are caves and gullies and bunkers." The word *bunkers* was stressed — enunciated so clearly that it was almost as if he were going out of his way to make it recognizable to someone with less-than-fluent Arabic. "We went there because there were good places to hide and fight if necessary," he said. "That is, if we couldn't escape to Pakistan."

"Do you know where on the map you were?"

"I was near Khowst" — a town on the very edge of the Pakistan border.

"Can you read a map?"

"A little."

"Can you read this map?" I pulled a map of the Tora Bora region from my blue knapsack. I'd printed it off the Internet.

He looked at the 8½-by-11 sheet of paper and followed some of the features on the map. I had translated the English of some of the towns and spelled the names on the paper phonetically in Arabic. The prisoner laughed when he sounded out the misspelled words, but said I had good penmanship.

The location he gave me for his time in the mountains was the same as he revealed to his first interrogator, thus passing one of our repeat-and-control questions. Bob further described the path to where he had stayed, saying there were stations and dugouts that locals kept supplied with water and basic necessities. But he quickly got to what he knew would pique my interest, an area in Tora Bora he'd described in a previous interrogation as a "former mujahideen redoubt." Tracing his path on the map, he took me to it practically by hand. The level of his cooperation was remarkable.

Somali Bob said he'd wandered the crags and peeked into the caves in those hills with a reverent curiosity. This is where the famous mujahideen defeated the Soviet juggernaut, and he was so full of admiration that he goaded me to acknowledge Islam's achievement on those billy goat battlefields. I expressed my authentic nod to the courage of those men but provoked him by saying, "Of course, it was the Americans who armed the mujahideen that won the war."

Somali Bob reacted angrily, as I suspected he would. He squinted his eyes and leaned forward: "Men win wars, not machines or guns. Allah would give us victory against the Russians if we had only the earth and stones to cast them out!"

With that rebuke, I shifted the conversation to details. I asked him to describe how to get to the redoubt and pulled out a more detailed map. With the stub of a pencil — the MPs weren't thrilled I had given him any writing implement — he started to draw away. He was a fairly talented cartographer, noting in legible Arabic the distance between different positions, using the metric system. He marked ammunition-running trenches and a well for an underground spring. He highlighted certain paths used by locals to bring supplies, and others that led to listening and observation posts. It was an excellent diagram. I wrote many notes in the margins of the map and on my own pad of paper. But while he marked up the map, my eyes were trained on him. I was studying his face and hands and body, watching for a nervous glance, a telltale gesture, or a shift in posture. He was giving us information that, if accurate, was certain to get his Arab colleagues killed. He had every reason to mislead us with his markings on the map, every reason to lie. I was waiting for some physical sign to give him away.

Lying has a body language all its own. It shows up in the eyes, affects the posture, triggers movement in the feet and the hands. It can alter the pulse, activate the sweat glands, and rob the mouth of moisture. It is part of a much broader lexicon of nonverbal signals that we rely on in everyday life, visual cues that give us insights into the moods and emotions of others. Our antennae to most of these signals are remarkably subtle. We can tell the difference between a polite smile, a pained smile, and a smile of sincere pleasure. We can spy a quarreling couple from a distance and tell by the way they are standing who is aggrieved and who is ashamed. We are so familiar with certain physical signals that our terms for them have become clichés: the cold shoulder, the come-hither look, the deadly stare. Dishonesty has its own collection of cues and its own clichés (lying eyes). But most of us are barely proficient at detecting even the most obvious of these clues, oblivious to dozens of other indicators that are so ingrained in human nature that they are rendered almost involuntarily.

Decoding these nonverbal signals of deception has been something of a holy grail to the intelligence community for decades. In 1963 the CIA produced an interrogation manual, called *Kubark Counterintelligence Interrogation,* that came to public light only decades later when the *Baltimore Sun* forced the agency to release it under the Freedom of Information Act. The manual (Kubark was the agency's code name) includes a list of possible physical manifestations of deception. "A ruddy or flushed face is an indication of anger or embarrassment. . . . A 'cold sweat' is a strong sign of fear and shock. . . . A pale face indicates fear and usually shows that the interrogator is hitting close to the mark. . . . A slight gasp, holding the breath, or an unsteady voice may betray the subject." Overall, it concludes, a person's body "is likely to be the physical image of his mental tension."

The Kubark manual was written at the start of an era of advances in the understanding of expressions and body language — an area of study generally referred to as kinesics. Subsequently, researchers have classified and categorized every conscious gesture and involuntary jerk they could identify, gradually creating a grammar for nonverbal communication. Paul Elkman, a psychology professor at the University of California Medical School at San Francisco, has devoted his career to the subject. Over years of painstaking work, he has isolated forty-three distinct facial muscles and three thousand combinations of their movements that correspond to specific emotions or convey some discernible meaning. Law enforcement and intelligence agencies have followed this research closely, with the FBI and CIA and the military consulting Elkman and others, as well as conducting studies of their own, hoping to divine secrets that would enable them to detect dishonesty in low-level criminals, high-ranking defectors, and everyone in between. They have found no foolproof methods, and probably never will, but have begun to piece together lengthy lists of reliably revealing clues. There are dozens of books on the subject — most written by cops for cops — and a cottage industry of kinesics courses have sprouted up all over the country. There are variations from one book to another, one course to the next.

But experts agree on at least two things. First, that you can never be certain that someone is lying merely by watching movements and gestures. And second, despite this caveat, there are dozens of physical clues that can alert attentive interrogators to points in a subject's story that should be viewed with deep suspicion.

To tell when a prisoner is lying, you have to start by studying how he carries himself when he's telling the truth. Though there is remarkable consistency across ethnicities and cultures in what expressions and basic physical movements mean, there is significant variation from one individual to another in what signal surfaces when. So the first step is to establish a baseline by watching the prisoner when he's discussing "safe" subjects, meaning nonthreatening topics on which he has little reason to lie — his children, perhaps, or his homeland. Once you have a baseline on how he behaves when he's telling the truth, you can look for departures from that pattern to signal when he starts to deceive. Often what you're looking for are symptoms of stress, because it isn't the lying in and of itself that triggers reactions in the body, but the anxiety that accompanies engaging in dishonesty. Different people have different thresholds. Some can barely call in sick to work without having their heart rates climb. Others don't see symptoms until they're on the verge of getting caught for a serious crime. But almost everybody has a threshold.

The focal point in interrogation, as it is with most interpersonal communication, is the eyes. Most people think of sustained eye contact as a sign of honesty, but that isn't always so in the booth. Smart prisoners realize that turning their eyes away from an interrogator may be interpreted as a sign of deception, so they do the opposite, and engage in unusually prolonged eye contact. We didn't necessarily look for one or the other, but for deviations from the prisoner's normal pattern. Blinking is another indicator. Sometimes rapidly blinking eyes are an indication that the mind is racing — which it tends to do when it is trying to keep a dishonest story straight. Forcing a prisoner to provide a highly detailed time line of his travels and activities — and then making him retrace that mental path starting at different points, perhaps even navigate it backward — makes it all the harder.

There are certain eye movements that are almost dead giveaways of deception. They have to do with where people cast their gaze when retrieving images from their memories. Science has yet to explain exactly why, but when people recall things they've actually seen — that is, when they are accessing real memories — they tend to look up and to the left. But when people try to picture something they haven't actually seen, they often look up and to the right, as if searching the corner of a mental movie screen. The latter eye pattern is called visual construction, meaning you're assembling images you don't actually have stored anywhere. Now, visual construction is a perfectly fine thing to do if someone has asked you to describe what your dream house would look like. But if a prisoner has been asked to describe the offices of the charity he claims to have worked for in Kabul and glances up and to the right as he answers, it's a strong indication that he's about to make something up out of whole cloth.

The CIA, in its Kubark manual, goes against conventional wisdom, saying that a prisoner's mouth "is as a rule much more revealing than his eyes." Biting lips or chewing on the cheek or a corner of a collar are obvious indications of unease. Frequent yawning can be a delaying tactic, an attempt to buy more time as a prisoner formulates an answer to a difficult question, or can suggest that a prisoner's metabolic rate has spiked to such an extent that he is trying to get more oxygen.

Most prisoners aren't even aware of all the nonverbal signals they're sending. The few who are rarely manage to keep everything in check. In an intense encounter such as interrogation, the brain is most aware of the parts of the body closest to it, particularly the face. More distant points on the central nervous system tend to get less mental attention. So it's not uncommon for a prisoner to manage to keep from revealing too much in his face but to forget entirely about what he is doing with his hands and feet. Early in the tour at Kandahar, I was watching Dan Corcoran interrogate a prisoner in one of the tents that served as our booths. When he was done I called him over to one of the empty tents in the JIF, where I was eating my breakfast after spending part of my morning eavesdropping on the interrogators. I asked him if his detainee had exhibited any signs of deception. He said no, the prisoner had seemed pretty straightforward. I took him back to the tent and lifted the chair where the prisoner had been sitting. There in the dirt was a deep groove where the detainee had carved a channel with his feet. Whatever was coming out of that prisoner's mouth was making him so nervous, causing so much internal stress, that he quite literally dug himself a hole.

The hands are often particularly active in times of profound agitation — tapping, drumming, massaging an arm or leg, grooming hair, smoothing out wrinkles in an outfit, fiddling with buttons. All indicate nervousness. But there are certain hand gestures that are particularly suggestive of deception. If a prisoner covers his mouth, or even lays a finger across his lips, it's often a sign that he is subconsciously trying to block what he is saying, perhaps trying to cover an untruth. Similarly, if he uses his fingers or hands to obscure his eyes, he may not like the images flashing across his mind's eye. If he tugs on his nose, it may be a sign that he is trying to pull uncomfortable admissions from his head. If he pinches his nose, he may be unconsciously suggesting that he thinks his story stinks. It sounds silly, the stuff of an amateur Freud, but experience has shown the correspondence. Perhaps the explanation is even simpler: the prisoner knows he is in trouble and is trying in some pathetic, unconscious way to mask his face from view. Emotions can be reflexive, whether we want them to be or not.

The act of smoking interferes with all these signals. So an interrogator has to make a call whether allowing a prisoner to have a cigarette will foster trust, help establish rapport, and bring him closer to revealing the truth, or whether it will absorb his nervous energy and soothe his anxiety, giving him a prop that could help him disguise his deception. Hasegawa, Davis, and Kampf were prodigious smokers, and I occasionally overheard them dissecting the smoking behavior of the prisoner for clues.

It's also important to observe the limbs in relation to the body. Someone who feels vulnerable tries to cover himself, crossing his hands in front of his genitals or crossing his arms across his abdomen as if to protect his internal organs. Shoulders thrown back are a sign of defiance. A prisoner who turns his body away, pointing his shoulder at his interrogator, is defensive. A surprising number of detainees actually tilt their entire frames toward the nearest window or exit in an interrogation room. The police books call it the "liar's lean."

Amid all these negative signals, we would also look for certain positive signs, indications that a prisoner may be preparing to tell the truth. For example, stroking the chin suggests contemplation and may indicate that a prisoner is considering coming clean. Huachuca teaches new interrogators that one of the most promising moves is when a prisoner tilts his head back and looks toward the ceiling, blinking rapidly, as if trying to prevent welling tears from leaving their ducts. The eyes may close for a moment and the prisoner may exhale before returning his gaze to his questioner with a look of resignation or sometimes relief. People coming to grips with strong emotions, reconciling themselves to difficult fates, also drop their heads down, lowering their eyelids and allowing their chins to touch their chests, as if summoning the courage for the confession to come. What happens next is key. If the prisoner then raises his head toward his interrogator and leans forward in some posture of supplication, he may be ready to talk. But if he comes out of these confessional sequences either looking up at the ceiling or down toward the floor and returns to a closed or defiant posture — crossed arms, averted eyes — he has likely regrouped and will continue to resist.

All these nonverbal signals are *indications* of a person's mind-set. Nervous tics and defensive postures and gestures can suggest that someone is lying, but there are alternative interpretations for every clue. A person can cross his arms on his chest because he is defensive and anxious, or he may do so simply because he is cold — an understandable reaction during the Central Asian winter at night. Yawning can be a sign of stress, or it may simply indicate that a subject is tired or — God forbid — bored. Interrogation can induce great anxiety even in the innocent. Someone fearful that his accurate account may not be believed can exhibit many of the same symptoms of someone engaged in deception. The key is the context, whether the symptoms surface consistently, or only in instances when the prisoner has a motivation to lie.

For all the lying that people do, most aren't very good at disguising their own deception or at detecting it in others. We struggle to spot deception even in those close to us: our spouses, relatives, friends, and coworkers. Even people in professions that require wading through deceit every day — police officers, judges, FBI agents, and CIA officers — do little better than chance when asked to view videotapes of witnesses and judge whether they are lying or telling the truth, according to studies by Elkman. Some believe our blind spot to dishonesty is an artifact of evolution, that our hunter-gatherer ancestors had little to gain by lying to other members of their close-knit clans or by accusing others of doing so. Other theories are that we just don't like to acknowledge the amount of deception we engage in or encounter — that it's a side of our nature we're not particularly proud of or eager to confront. Detecting deception is a skill that can be learned, but it takes a lot of practice.

The army does not concentrate on techniques of lie detection during initial training at Huachuca but does make kinesics training available to a small percentage of its intelligence troops as they move up the ranks. There were only a few of us at Bagram who had had the training. Hasegawa was one. I was another, having attended a three-day course a few years after I joined the reserves. I found it extremely interesting at the time but had forgotten much of it by the time I got to Afghanistan. It came back bit by bit during the course of the war. Interrogators who hadn't had the kinesics training gradually learned from experience in the booth how to spot physical indications of deception in prisoners. But we never became experts. And even when we were looking intently for physical clues, we didn't always find them.

I had studied Somali Bob's visage from the moment I entered the booth. I scrutinized his expressions and reactions during our preliminary chatter, trying to build a baseline, a frame of reference, on how he carried himself when he discussed safe topics, things he had no reason to lie about. I paid particular attention as he began describing the features of Tora Bora, the landmarks he could discuss without compromising his Arab allies. As we continued to more sensitive topics, I expected to see changes, signs of deception. I was sure I would catch his fingers involuntarily touching his face, or his eyes drifting up and to the right, while he described fortifications. I challenged him on key points and expected to see a completely different reaction than the honest indignation I'd witnessed when, to elicit a reaction, I said it was the Americans who had driven the Russians out of Afghanistan. But I didn't see anything. His intensity was the same. His posture didn't change. He didn't reach for his nose or let his eyes drift when I prompted him for more detail on the redoubt. No indication whatsoever that he was lying.

After my session with Somali Bob, I went to the marines' cartographic annex at Kandahar to get satellite imagery of Tora Bora to go with my report. A marine with Buddy Holly glasses flipped through images on his laptop until he came to a crisp shot of the ground, taken very recently. It was practically made for illustrating the positions the prisoner had described. Analysts had already marked it up with white arrows and lines pointing to features that they had already identified and that my prisoner had explained to me just minutes earlier. Back in the ICE, I was drawing a PowerPoint illustration of the redoubt, planning to attach the satellite shot as a reference, when I noticed a white line drawn around a certain area of the craggy hillside. There were analysts' markings on the circled terrain, and after a moment I remembered what they meant. Where my prisoner had plotted the supposed path of a water supply route — implying a safe course of travel for our troops and patrols — the army's imagery analysts had spotted dozens of antipersonnel mines. Somali Bob hadn't lied to me, not exactly. But he had omitted information. Either way, I hadn't caught it.

By early January, the level of activity at the base had picked up substantially. Cargo planes carrying troops, equipment, and, increasingly, prisoners were landing all night long. The thirty-seven prisoners who had been in custody in late December grew quickly to one hundred, then two hundred. Eventually it would get up to about five hundred.

It was odd, and telling in a way, that the number of prisoners didn't correspond to any visible action in the war. It wasn't like World War II, or even the Gulf War, when massive divisions overran the enemy, took them into custody by the hundreds or thousands, and quickly moved them to the rear. In Afghanistan, the action was often invisible. Raids on compounds in the middle of the night. Transfers of prisoners from prisons in Pakistan you didn't even know existed. A steady stream of detainees from Pakistan and other governments or Afghan warlords pocketing a nice wad of American cash for every prisoner they turned over.

In early January nearly 3,500 former Taliban fighters were being held by Northern Alliance forces at the prison in Sheberghan. A mobile interrogation team from Task Force 500 had been sent to Sheberghan to screen prisoners there, and many were making their way to the facility at Kandahar.

A growing number of detainees were also arriving straight out of Pakistan. The only way the interrogators at Kandahar knew this was by looking at the flight manifests to see where the flights had originated. They were coming from such cities as Rawalpindi, Karachi, and Lahore. Most were Arabs, presumably grabbed by Pakistan's intelligence service, the ISI, although there was no explicit documentation. Some had already been questioned by U.S. or allied civilian intelligence agencies.

The other major source of prisoners was Task Force Hatchet, a special operations group made up of Army Rangers, Green Berets, Delta Force, and Special Forces units from Australia, Great Britain, Denmark, and other countries. Even as conventional combat abated, Task Force Hatchet, often operating with local Afghan troops, was casting off in all directions on manhunts and sweeps that would grow in intensity in the coming months. The operations targeted safe houses, compounds, and even cave complexes where enemy leadership and resistance movements were coalescing.

This last source accounted for an increasing share of the new arrivals and also posed big problems for us, because the special operators — "too cool for school," as Fitzgerald liked to say — never stuck around to explain who they were delivering or even where they had been captured. They simply loaded prisoners on helicopters and, quite literally, left them on our doorstep.

Often we didn't even know to expect prisoners until a marine poked his head in the ICE and announced their arrival. A short while later, we would find ourselves in a tent with Arabs or Afghans, more or less asking *them* why they were there.

It took a while for us to realize that not all the prisoners being delivered to us were the enemy. We figured that if the Special Forces brought them, there had to be a good reason. But the truth was that the special operators couldn't distinguish the bad from the good in the raids, so they dropped them all on our doorstep to let us sort them out. They were bringing back a lot of fighters, but they were also bringing back a lot of farmers.

Fitzgerald was assigned to question an Afghan who had been scooped up in a Special Forces raid near Kandahar. It was pretty clear he was just a farmer — perhaps a farmer whose clan was involved with some opium ring connected to the Taliban, but a farmer nonetheless. His hands were just knots. He was missing teeth. And his skin was creased from season after season of exposure to the Afghan elements. He spoke Pashtu, and Fitzgerald spoke Arabic. So Fitzgerald tapped an interpreter named Walid, a computer teacher from Washington, D.C., who was among a number of native Afghans living in America who had signed on as linguists when the war started.

After an hour or so of pro forma questioning, Fitzgerald started to wrap things up. He closed with the same statement every interrogator memorized at Huachuca: "Everything you have told me today will be checked for its truthfulness and its accuracy. Knowing this, is there anything you want to change, alter, or delete?"

Typically, the prisoner just shakes his head no. But this farmer started yapping like crazy. His head bobbed up and down excitedly for several minutes as he unloaded what Fitzgerald assumed must be some urgent information. Fitzgerald began to get excited. Maybe this rote Huachuca warning really did trigger doubt and thoughtfulness in some detainees. But when the farmer was done with his monologue, Walid just looked at Fitzgerald blankly.

"What did he say?" Fitzgerald asked.

"It's nothing," Walid said. "He was talking nonsense."

Fitzgerald sternly informed Walid that his job was to translate, not decide what was worthwhile intelligence and what was not. Looking uncomfortable, Walid again tried to say it wasn't worth it. So Fitzgerald ordered him: "Translate."

"All right," Walid said reluctantly. "He's telling me he's been in camp now for a week and a half. At home he's got three wives. He said he's really lonely and you're a good-looking guy and you've got a nice mouth."

Walid paused before coming fully to the point: "He's wondering if you'd suck his dick."

Fitzgerald looked at the farmer, who was looking back with a very expectant grin, clearly waiting for an answer. Fitzgerald started to scrunch up in his chair, his mind racing for what to do. His instinct was to deck the guy. Then Fitzgerald looked over at Walid, who was holding his head down, trying to hide a grin. Walid started to laugh, and Fitzgerald blinked as it slowly dawned on him that this was Walid's idea of a joke. "You son of a bitch," Fitzgerald said, jumping out of his chair and pushing Walid over into the dirt.

The farmer looked on, bemused. He was indeed waiting for an answer, but to a different question. What he'd really said, Walid admitted, was that he was very happy the Americans had come to rescue his country, that he knew he'd be detained for a few weeks but was being well fed. He finished by saying he was a good cook and a good worker, and asked whether the Americans would give him a job at the base.

* * *

Daily life for prisoners at Kandahar, and for the MPs who guarded them, was one of unvarying routine.

Beyond their long johns, rubber shoes, jumpsuits, hats, and blankets, the only additional item issued to the prisoners was the Koran. Every prisoner got one, usually on his second day in the cage. The first thing they wanted to do was read the Koran. They spent hours at it. A good percentage of the prisoners boasted of having memorized the book while in custody.

The second thing the prisoners wanted to do was pray, multiple times a day. They would stand with their eyes closed, hands at their side, bring their hands to their temples, clasp them in front of their mouth, bow forward, put their hands behind their back, bow repeatedly, then kneel and touch the ground with their forehead. All the while they would be mouthing prayers.

There were giant signs inside the compound pointing the way to Mecca, with the word written in a dozen different languages just so everyone would understand. There were rules. No more than three prisoners in the same cell could pray at the same time: the MPs were worried that too many prisoners bobbing up and down would become a distraction. It was also too hard to tell if they were praying or passing information or coaching one another on how to handle interrogations. Talking to God in the cages was permitted. Talking to one another wasn't.

Breakfast came at 7:30 a.m. The MPs filled one of the big barns inside the mud-walled compound with heaps of halal rations, Islamic-approved versions of the ubiquitous ready-to-eat meals. The marines split open the heavy, brown plastic bags and divided the contents into enormous piles — peanut butter, cheese spread, crackers, main courses — then put the segregated items in brightly colored plastic mixing bowls. The bowls were enormous, about three feet across, and the MPs would drag them into the middle of the compound and line them up in a row on the ground.

The MPs would order all the prisoners to line up on the far end of each cage, then call them out one at a time, to let them move down the row of big plastic bowls, picking a single item from each. The prisoners had to eat the food right out of the envelopes, squeezing the sauces and processed meat products into their mouth. They didn't get any utensils, nor would the prisoners get the water-activated heating elements used to warm up the main course. If prisoners were being interrogated, the MPs would knock on the tent and announce that it was mealtime. That meant the prisoner had to be excused back to the compound or allowed to eat in the tent during the interrogation. The prisoners always preferred the latter, largely because the interrogators would sometimes let them warm up the food. Three times a day it was the same routine, with the same bowls and the same food. The prisoners couldn't believe it when interrogators would tell them in the booth that they ate the same food. Indeed, the halal meals the prisoners got had certain advantages over the standard MREs — the former often came with Froot Loops and always had bagel chips.

The marines spent nearly as much time emptying latrine buckets as they did filling up the plastic bowls. Every cell had six or seven buckets — just tin pails, really — sitting on the ground. The marines had guys who did nothing but retrieve those pails, empty them into a fifty-gallon drum, and set the contents afire with diesel.

Once a week there was Operation Wash Bob. (The marines and later the army MPs always called the prisoners "Bobs" for some reason.) They kept dozens of five-gallon jerricans full of water. They would grab a bunch of prisoners along with some tin buckets, soap and shampoo, and anti-lice powder and line them up at the edge of the compound where the marines had constructed a bathing facility with some pallets for a floor and some tarpaulin for a curtain. The prisoners were brought in three at a time. They'd pull off their clothes and squat down over the pails of ice-cold water, sudsing themselves and rinsing, with plenty of prompting from the MPs to clean the smelliest crevices. Then the prisoners would dry off with a big brown army towel, rerobe, and return to the cage. If the prisoners were lucky, they'd get a fresh pair of long johns, and their old pair would be tossed in another fifty-gallon drum for burning. It seemed as though the place was always on fire.

Twice a day the prisoners brushed their teeth. It was the same routine: line up against the back of the cell, come out one at a time, squat over a bucket, and slosh the toothbrush around. A lot of the Afghans had never seen such an instrument and didn't know what to do with it. The marines were always coaching them: "Okay, now the top . . . that's good . . . left side . . . get the gums . . . right side . . . spit!" Of course, the Afghans didn't understand a word, but they got the gist by watching the marines mimic the appropriate motions with their hands.

I was always struck by how paternalistic these burly marines would become with the prisoners. For a group of people who had to deal with burning their shit and looking after the prisoners in every way as if they were helpless children, they showed remarkable patience and — there's no other word for it — *concern*. They'd be going through the tooth-brushing routine and the marines would turn to an interrogator stopping to watch the spectacle and say, "I keep telling him he's got to do a better job on his gums. Those tooth problems he's having ain't gonna go away by themselves. Got to git some fluoride in theyhre!"

Of course, the marines also wore full combat regalia, with helmets, flak vests, and clubs, whenever they went near the prisoners, whether it was Operation Feed Bob, Operation Brush Bob, or Operation Wash Bob. The marines were wise to every prison trick and ruse. Every couple of days they would roust the prisoners from their cages and search their blankets, flip through the pages of their Korans, and shake out their clothes and shoes, looking for any hidden implements. They always found something, whether a sharpened Bic pen snuck out of one of the booths or just a wad of paper that wasn't torn from the Koran. Then, just to make sure the prisoners weren't getting too close with their cellmates, they'd mix up the prisoners and send them back into different cages.

Every two or three weeks, representatives from the Red Cross would come to the facility to interview prisoners. They coordinated their visits through the provost marshal's office, and we usually knew approximately — to within a few days — when they were coming. When the representatives arrived, they would look over the MPs' prisoner roster and pick twenty or twenty-five names. They always wanted to see every new prisoner in custody and usually wanted to revisit prisoners they had talked to last time who had complained of an ailment, a toothache, whatever, to make sure it was being cared for properly. They'd also pick some other names at random.

There was a small shed inside the prison grounds that the Red Cross used as their booth for interviewing prisoners, and neither we nor the guards were allowed inside while they were talking. There were usually two or three Red Cross workers involved in the process, and they always seemed overdressed — the men in collars and ties and the women in nice shirts. Their visits usually took five or six hours, and our whole operation would shut down for that period, because it took a lot of MP manpower to handle security and move the prisoners. When our visitors were finished, they checked in with the provost marshal as they left, passing along any concerns. The provost would then relay the information to us. If the Red Cross ever encountered complaints from prisoners that they were being mistreated, I never heard about it. The most common complaint from the prisoners was that they weren't allowed to pray en masse.

The Red Cross also gave prisoners little booklets of paper on which they could write home. The Red Cross teams would take batches of letters every time they visited, seeing to it that they were mailed. All the letters had to be screened by interrogators, every single word, before leaving camp. The letters couldn't contain any quotes from the Koran or even any vaguely poetic-sounding passages — too easy to be used as code to communicate with the outside. Often the letters were complimentary of the Americans. ("We get more food now than we did before we were captured.") Sometimes the letters seemed to be written with the interrogators in mind — strained references to topics that had come up in the booth, with passionate pledges that the prisoner had been truthful. "They continue to ask me questions about why I have come to Afghanistan, and I am telling them the truth. The truth, I tell you!"

We always made photocopies of the letters I reviewed and stuffed them in the prisoners' files. Sometimes they talked about their kids, about their families, about their worries. Stuff an interrogator might need to exploit.

Settling into a routine of my own, I began to try to find time for exercise. Running wasn't easy. The altitude, about 3,300 feet, made it difficult to breathe at first, an aerobic challenge compounded by the ever-present fumes from burning trash, most of it plastic or human waste. I struggled to get from one end of the mosque road, near the piss pit, to the far end, where three enormous bombed-out hangars delineated the farthest extent of the garrison, a distance of about three-quarters of a mile.

Along the way were tiny encampments of an ever-expanding number of countries sending troops to Kandahar. There was a Jordanian engineering outfit, a group of Aussies and Kiwis, a small but growing contingent of Germans, some Danes and Norwegians. Running along the road one half expected the Swiss Guards to show up with their pikes. It all looked like a kind of multi-ethnic martial fair.

If the running was miserable and hard, washing up afterward was no bonus. Field showers were supposed to arrive with the 101st, but they didn't. That left just one means of bathing: a disused *ham'am* not far from the MI sleeping tent. This was a concrete building, no bigger than a two-car garage, with a kind of ground-level trough in the center. There were spigots from a rusty pipe hanging over the length of the trough. It was meant to offer a place to clean one's hands and feet before prayer, not a full bath. Muslims would visit the *ham'am* to wash up before praying in the airport mosque a short walk away. For our purposes, soldiers had to fill a pail from a trickle of ice-cold water, then squat over the pail while using a T-shirt or other rag to wash up. Hair washing involved waiting to fill a second pail of water and the willingness to subject oneself to an ice-cold over-the-head pour. In some ways, the prisoners bathing here had an advantage — the marines fetched their water.

PRISONER 140

By mid-January, the war on terrorism was in full swing. Back in the United States, the Justice Department announced on January 15 that it had charged John Walker Lindh with conspiracy to kill U.S. citizens and providing aid to terrorists. A day later the United States indicted Richard Reid, an addled Al Qaeda figure who was wrestled into submission on a Paris-to-Miami flight after trying to knock the plane out of the sky by igniting a bomb hidden in his shoe. That same day a New York judge sentenced an Algerian man to twenty-four years in prison for aiding other terrorist suspects in a millennium plot to bomb Los Angeles International Airport. The makeshift detention camp at Guantánamo Bay got its third shipment of prisoners — the eighty being held there were among 433 in custody, with the vast majority of them at Kandahar.

Secretary of State Colin Powell arrived in Kabul on January 17 to meet with Afghan interim president Hamid Karzai, pledging that the United States would not abandon the fragile country as it had following the Soviet pullout a decade earlier. But the war in Afghanistan seemed to be moving in fits and starts. The skies were relatively quiet, with fewer sorties being flown; many nights passed without any bombs being dropped at all. Still, Pentagon officials were complaining that the job of scouring the cave-riddled redoubts along the Pakistani border was overwhelming combat troops, who weren't getting much help from ambivalent Pashtuns. At the base at Kandahar, marine demolition crews blew up caves and an abandoned mud house that had been used a week earlier by gunmen who had launched a night attack on U.S. forces just as the first planeload of prisoners was departing for Cuba.

As Powell met with Karzai, a fresh shipment of prisoners — mostly Arabs — arrived from Sherberghan. Among them was Prisoner 140, the German-Algerian who frustrated me in an all-night interrogation until he slipped at the end of the session, telling me in Arabic the name of the owner of the house where he had stayed in Jalalabad: Al-Jezari.

I was still reports editor but was becoming increasingly adept at persuading Stowe to let me slip into the booths. When I brought 140 back to the booth a second time, it was clear that his minor stumble had altered the dynamic between us. Perhaps 140 realized that his initial strategy — to scrub his comments of any identifiable detail — was one he couldn't sustain. In any case, the terse, one-word answers now gave way to an almost contrite, soft-spoken manner. He slumped in his chair a bit, abandoning the defiant, erect posture of the first encounter.

I adjusted my approach, too. Ordinarily, when a prisoner trips and discloses something he clearly intended to conceal, it's an invitation for a classic Fear Up, a fast-moving barrage that doesn't relent until the prisoner starts "remembering" the other details he'd been withholding, too.

But once you turn up the heat, you can't turn it down very easily. If it doesn't work, often you have to turn the prisoner over to a different interrogator with a clean slate and room to maneuver. And besides, to me, 140 didn't seem like the right candidate for the Fear Up. The one slip 140 made in the first session came at the least tense moment, when both he and I had stood up to leave. It was almost an afterthought.

On our second encounter, when the marine guard removed 140's cap from his head, I pointed to a cup of tea waiting for him on the table. We spoke for half an hour. He complained about being cold and asked for more blankets. He also complained about missing his wife, whom he had met in Afghanistan, and their little daughter. The two had fled to Pakistan and were likely in a refugee camp there. I said I would allow 140 to fill out a U.N. report with their names, so humanitarian workers in Pakistan could be on the lookout.

Prisoner 140 looked to be in his mid-fifties, which meant he probably didn't come to Afghanistan to fight. Perhaps he was involved in the drug trade or in helping finance Al Qaeda's activities, but he didn't seem bright enough, together enough, for that line of work, at least not at a high level. And in a country such as Afghanistan, with many impoverished but willing hands, there was no need for an expatriate lookout or runner. Why was he really here? I needed to learn more about 140's time in Europe, about the safe house in Jalalabad, and about the migration of Arabs who came to fight against the Northern Alliance.

I asked 140 whether he missed anything from his European hometown, and the prisoner quickly smiled and mentioned a well-known type of confection, little chocolate eggs — usually with a toy in them — for children.

"I have some questions about your time in Europe," I said.

"I thought you might," 140 replied. His comment suggested a greater awareness than I had assessed him capable of. By this time, everybody in America knew that some of the September 11 hijackers had come from Europe. But 140 wouldn't necessarily have known this. He wasn't getting newsmagazines or watching CNN.

At first 140 refused to discuss much about his time in Europe. He explained that he had strayed from Islam after leaving Algeria and that for him life began after he returned to his faith, years after he arrived in Europe. I insisted that for completeness, I needed to know about his life before his return to Islam. He complied, reluctantly. His description of youthful lawlessness was couched entirely in religious terms, wrapped in a shroud of regret. It was mainly regret for offending Allah and disgracing Islam, not concern for all the innocent people he had mugged.

After a stint in jail for drug peddling, he accepted an invitation to attend services at a local mosque notorious for its firebrand preaching. He claimed that he felt gravely out of place, "uncomfortable" with the message and self-conscious. But gradually he took a more active role in social and political get-togethers at people's apartments and Islamic centers in the city. Many of the radicals on hand were *arbeitslos* (unemployed), collecting state benefits even as they preached, often violently, against the government that was feeding them. Members of the group were always packing up and heading off to Afghanistan, only to be replaced by new recruits.

The group began putting pressure on 140 to make the trip himself, to fight the nonbelievers. At first 140 resisted, but finally, after a particularly inspiring Koran reading at someone's apartment, he agreed to go. Not to fight, he insisted, but to find a wife and "live a good Islamic life."

I moaned — only on the inside, of course — at this cliché explanation and pressed for details on 140's acquaintances at the mosque. The prisoner provided some fairly detailed descriptions of them and their apartments around the neighborhood where many of the September 11 attackers had made their plans. But when asked for names, 140 shook his head and said he knew only their *cunyas* — a kind of nom de guerre used by Arabs to protect their identity. These nicknames were universal among Al Qaeda operatives and were useless in tracking passports or other official documents. The prisoner also insisted that he wasn't an insider. He was too old, too much a latecomer to his own religion, for any of the serious militants to bring him into the loop on their plans. But 140 certainly traveled in the same circles as the September 11 plotters, and even though he professed not to recall any names, in other respects his memory was almost photographic. When he described a man who sold jihad videos, he explained precisely where in the man's shop the tapes could be found, in a secret compartment in a back storeroom.

I changed the subject, prompting 140 to describe his journey in more detail. He said he flew Pakistani Airways and landed in Karachi via Dubai. He stayed in a hotel that was practically a way station for Arabs headed to Afghanistan. Pakistani authorities stopped many of these travelers on their way through and had asked 140 if he was perhaps an intelligence agent of his native country. They also wanted to know if he was going to Kashmir. Satisfied with his answers, they apparently let him be.

Next 140 told me he moved on to a Karachi mosque, where transient Arabs and other religious pilgrims could always find a few days' hospitality. Not long after arriving, he was approached by a man who agreed to guide him across the border. A few days later they crossed into Afghanistan on motorcycle, a trip it was hard to imagine the frail prisoner in front of me surviving.

He made his way through a series of safe houses to his final destination: a house in Jalalabad.

The house was an enclosed, two-story structure, a kind of minicompound. There were apple trees in the garden and quite frequently a lamb or goat tied up near the open area for special meals. Owner Al-Jezari (the Algerian) was a plump bald man who wore traditional Afghan dress despite his name. There was only one weapon in the house, the ubiquitous Klash.

I thought back to my training at Huachuca and all the questions you are supposed to ask when a prisoner mentions a barracks. I started translating these questions to a safe house. Prisoner 140 was surprised at the level of detail I wanted. "Why on earth would you need to know that?" he would ask, then consent with a shrug and proceed. Often the best information comes when the prisoner doesn't understand why it matters.

Finally, I asked 140 to diagram the house, plot it out on a piece of paper in the booth. As he did so, I asked the prisoner how many people it could accommodate.

"Twenty-five."

"What makes you say it could accommodate twenty-five?"

"There were twenty-five sleeping mats."

I prompted 140 for landmarks around the house, to lock in the location and leave no room for him to try to change his story later or balk at what was coming next. When he was done, I pulled from my bag a large aerial picture of the section of Jalalabad surrounding the house. I'd ordered the photo from our marine cartographic team at Kandahar after our previous interrogation. Prisoner 140's eyes got very big.

"I take it you didn't take this photo," he said, poring over the image until he found a large hospital in the center of the city. From there he carefully traced his way down a road to a market and then onto a road running south toward the river. Halfway down he stopped and dragged his finger down an alleyway to a compound with some fruit trees.

"That one's dead," he said, pointing to one of the trees.

Beautiful. The Special Forces would no doubt appreciate that detail when they stopped in for a visit.

It was light again outside. Prisoner 140 had shed one of his blankets and I was down to my fatigue top and watch cap. I felt good about the interrogation. I'd gotten some good information — no closer to Osama, to be sure — and had certainly covered some distance in building rapport with a potentially valuable source. But as I made my way back to the ICE, I also knew that I was still getting only part of the story, incomplete information. There were nagging questions. Chief among them was why there were all those sleeping mats in the house. Prisoner 140 claimed he had been the only resident. There was a caretaker and many day visitors, but that was it. Indeed, during his two months at the house, he had seen no other immigrants, no other overnight guests. He also took to that map a bit too easily, showed a shade too much cartographic competence.

REPORTS

Report writing is the most miserable part of the job for interrogators. It's tedious. The protocols are arcane, hewing to formats that date back to a time when the information was transmitted by a kind of Teletype machine, and the approval process is generally humiliating. Every report is submitted to the reports editor — my job when I wasn't sneaking off into the booth — whose main objective always seems to be to tear apart people's best efforts, redacting, rewriting, and ridiculing everything he comes across. The reports editor and the interrogator may sometimes go back and forth for days over corrections and amendments involving both substance and style. But ultimately there is a purpose to all this, or at least sometimes there is. Interrogators may write lengthy narratives that are nice stories but have little intelligence value. They may list geographic coordinates in a confusing order, write their accounts in the present tense when everything should be cast in past, and put prisoners' comments in quotation marks when the arcane rules of intelligence report writing dictate that quotation marks are to be used only around the name of a ship.

At Kandahar, once a report had cleared the editors in the ICE, it was "dragged," in the metaphorical language of the computer mouse, into a folder that made it pop up on the computer screens in the Ops Section next door. There, another mini–review board, soldiers who got much of their satisfaction in life out of being sticklers for format, scrubbed the document again, prompting another round of give-and-take before they kicked it to the next level.

In Afghanistan the army had every device and information appliance available to the modern warrior, satellite hookups everywhere you looked and enough fiber-optic cable to have tripped all those fleeing Taliban as they headed for the hills. But the poor jokers in the Ops Section had to save all these precious interrogation reports on 3½-inch floppy disks and walk them across the bombed-out terminal to the tactical operations center (TOC). Protocol didn't dictate such hand deliveries — it was just that no one had bothered to wire the two facilities together.

In the TOC, a pudgy older man who used to be army but was now a contract civilian would collect the disks, reload them onto computers, and feed them into a machine that encrypted everything and beamed it to the Coalition Forces Land Component Command in Kuwait, the real headquarters for the ground war. Then CFLCC (or C-Flick, as it was called) would transmit the documents back to the States, where security-cleared "little old ladies" would check all the formatting, click a button, and blast everything off into the ether, making it instantly available to the alphabet soup that is the U.S. intelligence community.

Which report went precisely where depended on a high-tech subscription system that tacked onto every report a code that corresponded to some broad category of intelligence. In the ICE, interrogators would thumb through a big binder, looking up these codes for everything they were planning to report. They were hierarchical, so you'd start by finding the code for "enemy ground forces," then drag your finger down the page to the most narrow version of this category, where you could find, say, "recruiting of radical Islamic fighters . . . in northern Europe." Or maybe you had a report on currency forging or weapons procurement or chemical purchases. Everything had a code.

Out in that amorphous intelligence community were analysts who spent their careers specializing in extremely narrow subjects, and part of their job was to put their little classified routing addresses under every code that mattered to them. That way, when the ladies at Fort Gordon hit SEND on a report, it would automatically find its way to every analyst who cared.

Of course, all this formatting and transmitting took time, sometimes as long as a week. That kind of delay was impermissible if someone stumbled onto an urgent piece of information, perhaps a tip from a newly arrived prisoner that an ambush was planned for U.S. troops somewhere. In that case, the officers in the ICE would drop everything and stand over that interrogator's shoulder while he wrote up a SPOT report as fast as his fingers could type it. Then it was rushed to the TOC, bypassing the ordinary nitpicking, and blasted out to the entire community all at once, with a special flag calling it to the immediate attention of any specific group the interrogator thought might be interested.

And that was it. Your precious "piece of intelligence" was out there in the ether. And the worst part was, you never knew what became of it, whether it was laughed at by analysts back in Washington or seized upon by Special Forces commanders who built a covert raid around your information the instant they got it. The only way you really knew you had hit pay dirt was when your report was sent out one day and you were flooded with follow-up questions the next.

My report on Prisoner 140 ran half a dozen pages, with sections on the city he lived in and his route into Afghanistan, but the centerpiece was the information about the compound in Jalalabad. I had a map of Jalalabad digitally scanned, then circled the spot where the house was located. On the next page I did the same with the satellite photograph of the neighborhood. Then, on the third page, I rendered a highly detailed drawing of the house itself, diagramming the exterior walls, the position of every room, every doorway, even the supposedly unused sleeping mats. I also etched in the dead fruit tree.

Within days of my report on 140, the follow-up started to pour in. There was enormous interest from Washington in 140's recruitment in Europe. There were questions from the military command in Kuwait about 140's activities in Jalalabad. There was clearly an appetite for more from this Euro-Algerian, and I was spending a good chunk of my time preparing my game plan.

At the ICE one night, I discovered a package and some mail next to my laptop. The package was from Tanya, a girl I was dating back in London. It smelled of cocoa and was over-wrapped in that reassuring English kind of way (who still uses twine and brown wrapping?). I opened it to find a sweet note and the chocolate for 140 I had asked her to send in an e-mail note the week before. There was also a large selection of chocolate for me that I ate until I was Easter-morning sick.

When I arrived at the JIF, I thought I had walked the wrong way. The hobo fire was gone, as was the stack of palette wood that kept it going — just two army MPs dancing from foot to foot in a vain attempt to keep the blood circulating. The 101st had arrived and decreed all fires extinguished as a precaution against the growing danger of rocket attack.

Prisoner 140 seemed very pleased to see me when the knit cap was pulled away from his face. Over the protests of the new, more jumpy army MPs, I unlocked 140's shiny manacles, reached into a knapsack, and set the chocolate on the table.

"I thought you might appreciate this," I said. As it rolled closer to him, the prisoner smiled and said a little Arabic prayer of thanks. He took it, repeated the prayer, and unwrapped the colorful foil. The guard demanded that the little toy inside (a tiny brown plastic monkey) be impounded at once.

At first our discussion focused on the mosque in his home city, and 140 said he had remembered some details that might be of use, describing a number of new characters, including a person he called Rau'uf who had lived briefly in the apartment where some of the 9/11 planning had occurred.

Rau'uf's job, 140 explained, was to assist in coordinating the recruitment of central European Muslims who had volunteered for training in Afghanistan. Rau'uf and a handful of others collected welfare while simultaneously collecting donations for the cause. The donations and the state-paid welfare money (minus a small fortune for their living expenses) helped send young militants to Afghanistan.

Rau'uf, 140 went on, was a Moroccan who had spent a good part of his life in France. He had grown up in poverty, and his father had been tortured at the hands of the Moroccan authorities. But he had no love for the West, either. He was fond of visiting French and Spanish battlefields where Islamic armies had been defeated in the Middle Ages, and he pledged to reverse those accidents of history.

Rau'uf himself had traveled to Afghanistan, joined the Taliban's fight against the Northern Alliance, and returned with two fingers missing. When he came back to Europe, Rau'uf would raise his maimed hand as a kind of trophy, an Arabic red badge of courage. And, according to 140, three fingers were better than five when it came to encouraging angry young Muslims to make their way to Afghanistan.

Then 140 resumed describing his time at the safe house in Jalalabad. Discussing his duties, he mentioned a new revelation: he was sometimes engaged to take water and other supplies up to an Al Qaeda camp just outside the city. He also delivered supplies to a subcamp that was devoted exclusively to explosives and bomb making. It seemed that the safe houses not only put up fighters as they arrived in Afghanistan but were also responsible for their well-being while they went off to train.

But 140's memory again failed him whenever I pressed for details about payments or passage or whether there was an organized system in Pakistan to get volunteers over the border into the camps. And for all of 140's descriptions of the safe house, conspicuously missing was any reference to weapons beyond the Klashes that were stored there.

Frustrated, I changed the subject, probing 140 to see if perhaps he could be useful in other ways.

"How are you getting on inside the camp?" I asked.

"Thank you for the blankets," he said. I'd arranged for him to get extra blankets in his cage after he'd complained of the cold in a previous interrogation.

"Oh, you're welcome. But what I mean is, how are the other prisoners treating you?"

He seemed willing to discuss the general mood of the other prisoners, many of whom, he said, were coming back to the cage and claiming that they "had the Americans running around in circles." Then 140 went on to say that some of the prisoners making these claims weren't necessarily guilty of anything but were being difficult with interrogators for the entertainment of it.

Other prisoners, he continued, were coming back after hours of interrogation claiming they had "said nothing" to their inquisitors despite all kinds of bloodcurdling threats. At least one prisoner reported to his cellmates that the Americans had attempted to "drug him." (Truth serum had come up at Huachuca, where instructors told inquisitive students that drugs were highly unreliable, with no clinical evidence to suggest that they would make a prisoner say something under their influence that he refused to say otherwise. We never administered drugs to prisoners in Afghanistan.) I took some solace in these claims: such bravado probably indicated that some prisoners were talking and had to make up macho stories to cover for it.

He said the prisoners also spent a fair amount of time rating their interrogators, the way junior high school kids talk about their teachers. Chief Shami clearly had a reputation; the rumor in the cells was that prisoners who were completely uncooperative went to see "the white gray-haired man with the white mustache." The female interrogators, 140 said, were a real surprise. The prisoners assumed all of them were from the CIA. Cavanaugh was famous, too. It appeared that I, however, had failed to leave much of a mark.

It was so cold, I was afraid I'd lose my fingernails. Prisoner 140's lips were purple and there were mucous candles dangling from his nose and frozen to his mustache. I started to terminate the interrogation by offering a cup of tea. When I started to wrap it up, 140 got very agitated. "No, no, no! Don't go yet!" He asked again about his wife and daughter, but I could offer him nothing but the same old, tired assurances. "Will I go to Cuba?" he asked. It was the first time I had heard a prisoner use the word *Cuba*.

"What makes you think you'll go to Cuba?"

"That's where you're sending prisoners, isn't it?"

"Who has told you that?"

"Everyone knows."

"That isn't what I asked."

"The guards told us."

"Why would they do that?"

"I don't know. Maybe to scare us."

"Does that scare you?"

"I want to see my family — if I have to go to Cuba, I won't see them. Is that where we go from here?"

"That hasn't been decided yet," I said, not sure whether I should confirm the story or dismiss it, only for 140 to discover later that I had lied.

"If it's true, can you help me get to Pakistan, help me to see my family?" the prisoner asked, his eyes welling up. Putting the tea down, he stretched his hands flat on the table, inching toward me. The guard didn't see it as a threatening move, but I wished he would stop the encroaching hands.

"I want to help you," I said, noticing that my own hands were curled in fists and positioned defensively on the edge of the table. I corrected it, resuming the posture of consoler. Prisoner 140 sobbed and rubbed his head into his shoulder to clear away the tears. It was my Fear Down nightmare from Huachuca revisiting me ten years later.

"You know I'm a good man," I continued. "I don't want to see you separated from your family. I know how much it hurts. But you need to trust me and also trust the U.N. If you were to leave this instant — walk out the main gate of this camp — you would have a smaller chance of finding your family than if you wait here while we comb the lists of refugees in the camps."

"But I would go to the camps and look," he said, taking the suggestion literally that he might be allowed out the main gate. "I would go find them. Please, in the name of Allah, let me go find them."

"I didn't mean we could let you go," I said. "I meant that you would almost certainly get killed. An Arab in Afghanistan is a target for every soldier and Afghan with a gun. You would certainly die."

"But you could take me there. Your forces could take me there. I have been very helpful; now you can get me to the camps safely."

As we stood up, the MP offered 140 a chance to collect himself. I needed to collect myself, too. Beneath my (hopefully convincing) consoling posture, I was reeling from his account of what prisoners were saying in the cages after confronting interrogators. And as much as I would have liked to think otherwise, I was among those being toyed with. One part of me felt sorry for 140, wanted to believe him, wanted to reunite him with his family. But the other part saw all the holes in the story, the missing names, the missing weapons. There were subtle physical signs, such as the instinctive way he reached for his glasses (by now long lost) when he went to examine a photograph or map I put in front of him. That minor, absentminded move made me think he was accustomed to poring over documents, that he was more sophisticated than he was letting on. Most of the prisoners we encountered had never seen an optometrist. This prisoner was still telling half-truths and I was bringing him chocolate! What a sucker.

Outside it was still dark, but in the east the tiniest hint of silver could be seen. All the booths were occupied. The night shift was in-processing prisoners, yet another batch must have arrived. I walked over to return a lighter I had borrowed from the MPs and stepped into their conversation. One of them, a black kid from Detroit, was telling a story about how he had farted on a detainee, prompting his colleagues to break out in laughter.

In no mood, I lit into the MP a torrent of curse words and every ounce of outrage I could muster. The MP stepped back, stunned, and searched my uniform. The absence of any rank must have made his head swim with fear that he'd pissed off a captain or a major.

I stomped out, passing through the barbed-wire aperture that was the only entry point into the JIF. Halfway out, I turned on my heel to see the MPs brace themselves for the possibility that the crazy "officer" might be coming back for another round. The prisoners might not have been intimidated by me, but at least the night-shift MPs were.

Back at the ICE, Gary Heaney entered, flung papers across the room, tore off three layers of clothes, and threw himself into a chair near the stove. Heaney had by this point established himself as one of the stronger performers in the booth. He was one of the few with real experience, having done interrogations in

Bosnia in 1999 and 2000. Gary was a reservist and in his real life was a computer technician for a firm in Maryland. In fact, he had been working as a private contractor in the Pentagon on the morning of September 11. The plane struck the massive building's west side and plowed through three of its five concentric rings — C, D, and E — before coming to a stop in an open-air service way just short of the B ring. Heaney was in the B ring on that side of the building; the nose of the aircraft was pointing straight at where he was working on some routers. Like many people who narrowly escape disaster, he saw the hand of God in his survival. And a few months later he was in Afghanistan. He was one of the most levelheaded, even-tempered soldiers in the unit. In fact, everyone teased him about his good nature, calling him Gare-Bear. But as he stormed into the ICE that night he was livid. Turner had spilled the beans, Heaney said, had told a prisoner exactly where we all were — at the airport in Kandahar, Afghanistan.

Until that point, no one had ever told prisoners the location of the camp. Some had never been on a plane in their lives and actually thought they had been flown to the United States. Others might have suspected they were still in Afghanistan, but they couldn't see any landmarks from their cages and had no clue as to their precise location. That's the way it's supposed to be. If prisoners know where they are, they might be more likely to try to escape. If they get out, they can tell the enemy where our facility is located. Not to mention that uncertainty is a source of anxiety to the detainees, something interrogators can prey on, use to their advantage. Now Turner's guy would no doubt inform the whole camp that they were all still in Mullah Omar's hometown.

Heaney then launched into a litany of Turner's other failings — his fecklessness in the booth, his nonexistent charisma, poor questioning, lackluster ability to keep track of priority questions.

It was true that Turner had been struggling from the very beginning. Stowe, the night-shift senior echo, had tried to help by teaming him with Heaney. Clearly it wasn't working. For starters, it didn't exactly thrill Heaney to come out of his own interrogations, with reports to write, and then be sent right back into the booth to hold Turner's hand. Technically, Heaney was going in only as a translator, which ordinarily would have represented something of a break from the more taxing work of one-on-one interrogation. But within minutes Turner would be stumbling over questions or missing obvious follow-ups, and Heaney would have to step in. Pretty soon, Heaney was running the interrogation.

As Heaney went through his list of criticisms of his partner, others in the tent were getting their blood up, too, not only because Turner had given away the location of the camp but because his weaknesses indirectly harmed them. Interrogation is, at one level, a solitary endeavor. But in a prison, in a war, you win or lose as a team. Every blown interrogation leaves a gaping hole in the broader understanding of the enemy and sends ripples through the rest of the operation. One prisoner's disclosures can expose another prisoner's lies. Success hinges on winning prisoners' respect or playing on their fears — and neither comes easily if they start to think their keepers are a bunch of amateurs.

Heaney continued his tirade a good ten minutes, until Turner himself strolled into the tent, oblivious. Everybody went quiet.

The atmosphere at the next shift change was tense. There had been rumblings that the land component command, which was running the war from Camp Doha in Kuwait, was becoming concerned about the meager intelligence being gleaned from the prisoners. Pressure was also coming from the Pentagon to turn things around. Captain Rawles made some brief introductory remarks at the shift change, then turned the session over to Chief Tafford.

Tafford hardly ever came to shift change. He was a chief warrant officer, which meant he had opted out of the traditional sergeant's career track to become a specialist in his trade. His specialty, of course, was interrogation, and he outranked the Serial 93 warrant officers and just about everybody else in the ICE. Since December he had been in charge of a mobile interrogation team, a special group that would go out on missions with three or four troops and do tactical interrogation work in the field, away from the prison at Kandahar. He and a handful of other active-duty soldiers from the parent unit of Task Force 500 had been the first conventional MI assets in Afghanistan. With a full, red-tinted beard and puffy eyes, he resembled an Edwardian-era British royal. He was very tall, which was a good thing, because he was also grossly overweight. The big man was pissed. "I want to say a few words," he said. "I just want y'all to know why y'all *suck*. I don't know what's gotten into all of you, and I don't give a fuck. All I know is that you're going to straighten out and start to do your damn jobs."

Everyone shifted nervously or looked down at the floor or up at the ceiling. "Things have been going on here; shortcuts have been taken that make us look like horses' asses to everybody in the community. And this bullshit is going to end *now*."

Tafford went on, with liberal use of profanity, to say that he was not going to accept the lack of diligence and professionalism that he saw in the interrogators' reports, in their records, and in the booths. He delivered a brutal critique of the interrogation operation, then branched out to rip document exploitation, linguistic support, and analytical support. He said he had visited interrogation booths and listened in on what was happening inside. Soldiers were practicing "sloppy follow-up,

miserable approaches, and unpersuasive, ill-conceived attempts"
to persuade the enemy to give up information. There was no
energy and no purpose being exercised in this crucial job.

Then, in a misguided attempt to hammer home his message
with a reminder of his expertise and authority, Tafford tossed in
an unfortunate remark: "I am a CW2, *promotable*, and there
ain't nobody in this room except Chief Klein who doesn't have
to do what I tell him to do."

Everybody knew what *promotable* meant: that he was a chief
warrant officer 2 in line to become a chief warrant officer 3;
that he had, in fact, already earned the rank, but it hadn't yet
been formally bestowed. But I had never heard anybody tack
on the word *promotable* as if it were some legitimate component
of rank. Only a horse's ass would go around declaring that he
was a chief warrant officer 2 *promotable*.

Then Tafford capped it off with another big mistake.

"If there is any man here who disagrees with what I've just
said, tell me now, in the open."

Ed Roberts's arm went right up. Roberts was a sullen reserve interrogator from Florida who had been born in Syria
and clearly had decided somewhere along the line to change his
name. His native language skill already made him a fairly
prominent member of the unit, but suddenly he launched himself into the forefront of everyone's attention.

"I don't know who the hell *you* think *you* are, but the only
bullshit that's been said here tonight has come from *you*," the
furious Roberts said, thrusting his finger toward Tafford.
Roberts laid into Tafford for a good couple of minutes, attacking him for everything from abusing his privilege of wearing
civilian clothes to the fact that, in spite of his position as the
senior operations officer, he had elected assignments that took
him completely out of the task force's day-to-day business.
Roberts's tirade took everybody by surprise, including Tafford,

and it ended only when Captain Rawles ordered him to "take a breather."

Then Tafford, in his infinite wisdom, asked the assembled soldiers if anyone else shared Roberts's misgivings about the command and its administration. Bad move. Just about any other course would have been better than putting Roberts's rant to an instant Nielsen rating. More than half the people in the room raised their hands. There was a collective gasp. The atmosphere was almost mutinous.

Rawles desperately tried to conclude the meeting on a semipositive note, but the damage had been done. The contract linguists were angry and chattering away in hushed but sharp tones in the corner by the stove. The small document-exploitation team stormed into their adjoining tent to issue their own stream of curses. One of the newer arrivals, a female national guardswoman from California, was in tears. The day shift left the tent, muttering their disgust.

The worst part was that the thrust of Tafford's remarks was on the money. We *were* screwing up. We were extracting only a tiny percentage of the information locked in the minds of the prisoners a few dozen yards away. But nobody heard that. They were too offended and too distracted by Tafford's attitude. Once again we were blind to what was right in front of us. But all that was about to change.

THE RATMASTER

Tafford's disaster was followed a few days later by a major reshuffling of the interrogation staff. Fitzgerald and several others were reassigned to the day shift, which was short on Arabic speakers. The night shift would be reinforced by another group of interrogators set to arrive in a week: Serial 99, a mix of active-duty troops and reservists from all over the army.

The command also made the formal announcement of a change everybody had been expecting for weeks, namely, that the army's 101st Airborne Division would officially take over control of the garrison and the prison MP operation from the exhausted marines with whom they had been sharing duty. We felt bittersweet about the changeover. Admittedly, it was strange that a bunch of army interrogators had become so enamored of the marines they worked with. But they were an impressive, professional group of fighters.

We'd especially miss the marine liaison to the JIF. We had met the man we called the Jailer on our first night in Afghanistan, and his hunched back, the scar on his face near his mouth, and his short, round body seemed all too perfect, given his duties. But despite initial impressions, he was the picture of moderation. Routinely working one and a half shifts, he was forever advising his huge marines, assigned to escort prisoners to and from the JIF, to take it easy on their charges. He knew that any heavy-handedness could potentially interfere with the interrogators' plans, and he was right. The interrogators generally wanted the prisoners to get neutral treatment from the guards so that later on they still had the option of ratcheting up the anxiety or taking it down a peg.

With his flop of black hair and caustic sense of humor, Fitzgerald was Task Force 500's Hawkeye Pierce. And like the *M*A*S*H* character, he was often at his best when his wit was aimed at tormenting his superiors. The brunt of his insubordinate energy at Kandahar was the day shift's officer in charge, Chief Irvine, a middle-aged regular-forces guy who was at times half a step slower than some of the troops he supervised.

Fitzgerald called Irvine the Ratmaster.

Once Fitzgerald moved to the day shift, he quickly hooked up with Brian Talbot and Dan Lawson, two other young, too-smart-for-their-own-good interrogators. The trio shared a highly refined sense of humor and a certain disdain for authority — as well as an unusual talent for combining the two in small set pieces they would perform for any captive audience.

One of their favorites involved Fitzgerald's entering a tent with one hand covering his mouth as it spit out a hip hop beat, the other hand extended, fingers down, in the universal pose of rap orchestration. Then Fitzgerald would bust a verse:

"Who's standing atta?"

"Who's standing atta?"

"Who's standing atta?"

Then Talbot would burst in to finish the rap with the rejoinder:

"Attention? Attention? Attention?" his body jerking from side to side like a white army-uniform-wearing Flava Flav.

The fact is, Irvine wasn't a bad guy, nor a bad officer in charge. But Fitzgerald despised him for no better reason than that he was the boss. (As Fitzgerald would explain, hating the boss is a "time-honored tradition" in the army.) One of

Fitzgerald's favorite ways to goad Irvine was to launch into some asinine academic analysis of the army within the chief's earshot. Fitzgerald would start yapping about how volunteer soldiers such as Talbot and him — that is, soldiers who had signed up for one tour and had not reenlisted or extended their contracts — were "the moral equivalent of conscripts" who didn't know what they were getting themselves into when they signed up. Therefore, they were under no obligation to buy into all the Big Green brainwashed nonsense of the army, the mindless jeers, the incomprehensible acronyms. "The army is a totalitarian system," Fitzgerald would say. "There's a different word for everything. You become so institutionalized, you can't function. It's a green blob!" And soldiers who had re-upped, such as Irvine, someone who had been in for fifteen years, "had basically volunteered to be lobotomized."

Eventually Irvine couldn't take it anymore and would erupt: "That's bullshit! Don't listen to him, Talbot!"

One of the other Fitzgerald-Talbot-Lawson stunts would kick into gear whenever some brass-heavy officer made a visit to the ICE. Pentagon officials and officers from every branch of the service were always stopping in to see the nerve center of the interrogation operation. Everybody wanted to know what it was like to go face-to-face with Al Qaeda. Practically every day some fresh-faced junior officer would poke his head into the tent and warn everybody that Colonel or General So-and-so was going to be there in fifteen minutes. That would throw Irvine into an escalating tizzy. "I want this place cleaned up!" he would shout. "Look busy! Anybody not writing on a laptop should be writing in a notebook! If you have anything clever to say in your interrogation, save it and say it when the colonel pokes his head in! Move those water bottles off the table! Stack up that gear!"

While Irvine was rattling off all these commands, his insubordinate trio would begin snapping their fingers, scurrying around the room, and leaping over chairs like a scene out of *West Side Story*. To a tune Leonard Bernstein would never recognize, Talbot would start in softly with: "The general's coming, the general's coming, the general's coming . . ."

Then Lawson would pipe in: "Grab your gear! The general's here!"

Finally Fitzgerald would stand at attention in the center of the tent, put on a face so sad that it looked as if he was going to start sobbing, and break out in glorious falsetto: "I'm just a lonely private. . . . Who will hear me cry?"

In a panic that the colonel was going to walk in on this disgraceful scene, the Ratmaster would screech, "Quit it! Quit it! Quit that singing and dancing!"

OTHER GOVERNMENT AGENCY

T he day after the unit's December arrival, Lopez and I were walking through a wing of the terminal when he casually pointed to a cubbyhole of an office and said, "That's the 'Other Government Agency.'" We interrogators went along with local custom and called them as they wished to be called — OGA — but everyone knew who they really were.

It was one of a dozen or so offices that had been built out of plywood along one of the lengthy corridors inside the terminal. Inside were a couple of thirty-something guys wearing parkas and clicking away at laptops, and another guy in a thick flannel shirt. There was an American flag hanging inside, and a big September 11 poster on the door. It had silhouettes of the Twin Towers superimposed on an image in the shape of the Pentagon. Underneath were the words WE WILL NEVER FORGET.

A few days later, one of them came over to the ICE for what would be a semiregular schedule of visits. They always wanted to look at the latest prisoner lists to see if anyone new had arrived. Sometimes they wanted to talk to a prisoner, which the command would allow them to do, but only if they were accompanied in the booth by an army interrogator. We did that for a number of reasons. First, they were our prisoners and we would be on the hook for any Geneva Conventions violations in our facility. Second, they weren't sharing interrogation reports with us, so we needed someone in there to see what they were learning. Most important, we had to send people in because the agency needed us — not a single OGA officer we encountered spoke Arabic.

For a while the soldiers and officers in the ICE were impressed that OGA was around and stopping in now and again. But within a couple of weeks, most everybody in the interrogation shop started to resent the spooks. Their whole posture, once you spent some time around them, said "you work for us." The OGA folks were always smiley. They'd come into the ICE, saying, "Hey, how is everybody? Good. Good." Then, having dispensed with the small talk, they'd get straight to business. "Can we have that list?" They never offered any help, wouldn't check prior records or previous interrogation reports on detainees, and wouldn't share any information from any of their presumably vast databases. They were takers, not givers.

The OGA had its own interrogation facility set up in Kabul. Very few of the army interrogators ever saw it, but we knew it was there. Sometimes they would transfer prisoners the agency had already interrogated to Kandahar or Bagram. Of course, the army interrogators only knew this from the prisoners, who would tell us they had talked to our "agents." The OGA itself would never so much as pass on a note explaining how it had acquired a prisoner or what they'd gotten out of him. Thus, we figured they were turning over prisoners that they themselves couldn't break or had concluded to be of low intelligence value. If an army interrogator started to get some interesting information out of one of these transferred prisoners, the OGA sometimes showed up again to take him back.

The difference between the OGA and our European allies' civilian intelligence personnel was night and day. One of these allied organizations asked for a desk in the ICE very early on. A professorial middle-aged man named Martin worked among us most of the time. Unlike the OGA guys, he spoke Arabic. In fact, he might have been the best Arabist in the garrison;

he had spent years working in Damascus, Lebanon, and other stations.

Martin looked like a grown-up Dennis the Menace. He was about fifty-five, with gray hair around the ears. He wore unstylish metal-frame glasses, an L. L. Bean–style ribbed pullover with a zipper neck. He always wore a collared shirt underneath, thick, olive green corduroy pants, and lace-up boots.

He'd stroll into the ICE, spreading the typical cheer of his country: "Good morning, everyone. Good morning. Good morning. Good morning. What great things are you going to do today?" He was always darting off for some three-day visit to another locale and bringing back beer for select army officemates. (He'd bring in a backpack and say, "Chris, I have a desperately urgent report for you." Then he'd hand over the pack and I would reach inside and pull out a pack of Caffrey's in large cans. Martin would grin. "The problem is," he would say in a thick upper-crust accent, "it has to be *exactly* the right temperature." So I would put the cans in a plastic bag and submerge them in the water of the closest thing we had to a refrigerator in Kandahar: an Afghan cistern, a clay pot filled with water placed in a wide hole in the ground behind the tent.)

Martin wanted to see the reports and lists, too. But he went so far out of his way to be unimposing that it was disarming. He'd sidle up to me and say, "Could I possibly have a minute after shift change? I know you'll be exhausted. But could we just sit down for a minute? I found a few things hidden in these reports and I thought I'd better bring them to your attention. Now mind you, only someone with lots of time on his hands like me would have spotted this. . . ."

Then, gently, he would come to the point: "Did you notice, Chris, these two prisoners were from the same town? This guy's handler was Faryeed. That guy's handler was Faryeed. I'm betting they were the same man." In other words, "Hey, dumbasses, did it ever occur to you guys to connect the dots in your own reports?"

But that was the beauty of having him around. He was a giver *and* a taker. In fact, Martin and his countrymen were better than anybody at helping to run down information. If you asked them whether a certain prisoner was on a certain flight, they'd get back to you the next day with his seat assignment. If you asked the FBI, they'd say, "Give us three days," and never get back to you. One of the prisoners I interrogated was a guy named Rafiq whose name and background seemed to match up with someone who had done some time in a prison back in Europe. Martin's friends in his country's domestic intelligence service ran a check on the guy's fingerprints within days and showed that the two were not the same man.

Later on, aware that we were frustrated by the phenomenon of prisoners' just showing up on our doorstep, Martin and his gang started discreetly sharing with us what they could about the raids in Pakistan being carried out by Pakistani and U.S. intelligence agencies. These raids were responsible for scores of prisoners brought to Kandahar and Bagram. Martin had to tell us what our own intelligence services were up to. It was astounding.

But even Martin and his team weren't infallible.

In late February one of Martin's men was interrogating a man named Ali Hamza who, like so many others, had gone to Europe seeking asylum, only to plot its destruction while living in a government-funded council estate. Because of a shortage of MPs, our Tom Cavanaugh had to serve as guard in the booth. He was stunned when the interrogator gave up after encountering some "cheeky" resistance from the prisoner. The questioner shrugged his shoulders at Cavanaugh as if to say, "I did my best," and walked out of the booth. Cavanaugh stepped outside, lit a cigarette, and asked if he would mind letting "a dumb mick from Philadelphia" have a go.

Cavanaugh went back into the tent and surprised the English-speaking Ali Hamza by offering him a cigarette and pulling out his own notebook. "I don't give a fuck what you did, just tell me *why* you did it," Cavanaugh said, staring menacingly at the prisoner. Almost involuntarily, Ali Hamza began explaining his rationale for supporting radical Islam but continued to vehemently protest that he had done nothing wrong.

Cavanaugh shrugged again and told Ali Hamza that his guilt was a foregone conclusion and there wasn't going to be a trial anyway. "Just tell me why you decided to become a terrorist." Again, Ali Hamza started yapping, trying to explain what Al Qaeda actually meant to him. He tried to communicate the frustration Arabs felt and their loathing for the imperialist West, which they saw as marching inexorably toward a showdown with Islam. Cavanaugh kept asking, "Why?" and the prisoner kept expanding the scope of his answers until Cavanaugh emerged from the tent with a piece of paper. On it, Ali Hamza had diagrammed bin Laden's Afghanistan organization, even assigning numerical ranks to various figures according to their influence in Al Qaeda.

At the top of the chart was a box containing bin Laden's name, so notorious that it was legible even in Cavanaugh's chicken-scratch penmanship. Connected to it by a series of dots was another box containing the name Ali Hamza and his job title: translator.

In early February, as the marines prepared to turn the base over to the 101st, word spread through the ICE one night that the commander of the Twenty-sixth Marine Expeditionary Unit was coming in for a farewell visit. Practically a second later, Marine Corps Major General James N. Mattis pushed through the door to the ICE, a pistol strapped to his thigh, and launched into a speech that was simultaneously confusing, inspiring, and unsettling.

"About two days ago I went down into the center of Kandahar. And there I saw two little children flying a kite in an old soccer stadium," he said. "The Afghan guide who was driving us told me that under the Taliban, flying kites was an offense punishable by death. Can you believe these fuckers?! They would deny the little child an opportunity to fly a kite.

"That would have been reason enough to come over here and kick these fuckers in the ass. But they did that and a lot worse. And so it's important that every one of you understand what it is you are doing here. . . . You are helping us to *kill* the enemy. Let's not make any mistakes about this. Let's not try to sugarcoat it. You are assisting my marines to *kill* evil. To *bayonet* it, to *grenade* it, to *shoot* it with machine guns, to *cut* its eyes out and *shit* in the sockets. And you can take pride in that. You can take pride in knowing that you had a hand in gouging out the eyes and cutting out the tongue of evil." He added, "Let me apologize to the lady soldiers in the room; I'm not entirely accustomed to encountering you all during combat operations, and my language sometimes reflects that inexperience."

We were packed in the room with the somehow charmingly violent general. The arrival of a new rotation from stateside meant that there was hardly an inch to breathe. Mattis went on about how he was no "smart intelligence guy like you all" and would leave the "brainiac" stuff to us. How he was just a common infantryman, but he respected deeply MI's contributions and was grateful for all of our hard work. All these compliments were peppered with a combination of curses and further apologies for his inappropriate language to the "lady soldiers" present.

He closed with an invitation to ask him questions. There was a long pregnant pause. "Well, if one of you doesn't ask a question, I'm gonna call on some unlucky soul and order him . . . ahh . . . or her to ask one," Mattis said with a smile but leaving no doubt he meant it.

Having already established his reputation as an extrovert, Ed Roberts raised his hand. "Yes, sir, how can I help you?" the general said.

"Er, sir, I just want to ask you what the plan is for the prisoners that are in the compound just down a hundred yards or so away from us," Ed said, mounting a well-intentioned but poorly timed defense of the minority of prisoners in custody who, it had been determined, were not Al Qaeda or Taliban. "You know, sir, as well as I do, that a large number of the people who are in there have no business being there. Could you please tell me what you plan to do to get those people back where they belong?"

It sounded as though all the generators had suddenly stopped, as though the airplanes had all ceased to come and go. The tent was silent.

The general shook his head.

"Soldier, I take it you didn't hear my story about the kites. . . . Well, if there are no more questions, hope you all have a fine evening and that you continue to help us find and *obliterate* the enemy."

Before he could leave, the general was presented with a Russian army canteen (apparently a battlefield trophy from that ill-fated war) on which Colonel Lewis had somehow managed to have engraved a message of gratitude for his leadership. The general said thank you and disappeared.

The next interrogation I conducted was on a Syrian father-and-son pair who were brought in after a raid near Khowst. They were a suspicious duo, given that Khowst was a known rallying point for Taliban sympathizers and a key way station in the underground railroad for escaping Al Qaeda fighters.

The son was young, maybe seventeen years old. I targeted him first in hopes that he would be the most vulnerable. Indeed, he was: he cried most of the time, complaining that he missed his mother sorely and that he and his father were the only means of support for their family — all seventeen of them.

It was heart-wrenching stuff. Worst of all, it was a textbook case for a Fear Up. In Arabic I told him that we would be forced to hold him and his father indefinitely or turn them both over to the interim Afghan government. I suggested that the Northern Alliance had set up special jails for Arab outsiders like him.

"The Taliban jails for the Northern Alliance prisoners were awful, you know. The worst part was that they were over-crowded." I paused for dramatic effect. "That's the good thing about how the Northern Alliance runs the prisons now that they are in charge: there are many, many prisoners, but for some reason, no overcrowding."

The boy trembled so miserably that when he tried to sob, no sound came out.

"Now, Hesham, it is important for you to take control," I said, opening a metaphorical window. "It is important you decide what will happen to you and your family, who need you."

The boy was doubled over in his chair.

"Look at me, Hesham!" I shouted, craning my neck to get a look at his face, which was contorted, still shaking, still tearful. "You need to tell me why you and your father came to Afghanistan." But he wouldn't. He just sat there and wept.

I left the son and went straight into the next booth and sized up his father, who claimed to be forty-nine but looked 149. He confirmed that he had fourteen other children. He said he left Syria because he found his eight-year-old daughter smoking. This to him was the last straw in a long series of religious corruptions witnessed in that country. He had decided to pack up the family and move to Afghanistan in hopes of finding a better life.

Weren't there any out-of-the-way places in Syria, I asked. "No." Weren't there any places to go in, say, Turkey, or maybe

Iran? "No." So you more or less walk with sixteen members of
your family, including the cigarette-smoking daughter, and set
up home in paradise here in Afghanistan?

"Yes."

Terrific. This father of the year just wanted to get to a place
where he could ensure that his daughters never went to school
and that his sons could grow up and join the religious police
and make Daddy proud. The old man started to cry. He said
over and over and over again how sorry he was for the World
Trade Center attacks. He was truly sorry that anyone had corrupted Islam in such a way, but he had nothing to do with it.

"And what," I asked, "did you intend to do when you got
here? For a living, I mean."

"Allah would provide," the old man said.

"But did you have a backup plan at all? I mean, are you a
tradesman or something?"

Nope. There was just Allah. What a religion. How the hell
could the interrogators make any headway with a bunch of prisoners for whom this kind of insanity passed as a legitimate life
decision? I wanted to kick this guy under the table.

Of course, that was if his story was true. After thirteen
hours of interrogating the two of them, I had gotten not one au-
thentically reportable thing. I wrote two IIRs (intelligence information reports) about practically nothing just to keep face
with Mark Stowe.

The worst development accompanying the arrival of the 101st
was the requirement to wear "full battle rattle" everywhere we
went. Even walking the short distance from the ICE to the interrogation facility, we had to put on flak vests, helmets, LBE
gas masks, and weapons. More than once while making that
thirty-pace trip, I was accosted by overanxious 101st officers,
NCOs, or even junior enlisted, ordering me to button my flak
vest all the way up.

The new rules greatly increased the number of piss bottles lying around the tent. Nobody wanted to gear up just to go the fifty yards to the piss pit to relieve himself, so soldiers started grabbing empty water bottles and striding over to a quiet corner to do their business.

The danger was that after twelve hours of interrogation it was easy to mistake such stylishly packaged sewage as lemon-flavored Gatorade. More than a few MI soldiers were halfway to putting the rim of the bottle to their mouth before catching their mistake. And General Mattis thought we were brainiacs. This in turn created a new chore: sergeants were constantly barking at troops to take the piss bottles to the latrine and empty them.

The 101st also found it necessary to shut down the *ham'am,* where I had been indulging in periodic ice baths. This was made necessary by the inexplicable relocation of the water supply point from a well very near the ICE to a distant spot at the far end of the airfield, by the pirate-flagged engineers' area. The chief advantage of this new water point seemed to be that it was so far away that almost no one visited it.

Most days I would take an empty five-gallon jerrican from the tents to the water point, where a philosophical Screaming Eagle from Pittsburgh named Willis would fill it up from an enormous three-foot-high water bladder as big as an in-ground pool. Although this water was not potable, it was perfectly suitable for washing and laundry. The trip back to the tents with a full can was considerably harder, especially in full battle gear.

TALIBAN MINISTER

In Washington on February 7, President Bush declared that the United States would apply the rules of the Geneva Conventions to Taliban soldiers captured during the war in Afghanistan. But the White House added that these terms would not apply to Al Qaeda fighters. And neither category of captured combatant would be granted prisoner-of-war status. The administration was attempting to settle the controversy over how prisoners would be treated, a controversy that had been brewing since the war began and had heated up with each new arrival of detainees at Guantánamo. A shipment of thirty prisoners that same day had pushed the population there to 153, with all of them being held in cages at a temporary stockade called Camp X-ray.

The debate had triggered strong emotions among some figures within the administration itself. Secretary of State Powell had argued vigorously that if prisoners captured in Afghanistan weren't afforded the protections of the Geneva Conventions, it would be hard for the United States to insist that its soldiers receive those protections when they were captured. But to some extent, his pleas had been ignored by his boss.

The decision had little practical impact in the dusty prison at Kandahar, where the leaders of Task Force 500 had declared from the very beginning that the camp would be operated under the rules of the Geneva Conventions. The decision not to grant POW status was important, however. Such a grant would have required the United States to release prisoners at the end of the conflict. More important, prisoners of war are not legally obligated to tell interrogators any more than their name, rank, serial number, and date of birth.

Exactly one day after the White House made its announcement, the United States got its biggest catch to that point in the war: Taliban minister Ghul Jan Khan, who surrendered to U.S. forces in Kandahar. He was the first high-ranking Taliban official in U.S. custody. Tyler and Cavanaugh were assigned to interrogate him.

Ghul Jan claimed not to know the whereabouts of any key players, including bin Laden or Mullah Omar. Nor, he said, had he been aware of the September 11 attacks before they happened, aside from hearing some general talk that a "big attack" was afoot. But gradually he began to reveal some interesting information about bin Laden and Al Qaeda's movements in the immediate aftermath of the attacks.

He said there was frantic concern within the Taliban about how the United States would react. He confirmed reports from other detainees that bin Laden had visited the Al Farook training camp near Kandahar on September 12. The Ghoul, as he came to be known to us by way of the ever-nicknaming MPs, described a lengthy caravan of trucks and SUVs that went out to the camp to see bin Laden. The tall figure greeted his Arab volunteers by describing the success of the strikes on America and exalting the martyrs who had carried out the operation. There were great cheers and celebrations. But bin Laden said that "the work is not over" and that the long-term goals remained to defeat Israel and oust the United States from Saudi Arabia.

Much of this the interrogators already knew, but Ghul Jan disclosed an alarming new piece of information. He said Al Qaeda also had plans in place to attack U.S. gas stations, major bridges, and other landmarks. He said these attacks could be carried out by as-yet-undetected sleeper cells. This triggered a barrage of questions from Washington, which had been sifting through reports of such plots for months. (California governor Gray Davis had embarrassed himself in November by calling a press conference to declare that the Golden Gate Bridge was a target, only to have the FBI and CIA call the claim "unsubstantiated.") But having disclosed this minibombshell, Ghul Jan promptly clammed up, saying he didn't know any further details. He alluded to other "senior figures" he could contact — if he were released — and possibly coax into talking to the United States. Indeed, he said he had turned himself in merely to "test the waters" for the others.

When this offer was declined, he declared that he did not wish to be kept "hostage" any longer. It was as if he thought he had some sort of diplomatic immunity. When it dawned on him that he didn't have a get-out-of-jail-free card, the information he provided went from intriguing to dull and finally intentionally misleading. That, in turn, threw all his earlier statements into serious doubt and led many in the unit to suspect that he had dangled the bridge story in an effort to get the CIA into the booth so he could cut some sort of a deal.

But that didn't happen, either, and Ghul Jan became the first VIP prisoner at Kandahar. The Geneva Conventions require that officers be separated from the enlisted men, and he was a senior official (the situation wasn't precisely accurate, but the analogy broadly applied). But there was a more pressing reason. We knew that he would be recognized by the other prisoners, which could put him in jeopardy someday. If he told us where bin Laden was, for example, or even if we got that information from someone else, others would know that Ghul Jan had been in custody, and he might be accused of selling out the cause. One of the interrogation tents was converted into a private apartment for him, and he was stuck inside there all day every day, essentially under tarpaulin house arrest.

Ghul Jan's appearance coincided with a flurry of strange arrivals at Kandahar.

Just days earlier a plane full of prisoners touched down in the middle of the day, an exceedingly rare daylight delivery. Among them was a large consignment of Chinese Muslims known as Vighurs. It was as if someone had reached into the rain forest and produced a new species.

Fitzgerald was put in charge of interrogating them, but astonishingly he couldn't find anything on the U.S. classified computer networks about the group. On the public Internet, he found out that they were from far northwestern China and were agitating for an independent Muslim state. In fact, they called their territory Turkmenistan. The Chinese called it the Chang Ching Province. This gave Fitzgerald something to work with. He started his sessions by stating the obvious: that the United States might decide to turn them over to China, and, well, the Chinese reputation for welcoming back dissidents spoke for itself. On the other hand, if they cooperated, perhaps they might find a peaceful Muslim existence in the new Afghanistan.

Initially, what was most remarkable was their unimaginative cover stories, familiar claims of coming to Afghanistan to seek a bride or study the Koran. Because they didn't speak Arabic or Pashtu, they couldn't take Cover Stories 101 from the rest of the prisoners and didn't know that these lame excuses were Kandahar clichés.

But gradually a couple of the Vighurs started talking. They explained how their ultimate goal was to ignite a confrontation between the United States and China, or as a second choice, India and China. The point was to have China occupied elsewhere so the Vighurs could mount an insurrection and achieve an independent state. It all seemed awfully far-fetched, but the requests for follow-up questions flooded in from Washington, and every query that came in made it clear that U.S. intelligence was starting from practically zero with this group. They were so basic, in fact, that the Vighurs started to take some offense, apparently thinking their cause important enough to have warranted more OGA scrutiny than their apparent anonymity suggested.

The Vighurs' arrival came on the heels of another batch of prisoners who had left the separatist fight in Chechnya to come to the aid of their Muslim brothers in Afghanistan. It was the first time we had seen any prisoners who spoke Russian.

By this point, Turner was trying to duck assignments in the booth. And when forced to interrogate, he would typically return to the ICE forty minutes after leaving, saying that the prisoner was a low-level fighter and had no intelligence value. But as one of the handful of Russian speakers in the unit, Turner couldn't hide from this assignment. But Mark Stowe was wary, so he ordered Turner to put together a questioning plan and show it to him before he left for the booth. When Stowe got a look at Turner's plan, he was flabbergasted. There was nothing about the fighting in Chechnya or potential ties to Al Qaeda.

So I sat down with Turner to try to help him. When I cracked open the big binder in the ICE listing all the priority intelligence requirements on every subject under the sun, it was immediately clear that Turner didn't know how to navigate the book. After an hourlong tutorial, we finally had a questioning plan in place and Turner was ready to go. As he stood up to leave, I said, "Hey, Doug, how do you say 'gorge' in Russian?" As in Pansiki Gorge, an enclave in former Soviet Georgia crawling with Al Qaeda operatives and other Islamic militants.

He didn't know.

I wanted to head butt him. "Sit down, Doug. Look up all the words you're going to need."

"I'll talk around it," Turner said.

"Don't test my patience, Doug. Look up the words."

In full pout, Turner started thumbing through a Russian dictionary. By the time he was done, it had been three hours since Stowe had told him to get his questioning plan in shape. Nobody takes one hour, let alone three. Finally he finished up and headed down to the JIF.

But forty-five minutes later he was back. "The guy didn't know anything," he said. "He couldn't answer any of my questions."

Disgusted, I told Turner he was going back into the booth, except this time he would be accompanied by Kyle Sinclair, another Russian interrogator who had already plowed through a session with one of the new prisoners that night. Thirty minutes later Turner came back without his partner.

"What happened?" I asked.

"Sinclair sent me out of the booth."

Any other interrogator would have been so embarrassed by that outcome that he would have sat down there in the freezing cold, waiting for Sinclair to finish rather than come back to the ICE alone and defeated. But Turner's aversion to personal discomfort trumped his honor.

A short while later Sinclair came back and wrote a thorough report, with details on how many fighters were in the gorge and how they were getting their supplies. It also buttressed information other interrogators were getting indicating that despite Al Qaeda's efforts to take some credit for the fighting in the gorge, the Chechens didn't train with Al Qaeda. They weren't against Al Qaeda, but they didn't see themselves as aligned with bin Laden. More interesting yet was information on the woeful state of the Russian and Georgian armies. The prisoners said the Russians routinely approached the Chechens offering to abandon their equipment for cash or to trade ammunition for opium. This information occasioned follow-up questions from Washington like you wouldn't believe.

While Sinclair was writing his report, I asked him which of

the Russian prisoners was the most docile. Sinclair thought for a moment then offered the number of a prisoner who had broken right away. I turned to Turner and told him to grab the checkerboard.

"Go down there, play checkers with this guy, and learn to speak Russian," I said. I ordered him to do it every day, two hours a day. I assumed Turner knew the rules of that game, at least.

Chief Rodriguez practices running an interrogation control element (ICE) during a predeployment exercise at Fort Bragg in November 2001. The training proved good preparation for operations in Afghanistan.

Jonathan Lee, Chris Mackey, and Ben Davis eat a breakfast of MREs after the first night shift. The mornings saw a rise in the temperature on the high, arid plain where Kandahar is situated. At night the thermometer hovered just below freezing.

A barricade of freight containers and sandbags protects the ICE, just visible to the right of the center container. The Kandahar airport terminal is in the background.

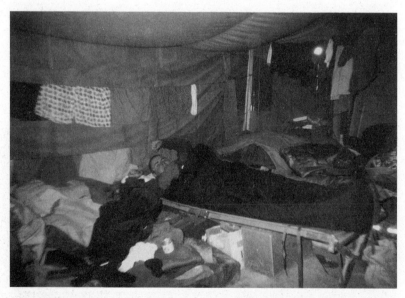

The basic accommodations for the interrogators resembled those of the prisoners. Mackey gets up for the night shift at Kandahar, February 2002.

After the closure of the "piss pit," engineers installed the ubiquitous "desert daisies" — pipes jammed into the ground and used as urinals.

Mackey brushes his teeth before hitting the rack after a long night shift; prisoners (many of whom never saw a toothbrush before surrendering or being captured) were made to brush their teeth by the guards just a few yards away. The sign over the interrogators' sleeping quarters says DEPARTMENT OF VIRTUE & PREVENTION OF VICE, a dig at the official name of the Taliban religious police.

Gary Heaney questions a prisoner in one of the booths. Heaney became a master screener whose assessments rarely proved wrong.

As a DLI-trained Spanish linguist, Henry Hasegawa was originally appointed the ICE clerk responsible for maintaining the interrogation board under which he is napping. He eventually teamed up with Ben Davis and became perhaps the most talented U.S. interrogator in Afghanistan. He also had another useful skill: the capacity to catch sleep whenever the opportunity arose.

Mackey and Hasegawa question the British cook, who feigned a stutter, a heart condition, and mental illness in an attempt to throw off his interrogators.

Geoff Fitzgerald on the end of the runway at Kandahar. A few days later he went "upriver" with the advance party to take over operations at Bagram.

The cavernous Facility at Bagram was the new home to detainee operations after Kandahar all but closed in May 2002.

Davis, Hasegawa, and Mackey take a break in the "reception room" just before another batch of prisoners arrived at Bagram in early June 2002. It was in this room that prisoners waited to be in-processed into U.S. custody. Interrogators were posted here to observe any prisoner behavior that could be used against them in the booth.

Major Gibbs, Mackey, and Chief Rodriguez pose for the camera in the ICE. This room served as the center of interrogation operations and the site of the morning meeting. Laptop computers with report templates ringed the room and hummed twenty-four hours a day, the conduits for sending collected intelligence to the community.

Ethan Kampf, the extraordinarily talented Arabic linguist and interrogator, takes a well-earned break outside the Facility. The porch on his left formed the entrance to the tents of Viper City, the official but little-used residence of the interrogation team.

Heaney and Davis wrap up questioning of one of the so-called Kissing Cousins. The interrogation booths at Bagram were a vast improvement over the tents at Kandahar.

Davis slumped in a chair the morning after the marathon interrogation of the Kissing Cousins. Most interrogators slept where they fell after routinely spending fifteen or more hours a day mentally battling with prisoners for crucial intelligence information.

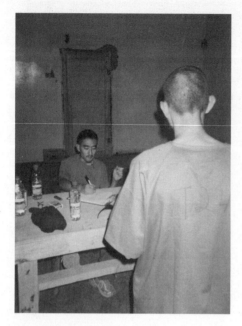

Hasegawa questions one of the "Bearded Ladies," a group of prisoners whose exploitation he managed. The meticulous detail and planning that accompanied this effort made it one of the most outstanding examples of applying all lessons learned against the enemy.

A last hurrah on the roof of the Facility. With the relief in place in August, an impromptu cocktail party at sunset showcases the contrast between the new arrivals (who were made to wear their uniforms in the booth despite experience showing the negative consequences) and those they came to relieve. From left to right: Jim Berrara, Chris Mackey, Christine Howe, Sean McGovern, Jimmy Kelleher, and Joe Rodriguez.

HASEGAWA AND DAVIS

On the first of February I was editing reports at the back of the ICE when I was approached by newly minted sergeants Hasegawa and Davis. "We'd like to talk to 140," Davis said.

My first thought was defensive. *What have I missed?* I asked the two young active-duty interrogators what they were onto. Davis laid out six interrogation reports on a table. "Look what I found," he said. He stabbed his finger at one report after another, and in an almost inaudible mumble pointed out that each of the prisoners was North African. Each had lived in Europe on asylum visas. Each had left Europe at almost exactly the same time to come to Afghanistan. Then he laid down two more interrogation reports, again North Africans but with different stories, lacking the common denominators of the others.

"These prisoners don't fit the pattern," he said. "But we will prove that they do and that they are lying." Prisoner 140, he said, was the key to helping them do it.

"Why?" I asked.

Then Davis pointed out something else the first six reports had in common. All described staying in a house in Jalalabad, and, of course, 140 had disclosed the name of the man who ran it: Al-Jezari.

I was impressed. The general approach was to get as much as you could out of a prisoner, write it up, and let somebody higher up in the food chain connect the dots. Truth be told, we weren't even supposed to be doing analytic research; interrogators are just collectors. And yet here were Hasegawa and Davis, each of them all of twenty-two years old, piecing together what would turn out to be a significant part of the Al Qaeda puzzle.

Hasegawa, a Japanese kid, son of a California cop, had served in Bosnia, making him one of the few in the unit who had any experience with interrogation in a combat environment. But he spoke Spanish, which wasn't of much use in Afghanistan, and the command at Kandahar had given him an assignment that kept him out of the booth. He was in charge of keeping track of the interrogation schedules. He spent much of his time marking on a big, white, dry-erase board who was headed into which booth, when the interrogation started, when it finished, and whether there would be an intelligence report. The other interrogators called him the minister of statistics.

Hasegawa sat on a milk crate in the ICE and would leave his whiteboard station only to go outside for a smoke. It was so cold outside that he would yip and dance around — "Shit. Shit. Shit. Damn. Damn. Damn." — then come bursting back into the tent with the cigarette half finished, put it next to his crate, and resume his post. He was a consummate soldier, a paratrooper, who loved the army, its numbered buildings, its ordered day. He was also sharp-tongued. Interrogators who came back from the booth a little too quickly would always get a snide reprimand from Hasegawa: "You back already? What? You figured out where Osama is and called it quits?"

Davis, with dark curly hair and blue eyes, was quiet and hard to read. At Incirlik, on the way to Afghanistan, Rodriguez and I had taken a private moment to assess the troops, and both of us had given Davis low marks. Interrogators tend to be extroverts, or at least have some aptitude for relating to other people. Davis seemed incapable of relating to others in his own unit. But he was a solid Arabic speaker and was machinelike in terms of tirelessness. From the moment we arrived at Kandahar, Davis was always working in the booth, writing reports, or, more than anyone else, doing his own research. He hated sloppiness and was a stickler for spelling names and places consistently so keyword searches would pick up connections. He wrote out names that others were messing up, such as *Djibouti,* and taped them to a tent pole in the ICE for general reference.

Hasegawa started leaving his post at the dry-erase board for short periods in January, wandering down to the JIF. Like me, he didn't want to spend the war as some office functionary. It made sense that he would hook up with Davis. They were the same age and rank and shared the same view of the operation — that it was messed up. Some of the leadership in the ICE appeared too worried about padding their stats — how many interrogations conducted, how many reports written — and seemed to pay too little attention to just how much crap those reports contained. These two were also disciples of Cavanaugh, king of the Fear Up Harsh. They could often be found sitting around a fire with Cavanaugh after shift change, listening to his macho accounts, taking mental notes.

By the third week of January, Hasegawa had pretty much disappeared from the ICE, passing off his minister of statistics job to whoever was closest to the whiteboard. From that point forward, he and Davis were a team.

After Davis spotted those patterns among the North Africans, he and Hasegawa persuaded Mark Stowe to give them control of interrogating all the Tunisians, Moroccans, Algerians, and Libyans in the camp; the interrogators who otherwise managed those cases were willing to cooperate and let them have a go. There were at least thirty detainees from this region, 10 percent or so of the prison population at the time. Hasegawa and Davis's first objective was to get the prisoners rattled, get them talking about one another — to engender panic, if possible — so they took the prison mug shot book and lined up one interrogation session after another, forcing all their subjects to look at every picture. Davis would study the prisoners' reactions while Hasegawa went through the monotonous task of asking, *"Hu-ah?" "Hu-ah?" "Hu-ah?"* (Him? Him? Him?)

The two would consider the prisoners' reactions in smoke breaks outside the tent. If they saw anything suspicious — a lifting of an eyebrow, a no that was a bit too energetic, an attempt to skip over a certain mug shot — Hasegawa and Davis would identify the prisoner whose picture had triggered the reaction and drag him into the booth. That prisoner, knowing he had been fingered, would either start talking to set the record straight or try to throw the interrogators off his scent by implicating someone else. Hasegawa and Davis were just looking for connections: who knew whom, who recognized whom, who blamed whom. Quickly they began to sift through the gestures and denials. Within days Hasegawa and Davis narrowed their focus to three North Africans, two Algerians, and a Tunisian, who seemed at once knowledgeable and particularly vulnerable, weaker than the others. They aimed to uncover with maximum precision how they had entered Afghanistan.

As Hasegawa and Davis started to show, everything came back to nationality. North Africans traveled together in schools, like fish, with their own networks, routes, and helpers, as did Yemenis, Saudis, and Pakistanis. This discovery supported other specializations. Anne-Marie Walker leveraged her talents on Saudis and Yemenis. Gary Heaney found success by putting time and effort into learning the ways of prisoners who hailed from the Levant: Syrians, Lebanese, and Palestinians.

Hasegawa and Davis discovered that in Rome, Milan, Paris, Marseille, and all over Germany and the United Kingdom, the European immigrant Arabs would congregate in ghettos, meet in coffee shops, and gather before and after Friday prayers at mosque. There, they would come into contact with leaders of opposition movements back in North Africa and "talk a little revolution," as the Irish used to say. Some could be persuaded to go to Afghanistan to fight. Others could be persuaded to go to Pakistan to study the Koran or convinced that they could find a bride in Afghanistan or Pakistan. Most were young, had arrived in Europe's cities alone, and quickly realized that there was a shortage of young Muslim women in a place like Bologna. More than one prisoner at Kandahar would assert that it was "common knowledge" that women outnumbered men in Pakistan. Once there, they would come under tremendous pressure to uphold their Muslim "duty" and train to fight in Afghanistan.

Most of the North Africans, Hasegawa and Davis discovered, had trained at a camp north of Jalalabad. This suggested a greater degree of segregation, of organization, than anyone had suspected. Why the exclusivity? Who was funneling all the North Africans into the same camp once they arrived in Afghanistan? One of the prisoners described a northeastern corner of Jalalabad, a neighborhood called Istakbarat. Tucked away in a complex of walled compounds, the prisoner explained, was a jumble of four or five garrison homes, one of which belonged to a man named Al-Jezari.

Here was the link to 140.

After securing my permission, Hasegawa and Davis arranged a session with my chocolate-loving Algerian. Needless to say, they didn't bring any candy when they spoke with him.

Having read through my reports, they knew 140's weak spot, his biggest worry: that he might never see his family again. He had squandered much of his life in petty thievery and drugs, traveled to Afghanistan under pressure, but had finally found something to care about in his wife and young daughter. Hasegawa and Davis had him convinced within minutes that unless he started talking, he would never see them again.

The frail man buckled, confirming the identities of other prisoners and describing their stints in Afghanistan. More significant, he owned up to playing a greater role himself. He had once mentioned to me that there was a room at the house he never entered, a room that belonged to the caretaker. Now 140 admitted that *he* had been the caretaker and that all those mats he said sat idle were for the constant stream of North Africans he was charged with putting up, feeding, and transporting to the training camp. And there were weapons after all: the root cellar of the compound was described like the Colt factory in Hartford.

Davis asked whether the house was exclusively for Algerians. Prisoner 140 said yes but added that many of his guests came straight from Milan. The North Africans were training so they could go back to their home countries and overthrow the government there. They weren't coming to fight the Northern Alliance, although some did; nor was Kashmir the center of their ambition, although some went there. They were in Afghanistan to learn how to build bombs to blow up buses and phone booths in Casablanca and Dakar.

Al-Jezari, 140 revealed, was a kind of Mafia boss for these North African volunteers from Europe, the gatekeeper to the camps. He would take volunteers' passports, officially "for safekeeping," but in reality so they couldn't go back home without going through him. He employed a group of forgers to amend the visa stamps or duplicate new passports altogether, so there would be no telltale months-long stays in Afghanistan, ensuring that their holders could eventually get back to Europe. Some helped move drugs along the way as part of a mutually beneficial financial relationship between the radicals and drug dealers of Europe.

Armed with all this new detail, Hasegawa and Davis started to reinterrogate more than a dozen North Africans and all the Europeans in custody. They were staying out in the cold practically all night long, calling for new prisoners through the handheld radio they carried with them. Every once in a while they would call back 140, who began to function as a stooge, telling them what was going on among the North Africans in the cages. He answered their questions reluctantly, but each time he did he grew more despondent at his cooperation. The North Africans were positively buzzing, convinced that someone had cracked their security and desperately trying to communicate with one another through the concertina wire. One prisoner, a Moroccan, told his day-shift interrogator that he had been asked to carry a message to another prisoner to "deny any connection with what happened in Rome." It was news to Hasegawa and Davis that *anything* had happened in Rome.

The two interrogators turned up the heat by planting the idea that the prisoners were going to be sent back to Algeria or Tunisia. This prompted waves of panic among prisoners afraid not only that they would be tortured but that their families would be rounded up and tortured, too. I was now frequently walking down to the JIF to listen in on Hasegawa and Davis from outside the tent.

"Where do you think we are going to send you!?" Hasegawa shouted at one prisoner. Davis ratcheted up his voice to translate, the only time in Afghanistan when he spoke above a mumble.

"I don't know — Cuba?" the prisoner replied.

"Yes, of course, you will go to Cuba, but we can't hold you forever. Where are we going to put you after Cuba!?"

"Here?" the prisoner would meekly ask.

"*Here!?* You think we are going to put you back in the country where you trained to kill Westerners? Wrong answer, Samir."

"I don't know. I don't know — where are you going to put us, sir?"

"You are from Algeria. Let's give you back to Algeria!"

"But, sir — praise be to Allah — but, sir, they will kill me and my family. You cannot have on your conscience the death of my sisters and mother."

Then Hasegawa and Davis really opened fire, demanding to know why the prisoner expected mercy when he had been happily training in camps in Afghanistan to kill the innocent.

"But, no, you do not understand," the prisoner babbled. "I was there for the Algerian Liberation Front, not for Al Qaeda."

"There's no difference to us," Hasegawa insisted.

And this is where Hasegawa and Davis learned another important lesson about how Afghanistan worked. In an effort to clarify his innocence and nonconnection to Al Qaeda, the prisoner told them that before the attacks in September, the Taliban were coming under pressure from the West about allowing training camps in their country. The Taliban at first ignored the demands but eventually started to restrict operations at camps across the country. Finally, in the spring of 2001, the ruling council, run by Mullah Omar, made the decision to ban all terrorist organizations *except* Al Qaeda.

All the other camps and fighters, the Vighurs, the North Africans, the Indonesians, and the Filipinos, had to get out. But bin Laden came to the rescue, offering the "commandants" of the other camps a way out: convert their facilities to Al Qaeda's banner and in return be allowed to stay in the country. It was a sort of Islamic fundamentalist leveraged buyout, and there would be a price: the benefactors would have to start supporting Al Qaeda's aims and assisting in the execution of its plans.

One of the assignments involved a poison attack on the U.S. embassy in Rome. When Hasegawa and Davis reported this, we looked upon the scheme with some suspicion. A bomb plot maybe. But poison? It didn't seem feasible, but we passed the tip along. Weeks later, in late February, eight Moroccans were arrested in Rome. In their apartment investigators found 8.8 pounds of a cyanide-based compound, potassium ferrocyanide, a tourist map with the U.S. embassy circled, and municipal maps indicating the location of underground utility lines near the embassy. Investigators suspected a planned attack on the embassy's water system. Though the Rome suspects were later acquitted, the talents of Hasegawa and Davis were never questioned again.

Another assignment Al Qaeda had for the North Africans altered the course of the war in Afghanistan before it even started. A number of North African prisoners said that shortly after their group cut its deal with bin Laden, they were tasked with killing the leader of the Northern Alliance, General Ahmed Shah Masood. On September 9, two days before the attacks on America, two North Africans posing as television journalists were granted access to Masood for an interview. Then they detonated a bomb inside their camera. One prisoner said the killing was "timed" with the attacks on America, presumably to cripple the Northern Alliance at a moment when the Taliban would be coming under considerable new heat. Another prisoner said that at the bomb-making annex to the main camp near Jalalabad, trainees were given a long list of objects in which bombs could be placed. One of the items on the list was a television news camera.

GUANTÁNAMO

———◼———

On February 10 the Kandahar team sent another batch of prisoners to Cuba. The criteria for who went to the Caribbean were the same as before. Prisoners who fell into any of three categories received "go directly to GTMO" labels and were put in a queue for a shackled seat on a C-17. The categories were: anyone on the FBI's most wanted list; foreign (mainly Arab) fighters; and Taliban officials. (Ghul Jan was an exception — the army wanted to keep him around to see if he could be used to get other Taliban officials to turn themselves in.) The order in which they were sent was simple, too: the lower their prisoner number — that is, the longer they had been at Kandahar — the sooner they were put on a plane.

For the most part, this was a perfect situation. The prisoners who were in custody the longest tended to be the ones who weren't being interrogated anymore. Indeed, most of the time they were becoming a significant hindrance, disabusing new arrivals of any fears they might have of harsh treatment by their U.S. captors.

Still, there were some unfortunate consequences. Hasegawa and Davis were pleading that certain of their prisoners be left behind. Some of their Tunisians were close to the interrogator's holy grail: a "schoolhouse break," meaning a complete surrender to authority and total cooperation. But once a prisoner's name was on a flight manifest, it was almost impossible to get it off. Part of the problem was that Task Force 500 didn't even control the list: it merely submitted names to the MPs. *They* were the official executives of the prison, and *they* controlled the list; technically, we merely "leased" prisoners from the MPs while they were in the JIF for questioning. The other problem was that once a manifest had been created, it was circulated to other corners of the army bureaucracy, which just wasn't capable of throwing things into reverse.

Prisoner 140 was on his way, too. I didn't know whether it would be wise to see him one last time or not, partly because I was feeling more than a little guilt. At Huachuca they taught you never to promise something you could not deliver. I hadn't exactly promised 140 that he would be reunited with his family, but the implication was clear. If he talked, there was a better chance of that happening. He would no doubt now feel betrayed.

Cavanaugh would never feel bad about this sort of thing. Hasegawa and Davis probably wouldn't, either. Here was a guy who had helped operate the terrorist production machine that Afghanistan had become. Hard to feel too sorry for a guy like that. Most of the interrogators truly detested the prisoners they faced, abhorred the perversion of Islam, and saw them as complicit in the September 11 attacks. Deep down, most of us found motivation in this antipathy, saw our jobs as opportunities to exact a small measure of revenge. Even Anne-Marie Walker, the tiny, midwestern blonde who wanted to be an elementary-school teacher someday, relished getting Arabs to rat out their "brothers," to turn on their cause. It made them look weak, which is what she and most of the rest of us thought them to be when they were isolated from the radical mosques and training camps. But with interrogation, you get a much closer look at the enemy than do other soldiers. Prisoners can be infuriating and pathetic and dishonest and despicable. Maybe you even hate them more than the soldiers who know them only through a sniper's sight. But they're humans. And their sins don't always make it easier to be dishonest yourself, even if it's for the greater good.

I called for 140 and went down and told him he was going to Cuba. He cried. He asked if he could pray. I said sure, and the prisoner dropped to his knees in the corner of the tent, collecting — in the absence of water — dust to start the Islamic cleansing ritual. I remembered I had brought some baby wipes for him to use for this very purpose and gave them to 140. His crying went on so long that my initial sympathy — which I struggled to suppress—was replaced with a desperate desire to get this over with. It was like breaking up with a girlfriend.

At last 140 sat back at the table and, though still sobbing, asked, "Why Matt?" — using my stage name — "Why are they sending me? I have done everything you and the others have asked."

I lied. "They are sending you to Cuba because they don't want anyone to know you have helped us," I said. "If we were to let you go right from here, you'd be dead and would never see your family again."

Prisoner 140 looked at me with huge, wet eyes and a runny nose. The smell of that baby wipe masked the usual prisoner odor. He pulled up the dusty blanket and wiped his eyes, leaving a patch of now muddy dust on his cheeks.

I showed him a picture of Cuba from the *Danbury News Times,* my family's hometown paper, which had arrived as packing material in a shipment of brownies. I told him to look out for "Sean" once he arrived.

"Good-bye, Samir. I wish you the very best of luck in finding your family again." I went back to the ICE and prepared a detailed report on our last meeting.

"Sean" was Sean McGinty, my childhood friend and Huachuca classmate who had recently e-mailed that he was headed to GTMO and then called on an unsecured military line to announce his arrival. In my final notes to 140's file, I hand-wrote a separate sheet: "Please give to the interrogator with the last four Social Security numbers 2525." On the paper I scribbled some useful details about 140, bits about his personality and background that wouldn't be in the intelligence reports. The information would be good for McGinty, and perhaps even 140.

THE TRAINING MANUAL

Throughout the war, Special Forces teams and other units were raiding suspected Al Qaeda compounds, safe houses, and Taliban ministry buildings all over the country. They brought back not only prisoners but piles and piles of documents, computer drives, and other records. They would stuff the material in empty MRE boxes and trash bags and haul them back to the document-exploitation (DocEx) team in the tent next to our ICE, which had its own crew of linguists as well as computers and scanners used to convert everything collected into digital files to be dispersed to the entire intelligence community.

When the pile would get too high, the interrogators would be drafted to help translate, taking stacks of papers to work through during their off time. The tedious assignment always prompted whining about why this person's stack was bigger than that one's, or why so-and-so got the pile with the most pictures.

One mid-February morning the DocEx crew dumped out a garbage bag full of papers and trash retrieved from the Al Farook training camp. Linguists and interrogators starting picking through the pile. Someone said, "Hey, look at this thing."

It was a stack of paper, about sixty pages, with two binder holes on one side. It had coffee stains and was rippled from moisture. Big chunks of it were handwritten, but it had clearly been photocopied. The top page had a rather surprisingly elaborate Al Qaeda symbol on it and the ubiquitous "in the name of Allah." Beneath that script was a handwritten note in Arabic: "Brothers, this is the book about prisoners."

At first everyone thought it was a book about what Al Qaeda would do to *their* prisoners. But as we thumbed through it we realized that it was the Al Qaeda guide for resisting interrogation if *they* were taken prisoner.

All hell broke loose when the command realized what had been found. Interrogations stopped, and anybody who could read Arabic was thrown into translating the manual. We spread it over every flat surface in the ICE and had the whole thing translated by the next day.

It was unbelievable. Here, laid out in neat Arabic print, was every tactic we interrogators had encountered in Afghanistan: the passive resistance, the blatant lies, the cognitive fog that shrouded every name or meaningful landmark in a prisoner's travels.

The book taught captives never to give away "another brother's name" and advised them to use *cunyas*. Prisoners were told to confuse their interrogators by using the Islamic calendar. It taught them to remain silent for a few days, then tell stories out of sequence, dribbling out erroneous information "in circles."

There was an entire section on the West. It showed a remarkable understanding of the American system. Hold out on providing any information for at least twenty-four hours, it said, to give "brothers" enough time to adjust their plans. The Americans "will not harm you physically," the manual said, but "they must be tempted into doing so. And if they do strike a brother, you must complain to the authorities immediately." It added that the baiting of Americans should be sufficient to result in an attack that leaves "evidence." You could end the career of an interrogator, maybe even prompt an international outcry, if you could show the Red Cross a bruise or a scar.

America's aversion to torture was presented as a symbol of American weakness. The West didn't have the stomach for such things, the book said, "because they are not warriors." Throughout, the tone was condescending. "Brothers, they will not understand our reasons [for fighting], and you must contrive to exploit their ignorance."

Other sections were dedicated to resisting other Middle Eastern interrogators' methods. These were clearly regarded as more formidable than Western approaches. Egypt, Jordan, Morocco — practically every country had a paragraph describing ways of obtaining information, often in language that seemed to indicate the author had firsthand experience. Included were hand-drawn pictures about positions "brothers can expect" to be placed in: sitting on the ground with their hands tied to their ankles; kneeling with a stick behind their knees, cutting off circulation to the legs; hanging from their arms tied behind their backs. One picture was like a Michelangelo drawing of the body, with each part labeled with a description of another horror. Gouge out eyes. Cut out tongue. It talked about filleting people, skinning their arms with knives. Dropping cement blocks on knees. Drilling kneecaps. Ripping fingernails off. Pouring boiling water on a prisoner's skin. There was even a picture of Chinese water torture, with a funnel releasing a series of drips on a prisoner's head. In Arabic were the words "Drip. Drip. Drip."

The manual offered little hope if drugs were administered. "Think about Allah if they drug you," it advised. "Brothers must ask for Allah's indulgence and keep in their minds the sure knowledge that the greater the struggle, the sweeter the reward."

Everybody wanted to see the manual — the command at Kandahar, the officers at Doha, people back in Washington. The interrogators divvied it up in sections and took turns reading it. We were buzzing about how we had already seen everything in the book played out in the booth. Every ploy it pre-sented was an echo of some experience we had ourselves en-countered.

The most infuriating thing about the Al Qaeda manual was that its core diagnosis was dead-on: the Americans would keep you in a cage eating halal MREs and giving you showers a couple of times a week. But when it came down to it, you could lie to them, refuse to talk, switch your story from one session to the next, and there wasn't anything they could do about it. In the long run, that was our strength. But at the time it felt like a terrible weakness.

INTERROGATORS' GAMES

Prisoners weren't the only thing delivered to the camp on a regular basis. The unit was getting a volume of mail from little kids back home that must have rivaled the quantity seen by the North Pole. They all had Crayola pictures and some had surprisingly belligerent prose: "Go Get the Bad Men" and "I hope you kill them all!" Injunctions to "come home safely" and "stomp on the bad bin Laden," coupled with pictures of soldiers shooting at men in beards, brightened everyone's day.

One stack of letters came from a Catholic grade school, Our Lady of Peace. The kids had drawn on ordinary sheets of white paper and had glued them to bigger pieces of construction paper, making colorful frames. One had pictures of airplanes dropping dozens of bombs and small figures at the bottom of the picture, all in turbans, fleeing for their life and flailing their arms. "We are praying for you, and said the Rosary in class for you today," the accompanying letter said. It was from Angela, age nine.

Anyone who didn't contribute to an outgoing stack of responses to the children was punished with extra duty. Chief Irvine would thumb through the letters, and if he didn't see a soldier's name, he'd say, "Well, we don't need anyone to move the water today. We've got a volunteer."

Writing real responses was a chore. But some of the interrogators delighted in writing mock replies that they taped to the original in an expanding gallery on the wall of the ICE. Talbot and Lawson were particularly talented at this.

"Dear Justin, I find your letter exhibits a disturbing propensity for violence. I prefer to see myself as a peacekeeper, not a soldier."

Talbot was an interesting case. He'd had a stereo shipped over from the States with his favorite CD: the soundtrack to *Rocky III*. Every morning, precisely at 7:30, just as the day-shift crew was coming out of their slumber, Talbot would crank up "Eye of the Tiger" so loud that you could hear the opening guitar licks three tents away: *dant, dant-dant-dant, dant-dant-dant, dant-da-daaaahhhh!*

He was a mass of contradictions. He'd studied sculpture in college, then enlisted in the army to learn how to interrogate Russians. He came from an enormous family of fundamentalist Christians from the South but ditched his family's church and converted to Catholicism. Needless to say, this was intriguing to Fitzgerald, who had ditched Catholicism and converted to Presbyterianism. But if they were going in different directions spiritually, they were remarkably compatible intellectually. They fed off each other, like a couple of brilliant improvisational comics.

The production that occupied them to no end was their Civil War general routine, in which they would mimic the pomposity of 1860s southern speech but mix in modern references. Fitzgerald, who greeted me in this manner the day I arrived at Fort Bragg, introduced the habit in Kandahar, and it grew like a weed.

At the end of the day shift, Talbot would announce, always within earshot of the hapless Irvine: "Suh . . . momentarily ah shall adjourn . . . and re-tah to my cot . . . where ah shall engage in ten minutes of hard-core pornography . . . and a marijuana cigarette." Being a good Catholic and a soldier, Talbot really had neither.

As the number of prisoners at Kandahar swelled into the hundreds, interrogators were coming out of one session and moving directly into another, day and night. But the grueling interrogation schedule was only part of the job. Interrogators under the rank of staff sergeant came off twelve-hour shifts and then rolled into one or two hours of "additional duties": filling sandbags, fetching water, stocking food, hauling trash. Picking up cigarette butts in the JIF, moving tents a foot or two so as to improve their alignment with other tents, burning paper, or organizing the supply tent were all ordinary and necessary parts of army life.

The FBI guys couldn't believe it. They would pop into the ICE, asking in which booth they might find an interrogator they needed to see right away, only to learn he was on kitchen patrol (KP) duty or something. Of course, the FBI agents were in a separate world. They rotated out every eight weeks or so and seemed naturally adept at making messes, not cleaning them up.

The trash detail was the worst. Whoever's turn was up had to help load all manner of detritus — unneeded pallets, empty MRE wrappers, piss bottles — into the back of however many Humvees it took and haul it to the far end of the post, where the marines had dug an enormous pit, at least fifty yards across and twenty feet deep. A dozen or so Afghans were employed by the army to keep that pit burning day and night, which they did by soaking huge sections with diesel fuel and then igniting them. Inevitably, some of us would be tossing our rubbish into the hole when an explosion would knock us against the bed of the Humvee. We'd grab our rifles and scramble for cover behind the vehicle. The Afghans would laugh and laugh at the big tough Americans running for cover, all because some half-empty propane tank had finally popped. The plume of smoke could be seen from miles away.

The Afghans were also world-class scavengers and couldn't keep themselves from venturing out into the yawning pit to retrieve the junk the army tossed aside. Who knows why, but they were particularly fond of the thick beige plastic bags that MREs came wrapped in. They washed out these small sacks with filthy water and lined them up in the sun to dry. They pulled out pieces of pallet wood and hunks of twisted metal — no doubt, much of this material was used to remodel their houses. Fitzgerald called it the End of Times garbage pit.

The extra duty was all a reflection of the army's extreme, and in some cases admirable, egalitarianism. Everybody had to do grunt work, whether you were pulling a trigger or pecking away at a keyboard. For most troops, the mantra was true: army life consisted of long stretches of tedium punctuated by brief periods of intense activity. If the combat arms troops weren't out on a mission, they had nothing else to do all day but drill and wait. For interrogators, there was no such cycle. Every day was a grind.

At least one shift had the benefit of working in daylight and of sleeping in the cool of the night. But the sunlight crew also had chores that the night shift generally escaped. One such involved pulling guard duty on a consignment of Afghan workers who were brought into the base every morning to do odd jobs around the camp. The workers were amazingly skilled. They could cut glass, fix plumbing with no tools and practically no materials, run electrical line wherever it needed to go. (One interrogator drafted a mock intelligence report saying that Afghans could build a nuclear reactor using a fluorescent light-bulb and a pair of dirty socks.) Two interrogators would hook up with a separate 101st Airborne detail to meet the hundred or so Afghans at the gate, then walk with them to whatever the job site was and supervise. Midday, the guards would give the crew a lunch break. They would gather in a small grove of anorexic trees and pass out halal MREs.

Afterward, the Afghans were given twenty minutes or so to lie under the scant shade. Most would take the opportunity for some rest. But inevitably, some of them would pair off and wander to the edge of the grove. One would lift up his billowing shirt, another would lower his pants. The other Afghans in the crew would hardly even notice. Homosexuality was pervasive among the Afghans, especially the Pashtuns in the south. Even when they weren't overtly engaged in acts of sex, they would cling to each other, hold each other's hand, and generally cavort in ways that would astonish Westerners and repulse soldiers. Some of the marines would laugh incredulously. Others would be moved to violent reactions. In one case, Fitzgerald watched a gigantic marine march furiously toward two coupled Afghans and pick them up and toss them in different directions like dogs, yelling the whole time in English the Afghans couldn't understand. The "female" of the two scurried away. The dominant male was sort of indignant and flipped his scarf over his shoulder and walked off.

There was a surprise announcement on the morning of February 10 that the first team from Task Force 500 would soon be on their way back to the States.

This was the latest in a series of false alarms about pieces of the task force being sent home or, in an alternative scenario being mentioned with increasing frequency, back to Germany or Kuwait to prepare for the next phase of the war on terrorism: the universally anticipated invasion of Iraq.

Like all the others, this announcement would soon prove to be erroneous. But it was official long enough to set in motion certain irreversible changes. For me there was only one that mattered. Anytime a unit is moved, it has to have a noncommissioned officer in charge (NCOIC). And even though this unit wasn't really going anywhere, Mark Stowe was named the officer in charge. And that, the company commander said before the assembled interrogators in the ICE, meant that I would take Stowe's place as senior echo.

Well, thank Christ, I thought.

THE EXODUS

By early February, much of Afghanistan was under allied control, or at least the control of warlords who were getting large wads of U.S.-provided money to play along. Hamid Karzai had been serving as president of the interim government for two months. But capturing territory and installing a new government weren't the main objectives of the war — crushing Al Qaeda was. And the Arabs were slipping away by the thousands, into Pakistan and beyond.

Since December, the intelligence requirements out of Washington — the national security community's shopping list for collectors like interrogators — had been largely unchanged. The 101st Airborne and Tenth Mountain Division requirements were focused on immediate threats: Where are the minefields? Where are the enemy fighters? Where are the weapons caches? Does the enemy have plans to attack U.S. bases? The broader intelligence community had the same questions as just about every American in the post–September 11 world: Where is Osama bin Laden? Where is Mullah Omar? What are Al Qaeda's other plots?

The closest we had come to locating bin Laden were reports from four prisoners claiming that the Al Qaeda chief was in Waziristan, bandit country just across the Pakistan border. The region's claim to fame was its renowned weapons craftsmen; gunsmiths there could make copies of just about any firearm, so refined that theirs were almost impossible to distinguish from the real thing. One prisoner said he saw the sheikh, other prisoners just said they heard he was there. I never heard a thing about Mullah Omar, not a single report on his location, throughout the war. Even though finding him remained a priority, the commanders in Afghanistan were much more persistent in seeking information on his lieutenants. It was as though they knew Omar was out of reach. Don't bother going for the touchdown. Kick the field goal.

In mid-February, for the first time, there was a barrage of new collection priorities. How were the Arabs escaping? Who was aiding this exodus through Pakistan? How were they being supported? Washington was hungry for information on activity in the Konar Province, the Paktika Province, and the Paktia Province, all hugging the craggy, porous border with Pakistan. What were the enemy troop strengths in those places? Where were the enemy observation points? Their listening posts? What did they have by way of antiaircraft weaponry? What were their countermeasures against unmanned aerial-surveillance drones? What concealment techniques were being employed? What would their standard operating procedure be upon making contact with U.S. forces? Some of the questions were striking in their specificity.

The day-shift senior echo and I ordered our respective interrogators to comb the prisoner files again, looking for anyone who had been captured in or near Konar, Paktika, and Paktia. Even if someone had been grabbed months ago and was sitting in the cages at Kandahar since then, we said, the interrogators were to go back in and question him again. Any scrap of information might be helpful. Sometimes a prisoner would just give you the name for one of the trails into Pakistan — "It's the Ibrahim route, named for a trader who used to bring goods into Afghanistan" — and a few days later Special Forces troops patrolling the area would start asking locals to point them to the

"Ibrahim route" so they could lay down motion sensors that could practically count the people traveling by.

As soon as the unit started submitting reports on all these questions, a second avalanche hit. Whereas previously there typically would be a handful of queries to handle a day, now there were a dozen or more landing every shift. And they were much more specific than the unit had previously seen. If you turned in a report that said a prisoner had gone through two mountain passes but couldn't identify which ones, a follow-up would land the next day saying, "*Find out.*"

They especially wanted to know about the friendly units along the Afghan frontier, trying to identify which were surreptitiously letting the Arabs pass. If you wrote a report that a prisoner had encountered such a sympathetic patrol, follow-up questions would shoot straight back: "Get a description of the guards, their vehicles, their uniforms, their weapons." One of the most interesting statistics the interrogators monitored was the going rate charged by these collaborating patrols. In January Arabs could buy off a border patrol for a couple of bucks. By February the rate for an escaping fighter was the equivalent of forty dollars.

There was also tremendous interest in border-crossing guides, the Pakistani equivalent of the "coyotes" who shuttle illegals into the United States from Mexico. If you wrote a report describing a guide — "170 cm, black beard, typical Pakistani dress, carrying 1x AK74 assault rifle with 3x 5.5 mil. cartridges" — some analyst would write back asking ten questions about the rifle.

We didn't know it at the time, but the burst of questions was a precursor to the most intense battle of the war, which would take place several weeks later, in early March. Major General Frank Hagenbeck, the Bagram-based commander of ground forces in Afghanistan, was preparing to throw U.S. forces into the cave-riddled mountains to which Al Qaeda fighters had fled. As he assembled the plans for Operation Anaconda, his commanders were scrounging for every bit of intelligence they could get.

In the midst of this barrage of questions on Al Qaeda's escape routes, a shipment of prisoners perfectly suited to provide some answers arrived: fifteen Arabs grabbed in a raid in the Pakistani city of Karachi. They had recently fled Afghanistan, making it all the way to the port city on the Arabian Sea, where they were found in a couple of safe houses in an ethnically Arab district.

Hoping to exercise my new authority and employ all the lessons learned by Hasegawa and Davis, I persuaded the day-shift officer, Irvine, to try a carefully orchestrated approach with this latest batch of prisoners. We would assemble a team of the best interrogators: Cavanaugh, Fitzgerald, Hasegawa, Davis, and Walker. The team would have a separate meeting at every shift change to share what they got and talk strategy.

Everyone would employ the same approach, the same pressure point: namely, that if a prisoner didn't talk, he would be turned over to the Afghan government, whose prisons were being run by the Arab-despising Northern Alliance. The Karachi Fifteen, as this group of prisoners was quickly dubbed, would be corrupted from the inside, interrogated and reinterrogated and encouraged to rat on one another until they were all more scared of one another than they were of their captors. Cavanaugh exhorted his colleagues to be "ruthless" for a change. "Don't be pussies in the booth," he said. There could be no freelancing on this one, because no matter how hard you tried to separate them, the prisoners always found a way to talk to one another in the cages, and when they spotted inconsistencies in the interrogators' threats, the whole plan would be blown. For all their success, Hasegawa and Davis had made this mistake, telling some prisoners at first that they were going to rot in Cuba, then later saying they were going to be sent to

North Africa. They figured the prisoners wouldn't catch on, but they did, and some rightly saw that these interrogators were likely making idle threats. The shifting claims had undermined their credibility.

The other ICE leaders and I waited for the first wave of interrogations to finish like bomber commanders waiting for squadrons to return. Five hours later the interrogators were dribbling back, and each had gotten fairly detailed descriptions of their prisoners' escape from Afghanistan.

The general story was this: When the bombing of Afghanistan began, many of the terrified Arabs living in Afghanistan gathered at safe houses for transport out of the country. This situation overwhelmed the network, more so since key players in the escape route (which was really the entry route turned the other way around) looked after themselves and bolted for Pakistan. Unlucky Arabs who congregated at such houses were captured by the Northern Alliance and were turned over to the United States at the beginning of the war.

Those who didn't stick around — usually the North Africans, Egyptians, and well-funded Saudis — made it to the border badlands in convoys of SUVs and junk trucks loaded with women, children, and fleeing fighters. The Karachi prisoners talked of the fear they felt every time they heard a jet overhead. They made it over the border mountains and into Pakistan through three passes along the frontier. Sympathetic tribesmen along the way gave precious water and food to the columns.

Several prisoners told stories of Pakistani frontier guards either waving the vehicles through or being bought off for tiny sums of money. The offending troops' units, uniforms, and vehicle markings were recorded by the interrogators for the analysts, with their ravenous hunger for such detail. Closer to the cities, however, the Pakistani authorities were more vigilant. They were known to take into custody the fleeing foreigners because of cash bounties being offered by the United States.

Sometimes they double-dipped, asking for bribes from the passengers, only to turn them in anyway and collect the U.S.-sponsored ransom.

In the cities, a cottage industry of Arab hiding had sprung up. Well-connected and cash-rich Arabs could count on good accommodations with access to the talented forgers for passport amendments and hard currency for ticket purchases. Poor Arabs migrated to the slums and were at the mercy of "custodians" who were often inclined to take the security service's "Judas shilling." Pakistani authorities prowled the marketplaces looking for locals buying large quantities of food—for Arab guests, it was assumed.

The hardest part for the poorer Arabs was getting passports modified. Many lost their documents to handlers back in Afghanistan who turned around and sold them on the black market. In Pakistan the cost of forged passports soared, especially Jordanian and Syrian passports, which were regarded as calmer, hopefully blind-eyed precincts. In basements and root cellars, people waited for the possibility that Arab "charities" would give them cash with a wink and a nudge toward a known passport forger.

Every significant piece of information was turned and leveraged on another prisoner in a series of We Know All approaches. As a result, the interrogators were making real headway, producing detailed reports and flooding intelligence channels with detailed maps and illustrations of tiny alleyways leading to hidden forgery rings and loan sharks supporting cash-strapped refugees. Players in this support system were identified with precision: "Ali is forty-two years old, short black hair, thin mustache. Eyes are always bloodshot because he works late into the night. He always wears a purple Reebok track suit and Adidas white shoes. His passport operation is based in a brass shop, the third stall on the left."

The Karachi Fifteen operation went full bore, all day and

night for six days. The team had so unnerved some prisoners that they went beyond exposing their routes into Pakistan and began revealing where they intended to go next, into cities in Syria, Yemen, and Sudan. But what was shaping up as one of the biggest exploitation successes of the war for us was short-lived. The OGA stepped in and plucked away the four most valuable prisoners, ordering Task Force 500 to put them on a plane and send them up to Bagram, where civilian questioners would take over. I was livid. We had broken these prisoners. I pleaded with Major Sutter, the executive officer of the Task Force, to deny the request — or at least delay sending them.

"There's no way to do it," he said. "They have to go."

I couldn't believe it. Once again, our civilian intelligence friends were takers, not givers. If I analyzed the situation rationally, I knew this was how it had to be. The assumption was that the OGA had the best interrogation specialists, not a bunch of twenty-something recruits getting their training on the job. And unlike us army schmucks, whoever was doing these OGA interrogations undoubtedly had access to top secret intelligence reports. They also operated behind a substantial curtain of secrecy. Whatever facilities they had, and wherever they were, must have been equipped to isolate prisoners much more effectively than Kandahar could. They therefore must have been in position to play all kinds of mind games. Most of all, the OGA had that *aura*. The army couldn't compete with that. Of course they were going to win every tug-of-war.

Still, we interrogators came out of each experience with the OGA less convinced of our civilian counterpart's supremacy. Every encounter took a chink out of that vaunted aura, and this case was particularly infuriating, not just because they were taking prisoners the army was on the verge of breaking completely but because we had already had a run-in with the agency over the Karachi Fifteen.

When the prisoners first showed up, it was clear they had been grabbed in an OGA operation. But once again, there was no explanation from the OGA where the prisoners had been caught, under what circumstances, why they were targeted. Nothing. Once again, we had to figure it out with help from some of our NATO ally friends and from the prisoners themselves. Many of the prisoners said they had already been questioned by Americans, meaning the OGA. That meant two things. One, the OGA had either underestimated these prisoners or tried to break them and failed, and two, they had not only been in on the capture of these prisoners but had to have had some reports on them from their interrogation sessions and weren't sharing any of it.

I was pissed. If those bastards weren't going to play as a team, then neither was the army. I decided to punish them the only way I knew how: I told the interrogators to start collecting on the OGA.

"I want you to find out anything that happened involving the OGA, especially if they did anything wrong," I said. "Find out what the threats were, see if they ran approaches with 'the dagger on the table' scenario."

Pretty soon my team started sending up reports. Some of the prisoners said the Americans who questioned them were keeping them up for long hours, wouldn't let them go to sleep. It was reported that they were using stress positions, making prisoners get down and do push-ups, making them stand up for hours, that sort of thing. It was mostly minor stuff, but maybe it would rattle somebody's cage.

The first person it rattled was Major Sutter, the deputy leader of the battalion, whose job was to coordinate the dissemination of intelligence from our command to the spy community.

"You think you're pretty funny, don't you?" he said to me, half joking himself. "These reports . . . you're a troublemaker.

You don't look like a troublemaker, but you're a troublemaker."
He told me to stop, in no uncertain terms.

Even so, at least some analysts in Washington seemed to appreciate certain information collected in this payback scheme. Hasegawa said one of his prisoners wasn't interrogated by the OGA, but rather by those across the border with whom the OGA was cooperating. The report indicated that these guys, as part of their established methodology, employed some kind of a nightstick that they lubed up and coated with hot pepper flakes. Hasegawa filed a report about it and got tons of what they called "S and M follow-ups."

The end of February did bring one true blessing. The 101st finally managed to bring a shower tent with them and, after several false starts, opened it to the general public. It wasn't easy to get in: the lines ran forever and the plumbing was always shutting down without warning. But nobody cared. The positive *wonder* of hot water on smelly, sweaty, dusty skin was rejuvenating. For many of us, it also meant that it was finally possible to go for a real run without smelling for days from all the grime that baby wipes or the trickle of water from our jerricans couldn't remove. I started to jog around the airstrip, minding the flagged but still undisposed mines and the array of bunker positions manned by bored 101st Airborne troopers. It was strange to venture beyond the confines of the ICE and the detention camp and see how the base that a few hundred marines had secured a few months before was now teeming with thousands of troops, with more arriving every day.

MISSILES IN THE BASEMENT

Less than a week later another batch of prisoners arrived from Pakistan, including two more from Karachi. This time, there was an OGA note, which we saw as both an encouraging sign and evidence that the OGA had failed to provide such information in all the other cases not because of some *policy* but because they just didn't feel like it.

The note was a typewritten page, with the heading FROM OTHER GOVERNMENT AGENCY on the top. There was no introduction, no classification marking, and, needless to say, no return address. The note indicated that the two Karachi prisoners were brothers who had been captured in a raid on a safe house filled with Arabs, passports, money, and weapons, including a surface-to-air missile launcher. We assumed this meant Stingers — a major intelligence red flag that vaulted the brothers to the top of the interrogation list.

The brothers were both Afghans. In their pocket litter was a charm bracelet that had tiny pictures of children and both men's wives. Every time their hoods came off they looked utterly shell-shocked. To help keep them that way, the MPs quickly separated them and placed them at opposite corners of the compound.

The brothers' initial story was preposterous. They contended that they were running a guesthouse for students at local madrassas, that any passports found there belonged to their guests, that there were no weapons in the house, and, finally, that they had absolutely no knowledge of any surface-to-air missiles whatsoever. Tim Atley and another interrogator named Singhal, who had recently arrived from the States, were put in charge of the exploitation. After two days of questioning, the brothers were sticking to their story but pleading to see each other. Atley and Singhal choreographed an encounter where the brothers would catch a fleeting glimpse of each other in the JIF. Both were shaken by this and strained to keep eye contact until they were out of sight.

In the booth Atley told the elder brother that there was good news: the harsh punishments discussed earlier — being turned over to the Afghan government and all the horrors that could possibly entail — were now "off the table because of your younger brother's decision to take responsibility for everything himself." The prisoner protested violently that is was "impossible" and that his brother would never admit to doing something he hadn't committed no matter what the consequence. "Lying would violate the tenets of Islam," he insisted.

Meanwhile Singhal went in again with the younger prisoner, and over a cup of tea discussed minor points of family and life in Karachi. As expected, the younger prisoner quickly brought up the brief glimpse he'd had of his brother and asked to be allowed to see him. Singhal told him that it was not possible just now, but he would be happy to carry a message to his brother if he wanted him to. The younger brother told Singhal that he would be "forever in his debt" if he were to tell his elder brother that he was "well" and that everything "would be all right in the end." Singhal said that he would do so but added that it would be helpful to have some piece of information, "something only your brother would know," to show his sibling that the message was legitimate.

The prisoner told Singhal, "If you tell him that I cannot wait to have my nephew sit on my lap again, so I can squeeze his rosy cheeks and kiss him on the nose," he would know that the message was authentic. Singhal then offered the prisoner a cigarette, knowing he was an addicted smoker, and left the tent without lighting it.

I fetched Atley from his booth, and we huddled out of earshot of the prisoners. Singhal transferred his essential bit of information to Atley, and both men rejoined their prisoners.

"We knew you wouldn't believe it," Atley said, picking up where he left off with the elder one. "That's why I asked your brother to tell me something only you would know as evidence of his decision to cooperate. He told me he 'could not wait to have his nephew on his lap, to squeeze his rosy cheeks and kiss him on the nose.' "

There was a long silence, at least fifteen seconds, before the prisoner blurted out: "I *need* to speak with Hamid."

Not a chance, Atley told him, as long as the two of them had separate stories. The elder brother began to sob with a hiccuplike up-and-down motion. Atley sucked in huge clouds of Marlboro Light smoke, holding it for pearl divers' minutes, and then shot it out across the table to his opponent. The silence that followed lasted close to five minutes.

When the conversation resumed, it was the prisoner who opened.

"How can you be so sure that we had weapons at my house?" And here Atley came up with a brilliant bit of improvisation. "We saw them with our satellite," he said.

"What do you mean 'you saw them with a satellite'?"

"We have a satellite that can see through things like an X-ray machine," Atley responded casually. "It can see through practically any structure and identify dense objects by shape or by remote chemical analysis of its structure."

"Could it possibly have been that the satellite machine saw my tools or pipes or my workbench?" the prisoner asked desperately.

"No, the satellite uses computers to differentiate between things," Atley said with calm confidence. "It could look into this tent and tell us what we had had for dinner. It uses technology that analyzes component parts of things for their elements."

"It could tell what we had for dinner?" The prisoner stared at him, only half believing the tall, smoking American's story.

"It can tell the difference between iron and steel, the difference between paper and plastic; it can tell if you are wearing dentures of if you have a gold tooth."

The prisoner thought about this for a minute and then said, "You may know that it is not uncommon for people in Pakistan to have guns in their house for self-protection." He began to cry again and slumped toward the field desk.

Then Atley screwed up. Instead of closing in for the kill, he terminated the session, offering the prisoner a chance to collect himself. I couldn't believe it. Atley had all but let this prisoner escape. We bickered over this turn of events on our way back to the ICE, where we sat down and tried to figure out a way to regroup and regain the initiative. A new tack would be required. We would have to find a way to stoke the prisoner's level of anxiety again, and then offer a window of escape and all but push him through it. In other words, Fear Up with Incentive.

To regain the initiative, we plotted out an elaborate sting. The elder brother would now meet two "FBI agents who worked with the Pakistani intelligence" in targeting the house with the help of Atley's satellite. The agents would be played by Singhal (whom he had never met) and Major Brooker, another latecomer to Task Force 500 who looked sufficiently old enough to play a number of roles in interrogations. Atley would be in the booth with them, with one job: forcefully remind the prisoner of the consequences of not cooperating. I would enter in the midst of this production to provide the "window," a false escape for the prisoner that would lead him exactly where we wanted him.

Just after shift change the next day, with the sun already heating up the insides of the GP (general purpose) tents, the elder brother was back in the booth. Atley had intentionally and conspicuously left on the table photographs of a federal penitentiary in Terre Haute, Indiana, which he had pulled off the unclassified Internet. When the prisoner had had sufficient time to examine the images, the team entered the tent and took their places around the table.

The prisoner appeared a little startled by the additional company and asked what the pictures in front of him were. Atley began to tell the prisoner that his life was going to change drastically over the next few months. Other witnesses, "both in this camp and others," had come forward to say that he and his brother were sheltering fugitive Arabs wanted in connection with terrorist activities. This evidence, coupled with the satellite-imagery evidence of weapons in their basement, was sufficient for the military court convening in Cuba to convict them. Because there was no actual evidence to suggest that the brothers had participated in terrorist acts, they couldn't be tried for a capital crime and executed. There was, however, enough evidence to put them away for life at the prison shown in the photos on the table. "But you really have to wonder," Atley added, "how long someone who harbored Arabs wanted in connection with the murder of three thousand Americans could last in a U.S. jail."

Using a high-resonance, high-magnification picture of the safe house, suitably blurred and vague, Brooker was able to persuade the prisoner that the satellite picked up dense metal compounds in the basement. Pulling out a sheet of paper with complex but nonsensical computer code, he then convinced the prisoner of the absolute certainty that the weapons were there.

The prisoner immediately resumed the previous day's sobs and pleas for mercy from Allah, entering into an all-too-familiar resignation pattern that was disadvantageous for us. Then I entered, dressed in civilian clothes, wearing sunglasses and carrying a backpack stuffed with files. Situated prominently on my belt was a holster with a giant Thuraya satellite phone.

Atley introduced me as Mike Burke (forgetting that my stage name was Matt) and said I represented the Justice Department.

"You have got yourself into a little trouble," I told the prisoner. "Did they explain to you your choices yet?" The prisoner tried to say something, fighting back tears, when I interrupted and opened the "window."

"You will be happy to know that my job is to try and keep you from spending the rest of your life in a U.S. prison eight thousand miles from where you live now," I said. "But the fact that you are denying what your brother is saying is a needless complication. One of you is lying."

I proceeded to explain that I would be willing to accept a variation on the brothers' story — namely, that they had reluctantly offered shelter to a single Arab, but then more and more showed up, until half of Al Qaeda was hiding at the house, with a full arsenal of weapons.

"My brother told you this?" the prisoner asked.

"No, we told your brother that rather than take full responsibility for running a safe house for wanted men, this version of events would avoid the both of you dying very lonely old men here," I said, thumping the prison pictures on the table.

"What will happen if we tell you something more?"

"You can't just tell us something more; you need to tell this man everything that you know about what went on in that house," I said, pointing at Atley.

Again there was a long silence. Then he crumbled. "The weapons belong to us," he said. "There was no missile launcher; it was an RPG [rocket-propelled grenade]."

Booker, Singhal, and I left Atley alone to hear a story that was practically Dickensian. The two brothers had been in

Karachi for years, operating a kind of import-export business between Pakistan and their homeland. After the American bombing started, they were approached by a cousin asking if they would be willing to take on a few refugees. Then an Arab showed up seeking safe harbor from the Pakistani authorities. Then more arrived and then still more, displacing the original refugees, who were pawned off on other relatives. Our planted story was right on. Or was it? Did he just latch onto what we had told him was an acceptable version of events?

The main preoccupation of the Arabs, he continued, was to put in order their travel documents and collect enough money to get a ticket home. There were Egyptians, a Lebanese, two Saudis, and a hand full of Yemenis. He claimed — of course — to know none of their names but provided detailed information about forgers and middlemen who operated in the city to assist the Arabs in acquiring papers and asylum requests in Canada and Great Britain. Whether or not the context was merely hijacked from my suggestion, this information was good enough and detailed enough to use.

Singhal then took Atley's notes and ran a We Know All approach on the younger brother, who, once he recovered from his surprise, confirmed the information and provided additional clarification and detail.

There were lots of questions from Washington and disbelief that the rocket launcher was in fact merely an RPG. Without access to the OGA reports, there was no way for us to know if a Stinger missile really had been recovered from the house. Getting information on Stingers was a major priority for a number of reasons, starting with the fact that anyone who had one could knock down a U.S. helicopter just as mujahideen fighters had done countless times to Soviet aircraft in the 1980s. The CIA had supplied Stingers to Arabs specifically for that purpose. And anytime we came across one now, it was regarded as a pretty good indication that whoever it belonged to was affiliated with Al Qaeda. The other information we collected was also useful. Atley and Singhal spoke several more times with the brothers, who were later allowed to see each other (under supervision, of course) over some local tea, and then sent on their way to Guantánamo.

The prison was such an isolated operation that it was sometimes easy to be oblivious to the events of the war. Operation Anaconda was an exception. We could see it coming for weeks, in part because we started getting tapped for duties regular soldiers ordinarily handled. There was talk about putting interrogators in bunkers along the airstrips and around the perimeter of the camp. I was ordered to assemble a guard roster and compile a list of who had which weapons: pistols, M-16s, M-203 grenade launchers. Somebody from the 101st came by to ask whether the interrogators knew how to use night vision goggles. Some of the interrogators were quite excited about the prospect of some martial action, but Sutter intervened with the command and shielded his group, arguing that their interrogations were too important and had to continue.

When the battle opened, the soldiers in the ICE huddled around a computer linked to MARK, a sort of live combat-operations chat room where bits of text, transcribed from actual radio communications, float across the screen from units involved in the action, whether airplane crews or grunts on the ground.

>>"They're putting fire on that ridge. You see that?"

>>"Roger. I see it."

>>"Can you put fires on that draw, just down from the saddle in the ridge?"

>>"Roger. I see it. We can light that area up."

The Anaconda fighting raged for a week, with American and allied troops being lifted up into the rugged mountains by helicopter to face hundreds of Arab and Afghan fighters dug

into caves and bunkers. On March 4 seven American reconnaissance troops were killed as helicopters tried to insert them
into locations that came under heavy fire. One Chinook was
struck by a rocket-propelled grenade as it landed and released
its troops. Most climbed back aboard for a quick escape, but
one was left behind. American surveillance footage showed
Navy SEAL Neil C. Roberts being dragged away to his death
by Al Qaeda fighters.

When the battle was declared over two weeks after it started,
there were reports of hundreds of enemy dead, although the
Pentagon claimed to have been not keeping count. If there were
any prisoners taken in Anaconda, they weren't delivered to
Kandahar.

AL QAEDA'S DOCTOR

It was always a bit of a mystery to the Kandahar crew what was going on at the other major army base in Afghanistan: Bagram. It was about 330 miles away, due north of the capital city of Kabul. Bagram was a former Soviet air base, far enough north that it was always the most secure Soviet anchor in the country, never really in jeopardy of being overrun until the very end. Bagram is on a plain surrounded by snowcapped peaks, a spectacular setting, the kind of real estate that in the United States might have been irrigated and covered with golf courses. The terrain is dry, but not desert like Kandahar.

The army had set up a detention facility there that in many ways was better equipped for handling prisoners than Kandahar. The interrogators at Bagram worked in an enormous old Soviet-built warehouse instead of in tents. The airstrip was long enough to handle the largest of cargo planes, unlike Kandahar. It was also considerably more secure, much farther from hostile Taliban and Al Qaeda territory. Even so, nobody was confused about the pecking order. Bagram's prison was a fraction of the size of the operation at Kandahar, a franchise operation staffed by just a handful of Task Force 500 interrogators and never more than several dozen prisoners.

Every now and then, we at Kandahar heard things about Bagram that made it sound either enviable or unsettling. The interrogators wore civilian clothes instead of uniforms. They worked just a day shift and slept at night, like normal people. Those of us at Kandahar never ventured more than a few hundred yards from the ICE, but our counterparts at Bagram seemed always to be hopping on planes for trips up to K2 for supplies or down to Kandahar for paperwork. Whenever they would pop in, they'd talk about how they didn't know how we put up with it at Kandahar, how eager they were to get back to the cool, free climate of Bagram.

It wasn't that Bagram was some sort of vacationland. It had been the launching pad for Operation Anaconda, and the Tenth Mountain Division and Special Forces soldiers based there were involved in all kinds of hairy stuff. A mobile interrogation team was based there, flying off in helicopters and landing in hostile territory and doing on-the-spot interrogations right in the thick of things. But the Bagram prison itself wasn't seeing much action, at least by Kandahar standards, and the interrogators there weren't subject to much scrutiny. Some of their notes read almost like practical jokes. "The prisoner didn't understand any of my questions," one said, "but I put on my Stevie Wonder CD, and he recognized that." Of all the whispers about Bagram, the most disconcerting allegation was that they were getting too cozy with some of the detainees.

This was never much more than just talk until mid-March, when Rodriguez came into the ICE, singled out Fitzgerald, and pulled him aside. A prisoner was about to be transferred from Bagram, Rodriguez said, and Fitzgerald was going to be assigned to question him. The prisoner had been in custody at Bagram since early winter, when he'd been captured at Tora Bora. The interrogators at Bagram should have had his story dead to rights by now. But for whatever reason, there was a need for a fresh start.

Rodriguez was typically cryptic about the whole thing. His years in intelligence had taught him ways of saying things without exactly saying them. In this case, he implied that Bagram

had botched the handling of this prisoner, had judged him to
be harmless, then learned too late troubling aspects of his story,
which linked him to Al Qaeda. By the time they realized their
mistake, it was too late to recover. They couldn't go back in and
reinterrogate him, because he was practically pals with all the
interrogators on staff. Rodriguez, more than anyone else from
our unit at Kandahar, had a line to the OGA, and Fitzgerald
got the sense that the members of that organization were involved in the decision to send this prisoner down to Kandahar.
But even gleaning this much from Rodriguez's comments required major reading between the lines.

The new guest arrived about 2200 hours. When Fitzgerald
came in for shift change the next morning, he began reading
through the prisoner's files. The prisoner's bio was spotty —
there was no narrative, no time line. He was described as a doctor, a good guy, someone who had certainly spent time around
Al Qaeda, but only as a medic, treating its wounded. There
were statements in the file that the prisoner had been very helpful, but whatever information he'd provided wasn't included
in the file. There was no indication he'd given up anything significant: in fact, there were recommendations for his release.
Having failed to achieve that, Bagram had given him VIP status, with special accommodations, including a private room to
sleep in.

The prisoner's name was Abdulsalam Al-Aimi, and he was a
British-trained physician who had been captured after the battle
at Tora Bora in December. He had been badly wounded in that
battle and probably would not have survived if American forces
hadn't found him. Later he would show Fitzgerald his abdomen, pocked with scars and red splotches from shrapnel.

As Fitzgerald glanced through these notes, he was approached by the Bagram interrogator who had escorted the
prisoner on the transfer, a laid-back, twenty-year-old named

Fields. He was wearing cool-kid skater clothes, had braces on his teeth that made him look even younger than he was, and a royal blue Superman hat. They walked down to the interrogation tent where the prisoner was being kept. The prisoner was lying down on a cot, and Fields snuck up behind him and grabbed him, exclaiming, "Gotcha!" They engaged in a few moments of horseplay, wrestling around like a couple of junior high school chums. Finally, they both stood up and Fitzgerald was cordially introduced. Al-Aimi was slight, about five foot five, with curly black hair. Fitzgerald thought he had the expression of someone who was comfortable among Westerners. Fitzgerald said something about how they'd be talking soon, and he and Fields walked out.

Fields insisted that Al-Aimi not be put in the general population cage, that he be allowed to remain in the tent. Somebody with some rank up at Bagram must have thought so, too, because the day-shift leadership were already on board with this decision. Al-Aimi would get one of the six booths as his personal apartment — occupying the second of two booths in what was becoming more a hotel than a JIF. He wasn't supposed to leave the tent, but he wasn't shackled and his tent wasn't guarded.

The next day Fitzgerald didn't so much show up to interrogate the new arrival as drop in for a visit. He was very cordial, almost deferential, appealing to Al-Aimi 's obvious sense of himself as an educated man. Fitzgerald was no Cavanaugh. Fitzgerald liked to leverage his own frustration, his own unhappiness with the army, the command, the mission. He would tell prisoners that he and they had something in common: they were both stuck in the same miserable place, that they were both desperate to get out and go back home, and the only way that was going to happen was for both of them to get on with the business at hand in satisfactory enough fashion for the U.S. Army to let them both go. For Fitzgerald, it was the most honest approach. Perhaps the prisoners who fell for it somehow sensed the underlying truthfulness of what Fitzgerald was saying. Perhaps that's why it was remarkably successful.

"This is how the game works," Fitzgerald told Al-Aimi. "We want your life story. As long as you keep telling us the same story — as long as it adds up — sooner or later we're going to have to make a decision on whether to release you. This could take a few months, and you're probably going to go to Cuba. But let me do you the service of writing an extremely detailed account of your life, so the next person who talks to you has no justification for doing it again and has to make a decision about you."

Al-Aimi at first tried to strike a tone of defiance. "You have no right to keep me here if you have no evidence," he said.

But Fitzgerald didn't flinch. "That's just the way it is," he said. "You got caught in a war."

Over the coming days the two would settle into an unusually congenial dialogue. Fitzgerald sought to emphasize the things they had in common, particularly their status as educated men surrounded by fighters with less schooling. Fitzgerald would bring him tea and snacks — leftover goodies from MREs or handfuls of Girl Scout cookies shipped from the States. Soldiers called this junk food "pogie bait," a reference to the stashes that military clerks (called "pogies") always seemed to have on hand. Fitzgerald also brought a chessboard, and the two men would play in the afternoons several days a week. Al-Aimi always won, but Fitzgerald didn't mind, because he talked the entire time.

Fitzgerald decided to keep up this preferential treatment for as long as he kept talking. And it wasn't long before Al-Aimi proved his worth.

One of the first things Fitzgerald did was show the prisoner the Kandahar "family album," the binder full of mug shots of the hundreds of prisoners there. Al-Aimi went through the whole thing methodically and positively identified at least thirty others in custody, describing where and when he'd encountered them and what their stories were, if he knew. "This guy was at Tora Bora," he would say. "That guy was in the hospital at Kabul. . . . I saw him at the Al Farook training camp." All of it was panning out.

Gradually, Al-Aimi came to believe Fitzgerald, that maybe if his story was recorded in enough detail, if his file left no unanswered questions, maybe he could avoid being shipped to GTMO. Indeed, Al-Aimi began to take Fitzgerald through his biography in excruciating detail. He would talk and talk and talk, making sure Fitzgerald got it all down, got it all right. Sometimes he would even quiz Fitzgerald: "Now, how many brothers do I have? What are their names?"

Soon they settled into quite a routine. Geoff would go to shift change at 0800, write a report, finish up about noon, then spend at least four hours with Al-Aimi in the afternoon, playing chess and taking notes. Here and there, Fitzgerald would slip up intentionally, testing his prisoner, and Al-Aimi would scold him, "No, no, you're getting it wrong. Here, let me tell you again." Sometimes he would even grab Fitzgerald's notebook away from him and write names, dates, places, and other facts himself, to make sure they were recorded correctly. At one point he asked for a notebook of his own and spent his off hours mapping out everything he would cover with Fitzgerald in their next session.

By now Fitzgerald knew a great deal about his chess partner. Al-Aimi was in his mid-thirties, from Yemen. He'd received a grant from the Saudi government to study medicine in the United Kingdom and Pakistan and had taken up permanent residence in Pakistan afterward, living there for years, working residencies in hospitals in Karachi until early 1999. Then, in 2000, he left Pakistan to return to Yemen. He claimed there was a problem with his grant that he needed to straighten out. He returned a year later and said he sought to resume his hospital training in Pakistan but didn't like the first job he found, claiming that there were new problems with his immigration papers and that he feared deportation. So, he said, he made an important decision.

"I wanted to become a *real* doctor," he said, "and thought it would be good to volunteer to help the poor people in Afghanistan." So he left Karachi and went to work for hospitals and clinics in Kabul and Kandahar, treating "anybody who came to me."

"Who came to you, Abdulsalam?" Fitzgerald asked.

"Mostly guys from the camps," Al-Aimi replied.

"What camps?"

"The Arab camps."

He didn't flinch as he said it or reveal any discomfort with where this narrative line was leading: that he was essentially a doctor for Al Qaeda, right up until Tora Bora, where he was treating the wounded until he was hurt himself. In his painstaking reconstruction of his personal history, he even owned up to several encounters with Osama bin Laden himself. The last was at Tora Bora, where the sheikh had thanked Al-Aimi for helping wounded Al Qaeda fighters, then urged him to leave and find safety, saying, "This is not your fight."

Very few Arab detainees could claim personal contact of any sort with bin Laden. Al-Aimi knew this would heighten suspicion of him. To Fitzgerald, it was a highly evolved defensive strategy. Al-Aimi had fingered other Al Qaeda in the camp, so he must have thought it possible that others could finger him. He knew it was possible that one of them had seen him with bin Laden, so he owned up to it preemptively. His version would be the first one to find its way into the reports, and he would be in a position to dispute any attempt to portray it as more.

An abbreviated version of this strategy had obviously worked wonders at Bagram. But there were two problems. One, when you stood back from this mosaic, the picture was disturbing. Here's a prisoner who spends years in Pakistan, makes a sudden return to Yemen — bin Laden's ancestral home — and then gets a sudden inspiration to move to Afghanistan and become Al Qaeda's team physician.

The second problem was that some of the tiles of this mosaic themselves were deeply troubling, more so than Al-Aimi probably anticipated.

For instance, there was the small matter of the entity that sponsored his move to Afghanistan: Al Wafa. Any Google search would show that this Saudi "charity" was on the U.S. State Department's list of organizations tied to terrorism, under U.N. sanctions, and suspected of funneling all sorts of money to Al Qaeda. Al-Aimi tried to brush this off, saying the West was so unsophisticated in its understanding of the Islamic world that it was seeing bogeymen where none existed. "You think we're terrorists?" he would say. "That's crazy! Your guys are so misinformed. Al Wafa does good work."

Harder to explain was his assignment for Al Wafa. Although he was treating plenty of wounded, he acknowledged he had other duties. Among them was managing procurement of medical supplies for the charity's hospitals in Kandahar and Kabul. For this, he made frequent trips between Karachi and Afghanistan, making sure hospitals ordered the correct supplies and then making sure they were sent and delivered.

When Fitzgerald asked what he procured from Karachi, Al-Aimi caught Fitzgerald off guard with his reply:

"I can write you a list of every kind of chemical," he said.

Fitzgerald had made no mention of the word *chemical*.

Al-Aimi took a pad and paper and in a matter of minutes wrote down more than a hundred chemicals and compounds, all in flawless English. There was nothing on the list that led directly to the conclusion that Al-Aimi might have been doing something more sinister, like ordering ingredients for chemical weapons. But that he was so quick to mention "chemicals" — almost involuntarily, really — and then list them so exhaustively struck Fitzgerald as more than odd. It was an area of detail in his account that he could easily have avoided, but he had nose-dived into it. To Fitzgerald, the psychology of that impulse was almost visible. It was like a person with a scar on his face that he is desperate *not* to draw attention to, but he can't keep his hands away from it.

Al-Aimi also let Fitzgerald in on another little secret. While at Bagram, he said, he had talked to "them."

"Who's them?" Fitzgerald asked.

"You know. Them. Your spies."

"What's the name of the organization?" Fitzgerald asked. But Al-Aimi refused to utter the three letters.

"What happened?" Fitzgerald continued.

"They made me an offer, but I turned it down," Al-Aimi said.

"What was the offer?"

"They'd let me go if I'd be their spy." He asked Fitzgerald if he could talk to "them" again. Fitzgerald said he'd see what he could do and pressed ahead with days and days of more questioning.

I had taken to my new job as senior echo with relish. My first move was to give Mark Stowe three days off to "pack" for the rumored trip back home, cementing a transition that wouldn't be undone even when everyone realized a few days later that there really wasn't going to be a trip back home. Then, with Stowe congenially marginalized, I immediately began boring in on my interrogators' questioning plans, challenging them, testing them, shaping them, and rehearsing them until I drove them to distraction. I kept a log next to my desk, dividing the pages in half. Down the left side I wrote methods and approaches used by my interrogators. Down the right I tracked whether and to what extent they had worked, with a little blurb on the intelligence gained in every interrogation on my watch.

I immediately overhauled the shift-change procedures. I started by rattling off the same statistics that Stowe always had — "We conducted twelve interrogations and five screenings" — but that was just the starting point for quick but detailed summaries of approaches and intelligence gleaned in every ongoing interrogation. Often I would point to the interrogators and have them give "two-second briefs" on where they were with their prisoners. They would respond with something like "Prisoner 257, captured in Kandahar by U.S. forces twenty-seven January, had a route of travel through Waziristan. Saw service in front lines near Mazar-e-Sharif. I'm using an Establish Your Identity approach. I've shown him the mug shot book. He's identified one prisoner in custody and another in Cuba."

It was critical to have everybody on the same page, to give each interrogator a glimpse of what was happening in the booths around him. It was the only way they were going to make connections, spot patterns, share ideas — see this whole operation as a team effort. It sparked all kinds of follow-up conversations among the troops. "What did you say you were getting from your guy? Can you sit down for a minute?"

Next I would launch into the daily situation report, or SITREP. The Department of the Army (DA) sends out a classified brief every morning and every night on all of the army's activities around the world. It's remarkably sophisticated, like a little computer-generated movie, with graphics and buttons and multimedia flourishes. (There was always an update on air strikes in Afghanistan — "There have been twenty-one aircraft sorties in the Kunar province . . ." — and as you read it a squadron of animated fighter planes would glide across the computer screen, leaving a cartoonish trail of flames on a digitally rendered map of Afghanistan.) I would summarize the pertinent parts every day, like a quick newscast, to keep the troops connected to the war going on outside the green canvas walls that confined them twenty-plus hours a day.

But for all the effort I put into staging this twenty-minute shift-change meeting every day, the part that the troops appreciated the most had nothing to do with interrogation summaries or bombing sorties. Their favorite part, hands down, came at the very end, when I set aside two minutes for a daily update on what was happening at Guantánamo. The interrogators at Kandahar were consumed with curiosity about this far-off station, which they regarded as some sort of Shangri-la with real toilets, real mess halls, and no freezing weather. There were two categories of Guantánamo news the Kandahar crew appreciated in particular: updates on GTMO's prisoner capacity and updates on GTMO reports filed.

The latter I presented purely for their entertainment value. The interrogators at GTMO were collecting some good stuff, critical pieces of intelligence that no doubt were helping Washington chart the course in the war on terrorism. But I generally skipped over all that and went straight for any scrap of information that might give the Kandahar team a momentary feeling of superiority over their Caribbean rivals. I generally didn't have to look very hard. A month after GTMO opened, it was still stuck on intelligence report number thirty. Thirty! Kandahar had hit that milestone within days. And it would have been one thing to be able to say that they were keeping their numbers down because they were reporting only the most serious and alarming findings, but that wasn't the case. They were reporting some preposterous stuff, items that would have been better off submitted to *The Tonight Show* than to the intelligence community. One report that came out of GTMO said the enemy was planning to poison cucumbers, somehow lace these vegetables with some toxin and presumably drive the West into submission, or at least cripple the pickle industry. Another report said that Al Qaeda was "interested in locating wreck of a

U.S. submarine sunk in the 1960s to recover plutonium from sunken vessel." The whole notion conjured up images of hardened terrorists trolling the world's waters, looking for the glimmer of some submerged hull. Al Qaeda as deep-sea divers! Where was the training camp for that? The Kandahar interrogators roared at these reports.

The other category of news, the updates on Guantánamo's prisoner capacity, was of more pragmatic concern to Task Force 500. GTMO had announced that it was closing its doors on February 15, with three hundred prisoners in custody and twelve more en route. That was all that Camp X-ray, the temporary holding facility, could handle. There would be no more shipments of prisoners until a new, larger facility, Camp Delta, was finished, which was expected to take months. The news had been crushing to us at Kandahar, because everybody knew we weren't going home until GTMO reopened. It also changed the mission at Kandahar dramatically. A prison pieced together with scrap and concertina wire and existing mud walls that really wasn't supposed to hold anybody more than a few days now was going to be the primary residence of hundreds of prisoners for months. And with no release to GTMO, the prison population ballooned quickly. At one point, the 101st engineers even had to open another wing, boosting Kandahar's capacity to about five hundred, just to absorb the steady stream of new arrivals.

Needless to say, the interrogators at Kandahar devoured any news on the progress of construction at Camp Delta, and there was an update almost every day in the DA brief. The updates were remarkably detailed, with aerial shots of Guantánamo, showing ground being cleared for construction, building materials piling up on the perimeter of the site, the structures of Camp Delta slowly emerging. And just when everything looked to be coming along nicely, the army would announce that it had hit some snag that made the Kandahar crew laugh

and cry at the same time. At one point the whole project was
delayed, according to a bulletin on the DA brief, because the
contractors at Guantánamo were waiting for shipments of
"appliances" for the interrogators' living quarters. *Appliances?*
What appliances? Well, in the fine print these appliances were
identified as refrigerators and air conditioners. When I disclosed
this tidbit, the troops went into a tizzy. *We're over here shitting in*
diesel cans, they said, *and they can't finish the job at Guantánamo*
because they're short of refrigerators and air conditioners?

Then came the coup de grâce. One morning the DA brief
actually had a photo of these "living quarters" that were sprout-
ing up amid the ocean breezes on Cuba. They weren't tents or
barracks in the traditional sense and certainly bore no resem-
blance to the squalor we were enduring. They were bungalows,
little beach cottages of the variety you might see on Cape Cod,
with what looked like porches and paned windows. There was a
diagram of the floor plan, like one you might be shown if you
were considering buying into a new condominium development. They showed bedrooms and bathrooms and kitchens.
(They were serious about those appliances!) I had the 101st
Airborne cartographic people blow the whole thing up into a
poster-size picture that we displayed at the next shift change.
The interrogators howled.

After a month of daily lengthy conversations with Al-Aimi,
Fitzgerald had constructed a biography more detailed than that
of any other prisoner the unit would see during the war. Geoff's
reports, which he typed away at for hours, ran well over a hundred pages. But the payoff was elusive. Without some contradictory fact, some hole in his story, their talks would only
produce more and more interesting, but less than incriminating, information.

So, after a month of daily visits, Fitzgerald cut them off, just
stopped showing up.

Al-Aimi was unnerved. A part of him surely must have feared that the hour upon hour he had spent pouring out every detail of his life had been wasted. Fitzgerald's whole approach had been, tacitly at least, a quid pro quo arrangement. Al-Aimi had done his part. And Fitzgerald just stops coming?

Al-Aimi stewed in his tent for several days, becoming increasingly alarmed, until one day he simply walked out, left his tent, and strolled over to the JIF control tent, the little command post where the MPs operated the radios and coordinated the movement of prisoners from the main prison to the interrogation booths. It was a short distance, fewer than ten paces, but no prisoner had ever had the audacity to leave a tent unescorted.

"Where's William?" he asked, using the name Geoff had used during their sessions. "William never comes to see me anymore. Where is he?"

The MPs were stunned. It's a wonder they didn't tackle him, toss him on his belly, and cuff him. But there must have been something about Al-Aimi's demeanor that made him seem less than threatening, because the MPs reacted with remarkable restraint, taking him by the arms and shuttling him back to his booth with a lecture, like a child being sent to his room. Talbot had been in the JIF and witnessed the whole thing. Of course, he thought it was kind of funny.

A few days later Al-Aimi ventured out of his tent again — he had been scolded for the first infraction, but not chained to prevent another — and wandered over to the JIF. This time he had a distraught look on his face, and before the MPs could leap up to grab him he said something strange.

"I know what you're trying to do now," he said. "You're waiting for me to fall asleep. But I won't fall asleep. You're waiting for me to fall asleep so you can move the machine."

Now it was beginning to look as if Al-Aimi was coming unhinged. When Fitzgerald heard about this latest episode, he blanched. What was going on here? And what in the world could Al-Aimi have meant by "the machine"? Fitzgerald wondered whether Al-Aimi had goofed up a translation. An Arabic word for *machine* is *alaah,* very close to the word for *God, Allah,* and the word for *spirit, aleh.* Could Al-Aimi have meant "move the spirit"? That would make a little more sense, but not much.

Fitzgerald gritted his teeth and paid Al-Aimi a visit, making up a story about how he had been forced to withdraw for a few days because his commanders were beginning to think he was becoming too sympathetic to the VIP guest.

Al-Aimi nodded. "We're all just fish," he said. "They reel us in and then they don't want us and throw us back." He was melancholy and anxious. He asked Fitzgerald why he couldn't just be released, and Fitzgerald leveled with him.

"Al-Aimi, they're not going to let you go from here," Fitzgerald said. "They're going to send you to Cuba, and this process is going to continue."

"But I'm innocent," Al-Aimi said.

"I'll ask if you can be released," Fitzgerald said. "But I don't know of any Arabs that are being released. Would you do that if you were us, Al-Aimi? Don't you think we're going to want to watch you for a while longer?"

Whatever part of Al-Aimi had come unhinged, he still understood the logic of that. Now he was really regretting spurning that deal the OGA had offered, whatever it was. He asked again whether he might get a second chance to talk to "them," and Fitzgerald replied that he had passed along the request but didn't know. The next day, and a complete surprise to all of us, Al-Aimi 's request was answered.

If the interrogators at Kandahar were getting a good laugh at the expense of the follies of their peers at Guantánamo, the brass at Guantánamo was not in such good humor about what was happening at Kandahar.

Maj. Gen. Michael E. Dunleavy, operational commander at

Guantánamo, took advantage of the lull in activity at his prison to travel to Afghanistan and visit the MI soldiers and the prison and interrogation operation. It was a bit like an executive at some assembly plant traveling out to meet his suppliers. That usually happens only when there's a problem, and Dunleavy made clear that there was. Dunleavy complained that Kandahar wasn't being nearly selective enough in filling out its transfer lists. Guantánamo, after all, was supposed to be reserved for the "worst of the worst." The criteria for transfer were pretty straightforward but didn't allow much wiggle room, and that was a big part of the problem. Every Arab was supposed to go, there was no getting around that without a signature from the secretary of defense himself. But not every Arab should have been sent. One of the cases that drove Dunleavy nuts was an Arab prisoner who had been scooped up after some battle in which half his head had been blown off. Nobody thought he would recover, but he did . . . sort of. He was so brain-damaged that he couldn't even talk — he just kind of sat there and drooled. The MPs called him Half-Dead Bob, a name that stuck until he got to Cuba, where the MPs there promptly renamed him Half-Head Bob. He was of no intelligence value, but he was Arab and he was a fighter, and rules are rules, so he had to go.

Not long after Dunleavy left, Task Force 500 was given new instructions. Now the interrogators were ordered to produce comprehensive reports on every prisoner in custody, each concluding with a recommendation that the prisoner be detained (by the Afghan government), shipped off to GTMO, or repatriated.

Producing these new reports in many cases meant going back in with the prisoners to get more information. The prisoners figured out what was going on, and many tried to be as helpful as possible. In fact, a number dropped their *cunyas* and volunteered their real names for the first time. No doubt, they thought this would help their cause, but it had the opposite effect. It simply confirmed that they had tried to deceive interrogators the first time around.

Trying to take advantage of this recanvassing to glean more intelligence, the interrogators started spreading word that Cuba was filling up and that those deemed untruthful would be turned over to the Afghans. It worked, and the unit started getting pats on the back from the command for the new information being collected. But the command in Kuwait was less impressed. To the senior officers at Camp Doha, the new reports just meant the interrogators were catching their earlier mistakes. As a result, some prisoners of dubious intelligence value were shipped to GTMO largely because no one at Doha trusted the reports recommending that they be released. In that respect, Dunleavy's effort backfired.

Fitzgerald walked into the ICE and did a double-take. Sitting in a folding metal chair was a woman with elegantly coiffed black-gray hair and big brown eyes, wearing a white top, a pair of fashionable jeans, diamond-looking earrings, and black leather shoes with heels. *Got to be OGA,* Fitzgerald thought.

The daytime editor confirmed his guess, saying, "This is Lilian, she's from the OGA, she's here to talk to Al-Aimi." Lilian had arrived in the ICE the previous evening, accompanied by a male colleague in a fishing vest who seemed to regard her as somewhat fragile, asking several times if she was okay before he ducked out for who knows where. The OGA had closed down its little cubbyhole in the terminal some time ago, so there wasn't anywhere for her to go but the ICE. The first thing she did was ask if one of the soldiers there could go fetch her "crate" from the tarmac. She couldn't carry it herself, so she left it there. Then she settled into a corner with the reports on Al-Aimi, flipping through Fitzgerald's phone-book-size file, as well as some materials of her own. At one point, I wandered over to introduce myself and sat down. She asked how things were going, what they were learning from the prisoners, then started asking about Al-Aimi. I told her I hadn't questioned that prisoner.

"What do you do here?" she asked.

I told her that I was the senior interrogator.

"If you're the senior interrogator, and this is an important prisoner, why haven't you questioned him?" she asked. I explained that the senior E doesn't generally go in the booth but manages other interrogators who do. We chatted for a while, and she seemed friendly enough, if out of her element. She looked more like an analyst than an operator, and not just because her wardrobe wasn't out of the Orvis catalog. I got the vibe that she thought I was angling for a job. The OGA people got that a lot, so much that they often assumed when they were chatting with some MI soldier, he naturally wanted to be in their shoes someday. As she got up to leave that night, she handed me her card and said, "We're always looking for people."

She was thumbing through Fitzgerald's report on Al-Aimi when Fitzgerald came into the ICE. After their introduction, Fitzgerald offered to escort her to Al-Aimi's tent. Before she could decline, Rodriguez butted in to say, "Geoff, you go in there with her."

As they entered, Al-Aimi gave Fitzgerald a nonplussed look. Fitzgerald shrugged his shoulders. They sat down, and the OGA soccer mom, who had been nothing but pleasant until that moment, suddenly adopted a new personality. She put on a stern face and summoned a hard edge to her voice and launched into a barrage of questions and accusations that caught Fitzgerald and the prisoner off guard.

We know Al Wafa and Al Qaeda were running an unconventional weapons program out of hospitals in Kandahar and Kabul, she said. She ran through the rap sheet on Al-Aimi, whom she characterized as an Al Wafa/Al Qaeda figure, apparently in charge of all manner of nefarious research in the basements of these medical facilities. She alluded to some information the OGA had that there might be plans to put these substances to use.

Then she started peppering him with pointed questions. What compounds were they working on? What were they going to do with them? Where were they coming from? Who else was involved? She brought up Al-Aimi's frequent trips outside of Afghanistan. "What were you really doing?" she asked. She leaned in, demanding that he come clean, admit that he was procuring poison for attacks on the West, rat out his boss and the others he had worked with in the hospitals, and expose the workings of Al Wafa.

It was impressive, in a way, that an OGA analyst could deliver such a performance, full of hostility and veiled threats and menacing looks. And she had come armed with information that Fitzgerald would have killed for — from the locations of the alleged labs in the hospitals to the rosters of Al Wafa figures surrounding Al-Aimi in his work.

The only trouble was, it didn't work. Al-Aimi just denied and deflected, and the longer it went on and the harder she pressed, the deeper he dug in. He kept looking over at Fitzgerald as if to say, "You gotta be kidding me." Clearly, this was not what he had in mind. In his earlier sessions with Fitzgerald, the prisoner had described his encounters with the OGA with some degree of admiration, saying he thought they were being straight with him and were sincerely interested in his help. But he couldn't bring himself to commit to do what they were asking, which probably involved working for them in some way.

A couple of times he tried to move the conversation — the harangue, really — in that direction. "I want to help you," he said. But Lilian cut him off, shaking her head and laughing at the mere thought of it: "There's no way in the world you'll ever work for us," she said.

Fitzgerald spent most of the session staring at his shoes. A month of his life was going up in smoke, a relationship with a terribly complicated prisoner dashed in half an hour by an OGA analyst who didn't understand what she'd just done, not to mention the teeth-clenching anger Fitzgerald felt at being shut out from all this intelligence sitting out there on classified computer networks about *his* prisoner. If he had been armed with even a fraction of the information Lilian had ripped through in the booth, details on the charity, the hospitals, the weapons-procurement program, Al-Aimi's alternate history, Fitzgerald could have leveraged all kinds of approaches. That missed opportunity was bad enough. The worst of it was that Lilian had basically conducted a scorched-earth interrogation, leaving little chance for another interrogator to recover. One of the main rules is that you never completely seal off the prisoner's escape route. You have to give him daylight, a reason to think he might have a future that isn't enclosed in concertina wire, a path that might lead to cooperation. Lilian had barricaded this escape route, telling Al-Aimi not only that he was never going to work for the agency but that he wasn't going to take a free breath anytime soon. He must have always known it was unlikely that he would be set free, just like that. But the possibility had been enough to keep him talking to Fitzgerald for a month.

It was a disaster, and in later, more reflective moments Fitzgerald would recall how it cemented one of his theories in life: namely, that there are no secret rooms where you open the door and step inside and find nothing but competence. Everybody bought into the OGA's aura, its omniscience. But it seemed to us that it was hollow.

Frustrated by Al-Aimi's refusal to crumble, the soccer mom got increasingly agitated until she got up to leave. Fitzgerald rose to his feet and searched his mind for a way to recover, a way to preserve even the tiniest link between him and Al-Aimi.

Instinctually, he turned to Al-Aimi with a slightly wounded look. After having spoken to each other for more than a month exclusively in English, Fitzgerald switched to Arabic, which the soccer mom couldn't understand, and asked in a confused tone: "What is all this?"

With this meek, semiconspiratorial question, Fitzgerald hoped to distance himself from what just happened and to grasp at any connection that Al-Aimi still might feel for his frequent afternoon companion. He was looking for any sort of sign, perhaps a look that said, "It's true, but we'll talk about it later."

But Al-Aimi looked at Fitzgerald, gave him a little grin, and said, "*Khalas*" — finished.

After the soccer mom left, Al-Aimi was moved out of his little apartment and into another secluded spot in the compound where he would still be alone, under the close watch of guards every day. For days Fitzgerald asked the guards for updates on Al-Aimi. They always said the same thing: he's reading the Koran a little bit and is very kind to the guards but spends most of his time staring at the ceiling. Within weeks, he was on a plane to GTMO.

KANDAHAR SHUTS DOWN

———■———

The arrival of spring is majestic in Afghanistan, one of the most spectacularly beautiful wretched countries on Earth. The snow starts to melt at the lower elevations but still clings to the peaks. Surprising patches of green poke up out of the dusty earth. The sight of an enormous springtime Afghan moon looming over the silhouettes of army tents can be incongruously breathtaking.

The army hadn't managed to keep any of its promises that the Task Force 500 troops would be sent home, but it had started dispatching troops in groups of two or three for a few days of R & R. The destination was one you'd never pick at your travel agent's office: Se'eb, the air force base in Oman, a sweltering belt of land between Saudi Arabia and the Arabian Sea. But Se'eb, which had gravel paths, real kitchens, air-conditioned tents, and rationed quantities of alcohol, was a dreamlike destination for troops in Afghanistan.

The senior NCOs and warrant officers were the last ones to get their turn. When my time came I was elated; the sixteen-to-eighteen-hour days with very little sleep were beginning to really drag me down. Best of all, I would be leaving on Saturday, March 16. There truly was a God: I would be able to celebrate St. Patrick's Day with beer.

The flight was to depart in the afternoon, leaving time to attend morning Mass. I turned in my rifle and Kevlar vest, neither of which was required at Se'eb. Without the weight of my combat gear, I practically floated into the garden in the center of the airport terminal, where a chapel had been set up. A German priest was there, puttering around with the altar when he asked for some help moving the benches around. I volunteered, in German. The priest seized me by the arm and asked if I would translate the Mass, saying his English was poor. *If the priests at Fordham could see me now,* I thought.

Afterward, three other interrogators — Corcoran, Vesecco, and DePaul — and I boarded a flight for Se'eb with a bunch of German Special Forces guys who wore funny, too-tight camouflaged shorts. When we arrived, we were shown to a giant air-conditioned tent, with row after row of bunks and large shelves holding fresh blankets and pillows for transients. The four of us from Task Force 500 made plans to get a couple of hours of rest, then take advantage of this exposure to semicivilization, find some real food, get something to drink. I didn't wake up until 2 p.m. the next day.

On St. Patrick's Day we made up for lost time. I skipped the American bar and dragged my comrades to the British zone. We drank Guinness from tall cans, sang Irish songs, and danced with some surprisingly good-natured nurses and RAF and air force girls. There were people wearing Hawaiian shirts and people with funny, floppy fly-fishing hats; there were carnival lights and a group of musicians who had assembled a garage band in the middle of the Arabian subcontinent. It was a giant, government-funded frat house, and it was the end of term.

The next day we wandered over to the car pool and bribed a couple of air force girls to take us into Muscat, the capital of Oman. We went to an enormous mall overrun by American expats and soldiers and gorged ourselves on American fare at TGIFridays. It was heaven. In three days at Se'eb we ate there four more times.

We returned to Kandahar to find the place in a surprisingly positive mood. Feeling that the threat around the garrison had diminished, the command had lifted the requirements for flak vests and Kevlar helmets. A field laundry had opened, and now seven items a week could be laundered by somebody else. I was also delighted to discover that a Sears dorm-size refrigerator I had ordered had made it through the mail to Kandahar. Finally, cold water for drinking.

Best of all, there was word that Task Force 500 would be returning home by April 15. There was every reason for the troops to greet this announcement with grave skepticism, after all the other false alarms they had endured. But this one was grounded in some external event that gave it some authenticity. Camp Delta would reopen in April — later in April than everybody expected, but still April — which meant that as soon as the prisoner population at Kandahar could be drawn down from its four-hundred-plus count to one hundred or fewer, the operation could finally close. Sutter called it the "collapsing bag."

It was like a changed camp. Everyone was elated. And then the other shoe dropped.

Lieutenant Finch, who had replaced Rawles when the latter came down with a flea-borne skin disease, took me aside to inform me that a number of troops had been selected to stay behind when the main body of Task Force 500 left for home. I and a handful of others would help wrap things up at Kandahar, then be sent to relieve the substation up at Bagram. Those selected included Fitzgerald, Rodriguez, Hasegawa, Davis, Heaney, Ethan Kampf, and Anne-Marie Walker. Finch asked me if I would volunteer for the assignment. I was dazed and deflated by this news. There was no way to look at it as any sort of "honor." It looked as though the command was picking a bunch of chumps — mainly reservists, judging by the roster — so that it could give its precious active-duty troops from Fort

Gordon tickets home. I couldn't blame them. The rumor of a coming campaign in Iraq or Africa — people were saying we might be headed to the Sudan or even Nigeria — was so strong that preserving Task Force 500 for a future mission seemed appropriate. No, I told Finch, I would not volunteer for this assignment. "But I will do whatever is asked of me."

That evening I found Fitzgerald sitting on the sandbags in the back of the large sleeping tent. I was tearing open an MRE, and Fitzgerald was rummaging through a box of goodies from home. It was a cool dusk; Fitzgerald was playing hooky from the ICE and his day shift while I was fixing "breakfast" and getting ready to start my night's work.

"I saw your name was on the list for Bagram, Geoff."

"That's what they tell me."

"You didn't have anything planned between now and October, did you?"

"Chris, I really *don't* want to go," Fitzgerald said, looking up to emphasize his seriousness on this point with an intense stare.

"Come on, Geoff; it's supposed to be beautiful up there. We'll have a good time, keep our heads down, and stay out of Iraq," I said, slipping my favorite meal — MRE jambalaya — into the cooker bag.

"Nah, I don't know if you get me," Fitzgerald said. "I mean I *really* don't want to go."

I knew Fitzgerald was serious the first time, but thought I might be able to short-circuit his gloom. But he was going to have it out. I could tell from the way his arms were hanging down between his legs in a kind of tired cowboy posture. He was tired in a sense that was more profound than the rest of the unit, deeper even than the dark circles under his eyes would lead someone to guess.

"I really hate this place. I hate the people, I hate the prisoners, I hate the fucking army, and I hate *you*."

"Yeah, but you always hated me, Geoff," I said, still hoping to dodge this gloomy discussion. Fitzgerald wasn't biting.

"This place is insane, Mackey. I'm telling you, it's insane in the membrane. Nobody has any goddamn idea what we're doing, and everybody figures the only answer is to redouble our efforts. I can't even begin to think about doing this bullshit until October. Look at everybody else. Look at the Bureau guys. Look at the OGA. Those jokers go home every few weeks. Somebody, somewhere in those organizations knows you can't just throw interrogators into this thing day after day without a break, exposing them to all this G.I. Joe versus Cobra crap day in and day out and expect them to keep on truckin'."

I was sorely tempted to remind Fitzgerald that there were troops getting killed in fights like Operation Anaconda, soldiers who were suffering all manner of deprivation and danger while the interrogators were essentially working in an office. But I could see in his posture, more clearly than I had until that moment, that interrogation was debilitating work, too, in its own way. The interrogators were swimming in deceit, all day every day, not just the prisoners', but their own. And that took its toll, to engage in cynicism, dishonesty, and deception in quantities that would be considered pathological in the real world, day after day after day. I was shielded from this strain to a certain extent. My increased responsibilities meant I was spending far more time administrating than interrogating.

I tried to soothe Fitzgerald, telling him what an asset he would be in Bagram, how important his contributions would be there. But Fitzgerald was resolute. He said he was going to start creating a paper trail so the army could never claim he hadn't made it perfectly clear that he objected to this Bagram assignment. He was going to write a letter to the reserve unit, still languishing back at Fort Bragg. He was going to write his senator, too.

I didn't have the energy to argue. I wasn't thrilled about going up to Bagram, either, but I wasn't going to write my senator about it. This was an aspect of Fitzgerald's personality that I found more than a little pathetic: this capacity for self-pity. He was the smartest, funniest, and in many ways toughest person I knew. But everything conspired at that moment to extinguish any sympathy. So I took my superheated jambalaya out of the cooking pouch and excused myself with a halfhearted platitude.

"Don't worry, Geoff," I said, "everything is going to be okay."

Hasegawa and I teamed up for one last interrogation at Kandahar. I was happy to work with him, increasingly impressed by his talent. The prisoner was a Moroccan named Ahmed who had lived seventeen years in London and claimed he had a heart condition. The doctors had checked him out and found nothing wrong. But whenever Hasegawa and I started in with a line of questioning, Ahmed would wheeze and hold his chest and beg to be allowed to catch his breath. When he wasn't feigning another heart palpitation, he was going on about his seventeen years in London, where he worked as a chef at Planet Hollywood.

Just to be safe, Hasegawa and I had another doctor take a look at Ahmed, and he too found no health problems. So we plowed ahead, pausing every time Ahmed claimed he needed a moment to catch his breath, then continuing on, making it clear that we could carry on with this act just as long as Ahmed could.

The only thing that got Ahmed's attention was when Hasegawa and I told him that we were considering turning him over to the Moroccans. "They would certainly kill me!" Ahmed said. Hasegawa and I didn't argue that it wasn't a possibility but calmly explained that what the Moroccans did with their own citizens was their business.

At last Ahmed said that he could remember perhaps something of importance. He went on to describe the fall of Kabul and his participation in the Arab exodus from the city. Hasegawa and I got Ahmed to pinpoint the villages he and other fleeing Arabs had stopped in and to tell which had given them the most sympathetic reception. At the end of his story, after nine hours of interrogation, came the first significant nugget: he and the others had been delayed at one particular village because a small party of Arabs was going in the other direction — into Afghanistan. But when Hasegawa and I pressed for more detail on this tidbit, Ahmed suddenly became possessed of a stutter that he claimed to have effected purposely as a child to empathize with a friend afflicted with the condition for real. Now, he claimed, the stutter he concocted as a youthful game came and went and was beyond his control. Fed up and exhausted, we called it a night.

The next shift Ahmed dispensed with the stutter, only to claim yet another malady: mental illness. (This seemed perhaps a little more believable, given his last attempt at throwing us off his trail.) He said he had gone from mental hospital to mental hospital in the United Kingdom and was under a doctor's care when he ran away from one such facility to go to Pakistan. The only thing that gave this claim even a modicum of credibility was the fact that he managed to name the pharmacological drug he was taking.

Hasegawa and I pressed on, but now we had to put up with mental "spells" and other antics that made questioning Ahmed an unrivaled pain. What a war.

Of course, our worry was that Ahmed might tell the rest of the camp how much success he was having with this tactic. The next thing you'd know, there would be prisonwide coronary and schizophrenia epidemics, not to mention an outbreak of stuttering. So we put the Arabic-speaking Ahmed in a cage with

Fitzgerald's Chinese-speaking Vighurs. If he could tell them about the technique, more power to him.

By mid-April small groups boarded C-140s for home. Soon there were just five interrogators on the night shift, and the others spent most of their time finishing up the repatriation reports Dunleavy had ordered and looking for any last-minute "open" items in the follow-up questions from the community.

We on the night shift just tried to keep it all together in the waning days of our operation. Turner, whose failings had finally gotten him all but banished from the booth, had found a new job scanning prisoners' files so they could be transmitted to Cuba. All night long, sometimes for eleven of the twelve hours of the shift, he copied page after page of interrogation reports, slapping them on a scanner, zipping the files for transmission.

Whenever there were new prisoners, Heaney and Corcoran would rush down to the in-processing tent to take care of them. Most of the new arrivals at this stage were Afghans, practically all captured in raids conducted by international Special Forces units from other countries that had sent troops to Kandahar. The few incoming prisoners added to a population of longtime residents who had been questioned, assessed, and practically tied with ribbons awaiting their shipment to GTMO.

The steadily diminishing head count in Task Force 500 also meant a lot of extra work: tents had to be taken down, gear consolidated, and pallets of specialized equipment arranged for air transport. The temperature during the day was now routinely soaring over a hundred degrees, and sleep was practically impossible except for the hour and a half directly after the night shift ended and the hour or so before the next night shift began.

The five soldiers who made up the night detail all had raccoon eyes and borderline narcolepsy, and I was certainly no exception. The MPs were having to prod interrogators awake in the middle of interrogations. When a shortage of interrogators one night forced me to screen some new arrivals myself, I became intensely frustrated with one prisoner who refused to answer any of my questions. The prisoner just kept looking at me, repeating, "I don't speak, I don't speak."

Assuming it was another ploy, I looked at the MP, a tall, thin, red-haired man from the North Carolina National Guard MP Unit, and rolled my eyes. "Another prisoner pretending to be a deaf mute," I said.

"Or maybe he just doesn't speak English," the MP said. I blinked for a moment and realized I'd been posing all the questions in English, not Arabic.

After Turner, Heaney, and the others departed for Bagram, I was the only night shifter left at Kandahar. Occasionally there was a note from the newly arrived Bagram team. Fitzgerald, who left in a funk but appeared to have leveled off a bit, described the place as "lawless and crazy." There were Afghans roaming all over the camp, riding bicycles with pinwheel sparklers while others were driving big diesel trucks painted purple and bedecked with ornaments hanging off bumpers, mirrors, and every other appendage. Soldiers kept lights on in their tents all night, practically inviting mortar attacks. There were Special Forces guys running around in thongs and sunglasses, and Australians in bush hats with no shirts and their version of those goofy small shorts. The interrogation operation, if you could call it that, seemed to consist largely of dragging deck chairs up onto the roof of the old Soviet-built warehouse and sunning yourself and playing Frisbee. It was, Fitzgerald said, "like going upriver in *Apocalypse Now*."

But there was some good news: the temperature there was more than thirty degrees cooler than in Kandahar. From their description, it sounded like a kind of paradise, where snow-capped mountains ringed a lush valley. The prison was a real building with real walls and doors and cool cement floors.

Inside only nine or ten prisoners awaiting transport occupied the time of ten interrogators.

In Kandahar newcomers were still trickling in. But for the most part the five hundred–plus occupants of the detention facility had been "tactically exploited" and were simply waiting for the big birds to take them westward to the Caribbean. When Camp Delta finally opened on April 29, it was as if someone had pulled the plug on the mud-walled basin that served as the prison at Kandahar.

As the camp emptied, I waited for the plane to take me north.

My tent was now almost entirely empty, with only Corcoran and Lee left. I stuffed my gear into my duffel bags and rucksack and boxed my precious refrigerator in its original shipping container. Corcoran reluctantly put his Game Boy down and helped take my equipment to the runway. There, in an area roped off with engineering tape, I waited with some Special Forces soldiers from Germany.

I had been waiting there for an hour when there was a tremendous commotion on the tarmac. A consignment of twenty MPs in full battle gear — helmets, vests, chemical masks lashed to their hips — took up positions on the concrete apron where passengers boarded flights. Two other MPs took up machine-gun positions with their 5.56 milimeter squad automatic weapons. A kind of six-wheeled golf cart traveling at only a few feet per minute and carrying a stretcher inched toward a waiting cargo plane, with MPs scurrying alongside like a Secret Service escort. The tail end of the airplane opened and the MPs hoisted the stretcher aboard the plane. Then, just as suddenly as they appeared, the MPs scattered and the air force crew came to fetch the others waiting for transport to Bagram.

I struggled to carry the rucksack, the duffel bag, and the refrigerator into the plane. As the air force crew assembled all the equipment and strapped it onto a pallet, I prayed they wouldn't crush the precious Kenmore cube. As I stepped around the pallet, I nearly tripped over the passenger of the golf cart.

There, strapped down in the center of the plane like Hannibal Lecter, was the prisoner I had seen on my very first night in Afghanistan. The one the guards had thrown apple cores at to calm down. The prisoner, known as Crazy Bob, had been sent on to Cuba in the interim. But the GTMO crew had apparently decided that a detainee whose main activity was eating his own shit wasn't of much intelligence value and had sent him back to Afghanistan to be that fledgling country's first official ward of the state.

It was time to head upriver.

PART

BAGRAM

The flight from Kandahar to Bagram, from the edge of the Rigestan Desert to the steps of the Hindu Kush, is about 330 miles. As we drew closer, our noisy C-130 plane began to hug the jagged topography, following the contours of the ground in a defensive maneuver air force crews call "nap of the earth." I started to feel the effects in my stomach, and I wasn't the only one. The prisoner, his arms secured by straps and his eyes covered with spray-painted goggles, began to throw up. Two airmen from the flight crew scrambled to prop him up and turn his head so that the vomit could escape his mouth. I wasn't thrilled that to tend to this airsick passenger the crew members had to leave their stations at the portals, where they were supposed to be scanning for surface-to-air missiles. But I didn't want to be at the scene of a detainee's death any more than they did.

Finally, the C-130 landed and rolled to an abrupt stop. It was midafternoon as we disembarked and waited at the edge of the runway while Crazy Bob was deplaned amid a considerably smaller security detail. He was hauled off in one direction, and the rest of us were taken to a makeshift terminal — a long tent with a reception desk, some folding chairs, cots, and a large-screen television playing violent, martial-arts DVDs around the clock. Greg Olson, a counterintelligence agent with Task Force 500, had been sent to meet me. He helped load my stuff in the back of a small utility vehicle and took me to Task Force 500's Bagram Team headquarters.

Fitzgerald was right. Bagram was at once remarkably beautiful and alarmingly chaotic. The air was dry and thin from the altitude — nearly a mile above sea level — and at least fifteen degrees cooler than Kandahar. There were trees, and the shade they created was such a novelty that at first I couldn't quite tell why there were dark patches on the ground.

There was a lot of history here. Alexander the Great established a fort near Bagram in 329 BC. A few thousand years later, the Soviets turned it into a major base of operations for their occupation of the country in the 1970s. More recently, control of the base had changed hands numerous times in years of fighting between the Northern Alliance and the Taliban. It had served as the Northern Alliance's southernmost position for months until U.S. warplanes showed up in October and the Northern Alliance forces rolled south.

Now the base was buzzing with not only thousands of soldiers in their desert fatigues, but also hundreds of Afghans moving about in pantaloons and headdresses. The Afghans were walking around with no guards or escorts, pedaling by on candy-colored Chinese bicycles and rumbling past in giant Russian-built ZIL trucks with ornaments hanging from their bumpers, mirrors, and fenders. Allowing the Afghans such free rein of the base was part of the deal demanded by Gen. Baba Jan, the local warlord who controlled the surrounding territory. It was all extremely disconcerting for a new arrival from Kandahar, where the sight of an unescorted Afghan would have warranted drawing a weapon.

Headquarters comprised two perfectly rectangular buildings with pitched roofs. They were dubbed Motel 6 by the troops because they looked like cheap roadside accommodations. There were soldiers lounging around on the front steps smoking cigarettes. Inside, the company commander and first sergeant greeted me in civilian clothes. They seemed happy to see me and ordered Olson to drive me to the detention facility. We hopped back on the six-wheeler and rode up the base's main road, which ran parallel with the runway, though the road was a bit higher in elevation and several hundred yards away. Between the airstrip and the road was the bulk of the base: the tent village where the troops lived, the mess halls, and the aircraft-maintenance hangars. As we rolled along, Olson swerved to avoid women in burkas, children brandishing fistfuls of Afghan money they were selling for "one dollaha," and bare-chested Special Forces troops jogging with giant weapons I had never seen before.

We turned down a rutted road into a sea of green canvas triangles staked into the ground, a soldier village the troops called Viper City. Dust was everywhere, and all the tents flapped in the chalky breeze. *At least there is a breeze,* I thought. Olson showed me to my tent, which had recently been abandoned by a helicopter attack squadron that had been sent home. It all looked extremely comfortable, and I set up my cot and plugged in my refrigerator to a purring generator. Then we were back out on Disney Drive, named for a twenty-one-year-old army specialist who had been killed in a welding accident at the base months earlier. Four hundred yards up, Olson made another left, this time into the outstretched palm of an MP bearing a riot shotgun. After checking our ID cards and my rucksack, the guard waved us through, and we approached a low-slung building large enough to cover a city block. It was a white cement structure with a flat roof. Most of the windows were blown out and boarded up with plywood. It was clearly Soviet-built, not Afghan, all hard corners and metal and concrete, the kind of building you might find in an aging industrial park. A walkway cut through four stacked loops of concertina wire led to a plywood door on which the words NO ACCESS had been scrawled in red spray paint.

Inside was a kind of vestibule, where a few MPs sat playing cards. One, a giant called Lupas, stood up, checked my name on a clipboard, and let me through. He was about to take me upstairs when I heard the familiar voice of Edward Roberts, our Syrian-born interrogator, who was bearded now and wearing a black T-shirt and black jeans. We shook hands and ascended the stairs in light so dim I had to feel my way while my eyes dilated. Several of the steps were broken, and twice I almost fell back down on top of Olson. Reaching the top landing, we turned right onto a long second-floor walkway. Along the right side were eight rooms, spaced evenly over the hundred-yard length of the corridor. Along the left was a wall of blankets, which hung down from rusty I beams. Roberts parted one of the blankets to reveal an almost Orwellian scene.

Below the balcony was a massive open space, the former factory floor for a Soviet aircraft machine shop. Massive presses and other equipment had been shoved to one side of the floor to make way for five concertina-wire cages, each about sixty feet long and thirty feet wide. The roof was forty or fifty feet above the shop floor. In the distance, on the back wall, was an army-constructed wooden catwalk, itself wrapped in concertina wire to prevent prisoners from surmounting it. Each of the five cages had a handful of prisoners in orange jumpsuits. The only way in or out was through a sally port of welded bars that provided passage through the barbed wire. Each sally port had an inside gate and an outside gate, and just enough space between the two for a person to stand. Prisoners could open the inside door when an MP pulled a string releasing a simple locking mechanism. The prisoners would then wait in the sally port until the door behind them was pulled shut, again by string. They would then extend their arms through the bars for an MP to apply the shackles, and finally the MPs would open the outer door to the Facility floor.

I looked down from the balcony hallway for some time.

Some of the prisoners were standing and praying, others were reading the Koran, and still others were sleeping on clumps of blankets. I was about to comment when Roberts tapped me on the shoulder and put his finger to his mouth. He then motioned behind him, where, in the first room along the balcony, I saw a scruffy-haired prisoner wearing civilian Afghan clothes. He was lying on a bunk and reading a crossword-puzzle book in English. When he noticed us, he stood up and walked out of his room and offered his hand. With a polite little bow he introduced himself as "Papa Smurf," a moniker that was never fully explained, although Roberts's theory was that it was the code name U.S. authorities had assigned to him on their list of "high value targets" before he turned himself in. After a moment of small talk, Edward gestured for this character to go back into his room, and we headed down the hall to see the rest of the team. Papa Smurf smiled from his doorway and watched us walk away.

Roberts explained that Smurf had been a Taliban cabinet minister, but was not hard-line Taliban. In fact, he had played a role in the rescue of two Bible-thumping female missionaries just prior to the start of hostilities between the Taliban and the American forces. Now he was under a sort of house arrest. To my relief, the rest of the rooms were set up for interrogations, with tables, Coke-can ashtrays, and two chairs apiece. Only one was occupied. Davis and Hasegawa were confronting an intelligent-looking, neatly groomed Arab. It took me a minute to realize that part of his intellectual aura came from a pair of gold wire-rimmed glasses. It was the first prisoner I had seen so accoutred.

It was all very casual here. All the interrogators were in civilian clothes, and when an echo wanted a prisoner, he or she signed him out on the board inside the ICE and wandered down to the cages to get the detainee. The in-processing room was a dank space downstairs, illuminated by a single fluorescent lightbulb. A giant American flag hung between two hand-painted images of the NYPD and NYFD badges. There was a painted square on the ground where prisoners were to stand while the doctor examined them, and painted lines indicating where to go to be photographed. It was all very efficient.

Chief Rodriguez greeted me and took me out the back door, which led into a small overgrown garden area, warning me not to wander off the path because the surrounding land had not been fully swept for mines. A gate had been cut through the concertina wire to create a shortcut to an enormous Soviet aircraft hangar that dwarfed everything on the base and was two or three times taller than our makeshift prison. It was so large that the army had erected a small village of offices and facilities on the cement floor inside. At the very center was a plywood building that served as the headquarters for U.S. operations in Afghanistan. We called it the "Puzzled Palace," a play on the National Security Agency's "Puzzle Palace" nickname. It looked like an oversized clubhouse for kids, except that there were no windows and it was wrapped in its own cocoon of concertina wire.

But even as I was studying the plywood lair, my senses were drawn to another, adjacent facility: the command staff chow hall. They had started serving hot meals at Kandahar midway through our stint there, but they weren't real meals, just MRE in giant containers heated up and dumped on your cardboard tray. Here at Bagram they were serving honest-to-goodness grub, the likes of which you would find at any garrison stateside: eggs, bacon, beans, fruit, toast, hamburgers, milk, juice. It was paradise, and just a few dozen yards from the prison.

Turner, who had joined Rodriguez and me for this part of the tour, told me that the main chow hall, in the dusty tent village, would be open in half an hour, and we agreed to go have a look and get a bite to eat. Back in our sleeping quarters, I got my gear situated and changed out of my uniform. The box of civilian clothes from home contained a wardrobe a bit more formal than everyone else's: my mother sent me collared Brooks Brothers work shirts and Gap chinos. I had told her we were indoors now, and that meant "office" to her. Never mind, I thought; we'll just be here a few weeks, and it'll be back to work in suits in London.

Unpacking complete and with a restless Turner in tow, we left for the chow hall, where I had my first real food since Christmastime: pork loin, scalloped potatoes, and canned carrots. It was May 8.

Bagram did not impose the same hardships as Kandahar. The interrogators worked indoors, and there was real food, Porta-Johns and real showers. But Bagram was a much more depressing environment. It was, in every sense of the word, a dungeon.

Medieval sounds echoed through the cavernous space: chains jangling between prisoners' ankles and wrists; gates and latches slamming and locking; violent shouts from interrogators; high-pitched whines from the wind slipping through cracks in walls covered with barricades that allowed only slivers of daylight to enter. There was Russian writing all over the walls inside the place. Even though the building sat up on something of a slope on a dry mountain plain with no moisture in sight, there were stains and crusty markings and trails of rust running down the walls, making it appear that the whole place had at some point been underwater. The Soviet machines pushed to the back of the shop floor loomed in the shadows like Cold War ghosts. It was impossible to spend any amount of time inside that facility and not have it affect you psychologically, to not be at least somewhat creeped out.

There were other corrosive new forces at work. The detainees we'd encountered at Kandahar seemed docile compared to those we were confronting at Bagram. Maybe it was because the Kandahar prisoners were taken early in the war — they were the low-hanging fruit, if you will. At Bagram, we were getting detainees who had eluded us to begin with, who were trying to get back *into* Afghanistan, or who were captured by other means. There were, of course, hard cases at Kandahar — some who refused to talk, and many who duped us. But it was at Bagram that I encountered the first prisoner who told me to fuck off, the first prisoner who threatened me, and the first prisoner who spit at me. They were more hostile toward us, and the interrogators' hostility toward them increased in turn. I was never sure how to react to this hardening, never sure whether it would help or hurt our performance as interrogators. It made me wonder sometimes whether we were becoming like the troops in Vietnam who had become so prejudiced against "gooks" and "slopes" and "Charlie." I always thought of them as so woefully unenlightened. In one of the amateurish videos they showed us at Huachuca, U.S. interrogators would actually conclude a Vietnamese was VC if he didn't know who had won the 1962 World Series.

NUMBERS

When prisoners were taken into custody, they were assigned ten-digit serial numbers that formally entered them into the U.S. detention system, and were also used in the official records of the Red Cross. But this was just the beginning of a record-keeping thicket that sprang up around every detainee and created a host of problems.

After in-processing, prisoners were given "MP numbers," the digits scrawled across their jumpsuits that corresponded to their order of arrival and were used by the guards for daily head counts, medical logs, and other records. The trouble with assigning prisoners sequential numbers was that detainees with high numbers (rookies) quickly figured out that it was smart to approach prisoners with low numbers (veterans) for advice on countermeasures to use in interrogations.

After that, the interrogators assigned prisoners yet another series of digits called "source numbers," which were used to identify prisoners on intelligence reports. (Intelligence reports generally don't use prisoners' names to protect their identities in case a report were to fall into the wrong hands.)

There was all sorts of confusion at Bagram whenever a prisoner was transferred up from Kandahar because the sequential number he'd been assigned in the south didn't correspond with his order of arrival in the north. And though you could give the prisoner a new number at Bagram, the MPs still had to keep track of his old number because it corresponded to all of his medical records and other data. (Never mind the cases in which prisoners started at Bagram, were sent to Kandahar, then returned to Bagram.)

The system could reach comical proportions. In a videoconference one afternoon between Bagram and GTMO, the GTMO team started reading out all the numbers assigned to a certain prisoner. Every one of the participants in the conference knew the man by a different number: the OGA had one, the guys in the Pentagon's Special Intelligence Section had another, and the FBI and the DEA had different numbers still. GTMO itself had given the prisoner *two* numbers. When the speaker asked if everyone knew which prisoner was being discussed, I had to say no, and asked if there were any other numbers he'd gone by. Indeed there were. It turned out it was Ahmed, Prisoner 220, the British chef with the phony heart condition.

None of the numbering nightmares would have mattered much if the only consequence were bureaucratic inconvenience. But there was a more serious problem: once prisoners were wrapped in this red tape, it was almost impossible to extricate them. Nobody wanted to be responsible for holding innocent people in custody, but there was a more powerful concern that haunted every officer in the system. Nobody wanted to be the one who signed off on the release of some prisoner who later turned out to be the missing twentieth hijacker. For most officers the safe course was obvious: don't let anybody go.

It wasn't until June that our command at Bagram figured out a way to solve the problem. They came up with a whole new prisoner category called "persons under U.S. control," or PUCs. The whole idea was to create a sort of limbo status, a bureaucratic blank spot where prisoners could reside temporarily without entering any official database or numbering system. We could keep them in this temporary status — designated by a new number beginning with T — for up to fourteen days, giving us time to make a call. If they looked like they might be of some intelligence value, we'd officially enter them into the system and assign them a permanent number. If not, we could release them without first having to get signatures from CFLCC headquarters in Kuwait or, in some cases, even the Pentagon. There was a glorious symmetry to the whole thing. To keep prisoners from getting tangled up in one numbering system, we had to create another.

The upside of the new PUC system was that we finally had a means of releasing worthless prisoners back to their farms and families. But there were also drawbacks. For one, it had the odd effect of making interrogators *less* decisive in their initial analyses of newly arrived prisoners. Because they had fourteen days to figure out what to do with a prisoner, they had an incentive to be noncommittal until the very end of that two-week period. As a result, interrogators hedged their early reports, because only vagueness would allow them to swing in one direction or another at the end of the evaluation period.

The PUC system became more important as time went on because as the war progressed, we found ourselves releasing a larger percentage of prisoners. In our first weeks at Kandahar, we hardly released anybody. As time went by, we released a higher percentage, largely because the ratio of Arabs to Afghans diminished. The provost marshal's office, which ran the "repatriation" process, talked about soon-to-be released prisoners the way zoologists discuss the release of domesticated animals into the wild. Could they manage on their own? Would they be accepted by their tribe? Had we altered their diet too much?

The diet concern, as it turned out, was real. The doctors at Bagram told us that our food was laced with quantities of salt and preservatives and strange MRE juices that gave the Afghans' intestines fits. We had also totally reprogrammed their metabolisms, keeping ordinarily highly active people cooped up in cages day after day and giving them more drinking water each day than they would ordinarily consume in a week.

Released prisoners got a grab bag of consolation goodies from the army: galoshes, parkas, boxes of Froot Loops, and bottled water. But our civilian translators — many of whom were native Afghans whose families had fled to America during the Soviet occupation — thought these going-away prizes were woefully inadequate, so they would "pass the hat" in the ICE and collect sometimes forty or fifty dollars from the echoes and other translators to dole out to the homeward-bound prisoners. (I called it "moola for the mullahs.") Inevitably, the Afghans would start wrestling each other over the small fistfuls of cash and argue with us that injuries or hardships warranted a larger payoff.

While this melee was under way, the provost marshal would appear and give a little stump speech: "You will VAY-kate at your point of capture and be re-MAN-ded to your own re-COG-na-zence!" He meant that the prisoners were to be returned to the same spot where they were taken into custody. Our civilian translators would give him an "Are you kidding me?" look and translate the staccato speech into something the soon-to-be-released prisoners could understand. In most cases, Special Forces had already visited the drop-off point to tell the local villagers of their friend's or relative's impending arrival.

Some of the prisoners would protest. "But my enemies will be there to kill me!" or "I owe money! They will be waiting for me!" Sometimes they would act as if they were at the counter of a travel agency and ask to be delivered to some other location. All of this must have sounded very reasonable to the Afghans, but the provost marshal always looked miffed. We had imprisoned them unnecessarily, but the marshal seemed to be expecting a bit more gratitude. The combination of the money tussle and the destination shopping made some of the interrogators feel the same way. "Fuck 'em all!" Hasegawa would say. "Fuck all ya'all!"

TASK FORCE HATCHET

There were only sixteen prisoners in the cages at Bagram, and they had been largely exploited. There were some follow-up questions coming in from stateside and local commands, but overall it was a pretty relaxed situation. We were told we would probably be in Bagram for fifteen to twenty days before relief arrived from the 525th MI Brigade at Fort Bragg — all the troops we'd left behind in December. There was a chance we might be made to stay another tour alongside them, but even then, we figured at the very least they would send us home for a little rest.

True to form, Hasegawa and Davis had hit the ground running. They were engaged in following up on questions from the community on Aier, the Afro-Caribbean British prisoner. He was talking anew because of an effective ruse. He'd been led to believe he was coming up to Bagram to meet with the OGA. Posing as if they were from that organization, Hasegawa and Davis got him to give up good details about Al Qaeda's recruitment and procurement operations in Europe, as well as new information about bin Laden's security detail and movement habits.

There were other familiar faces. Fitzgerald had just emerged from an interrogation, but having already adapted to the Bagram pace, he was in no hurry to write a report and instead cracked open a *Weekly Standard* and puffed on a stubby cigar. Heaney was wandering around in a tie-dyed T-shirt and carpenter jeans, whistling as he hooked up the laptops I had brought with me from Kandahar. Without much fuss, Roberts, who had been serving as noncommissioned officer in charge, turned his authority over to me. For the first time, I would have the room to run the show entirely as I wished, so long as it met with Rodriguez's approval, but that would be easy: he and I saw eye to eye on almost every administrative and operational detail.

Six days later, I was late to my own morning meeting after taking a few moments too long to savor breakfast: French toast sticks with powdered sugar and syrup, and real Tropicana orange juice. The guards smirked at my gingham Thomas Pink shirt and Brooks chinos as I rushed into the center, tripping on the same stairs that had caught me days before. Papa Smurf, smiling gaily as always, was there to welcome me at the top of the stairs, asking me to repeat my name. Roberts had introduced me as Chris (thanks, Edward), but I restyled myself as "Mike Burke," sticking with the slightly altered name Atley had mistakenly used when introducing me to the two brothers at Kandahar.

The meeting was interrupted by a runner telling us we would soon be getting a visitor from Task Force Hatchet, the code name for a team of Rangers and special operators conducting raids across Afghanistan in search of leadership figures, including bin Laden. Rodriguez and I looked at each other in bewilderment. Why would an officer in charge of *that* group be paying *us* a visit? Fifteen minutes later, three men showed up. Only one of them, an air force colonel, was in uniform; the others were in civilian clothes. I met them at the entrance, and they asked if there was somewhere we could go to talk. I was generally reluctant to take guests up to the ICE and had no idea what this trio wanted, so I tried guiding them into the screening room not far from the entrance on the ground floor. But they were plainly uncomfortable in that open space and asked whether there was an office. So I led them upstairs to the ICE, where

Rodriguez was sitting down at a computer and there were a handful of interrogators milling about. "We really need to speak privately," the air force colonel said. After everyone but Rodriguez had left, we pulled some chairs into a circle. "There are a lot of people at a lot of levels complaining about a lack of cooperation between our two groups," one of the men in civilian clothes said. "We're never going to win this thing unless we work together."

The older of the two men in plain clothes paused and found a chair. He was wearing a fishing vest, a baseball cap with no logo, and hiking boots with red laces. He said his name was Steve and that he was the senior intelligence officer in Task Force Hatchet. In very broad strokes, he told us about his background, that while he was trained in counterintelligence, he had done his share of interrogation work and knew it well.

"What we're talking about here has not happened before," Steve said, leaning forward on the edge of his chair. "We do not operate with anybody who is not one of us. Ever." He proceeded to talk in very general terms about creating a new arrangement between his unit and our interrogation operation. He said there was an upcoming mission and that he wanted to share information with us about it. He finished by saying he needed to consult his command on how far he could go, how far into the loop he could bring us.

"I'll be back," he said.

I figured this meant maybe we'd see him in a week or two. But Rodriguez didn't want to end on that ambiguous a note and asked Steve specifically when he thought he might return.

"Soon," Steve said.

"Days?" Rodriguez asked.

"In an hour," Steve said.

After the three men left, we let the interrogators back into the ICE. Rodriguez and I grabbed Cokes and walked downstairs and out the back door of the Facility. Neither one of us knew quite what to make of this visit. We were elated to have any contact with the Special Forces. We'd been complaining since we hit the ground at Kandahar that it was crazy to have prisoners dumped on our doorstep without any explanation. And here these guys seemed to be suggesting that they might let us in on some of their raid plans *before* they were executed. Maybe our complaints had percolated up, perhaps they were among those "complaints from a lot of levels" cited by the the older guy in the fishing vest. And yet our visitors were so vague, and their culture so secretive, that Rodriguez and I were also preparing ourselves to be disappointed by their definition of cooperation.

We went back up to the ICE and the phone rang. The MPs were calling from the entrance. This time Task Force Steve had come alone. I went down and signed him in and brought him upstairs, but instead of going into the ICE, this time we went into an adjacent room that we used mainly for storage — it was identical to the other booths, but we never used it for interrogation because we were worried prisoners might overhear our conversations in the ICE next door. The storage room was loaded with supplies and gear, and Steve walked carefully around the room, inspecting the walls and the corners and the boarded-up windows as if he were searching for electronic bugs. Then he set a large tube he was carrying on the table in the center of the room and pulled out four satellite photos that had been blown up poster size. They were all in black and white, three feet tall by three and a half feet wide. The photos depicted a compound on a level patch of arid land with a dried-up riverbed snaking behind the buildings. Each photo he pulled out zoomed in closer on the compound. The first one he rolled out showed the surrounding terrain, at least a mile in every direction. The last one showed nothing but the innermost buildings of the compound itself, magnified so that you could make out small rocks and footprints. The photos were marked with white circles and arrows, and designations like "rally point Tiger." Steve walked us through the plan: Army Rangers would cordon off the perimeter, and the Special Forces would move into the compound itself. The strike would happen that night, he said, and the attacking force was already in the air.

The target of the raid was Mullah Berader, the senior military commander of the Taliban. Berader was directly linked to the highest echelons of Al Qaeda, including bin Laden. He was a warrior, someone who represented a serious threat to American forces because of his presumed ability to organize resistance forces and orchestrate attacks. And like Mullah Omar, Berader was so shadowy a figure that the United States had no pictures of him, only OGA sketches drawn from descriptions given by Afghans who had encountered the man. Task Force Hatchet probably would not be able to identify Berader at the scene. The first objective for the interrogators, Steve said, would be to figure out if Berader was among the prisoners his troops brought back.

Rodriguez and I were torn between feeling almost giddy because we were finally part of an operation on the front end and panicked because we had only a few hours to prepare. Steve asked us to describe our process and winced at the amount of time he saw consumed with each step. Then he asked to hear our questioning plan for Berader, and we had to admit we didn't have one. "Don't you think you should have that ready?" he said. What could we say but yes.

Steve had asked us to come up with a list of our top people. Rodriguez and I agreed that would include Hasegawa, Davis, Kampf, Fitzgerald, and Walker. We pressed Steve to brief the interrogators so they could hear the details of the operation from him. When he reluctantly agreed, I had Fitzgerald and Davis fetch pieces of plywood so we could tack the satellite photos up on a board for the troops to see. Steve opened by asking the assembled echoes: "Who here knows Berader?"

Thankfully, all their hands went up. We didn't have a detailed questioning plan on the shelf, but at least everybody knew who the bastard was.

Steve discussed the raid and said that if Berader wasn't among the prisoners brought in, the objective would be to find out as quickly as possible from the detainees they did catch whether Berader had been at the compound and where he had gone. Steve figured that the interrogators would have about seven hours to break the prisoners. After that, any information they got would be too stale. Steve mentioned that a second team of Task Force Hatchet troops would be standing by all night, ready to launch a follow-up mission. The deadline seemed kind of arbitrary, and I wasn't the only one who didn't understand how Task Force Hatchet could expect to have a second shot at Berader if they didn't catch him in the compound.

When Steve left, the room was quiet. There was a seriousness and focus that I had never seen affect the group as a whole. I told most of the interrogators to go find cots in the Facility and try to get some sleep while Rodriguez and I spent the next several hours streamlining our system. The sixteen prisoners already in custody were moved into the two cages at the end of the shop floor, leaving us with the other three cages for segregating the new arrivals. Two huge pieces of plywood were recovered from a dump site and brought into the ICE so that we could tack up additional mug shots and screening summaries. I wanted to rank the incoming prisoners in descending order, with Berader at the top of the plywood panel like the star on a Christmas tree.

The field phone in the ICE rang around midnight. I woke up the troops and let Heaney and others head down to their in-processing positions while I gave Turner some last-minute instructions and fired up the computers for what I hoped would be an avalanche of reports. When I made it downstairs, I saw fifteen prisoners kneeling along the wall in the reception area, their heads in sandbags and their foreheads pressed up against the wall in front of them. Their hands and feet were bound with thick, white plastic zip ties. Two prisoners had wet themselves, and another had shit his loose-fitting native Afghan garb. The room had already acquired a terrible stench that seemed to make the moldy paint peel back.

Turner was watching the prisoners lined up against the wall, taking notes on who was crying, who had soiled them-selves, and who was praying — all indications of anxiety that would help us figure out which prisoners to interrogate first. Next door in the in-processing room, an army doctor named Barjeeb was poking his rubber-gloved finger around an Afghan's mouth. The prisoner's photograph was taken while Pearson rummaged through a stack of Afghan money, playing cards, and other paraphernalia removed from the prisoner's pockets. I selected Pearson because I knew the presence of a woman would be unsettling for Muslim prisoners, especially as they were being strip-searched. After getting his new garb, the pris-oner was hit with a verbal volley from Heaney, who was really getting the hang of the screening chief job. Even the prisoners in the cages were jolted out of their sleep. Within minutes, every prisoner in the place was awake and pressing against the barbed wire wondering what the hell was going on.

The MP moved the first batch of prisoners into interroga-tion rooms, pushing them along so quickly the zip ties around their legs went taut each time they took a step. In one of the booths, Kampf was standing at a field table. Behind him on the wall was a large color poster of the Twin Tower attack I had printed at the mapmaking center on base just for this occasion. Against the backdrop of a blue sky, a stream of flame could be seen slicing one of the towers. As we took the bag off the pris-oner's face, his eyes widened at the sight of the poster, and he blurted, "I NO AL QAEDA."

"Shut the fuck up!" Kampf shouted, and he was echoed at equal volume by his Pashtu interpreter. The prisoner again tried to interject, and his hands came together in Islamic supplication in front of him.

"Why were you at the compound?" Kampf asked.

"I was just traveling, and the owner of the compound is known to be receptive to guests," the prisoner said in Pashtu.

"Where are you traveling from?"

"I'm coming from the north, I swear to Allah on my heart and limbs."

"Why are you traveling from the north?"

"I am trying to get work from a farmer or a builder, and I am told that there is work here."

"You told the first American you spoke with that you had no military experience," Kampf said, seizing on the fact that it was extremely rare for any twenty-something male from the northern part of Afghanistan to escape military service.

"I am not in the army. I am not well; I could not serve."

"You have two choices. And you are going to have to make a decision that will affect you for the rest of your life before you leave this room. If I think you are lying, I will turn you over to the Afghan interim administration. They can do with you whatever they want because I am confident that their decision — whatever it is — will guarantee that you are never again able to bother our forces."

"I swear to Allah and on my mother's grave I have never done [sic] in the army."

"Then I take it you're going to make a decision that will be very hard to live with."

"I am telling you the truth, I swear to Allah, I swear on my mother's . . ."

"We have sixty prisoners," Kampf interrupted, purposely distorting the number. "One of those prisoners is going to tell us the truth. That person goes home tonight. That person is not a threat to us; that person is not a threat to peace in Afghanistan. The rest of you become irrelevant."

I listened to Kampf rattle the prisoner, who was displaying classic signs of defensiveness. He was leaning back but had his arms clasped from the elbows to the wrists in front of his body. He was touching his face as he spoke and inching backward, up against the suede desert boot of the MP who was standing behind him.

Back behind the green wool army blanket that served as the door between the shop floor and the main reception area, I discovered Chief Rodriguez talking to two men in desert camouflage, Majors Hartmann and Vaughn. Hartmann and Vaughn constituted some sort of liaison between Task Force Mountain — the real war fighters — and the interrogation facility. Hartmann was a reservist, an attorney from Queens, and Vaughn was active duty with a combat infantryman's badge. They belonged to a team called the Joint Working Group, and officially their job was to keep on top of any intelligence collection that might aid the hunt for enemy leadership. But Hartmann and Vaughn had taken that narrow charter and parlayed it into pseudoauthority over every aspect of military intelligence at Bagram. Both Lieutenant Colonel Lewis and Major Sutter had warned us about interference from the Joint Working Group — which was not in our official chain of command — before we'd left Kandahar.

Hartmann was speaking to Rodriguez in short and sharp tones, asking why he had not been told of the arrival of a new batch of prisoners, or of the changes we were making to the in-processing procedures. His silent but angry-looking companion gnawed on a large plug of chewing tobacco. The scene, just out of the newly arrived prisoners' earshot but very much in front of the troops, was making Rodriguez extremely uncomfortable.

We adjourned to the ICE, and Hartmann was still going at us when the phone rang again. We went downstairs to meet Steve, who told us he wasn't sure Berader was among those in custody. We checked the mug shots of the new prisoners against the OGA sketch of Berader to see if there were any similarities, and there were three who looked as if they might just match. All had features strikingly close to Berader's — huge beard, large ears, Roman nose — but we couldn't be sure. Chief Gordon, a holdover officer just waiting for his trip home, proposed that we show the mug shots to Papa Smurf, who, because of his job with the Taliban, would have met Berader. The whole idea made me very uneasy — relying on a prisoner, a former Taliban official no less, to answer a crucial intelligence question. But we were under enormous time pressure, and Steve, already comfortable enough around us to offer advice, said, "Go for it." We laid out the mug shots for Papa Smurf and told him to tell us who they were. He studied the photographs, which had been intentionally mixed with other, random prisoners as a control measure, but he couldn't identify any of them. After a few moments he looked up with a grin and said, "You are looking for Berader!"

That told us all we needed to know: we didn't have him. Steve pulled me aside and told me that we had used more than one and a half of our seven hours. He needed to know who owned the compound they had raided and whether there were other safe houses to which Berader might have fled. I exhorted the interrogators to keep the pressure up. They were screening prisoners in ten-minute sessions and handing the sheets to me. Back in the ICE, I started ranking the prisoners, picking the ones we should hit with full-scale interrogations.

There was no time for a break. I knew the interrogators would continue until they couldn't stand, but the civilian translators would all quit and demand time to rest. Gordon approached me to say that we should be using Smurf as a translator. I looked at him with honest incredulity, thinking back to the Vietnam video at Huachuca. It turned out this was something the Bagram crew did routinely. I agreed to let Smurf assist the doctors in the medical screening room, but wouldn't let him in the booth.

The interrogations ran full bore on the new group of prisoners, whom we dubbed the Riverbed 32, until 0645, when I told everyone to quit what they were doing and get together for an assessment and collective info dump. We sat in a big circle. Turner went first.

"There are thirty-two men, aged from seventeen to . . . according to the in-processing report . . . one hundred ten," he began. He proceeded to tell us which of the prisoners, by number, appeared to be the most afraid. He had also recorded everything he had observed from the balcony overlooking the prisoners' cages in exquisite detail. Turner even noted one prisoner who tried to take a leak but couldn't. There were too many people around, and he froze. We all thought that this was a sign of a prisoner overcome with anxiety, someone we should target right away.

Then everyone had a turn, each interrogator describing what he or she had encountered either in the booth or at his or her particular station. Steve, the mysterious special operations guy, was careful not to usurp my authority, but he probed the interrogators' reactions and first-blush analysis. He was impressed when his questions were met with confident answers and with an air of matter-of-fact experience and authority.

"How does the group interact — are they deferential to anyone of their number?" he asked.

"They are naturally deferential to the older men, but there is a dynamic between the Pashtu transients and the Hazrati locals," Kampf said. "I think we can see that these people are familiar with each other, and the story that they were migrant laborers is probably bullshit."

We discussed every prisoner in detail, one by one, recording everything on each prisoner's summary sheet and sliding it into

the document protector stapled to the plywood. We then affixed wallet-sized copies of the prisoners' photographs to help
us remember whom we were speaking about. That exercise
complete, the interrogators retired to the "Echo Lounge" (as
we called it), a large room next door to the ICE with no windows and an unmilitary ramshackle of cots and boxes of bottled
water and other crap that had accumulated since the seizure of
Bagram airfield. I set to work with all of the information at
hand, occasionally creeping into the musty lounge to wake
someone for a clarification. I had the order-of-merit list, defin-
ing the application of interrogation and translation resources
on the prisoners, complete at about 7:30 a.m.

I was about to get everyone back up and ready to go into the
fight once more when Olson, the youngster who picked me up
in his golf cart the day I arrived in Bagram, darted into the ICE.
"First sar'ent says you guys gotta form up for the change of
command, Sar'ent Mackey."

Sometimes in the army you can feel like you're part of the
most glorious organization on earth. And then something happens to remind you that you're also stuck in a big, green, insen-
tient machine. Here we were, working hand in glove for the first
time with Special Forces, racing against the clock. And Olson
was arriving to inform us that we were wanted at the complete
opposite end of the base for a change-of-command ceremony,
the military equivalent of a middle school graduation. And, because it was the army, we had no choice.

Our adopted parent unit, "C" Company of the 500th Military Intelligence Battalion from Fort Stuart, was honoring
its commander's departure and the appointment of a new commander, Captain Bournworth. We were supposed to form up
for a rehearsal at 0700 and change the command officially at
0900. We were already half an hour late for the practice. I
rounded up everyone who wasn't in the booth questioning a
prisoner, and we headed to the tent city to get into our uni-

forms. Only one person was missing: Roberts. I had left him to sleep in his tent even though the extra interrogator would have served us well during in-processing and initial interrogations of the Riverbed 32. But he was so miserable and whiny that I had privately decided to isolate him. I found Roberts on his cot, pretending to be asleep.

"Sergeant Roberts," I said.

Nothing.

"Sergeant Roberts! SERGEANT ROBERTS!"

Still he didn't budge. So I shook his foot, and he jerked it away. "Don't touch me, man!"

"Sergeant Roberts, let's move. Change of command."

"I'm not going."

"Oh, yes you are. Get up."

"Who says we've got to go to that stupid thing?" he said.

"I say we do."

No movement.

"Sergeant Roberts, GET UP!"

He didn't budge. I wasn't going to pull him out of bed and dress him like some little kid racing to catch the bus. I had issued an order. We'd see if he followed it. I left.

We trucked down Disney Road as far as it would go, past all of the U.S. encampments, past the Spanish hospital, past the Italian air force contingent, and finally past the high, neat walls of the Royal Marine fortress with its towering parapet. We trundled along a path of fine sand, barely wide enough for a Humvee, until we entered a field of tumbleweeds and earthen mounds that served as a graveyard for rusting Soviet MIGs and HIND helicopters. Finally, we broke into the widest of open spaces at the far end of the Bagram airfield. We were in open country — the first time I wasn't within a few paces of a defensive structure since I had arrived in Afghanistan. It was a bright summer's day, and we could see for miles. There was still snow on the highest peaks in the distance.

Perched out at the very tip of the runway was a cluster of soldiers and two flags. The troops were placing folding chairs in neat columns and rows. Our guys, though exhausted from the all-night attack on the new arrivals in the Facility, seemed to gain energy from the majestic setting. Here we were, a rag-tag group of a few dozen reservists, national guardsmen, and active-duty troops pantomiming a European-inspired military custom with all the pomp and ceremony we could lend to it. The army's "Caisson Song" reverberated against (very appropriately) the nearby cement bomb-proof casements where Soviet ammunition and rockets were once stored. I was surprised by a swell of pride, a sense that we were explorers on some new continent, carrying our flag to this dangerous and desolate place. Even the uninspired speakers fit the mood with their "you're American heroes" clichés.

Afterward, I managed to steal three chairs for the ICE and headed to the county fair–size big top, where a special meal of local lamb and rice dishes was served up by civilian translators. After a few quick bites, I rounded up the troops, including a dour but nevertheless present Roberts, and returned to the Facility for our next round of attacks. Back at the ICE, Steve was in my face, bull-crazy mad that we had lost three hours' time. When he heard my explanation that we'd been pulled away for the ceremony, he stormed out to vent his anger on my command.

In the seven hours after the prisoners arrived in our custody, we had discovered a good deal about them, but not exactly what Steve and his gang had been hoping for. We did not have Mullah Berader — of that we were confident. We discovered that the compound was owned by a man called Abdul Fawaz, a local potentate and Taliban supporter. His sprawling estate featured a castlelike adobe wall and even a kind of drawbridge — a trailer bed that was rolled out across a ravine so that visitors could cross, then rolled back when it was necessary to make the road to the compound impassable. Inside the compound was a cache of arms large enough for an infantry company of 180 men. Later, American troops discovered crude Russian night vision goggles on the bodies of dead sentries.

All of the compound's residents had been sleeping on the rooftops when the shooting began. Some ran, but most ended up in the arms of the raiders, who had formed a cordon around the ranch. Those who tried to duke it out were subdued or killed. In all, five or six enemy combatants and two civilian by-standers were killed, including a village elder. We tried to plot where each prisoner had been in the compound when the raid started, hoping to identify, quite literally, the inner circle. But the prisoners who were inside the compound were loath to admit who was in charge, and it was taking a long time to put together our little plotting diagram because we only felt confident marking an individual prisoner's position when we had it from multiple sources.

Fitzgerald, Kampf, Hasegawa, and Davis were focused on the four prisoners we thought most likely to have information about Berader, based on where we thought they were when the raid went down, and also on the intimations of their fellow prisoners.

Hasegawa and Davis were in with a man who claimed to have fought the Russians when they were in Afghanistan, and the two of them feigned deep respect for his achievements. The wrinkled old man told the young interrogators about his exploits shooting down Russian helicopters like "the bat eats gnats," a phrase that quickly entered the lexicon of the ICE. The man claimed to be a kind of sharecropper who had lived at the compound for years.

"There were bad men at the compound with you," Hase-gawa said. "Tell me why they come to Fawaz's compound."

"There were many people there. Not all of them live there."

"How many transients were there?"

The prisoner stumbled a moment before Hasegawa and Davis realized the man could not count.

Switching to another topic, Davis asked why there were so many weapons at the compound.

"We have to protect ourselves from bandits."

"Which bandits?"

"There are bandits everywhere."

"Then you will be happy here; there are no bandits in our camp."

"Well, we need to go back! We have to look after our wives and children; the bandits will get them because you took all the men."

"The Afghan soldiers will look after your families," Hasegawa said, knowing the prisoner would not exactly be reassured to be told that Northern Alliance troops, who were bitter rivals of the Pashtuns in the south, would be guarding his women.

"NO! They will rape them. They will steal from us."

"Well, in that case," Hasegawa said, "you have to go home right away."

"Oh, yes, thank you. I need to go home right away. Yes! I knew you Americans wouldn't keep us," the man said with a naïveté that diminished his stature as a tough mujahideen.

"Excellent!" said Hasegawa, preparing his pen and papers. "Who came to visit you from the Taliban?"

"What do you mean? I thought you were going to let us go now."

"Oh, we will. But as I said, there's the matter of the Taliban who came to visit you."

The old man slumped down in his dusty, red plastic chair.

In the next room, Kampf was speaking to a man missing a leg and a thumb; he was about thirty years old, with a thick black beard and a pockmarked face. He told us the leg was lost when he stepped on a mine in the Soviet era. He couldn't explain why it was still scabbed over, oozing pus and requiring treatment from our medics twelve years later. "It does that," he said, with remarkable confidence in his ability to lie.

Kampf had shaved his head bald, and his tan only darkened his olive complexion. He had on the table next to him all of the prisoner's personal possessions, which included a huge stash of Afghan and Pakistani money and more than a thousand U.S. dollars. The man claimed to have been on the pavilion/deck area, but U.S. raiders insisted the one-legged man had been in the compound and had engaged them with an AK. Kampf was using a new approach I came up with: "If you tell us you are with the Taliban, you become a prisoner of war and we have to let you go when the hostilities are over between us. If you continue to claim your innocence, then we will try you as a war criminal. A man dressed in civilian clothes, heavily armed, resisting the Americans, and in a house with enough arms, ammunition, and money to fuel a small revolution — this isn't good."

The prisoner listened and was visibly shaken when the words were translated into his native Pashtu.

"It's very hard to tell what the Northern Alliance would do with a man in your condition," Kampf said. "The labor camps are not exactly set up for the handicapped."

Next door, Fitzgerald's prisoner, 141, was a particularly interesting character. First he tried to tell us he was a migrant worker; then he claimed he was a caretaker at the orchard near the dried riverbed. He said he'd been captured out on the pavilion/deck area. But other prisoners who we knew had been on the deck said he wasn't there. One of the oldest prisoners, a man with a long white beard, had explicitly told us 141 was inside.

Fitzgerald calmly informed him that U.S. forces were inclined to categorize him as a Taliban sympathizer, and suggested that the most likely future for him would include being turned over to the new Afghan intelligence service in Kabul for further questioning. When Fitzgerald broke to go to the ICE for some coffee, I asked him what was up with 141.

"There's something there, I'd say," he said.

"Does he know Fawaz?"

"Yeah, I'd say so."

"When you say 'I'd say so,' what exactly has the prisoner said to lead you to this conclusion?" I asked, mocking the schoolhouse cadence and questioning precision.

"He told me he's married to Abdul Fawaz's sister," Geoff said with his back to me, stirring his coffee with a Bic pen. "I'm on him now about a weapons cache hidden in a false wall of the house. He says Berader was there but disappeared on a motorcycle just before the raid went down."

I walked down the balcony and knocked on each interrogator's door. "Telephone call for you," I said at each one. "Fitzgerald found out Berader was there in the compound, but escaped on a red motorcycle just before the raid; we have Abdul Fawaz's brother-in-law."

Each interrogator then imparted some small bit recovered from his or her prisoner. It was beginning to come together: the compound was full of Abdul Fawaz's family members, nearly all supporters of the Taliban. Fawaz had been in charge of the local militia draft during the days of the regime. And he had been there when the raid went down.

The interrogations continued all day and into the night. At 2100 local, I called a halt to operations and held a meeting in the ICE. The interrogators were exhausted, and as they slumped onto the floor, they let handfuls of notes and pens and dictionaries fall to the ground with them. Heaney and Pearson sat at the laptops to write their reports but fell asleep on the lip of the table. Chief Rodriguez had to wake them and press everyone to finish the write-ups for Task Force Hatchet. In twenty-one hours, we had managed to in-process, screen, and interrogate every one of the Riverbed 32 at least once. The most important prisoners had been under interrogation for more than nine hours. (All of that *and* a change-of-command parade.) But the information we had gleaned, while helpful, was far short of a breakthrough. We knew the compound had caches that had gone undiscovered by the raiders; we knew there were a number of volunteers for the post-Taliban militia that were sheltered there. But information that would help Task Force Hatchet and the Joint Working Group capture Berader was not forthcoming.

Steve, Chief Rodriguez, and I huddled afterward to discuss our overall progress. I didn't want to let up, but the interrogators were tired and even if they could have kept going, we absolutely had to give the civilian translators a break. Steve was willing to go along with that as long as we didn't let the prisoners rest. He wanted them to stay in the booths, each with an MP, to ensure they did not sleep. Rodriguez and I protested that this would violate the Geneva Conventions. You can't punish a prisoner, even by denying sleep, for refusing to answer questions. But Steve was adamant. "We've got these fuckers on the run," he said, and we shouldn't let them recover.

Fitzgerald was sitting on the edge of a cot in the Echo Lounge, half watching a movie that looked like a cranked-up version of *Miami Vice*. I went into the dimly lit space and asked him to join me in the office.

"Geoff, I want you to go back in with 141," I said.

"Who's translating?" he asked.

"Nobody," I said.

"What do you expect me to do, draw him pictures?"

"I don't care what you do, just stay with him until the translators are ready to join you again."

Fitzgerald looked at me with his patented fishy eye — one

of his orbs tends to wander when he's tired. Prisoner 141 was still sitting at the table in the booth, eating dry Froot Loops from his breakfast meal. When Fitzgerald entered, 141 looked up and started to say something. Fitzgerald ignored him and pulled out a history book and started to read aloud. The prisoner continued babbling in Pashtu for some time before he realized Fitzgerald wasn't listening. Every once in a while, the prisoner would try to interject, try to get the upstate New Yorker's attention, but Fitzgerald just carried on, reading and flipping pages. Kampf, Hasegawa, and Davis went in with their prisoners and did the same, only without the book.

They carried on this way for another three hours. When I went to check on them, they were still at it, but in what looked like slow motion. Their eyelids drooped, their shoulders sagged, and their vocal cords were shot. After three and a half hours, we couldn't sustain it any longer, and the translators weren't anywhere near ready to resume. So, at a moment when Steve wasn't around, I decided we'd call it quits. We gave each of the three prisoners we had focused our energies on a can of our precious Coca-Cola, hoping the caffeine would inhibit their sleep, and left them in the booths alone with an MP at the door. The interrogators stumbled into the Echo Lounge and fell down on the cots like dead men.

I fell asleep myself shortly after 0100, while Rodriguez and a young interrogator, Sgt. David Santos, edited the reports submitted thus far. An hour or so later, I was awakened by a boom box blaring Prince's "Raspberry Beret." Thinking it was one of our troops, I set off with a vengeance to find the offender. The sound took me down the walkway toward the booths. I discovered the MPs had 141 up again, and were making him stand in the middle of the room and blaring music at him. For good measure, one of the guards slammed a big walking stick into the cement floor over and over again with a terrible crash. Irate, I pulled the guards outside and asked what the hell they were doing. They had assumed, they replied, that we wanted 141 to stay awake. I told them to let 141 lie down. But not before giving him another can of Coke.

At 0330, I woke up the interrogators. They groaned and stumbled and flopped their way down the back stairs to use the water buffalo spigots — valves off the back end of an army water trailer — for teeth brushing and whore's baths. They reappeared in the ICE with wet hair and fresh T-shirts. Rodriguez, who apparently never went to sleep at all, had a pot of coffee ready for them. They drank while I gave them their instructions and giant, menacing bugs darted about the ICE, banging into the lights. The echoes jotted down their questioning plans while the MPs roused the prisoners. I set off to fetch the sleeping translators from Viper City. Everyone was back in the booth by 0400. The sun was still hours away.

The results were good. Kampf's one-legged prisoner, cranky and with sleep still in his eyes, admitted to having fought for the Taliban and said that he was recuperating from war wounds at Abdul Fawaz's compound, where his father — a mullah, but not Mullah Berader — lived. He confessed he had lost his leg when a U.S. helicopter attacked his SUV convoy in January. He told us that Berader had been to the compound before, but he couldn't remember when.

Hasegawa and Davis's old prisoner slowly crumbled. He, too, had seen Mullah Berader before, always arriving by motorcycle, always with one other man in his company. The two men had carried the snub-nosed AK-74 rifles favored by the leaders of the Taliban and Al Qaeda. Berader had visited Fawaz's compound even before the U.S. intervention. While explaining this, the man slipped and mentioned that a satellite phone had been left in the compound while the prisoners were zip-tied and toted off to our prison. (He also revealed that Abdul Fawaz had ordered sentries to take positions some distance from the compound. Equipped with walkie-talkies, they were to alert him if choppers were heard approaching. It appeared the plan had worked, enabling Berader, Abdul Fawaz, and several others to escape.) When I went to alert Fitzgerald, he came out onto the balcony and passed along news of his own: one of the other prisoners in the cage was a Taliban runner, an errand boy who carried messages for members of the deposed regime. Prisoner 141 was trying to throw Fitzgerald off his trail by pointing to more interesting quarry in the cages.

I put Walker on the case. Reexamining the prisoners' possessions, she found a small notebook. In it were names and contact details written in pencil, along with little quotes from the Koran and other scribbles. None of the prisoners' items had been marked — the capturing unit had apparently skipped this tedious but important part of its job — making it almost impossible to determine who owned which pieces. But the notebook had a partial name scribbled on the inside cover that matched the name 141 had given us during in-processing. Prisoner 141, whom we called "the Runner," was about twenty years old. For her part, Anne-Marie looked about seventeen, especially having given up the battle dress uniforms at Kandahar for a civilian wardrobe. After ninety minutes in the booth, Walker came out to see me. The prisoner would not acknowledge that the notebook belonged to him.

I went in to have my own bout with 141, and without really asking, Steve crept in behind me. He wanted to see what I, a reservist, was made of. Making sure I did not disappoint, I strode into the booth like a drill sergeant and sat down.

"How old are you?"

"Nineteen."

"Are you married?"

"No."

"Do you want to get married one day?" I was only a few inches from his face. I could smell his "dinosaur" breath, as Heaney called it.

"Yes."

"Do you want to have children?"

"Yes."

"Do you want to make a little money, buy a Toyota, and look after your family?"

"Yes."

I turned and kicked a full two-liter bottle of drinking water across the room so hard it burst, startling the prisoner and wetting everything, including my leg.

"If you don't tell me the truth, I have to turn you over to Afghan soldiers," I said with a severe scowl, my head cocked, index finger hammering the air just an inch above his jump-suited chest. "They are here right now. They will take you away, and you will never get married. You will never have children; you will never buy a fucking Toyota. And do you know why? DO YOU KNOW WHY YOU WON'T DO THOSE THINGS?"

"Yes."

"Tell me why you won't be able to do those things, Faruk, tell me why."

"Because the white man in the back of the room is here to kill me," he said with tears streaming down his face. It wasn't exactly the answer I was looking for, but it would do.

"Faruk — no matter what you think about me, no matter what you think about the USA, or about the Taliban or about Massood — the main thing is you don't want to end up like Massood. Right?"

"Yes."

"Because no matter how you feel about me or about the Taliban or about the USA, there's nothing you can do about those things if you end up like Massood, right?"

"Yes."

"Tell me about those messages, Faruk. Tell me about the messages, and we will send you home."

"If I tell you, what will you do?" he asked through the tears. *Hallelujah!* I thought.

"If you tell me I will work to get you out of here and back home. Where is home?"

"Near Jalalabad."

"I will work to get you back to Jalalabad," I said.

"But if I tell you, they will know I said it."

"Not if you tell us now; if you tell us now, you will not have been in custody long enough for anyone to suspect you told us anything."

He considered this for a minute, and then started to talk about a friend in Jalalabad.

Steve interrupted. "I need to speak with you *right now*," he said to me. I looked at him as if to say, "Asshole, I just broke this guy, will ya give me a second here?" But we stepped outside.

"Great work," Steve said. "You've got him going. Now let me in for a second."

Again I looked at him with a mixture of annoyance and bewilderment.

"I've been doing this for years, Chris. I was interrogating people at Field Station Berlin when you were in diapers. Just let me say a few words to him. I won't even need a translator."

I knew what he was up to: classic good cop–bad cop.

The door to the room flew open, and Steve rushed in.

"You little shit!" he shouted in English. "You little SHIT! You think you're gonna get away with this because he's a nice guy? You think you're gonna lie to ME?" Despite Steve's declining his services, the translator muttered away in the background. "You tell him whatever you want to," Steve bellowed while pointing at me. "I know the truth. When he's done with

you, I'll look at your fucking lies and then I'll GET you. I'll get
you, you little shit, and it will be the worst day of your LIFE!"

The prisoner was shaking and babbling so fast the tired
translator didn't even bother to keep up. "He's basically praying," he said.

Steve is not an imposing figure. He looks a bit like Mr.
Drummond from *Diff'rent Strokes,* with graying temples and an
average build. But he had completely transformed himself into
a ferocious presence. His face turned red, his voice lowered,
and his hands cut through the air like a food processor. He also
violated the rules: he touched the prisoner. In the course of his
act of mania, he had grabbed the prisoner's jumpsuit, gathered
the excess material in a wad, and shook him. I was alarmed,
and stepped forward to intervene. When I did, Steve stopped
his tirade and stormed out.

Rubbing his eyes against his shoulders and leaving wet spots
on the light-blue material, Faruk told me that it was a custom in
Afghanistan to carry mail for people when traveling. (With no
official postal service, that's how messages or small packages
were transferred.) The prisoner asserted he had made it known
that he was traveling from Jalalabad to Khowst, and had been
asked to carry a message to Abdul Fawaz's house. He didn't
know what the message was, or why he was transporting it. He
was just told that when he got there, they would know him, and
he should turn the letter over to whoever asked for it.

I was miserable. This wasn't the truth. The tears, the shaking, the threats from Steve, none of it had worked. I pressed
him. Who had given him the note? Did they prepare the note in
his presence? Was the recipient supposed to be an Afghan? No
answers. Not gaining any ground, I told him I was going to
check with our "communications intelligence" people and left
the room to get some air.

A couple of minutes later, the translator joined me on the

balcony, leaving the prisoner with a tiny female MP. We held back the curtain and looked at the large mass of prisoners below — mainly sleeping, some praying. There were three times the number in those cages as when we first arrived at Bagram.

"He says he's ready to tell you the truth," the translator said.

"Who is?"

"The kid, in there. He says he's ready to tell you the truth."

"What?" I looked at the translator, with his puffy face and crew cut. He was about thirty-six years old. He worked as some kind of IT teacher in Virginia. He was wearing a Reebok T-shirt with huge sweat stains under the arms.

"He says he doesn't want you to get in trouble with the 'guy who yells.' He wants to tell you about the note and the guy he was supposed to deliver it to."

I went back into the booth. The youthful prisoner, still in his hand and leg irons, stood against the wall. A plumber's droplight hung from a clothes hanger and bathed the room in stark whiteness. Moths fluttered around it and occasionally bumped into the jumpsuited boy.

"You have something to tell me?"

"Yes."

"Tell me now."

"I was running a notebook and money to Fawaz's house. I have been there before. He is a good Muslim [meaning hospitable to travelers]. I have been at the house for two days, and I waited for the man to pick up the note. The soldiers came, and I could not deliver the note."

"Who was the note for?"

"I don't know who he was, but I was told he would be riding a motorcycle."

The information we got from the Runner was good. The man who had given him the note was an injured Taliban "general" who was living in a basement to avoid capture by our forces.

The general was closely allied to Gulbuddin Hekmatyar, a renegade warlord who had recently returned to Afghanistan from Iran and was bent on ousting the Americans. Hekmatyar was a bad dude, one of the leaders of the mujihadeen that ousted the Soviets. When the Soviets pulled out, the Pashtun Hekmatyar became prime minister in the fledgling government, but he was also an intense rival of the Tajik president, Burhanuddin Rabbani. Their power struggle rekindled a civil war in which Hekmatyar's forces shelled Kabul, killing thousands of its residents, before the rise of the Taliban forced Hekmatyar to flee to Iran. He returned to Afghanistan after the Taliban fell and promptly became such a menace to the coalition that the OGA tried, but failed, to kill him with a missile fired from a Predator surveillance plane.

The runner's note contained complete contact details for a dozen Hekmatyar supporters. There were multiple contact details for each person on the list — reflecting the enemy's mistaken belief that our signals surveillance could be avoided by switching lines. It might have been effective if U.S. intelligence was just tapping individual lines. But in reality, U.S. intelligence was vacuuming up virtually every word uttered by the enemy.

A few days later, when I was following up on some questions with the Runner, I brought him a book from a collection our troops had retrieved from a house in Kandahar. They were tourist books about Afghanistan, from the mid-1970s, older than most of the soldiers I was surrounded by. The faded color pictures depicted an Afghanistan before Soviet intervention. There were pictures of the Hotel Intercontinental, with its bar and pool. There was a picture of an Afghan tour guide wearing a New York Mets hat. One photo showed a line of Western tourists riding donkeys down a mountain path. There were also photos of bazaars, uniformed schoolchildren, and Bedouin-esque "belly dancer restaurants," all relics of a formerly energetic, optimistic society. I didn't know much about the troubles that led the Russians to invade, but the book left me with the perception that this crappy place had been derailed from a brighter future.

I let the Runner look at the book while I was jotting down some information he had provided. He was taken by it, asked me all kinds of questions about it that I couldn't answer. Long after our interrogation, when I would pass by the main cages late at night, he would spot me and approach the wire. "Can I see the book again?" he would ask in Pashtu, motioning his hands as if he were flipping through a book's pages. One time, in a fit of compassion, I had the guards take him upstairs. I sat in a chair and wrote a report, unrelated to him, while he flipped through the pages again. There was no translator, so I could not understand the questions he asked me. I used that old book several other times, and it always provoked a response that demonstrated to me these people had a desire to be part of a real country. They wanted lights that worked and food on their plates and hospitals with doctors and medicines. Instead, they had gotten swatted by the wrecking ball of history and their own self-inflicted wounds. Some of them were the enemy, full of hate for Americans like me. But often it was easier to feel sorry for even those guys than it was to hate them back.

Ultimately, we had managed to gather useful enough information to form the basis of a follow-up raid. Satellite phones and another cache of weapons was found, including antipersonnel and antivehicle mines, as well as rocket-propelled grenades. When those Special Forces troops returned, Steve asked if he could bring them up to visit the Facility and see interrogators in action. I agreed, and Rodriguez did, too. The interrogators, notably Walker, were not so keen on the idea, believing it would distract the prisoners. It also treaded a fine line of the Conventions, which forbid making POWs the subject of "curiosity." But Steve's men had captured these prisoners in the first place — they weren't coming to see what a detainee looked like. And besides, they might be able to help us determine whether certain prisoners were being truthful about where they had been taken on the compound, and about what they were doing. I was happy to allow these men to see the fruits of their labor, to see what an intelligence feeding frenzy looked like. It was also good that they saw how we treated the prisoners. Some complained that we treated them so well.

HOW FAR TO GO

The instructors at Huachuca taught us that physical coercion is not only illegal and immoral, but ineffective, that you can't trust information gained by torture because prisoners will say anything to stop the pain. History shows there have been many skeptics of this theory, and exceptions to this rule.

In ancient Athens, slaves had to be tortured in order for their testimony to be admissible in legal proceedings; the Athenians thought slaves incapable of telling the truth under any other circumstances. Accounts of the military campaigns of the ancient Greeks suggest that they found death threats and brutality highly effective in prying information from the enemy. After losing the battle at Cunaxa in 401 BC, Greek forces were desperate for a safe route of retreat from what is now southern Iraq. Xenophon, the Greek historian and military commander, had his men interrogate two Persian prisoners for information on possible paths of escape. The first prisoner refused to answer despite "all sorts of terrors applied," Xenophon wrote in his account of the campaign, *Anabasis*. So Xenophon ordered his soldiers to cut the man's throat in front of the other prisoner, who quickly became cooperative.

Civil War correspondence in the U.S. National Archives suggests certain officers routinely used physical coercion. "I herewith forward to you under guard two 'tough cases,'" begins an August 31, 1864, letter written by Capt. John McEntee to

Col. George Henry Sharpe at the Army of the Potomac head-quarters. McEntee proceeds to express skepticism of one pris-oner's claim that he was a deserter from the South. "I had him tied by the thumbs all day yesterday and still he sticks to this story," McEntee writes. The other prisoner is described as de-ranged. "I think it useless to abuse the man," McEntee says, adding the prisoner was "tortured here and it made a perfect lunatic of him for twenty-four hours." This, of course, pointed out one of the fundamental weaknesses of torture, even if McEntee missed the connection: harming a prisoner can de-stroy any chance of getting information.

U.S. troops battling insurgents in the Philippines at the turn of the twentieth century employed a technique called the "water cure," in which a victim's mouth was held open — sometimes by pinning a bullet between the upper and lower jaw — and water was pumped into the prisoner's belly through a rubber syringe. Once the prisoner's abdomen was painfully distended, soldiers would pound the victim's stomach with their fists or feet until the water shot out of his mouth. One victim "screeched terribly and his eyes were all bloodshot," said one of several army-enlisted men called to testify before a Senate committee investigating the matter. When the prisoner still refused to dis-close whether he had sent warning to local insurgents that American troops had arrived, the Americans "took a syringe and squirted water up his nostrils. He would not give the infor-mation then and they put salt in the water. Then he was willing to tell."

At the U.S. Army Center of Military History at Fort Mc-Nair in Washington, there are piles of records gathered by U.S. intelligence on the interrogation techniques of other countries. The file on the former Soviet Union is particularly thick, with gruesome accounts from German and other prisoners who were either released or escaped Soviet custody after being imprisoned during World War II. Prisoners described being offered cigarettes by Soviet interrogators, only to have specially designed, sharp-edged cigarette cases slammed on their fingers, cutting them to the bone. One prisoner interrogated by the Soviets described being stripped to his shorts, confined in a frigid room with sharp stones on the floor, and forced to stand at rigid attention for days. "After I had spent two days in this position, I felt terrible pains in the abdominal region, and in particular the region of the kidneys: my hands and feet swelled considerably. . . . After one hundred eight hours, I was taken back to the prison more dead than alive." In subsequent sessions, the prisoner said he was bombarded with bright lights, and slapped on the head until incoherent. The Soviets could be even more brutal when interrogating their own, according to a 1952 Department of the Army study that was declassified in 1984. It includes accounts of prisoners who said they had their fingernails pulled, teeth drilled, or had two-inch needles hammered into their skulls. Some were locked in sealed chambers that were slowly drained of oxygen. One technique dubbed "pulling off the glove" involved thrusting a prisoner's hands into boiling water and then peeling off the scalded skin.

Our civilian intelligence services, always inclined to take a coldly analytical approach, concluded decades ago that threatening to inflict pain produced much more anxiety in prisoners than pain itself. "Most people underestimate their capacity to withstand pain," reads a passage from a 1983 CIA interrogation manual released under the Freedom of Information Act. "Sustained long enough, a strong fear of anything vague or unknown induces regression. Materialization of the fear is likely to come as a relief. The subject finds that he can hold out, and his resistance is strengthened." The manual goes on to describe multiple ways of inducing anxiety: exposing prisoners to extreme heat or cold; forcing them to hold stress positions for hours on end; depriving them of any sensory stimuli. Disclosure of the document in 1997 caused an uproar, but the government said it had repudiated techniques of mental torture and coercion in 1985. Since September 11, U.S. intelligence services continued to insist that they did not engage in torture, although some officials have acknowledged that techniques including sleep deprivation and refusing to provide pain medication to wounded detainees are again considered fair practice.

Back at the reserve headquarters in Connecticut, I used to hear old-timers tell stories of Vietcong prisoners being administered electrical shocks by their South Vietnamese captors. Of course, the war in Iraq in 2003 provided numerous disheartening examples, from the lieutenant colonel who fired shots from his 9 millimeter pistol to scare an Iraqi captive into surrendering details of a planned sniper attack, to the gruesome abuses at the prison at Abu Ghraib.

When we arrived in Afghanistan, I had an unshakable conviction that we should follow the rules to the letter: no physical touching, no stress positions, no "dagger on the table" threats, and no deprivation of sleep. The night I had arrived in that bombed-out terminal at Kandahar, I didn't know for certain what a real interrogation would be like, but I knew that it was possible to make bad decisions in the heat of the moment, that it was easy for emotions to overwhelm good judgment. Following the rules to the letter was the safe route. Even entertaining the idea of doing otherwise was inviting "slippage."

But, as I realized now, the trouble was that the safe route was ineffective. Prisoners overcame the Huachuca model almost effortlessly, confounding us not with clever cover stories but with simple refusal to cooperate. They offered lame stories, pretended not to remember even the most basic of details, and then waited for consequences that never really came. The notable exception was Cavanaugh, who compromised the Huachuca method from the start by constantly running loud, Fear

Up harshes and, on occasion, putting prisoners in stress positions. Although I do not think he ever placed the dagger on the
table, he came as close as anyone would have done. It helped
that his sheer physical presence was enough to make some prisoners question their initial conclusion that no harm could
come to them in American custody.

Later on, Davis and Hasegawa combined the Cavanaugh
method with a more sophisticated "back office," taking his inel-
egant but effective Fear Up franchise and adding new layers of
technique. They conducted exhaustive research, designed exploitation plans based on nationality, then picked off prisoners
in their mug shot book by turning one against another until the
wall of deception crumbled.

Other innovations weren't as effective as we'd hoped. We
tried to get around the dagger-on-the-table prohibition by using
a loophole in the Huachuca rules. Our instruction barred direct
threats against a prisoner's life. There was, however, the special category of "Establish Your Identity" approaches. In these
cases, prisoners caught in suspicious circumstances — out of
uniform, far from their own lines — could be accused of spying
and told point-blank that spies were executed. In Afghanistan,
we faced Establish Your Identity profile prisoners every day.
We *never* saw prisoners in uniform. Instead of accusing them of
being spies, we told hard-core holdouts that we suspected they
were terrorists, and that terrorists could be executed. But for
many prisoners, death was not what they feared most. Confronted with the "you may be convicted of terrorism" argument, some retreated into an Arab-Islamic fatalism that could
be almost impossible to reverse. They would surrender to Allah
and refuse to utter anything other than Koranic quotes and divine supplications. I called it the "reactor shutdown" syndrome.

Of course, these changes really amounted to minor tink-
ering with technique, tiny encroachments on the rules. But
during the coming months in Bagram, a combination of forces

would lead us — lead me — to make allowances that I wouldn't have even considered in the early days at Kandahar. The first involved our policy toward sleep deprivation.

When Task Force Steve urged us to keep those Riverbed 32 prisoners awake, it was the first time in the war that anyone of higher rank had challenged the leadership in the ICE in such a way. Until then, every signal we interrogators got from above — from the TOC across the airport hallway to the colonels at CFLCC in Kuwait to the officers at Central Command back in Tampa — had been in the opposite direction, warning us to observe the Conventions, respect prisoners' rights, and never cut corners. Steve respected our chain of command and wasn't ordering us to put these prisoners on sleep deprivation, but he made it clear to me that we would be letting him down, letting down Task Force Hatchet, if we were to take our foot off the gas pedal.

There clearly was pressure. We'd desperately wanted to work more closely with the Special Forces for months, and here we were in the midst of our first big joint effort telling them we needed to shut things down on our end for a while so our crew — and therefore the prisoners, too — could get some sleep. We were about to confirm the suspicions they no doubt had long before they even approached us that we MI types couldn't be counted on, that we just weren't made of the same stuff.

Steve had made it clear that he thought we were being overly deferential to the Conventions, that we were unnecessarily depriving ourselves of effective techniques that, he implied, were used routinely by other interrogators in other wars. He spoke with authority and experience. Not that we were ever told exactly what that experience was, but he talked in almost academic terms about patterns of prisoner behavior. He told us at one point that hard-core prisoners were unlikely to start cracking until about fourteen hours into an interrogation, and it was clear that he wasn't just pulling this number out of his head. Our experiences at Kandahar and in the early weeks at Bagram told us he was right. It had become increasingly clear to us that some of the best intelligence we were collecting was coming in the latter stages of lengthy interrogations.

Of course, there was some common sense behind it: tired prisoners were simply more prone to slip. The Geneva Conventions don't spell out how much sleep prisoners are to get. They're not that explicit. What they do say is prisoners can't be coerced into talking or punished for not being cooperative, and these guidelines — as our Huachuca instructors always made clear — prohibit sleep deprivation. I never wavered in my commitment to the Conventions, but I did begin to say, "Well, how can we justify this?" It was like confronting a tax question back at the office: this is what we want the answer to be. How do we interpret the tax code so that we have "substantial authority" to justify the conclusion we want?

After no small amount of deliberation, I began to see a solution, or, some might say, a rationalization. The prisoners usually got twelve or more hours of sleep a day, and the most debilitating thing they did in their time out of the booth was read the Koran. Their interrogators got four or five hours of sleep if they were lucky, working fifteen or sixteen hours a day in the booth and then confronting two hours of regular army duties like KP or maintenance. In my mind, there was no getting around the fact that keeping a prisoner awake was a negative consequence, a form of punishment the rules would not countenance. But what if the interrogation itself drags on? When does an interrogation in and of itself become a negative consequence?

The abiding theme of the Conventions is you can never treat prisoners worse than you treat your own men. And it was in that interpretation that I saw some wiggle room for us. It would be one thing if we were doing something to rig the game, like tag-teaming prisoners with multiple interrogators. What if we made it a rule that interrogations could go as long as the interrogator could hold up? The more I thought about it, the more reasonable it seemed, the more *defensible* it seemed. If the interrogator followed the exact same regime — slept, ate, pissed, and took breaks on the same schedule as the prisoner — there was no way to argue that we were treating prisoners any differently than we treated our own men. If that was sacrosanct, then we would be immune from all but the most unrealistic criticism. Because the odds of abuse were high, this tactic was to be a method of last resort, and I insisted that interrogators get approval from Rodriguez or me in every instance in which it was used.

What to call this technique proved to be a sensitive question. I insisted on the euphemism "adjusted sleep routine," or ASR, and once made Kampf do push-ups for calling it "sleep dep" one too many times. But ultimately, neither of those names stuck. The one that did came from a coalition intelligence sergeant named Kim Dawson, who arrived at Bagram some time later. He was a very enthusiastic guy, always pushing us to be more aggressive in the booth. One time, he was giving some interrogators pointers in the ICE. "You've got to scare them," he said, "get right up in their faces and *monster* them." From then on there was only one word that we used for keeping prisoners in the booth until they or their interrogator broke: *monstering*.

OUR ALLIES

The Brits had a brigade of Royal Marines at Bagram. They were a rugged, hugely professional bunch, a wiry people with inexhaustible stores of energy. Their packs towered above their bodies, while their sturdy little "bull pup" assault rifles looked as if they could fit in a pants pocket. The British always seem to get healthier when they leave their island, and this was no exception. When they weren't off traipsing around the Afghan mountains, they could generally be found on any flat surface, sunning themselves to a golden brown — or, perhaps more frequently, a painful pink. They invaded the bodega-sized PX every day like locusts, pushing aside even the bear-sized Australians and emptying the place of precious Gatorade and Doritos.

All of our coalition partners had some kind of intelligence asset in Bagram, but these were small contingents. Our closest partner had all of seven soldiers. They had their own "Facility" within the walls of the Royal Marine compound near the end of the airfield, a mile or more away from the American prison. It consisted of four small cargo containers arrayed in a cross formation, with the open ends facing each other. In the center was a camouflage canopy connecting all the cargo containers within its drape. There was also an administrative cargo container (their equivalent of our ICE) off to the side.

For all of the work to set the intelligence facility up, it never held any prisoners. Indeed, the British never captured a single soul. Instead, the containers were used for secret rendezvous with Spanish nurses and, reportedly, the occasional journalist. They were also home to some fantastic, memorable parties (of which I do have firsthand knowledge), but they were never for holding any Al Qaeda or Taliban.

The ranking noncommissioned officer in our ally's human intelligence unit was Bill Ellis, a forty-one-year-old warrant officer who had to work hard at slowing down his north-country accent for our benefit. He was about five foot nine, with a receding hairline and a ready smile. Ellis was a man who really did write the book on interrogation methods: he was the chief instructor at his country's interrogation school and had been teaching the trade all over the world for twenty years.

"Billy," as he insisted on being called, would have to look beyond his facility for any action in Afghanistan. And we could certainly use a man like Billy. Major Sutter, working with the command in Kuwait, arranged for Billy and his crew to have carte blanche. While senior officers of our own forces were obliged to file request for entry, wait for an escort, and leave their weapons at the front door, Billy and his team could enter without escort, take their weapons with them upstairs, and even summon prisoners as my own troops could. They were also permitted to interrogate prisoners without a U.S. Army monitor, a privilege never granted to the FBI or OGA (oh, the feathers this ruffled!). The reason for this was simple: we trusted them, and they shared everything they got with us.

Even under this arrangement, our guests were content to get most of their human intelligence from our reports, just as our ground commanders in Afghanistan did. When their interrogators went into the booth, it was generally to question prisoners who had spent time in their country, or in other parts of Europe. At the most, the number of such prisoners in custody was four.

For all of the privileges I extended to Billy, he did his own turns for me. The most important of these was his decision to place his four Arabic linguists at our disposal. That meant I could free up Davis, Fitzgerald, Heaney, Pearson, or Kampf, who otherwise had to go in with the non-Arabic-speaking echoes, including Hasegawa. More important, I could get my troops out of in-processing roles, document-exploitation assignments, and medical details in which they had to trail doctors on their daily rounds and translate for wounded prisoners.

Most of the men on Billy's team were soldiers in the territorial army, his country's equivalent of the national guard. They were generally much older than our troops, and often a bit professorial. Sometimes it seemed as if they were more interested in the experience of war — the opportunity to see far-off lands, encounter exotic peoples — than in winning it. Billy was a little different. He had been around Americans, particularly American soldiers, for a long time. He appreciated our best traits and tolerated our many excesses. It sometimes seemed to me, even among the tough, stout Royal Marines, that most of them regarded the American war mentality — our ferocious desire to *defeat* the enemy — as a little sophomoric, as if jingoism were beneath them. Billy understood this, and when he wasn't playing to our galleries, he must have been explaining the circumstances to his own bemused troops.

Billy and I became good friends. After the war, I would see him awarded an Order of Chivalry bestowed by the sovereign at the palace. But it was actually one of Billy's countrymen from the civilian intelligence service who would help me carry out one of our most delicate undertakings at Bagram.

At sunrise, Disney Drive was made for running. It was free of the bustle of 1950s trucks piloted by mad Afghans, and the choking dust of the place was still damp and settled. I loved to run to the far end of the airfield (pistol by my side) and watch the sun poke up over the snowy mountains. Well down Disney

Drive, past the British camp, the road turned into a path that at one point was crossed by a wide stream. Hasegawa had made me paranoid about crossing streams at Bagram with his stories of plastic Russian mines flowing in the current. Sometimes I would wait for a passing army truck so that I could cling to the fender to make my way across. On one of these morning runs, I bumped into a tall, youngish-looking Brit, also in civilian clothes, and also out for a jog.

"Hello, good morning!" he said with very unmilitary friendliness.

"Hey, how ya doin'?"

"American! How do you do? I'm Simon."

We chatted for a bit, and he came around to asking me where I worked. I told him I worked "near the Task Force Mountain headquarters. I'm a translator."

"Really? Do you speak Dari?"

At this point I knew I was probably dealing with an intelligence person. In fact, I'm sure that was Simon's intent in asking that question. Simon was winking at me verbally: most regular troops didn't even know there was such a tongue as Dari.

"Nah, I speak Arabic. What about you?"

"I also speak Arabic," he replied. "I work over there, in the Royal Marine camp."

We talked for a moment longer and then parted company, he bound for the main cantonment area, and me off to the far end of the airfield, near the change-of-command site and a sizable party of engineers busily clearing mines.

Simon came to the Facility a few days later. We were still involved in clearing open items with the Riverbed 32, and as I escorted him to the ICE, he paused at each doorway, glancing into the occupied booths as if he were storing the images for future reference. When I explained the Riverbed 32 to him, he wasn't too interested. That sort of prisoner was the business of the Americans, obsessed with "leadership takeouts," as his countrymen called them. He was visibly intrigued, however, when he learned I had been called up from a job in the UK, and more so when he discovered I had been with a firm he knew. In fact, one of his fellow agents in Kandahar had been a senior manager at my accounting firm in London in a prior career; his office was in the same building as the one in which I worked.

Like Billy's uniformed troops, Simon's civilian agents were afforded absolute rein of the house at Bagram. We called them (like all non-American intel types) FIS agents — agents from a foreign intelligence service. They had proved themselves in Kandahar as well-mannered guests. And unlike members of our own civilian intelligence agencies, they were more than willing to let us read their reports when they were finished. In fact, sometimes I would simply have Turner put their reports into U.S. format and submit them as if he had performed the interrogation himself — a bit of plagiarism that no doubt bolstered his reputation among report readers in Kuwait and Washington.

Simon was there to speak with Aier. Aier was a convert to Islam, Afro-Caribbean by birth. (He of course spoke perfect English.) The guards used him to communicate with the Arab prisoners when one of us was not around, but Aier retained a remarkably positive reputation among the other Arab prisoners. Since he admitted his fairly high-level involvement with Al Qaeda, he was the target of all manner of follow-up questions from the community, and he attracted the attention of both Billy and Simon. They could chat with Aier as much as they liked, as long as they didn't give the game away: Aier was still being interrogated by Kampf, and Aier thought Kampf worked for our OGA.

Both Billy and Simon managed to achieve the status of family with our crew. It didn't hurt that they frequently arrived with goodies. Their mess hall had even better food than ours — I

can remember eating there and actually crunching into perfectly cooked green beans. And Billy's capacity to steal jelly
doughnuts from his force's sergeant's mess and bring them to
us was cat burglar–like. Simon managed something even more
impressive. One evening, after he'd finished talking with Aier,
he said he had a "special treat" for me. We made our way to the
roof of the Facility on a severely damaged fire-escape ladder.
Once we reached the open space on top, he pulled out Bombay
Sapphire gin, India tonic, and a real lemon.

Simon was no doubt cozying up to me for information and
continued access. Indeed, he was doing exactly what people in
his line of work are supposed to do. But it was a quid pro quo
relationship. I needed him, too, and not just for Bombay Sapphire and tonics (I called it my "special mefloquine" because
gin contains the same ingredient as the anti-malaria drug we
were supposed to take on "Mefloquine Mondays"). I wanted to
continue to have access to help from his country's police, domestic security service, the FIS organization he belonged to,
and, of course, Billy's team down the road.

We were running a very different prison at Bagram than we had
at Kandahar. For starters, we developed a tiered system that relied more heavily on our top performers. Kampf, Fitzgerald,
Davis, Walker, and Hasegawa became more like project man-
agers, and they were given responsibility for groups of prisoners. Each group had, say, a half dozen or so prisoners — who
were usually captured together. Our echoes coordinated the interrogations of the prisoners in their groups, making sure the
echoes working for them were using the right approaches and
cooperating.

We also did away with shifts. Interrogators could take their
prisoners into the booth whenever they wanted. The only rule
was that every interrogator had to perform at least two itera-
tions a day, even if they were on the same prisoner. Some troops

liked to have their first interrogation right after the morning meeting, then write the report and do a second sequence in the afternoon. Others preferred to go about it quite differently. Davis liked to go to sleep after the morning meeting and then do marathon interrogations all through the night. He felt this upset the balance of the prisoners. Every interrogator was in the booth at least eight hours a day, with the exception of Heaney, who had heavy in-processing responsibilities in addition to serving as our computer network administrator. Given that each interrogation required about an hour's preparation time, and that the subsequent report was worth about four hours' time, plus the interaction with me before and after an interrogation and the follow-up questions from the Community and Santos's "catches," and finally the hourlong meeting each morning, each interrogator had an exhausting fifteen- to eighteen-hour day. In the two weeks since the Riverbed 32 raid, the troops were more tired than at the height of operations in Kandahar.

Because of the heavy schedule, the interrogators were rarely in their tents. They slept where they fell, inside the Facility, after their duties were complete. Our cots in Viper City were now coated with fine dust, and all of our equipment, save the weapons that we carried with us, looked as if it were resting in a newly discovered chamber for a pharaoh.

SNITCHES AND RUMORS

Sometimes running the detention facility at Bagram was like watching a nature program on television during which some beehive or anthill is cut away so that cameras can monitor everything that happens inside. The way the balcony looked down on the prison floor — it was two stories up, but it felt more like three — added to this effect. You got a feel for the rhythm of the population, a sense of the roles certain prisoners played: the leaders, the followers, the loners, the talkers, the cool customers, and the worriers. In those nature programs, some external trauma — a fire, a downpour, a predator — always comes along and agitates the colony into fits of activity and anxiety. We tried to agitate our colony on a regular basis, and one of the main ways we did this was by constantly spreading confusion.

We started rumors that Cuba was filled up, that some prisoners would have to be sent to their home countries. We started another rumor that an Afghan general was coming to examine the Facility to judge how many guards he would need to look after the prisoners when the U.S. troops left. We were always trying to create divisions among the prisoners, to make it seem as if one side or one subgroup was betraying another. We used to say that this or that Middle Eastern gestapo had opened up an office at Bagram in order to collect bigger U.S. bounties by grabbing more Arabs trying to escape. We'd say that Afghans were testifying in courts that they'd helped Arabs escape. We said that the United States and other countries had created terrorist courts. And because the prison population turned over with the shipments to Cuba, there was never a group of prisoners who had been around long enough to get wise to our game.

One of the most effective rumors we spread was that the United States was paying Middle Eastern countries $100,000 for every one of their nationals they took off our hands. It wasn't true — we never did anything with prisoners but keep them, release them, or send them to Cuba — and the supposed price was preposterous. But the mere idea that money was changing hands positively convinced the conspiracy-obsessed Arabs the rumor was true. Within a few days, it had morphed, and prisoners started whispering that we were *selling* prisoners to other countries. Then it got even better. When the Red Cross came through for the next of their biweekly visits with prisoners, one detainee mentioned that he had heard we were selling prisoners to their home countries. Unwittingly, the Red Cross said we weren't *selling* anyone, we were just giving them over. I have no idea where they got that information, or why they said that, but it was wonderfully helpful to us.

We also performed experiments to see how information flowed within the camp. When the MPs were shuffling prisoners around, we'd put a North African at one end of the cages, place another from the same country on the opposite end, and see if a rumor could make it across the sea of Arabs, Pashtuns, and Hazratis between them. When a prisoner had left for GTMO, sometimes we'd take a bit of whatever intelligence we'd gotten from him and leak it back into the cages. If he had told us the Arabs weren't hiding out in Faisalabad anymore because the Faisalabad authorities were thought to be in bed with the OGA, we'd slip that back into the general population. Inevitably, some group of prisoners would know the story was true, and that would help convince them that whether they talked or not, their cause was being sold out, piece by piece.

As our efforts became more sophisticated, we created an unofficial body of "rumor creation." After morning meetings, I'd pull aside Hasegawa, Kampf, and Rodriguez, and we'd spend twenty minutes brainstorming rumors, starting with the objective — the impact we wanted to have — and working our way back to figure out what little planted piece of information was most likely to achieve that end. If there was a certain group we wanted to unnerve, we'd look at our "wall of shame," our giant board of mug shots from the FBI and Interpol and the OGA, and pick someone whose capture might alarm a certain demographic in the camp. Then we would plant the rumor that he was in custody. Sometimes we'd let it "slip" in an interrogation and let the prisoner spread the rumor unwittingly. Other times we'd tap the MPs to spread the deceit, often by having two of them chat about some falsehood in earshot of the prisoners. And still other times we'd just ask one of our cooperative detainees to start the rumor for us — and then watch very closely to make sure that he had.

Of course, inserting information into the prison population is only part of the equation. You also have to be able to extract it. And that means finding reliable volunteers. You look for prisoners with vulnerabilities you can exploit. It can be someone with something they need to hide from the rest of the population, someone who let the cause down in some way, or a prisoner claiming a particularly pressing hardship. "You say you desperately need to get back to your family? We're thinking about it. But as evidence of your willingness to support my country and its efforts to liberate Afghanistan, I need to ask you a favor." The longer we spent at Bagram, the more we came to focus our volunteer recruiting efforts on two types: the sycophants who were always telling us how much they loved

America ("Prove it.") and the Afghans we were going to release ("I need something from you before you go."). Many of them were truly favorable to the American cause, and willing to help, even after being captured and held in custody.

One of our more useful volunteers was an Iraqi who had been transferred up from Kandahar. We worked with him partly because of his nationality. Iraqis can move among other Arabs more easily than their peers from other Gulf states, and they generally don't provoke the same rivalries, suspicions, or negative reactions from, say, a Tunisian, as Egyptians or Saudis or Kuwaitis do. The Iraqis have a culture that predates and, in some ways, transcends Islam, and they are regarded as fairly well educated. Their country's fights against mostly Shiite Iran and the United States enhanced their reputation. And besides, the fact that our Iraqi had been transferred up from Kandahar meant we knew him better than the rest of the Bagram prisoners did.

He was a miserable little man, a pathetic liar who claimed over and over that he was in Afghanistan doing humanitarian work for the Saudi Red Crescent. So we looked on the Red Crescent Web site, took down some basic information, and put dozens of questions to him. He couldn't answer any of them. He didn't know a single soul within the organization. He told us he had joined in Riyadh, but he couldn't describe where their offices were. Of course, lying is not necessarily a disqualification for helping out in this capacity. You never base a decision solely on what a collaborator tells you, and you never expect the complete truth. You're just happy if some of his information pans out.

This prisoner, 230, was thirty-four years old, but he looked much older. His name was Heesham, and his face was scarred from acne, his nose round like a drunkard's. His hair was wavy, and his big eyes were perpetually bloodshot (because, he claimed, he was "always on the lookout for agents"). But de-

spite his mild paranoia, he was extremely eager to help. Davis
had been speaking with Prisoner 230 since his arrival, collecting information on Iraqi units and dispositions — always a top
priority for U.S. intelligence. Davis hated this because it meant
writing complex reports with full order-of-battle tables and
tons of geographic dispositions. Davis rolled his eyes when I
told him to introduce me as the deputy chief of the CIA office
in Bagram. Oblivious to his own odor, 230 smiled and bowed
and tried to kiss Davis's hand; Davis rolled his eyes again and
wiped his hand on his pants as one would after a dog's greeting.

Davis's Arabic was strong when he got to Afghanistan, and
it had been improving ever since. By this point he had acquired
the rich, dulcet tones of a Gulf Arab. He used his hands a lot
when he spoke, as if he were picking the words off a shelf. Davis
told the Iraqi that I was his boss and that I was here to discuss
why he had lied about his reasons for being in Afghanistan.

"I wanted to protect the group I am working for," he said.

"Do you mean the Saudi Red Crescent, Heesham?" Davis
asked.

"No — I was working for someone else, who Allah and I
know and so do you."

Jesus, I thought, it was going to be another prisoner "Yoda
chat," with nothing but cryptic references, Koranic quotes, and
Arabic haiku.

After several minutes of verbal wrestling, Heesham said he
had been working for something called the "Islamic Development Organization." I could see Davis mentally typing the
name into the classified Internet search engine.

"I was in Afghanistan to see that our funds were reaching
the appropriate parties, none of whom America would have
problems with," he said. And then, suddenly, he changed the
subject: "Can you find me a children's book? I'd like to start
improving my English."

Davis was unfazed and proceeded to question him about this new organization, and this time he got real names, places, and contact information. All along, 230 expressed eagerness to provide anything he could to root out "the terror makers," as he called them. He was as obsequious as they come and seemed genuinely scared of us. As we talked, he held his midsection as if he were giving himself a hug and leaned back and forth rhythmically, filling the gaps in our conversation with a nervous murmur: *mmm . . . mmm . . . mmm.*

After Davis finished up his collection on the "charity" and its works, we went back to the ICE and gave the contact details over to our signals intelligence people for exploitation. While all of that went on, I told Rodriguez that I thought we might have our man, and that I would set to work on him later that night. At about 0300, after the ICE had cleared out, I called for Heesham.

"I'd like to talk to you about your future," I said. "I think it's important to do this because I don't want you to be confused."

"I am very, very worried about this, *ya-fundem,*" he said, using the very formal Arabic equivalent of *sir.* "I have a lot to offer you, but I am afraid."

The statement was tantalizing, but I didn't bite. There would be time for that.

"You should be afraid, Heesham, because we are very unsure what to do with you."

"I can help you, but you need to look after me."

"Yes, you've said that, but you know how these things work."

"No. What do you mean?"

"There are a lot of possibilities for you. Maybe you will end up in Italy. Maybe you will end up on a horse farm in Virginia, or maybe you will be taken to the border of Iraq and turned over to the authorities there."

With horror in his eyes, Heesham leaped forward, attempting to take my hand. "I want the Italy one, or the horse one," he said.

"I thought as much," I said, trying to keep from laughing. "We want to consider all of this, but of course there are two parties involved, aren't there?"

"Yes, you and Mr. John," he said, referring to Davis's stage name.

"No," I said. "You and me. We're the two parties. We have to trust one another, and trust cannot only be spoken of — it must be something we see in each other — something we *witness*," I said, using a word I'd looked up in the Arabic dictionary.

"Yes, yes, I agree. Do you have a cigarette?"

I pulled out my pack of Marlboro Lights and what might have been the last working lighter in the ICE.

"I'd like you to help me to help you," I said, wincing at my Jerry Maguire cliché. "I like to think the way we build trust is to *evidence* trust. Do you agree?" *Evidence* was another word from the Arabic dictionary.

"Yes," he said eagerly.

"Fine. I am going to send you back downstairs. We'll speak again soon, and you will have an opportunity to show me trust, and I will have the opportunity to show you trust, too."

Two nights later, we were together again; this time I was armed with a chicken dinner, mashed potatoes, green beans, and a little frosted cake. (Only the mightiest army in the world could make frosting in the foothills of the Hindu Kush.) My guest was appreciative to the point of groveling, and wished every blessing on me, my wife, and all of my progeny. Before I could nudge the conversation toward the mission I had in mind for him, he started talking about some boxes he saw in the Iraqi port of Um Qasr in July 2000. These, he insisted, were almost certainly chemical weapons. Now here I simply had to take the bait, although I quickly regretted it. Did he know where they were manufactured? No. How they were deployed? No. What they were doing at the port, where they were being shipped, specifically what they contained? No, no, no.

"Then why did you think they were chemical weapons?" I asked.

Because, he said, some of the crates were dated, "like milk." He pointed to the "use before 2006" stamp on top of the irradiated milk carton from which he was drinking. He described in detail all the security surrounding the mysterious boxes, the markings on the trucks, the number of troops on hand from the "Saddam bodyguards." We were together almost three hours when at last he ran out of information. Then he looked up at me with an expression of satisfaction, sure he had done his part in our negotiated exchange of "trust."

"Okay, Heesham. That's very interesting, and I'm grateful for your helpfulness. You know it will take us some time to follow up on all this information. I will send it to the 'Iraq Department' [*Kussum Al-Iraqi*] within my organization. In the meantime, I'd like you to think about something closer to you and me. I'd like you to think about the people in your prison box."

"Box?"

"Yes, the box of people you are in"

"You mean *cell*?"

"Yes. Think about the other people in your *cell*. I want you to listen to what they are saying. Just listen. Don't ask anyone anything. Just listen to what's being said. I will talk to you again in two nights' time. You tell me what you have heard."

"I have heard things already."

"Is anyone trying to escape or kill a guard or one of my friends in civilian clothes?"

"No."

"Okay, keep it to yourself for now. Just go back and listen. Do you understand what I'm asking you to do?"

"Just listen, *ya-fundem*."

"Good. Just listen."

"No, no," he said. "*Just listen!* I will tell you what has been said already."

"What?"

"Just listen, *ya-fundem*. There is an Egyptian who —"

"LOOK, I want you to just go down there and listen. I don't care what's been said so far, unless it's something about an escape or someone trying to kill someone else. Do you understand?"

"Yes."

A transaction I expected to take minutes had stretched past four hours, and Heesham was driving me crazy with his inability to clue in to the arrangement. Worse, I had lost my cool and shut him down — a real rookie move — while he was offering information from inside his cell. Here I was trying to recruit our first real collaborator, and he's staring at me with confusion all over his face, not to mention a good helping of congealed, yellow army chicken gravy.

"Now for my part of showing you my trust," I said, trying to get this conversation back on track. I produced a pile of United States visa application forms I had pulled off the Internet. They were just for ordinary visitors, but they looked official, so I didn't care.

"Okay, these forms are the ones we need to start filling out if we are going to decide where you will go. They are very important. But we should wait until next time to start filling them out. You don't want to do this when you're tired because you might make mistakes, and the forms have to be perfect. Do you understand me?"

"I am not too tired, *ya-fundem*. Don't wait on my account."

"I'm sure you don't realize how tired you are, and we need to make sure these are perfect."

Whether he was too tired or not, I was exhausted, and there was no way I was going to go through the forms with him at this point. And besides, my Arabic was in full retreat, and figuring out how to ask him about mothers-in-law and past work history was beyond me.

Again, Heesham started in. "I'm not too —"

"LOOK" — I cut him off again — "we'll start on these tomorrow or the next day."

"Okay. After I listen."

"Yes. After you listen."

I left the room ready to jump off the balcony.

PRISONER 237

September 11 imagery had surrounded us from the moment we hit the ground in Afghanistan, from the posters that the FBI and OGA guys kept on their doors at Kandahar to the Crayola pictures we got from elementary-school kids and hung on our walls. But we never came across a prisoner we thought might have some connection to that horrible attack until early June at Bagram.

He was delivered in the middle of the day by Special Forces troops who looked like skateboarders in their baggy pants and kneepads. They said the prisoner had been picked up over the border and briefly held by local authorities before being transferred to our custody via the OGA. He was a Saudi who had gone to high school in the United States and later studied aeronautical engineering in Arizona. None of the September 11 hijackers had trained there with him, but a number of them had trained elsewhere in Arizona. And there were all sorts of intriguing connections. In July of 2001, an FBI agent in Arizona had written what became known as the "Phoenix memo," an e-mail sent to bureau headquarters months before the attacks, warning that Al Qaeda might be sending operatives to U.S. flight schools to train for terrorist actions. The memo was triggered by the agent's discovery of an incongruously large number of Arabs enrolled in area aviation programs, including ones near this prisoner's university. Hani Hanjour, the hijacker who piloted the plane that crashed into the Pentagon, had gone to flight school in Phoenix, about one hundred miles south of where Prisoner 237 had studied. It looked like we had a major catch.

Rodriguez wanted to put Hasegawa and Davis on the case, but I was less enthusiastic about the idea. They were without a doubt the most successful interrogators in the unit, but much of their success was a result of their North African specialization. Anne-Marie Walker had developed a similar specialization on Saudis and Yemenis. She was also accustomed to dealing with celebrity guests. At Kandahar she had caught a high-ranking Al Qaeda figure masquerading as an ordinary Arab volunteer fighter. I also thought there was a tactical reason for giving Anne-Marie the job. I knew that a petite, blond-haired American girl with ice in her veins was the last person 237 would ever expect to see in front of him.

Anne-Marie was glad to get the nod, and she immediately began assembling a smart interrogation plan. But then she threw me a curveball and proposed that she go into the booth accompanied by Paul Harper, an army counterintelligence agent who had basically been assigned to the prison on a full-time basis as an analyst. Harper had a quick mind and good instincts. He was also Anne-Marie's boyfriend. Rodriguez and I, as well as the Task Force 500 command, had known about it for some time. Such relationships are severely frowned upon by the army, but we were willing to turn a blind eye to it so long as both of them maintained a sufficient level of discretion. They had managed that so far, aside from one embarrassing encounter when I went looking for Anne-Marie in her tent and found the two of them "resting" on her cot. My instincts told me to say no to this proposed partnership, but Anne-Marie had spent some time preparing her case. She argued that this interrogation would require substantial analytical support and that Harper, with his top secret clearance, had access none of the interrogators did. I wasn't entirely persuaded, but I didn't have a compelling reason *not* to allow them to work this one together, so I gave in.

As the clock ticked and mealtimes passed with no update from Anne-Marie, it dawned on me that she and Harper had been in the booth with 237 for seven hours. I began to get excited, hoping that perhaps Anne-Marie had produced another coup; maybe she was in the midst of breaking a disappointed would-be highjacker, his participation in the plot thwarted by some incredible chain of events now being recorded by her pen. But after eight hours, Walker and Harper emerged exhausted and frustrated. Anne-Marie was so shaken by the encounter that she suggested that she shouldn't go back in. The prisoner was "too much," she said. Paul disagreed. He claimed to see indications that this fair-skinned, black-bearded Saudi was wearing down.

Other interrogators in the office, including Davis, Kampf, and Heaney, gathered around to listen to the back brief. By Anne-Marie's account, 237 was as smart and smooth as any prisoner we had encountered. He spoke flawless English, with barely the trace of an accent, and unlike other prisoners, who were rattled when confronted by a young female interrogator, 237 was dismissive and aloof. He just shook his head and refused to answer some questions, as if they were unworthy of his time and attention. He had the manner of someone with city hall connections waiting for the new cops on the beat to realize the magnitude of their mistake in detaining him. At one point, he offered to provide names, addresses, and telephone numbers of American citizens — his former teachers, classmates, and landlords — saying they would corroborate his story and dispel any suspicions we might have about his past.

And yet, here he was in Afghanistan, engaged in deception tactics that were so clearly out of the Al Qaeda resistance manual that Anne-Marie could practically recite chapter headings.

For example, though he'd spent years in America, he pretended to be incapable of using anything but the Muslim calendar. He would be quite docile for a stretch, then suddenly become very boisterous, arguing we had no legal authority to keep him in custody and demanding a clear explanation of his rights. It was strange to see a prisoner trying techniques that we hadn't encountered in months. We thought perhaps he had been on the run and isolated from the fleeing Arab scene in Pakistan's cities, where more sophisticated resistance techniques were being devised and spread by word of mouth. Heaney, the computer consultant, likened 237's lies to a "virus from 1996 trying to get past modern virus-protection software."

Although the prisoner was insisting that he was innocent — and that he had gone to school in Arizona simply to study aeronautical engineering — he made little effort to obscure his extremely suspicious subsequent travels and activities. He had been to Afghanistan numerous times, stayed at Pakistani madrassas, and was spotted hanging out with other Middle Eastern terrorist organizations. There were sparse OGA reports on him — as if he were enough of a well-known figure in Al Qaeda that they had an existing file on him, with information from other sources. One report said he had been associated with Hamas. And he made no effort to conceal the fact that he was an admirer of the Taliban, praising the purity of its Islamic rule and rattling off statistics on how crime had declined and the number of schools had risen during the regime's tenure.

Of course, I was very concerned that my chosen interrogator hadn't cracked 237 — and that she was so rattled she felt uncertain she ought to continue. But I dismissed Anne-Marie's wobble and told Rodriguez that I wanted to allow her a chance to refine her strategy. She started working out a new game plan while Harper set about using his access to the top secret Internet to research the upper echelon of Al Qaeda for clues about where this prisoner might fit in. Carlson, our assigned analyst, reviewed the mug books and past reports in search of a clue or description from some prisoner in the past that might fit the restless bearded man next door.

When Anne-Marie and Harper went back in with the prisoner, he threatened to go on a hunger strike to protest what he characterized as our "outrageous treatment." This was worrisome because we had seen reports that prisoners at GTMO were on hunger strikes and that medics had to feed them via intravenous drips. I had stayed away from the booth for Anne-Marie and Harper's first session with 237, but this time I positioned myself outside the door to listen. The prisoner was just flicking away her questions with unresponsive questions of his own. At one point she asked why he was active in the Islamic society at his university.

"Why does someone join a fraternity or a sorority?" he asked in return.

"You're not in a position to ask me questions!" Anne-Marie said.

Right away, I was disappointed with how Anne-Marie was handling things. As a rule, she was extremely disarming when she entered the booth. She was so petite and youthful, she was like someone's little sister. But she was a thinker, and at Kandahar she lured prisoners into making mistakes because they underestimated her and got themselves caught up in skeins of contradictory claims. She was so good at keeping her cool that the prisoners would lose theirs. But now, for some reason, she was straying from this approach, adopting the manner of an angry, at-her-wit's-end mother. And Harper's one-dimensional, confrontational style was only reinforcing this unproductive dynamic.

When they came out, the report they delivered was in the

defeated tone of a postmortem. "The prisoner exhibited continued resistance to interrogators' attempts to unseat him from current positions, which we regard as fabrications." In other words, they had failed to break the prisoner and didn't have a clear idea how to proceed.

Three or four weeks into my tour at Bagram, the telephone rang just after shift change. The MPs said there was a Mr. Josh Rhodes to see "the officer-in-charge." Rodriguez was out, so I went down and introduced myself as the senior sergeant. He was a very unassuming man, very sober. I knew what he was here for the second I saw his very expensive-looking luggage. He was from the U.S. Army Intelligence and Security Command, and he came with his lie detector.

We had been told at Kandahar that we were supposed to get one of the machines, but it never materialized. Rodriguez, who had a bee in his bonnet about lie detectors, was happy about that. He dreaded the effect the machine would have on the troops, believing they would become dependent on the device and stop trusting their own instincts and judgment. "Jeez, Mack, can't people just do their jobs?" he asked.

I was aware of the scientific community's skepticism of the effectiveness of the lie detector, that studies showed it was a far-from-foolproof indicator of deception. But I didn't agree with Rodriguez — we had to take every possible advantage. Just hooking detainees up to the contraption would probably scare some truth out of them.

When Rodriguez returned, I hid my enthusiasm. "Chief, this is Josh Rhodes," I said. "He's here with his lie detector."

Out of nowhere, Turner butted in with a loud buzzer sound. "AHHHNT!" he said, shaking his finger at us. "It's a 'polygraph.'"

We looked at him as if he were insane. He just smiled a rather worrying smile and went back to the laptop screen.

Rhodes asked for a summary of each prisoner we wished to submit for the polygraph, so I sent out word for all the echoes to submit recommendations by the end of the day. It was going to add hours to their workload, but I figured it would be worth it. But when Rhodes approached me the next afternoon, he said there wasn't a single prisoner who qualified. I was stunned. Rhodes said there had to be "measurable truths" we were trying to establish and that the cases we had recommended did not meet that criteria. It was this sort of bullshit that again and again made me wonder if we were actually going to win this war. He had come to Bagram — no doubt at great expense — taken my interrogators' off-line to prepare recommendations, only to tell us that not one of the more than one hundred prisoners in custody was a candidate for his machine. If Rodriguez hadn't intervened, I would have thrown Rhodes out of the Facility, but he ended up leaving on his own.

Our next guests from intelligence looked a little like my father when he worked as a lineman at the phone company years ago. There were two of them, both with tool belts that had terraced compartments loaded with gadgets and tools. One of the men had a "Marine Corps Birthday Run — 1994" T-shirt on. (Okay, okay — you were in the service at one point, too. Got it.) The other was carrying two full-sized flashlights, even though whenever he needed to illuminate something he used a tiny one on his key chain. They were nice guys, and Chief Rodriguez was delighted to inform me that they were here to talk to us about bugging the interrogation rooms. I suggested we also bug the prisoners' cages on the main floor.

These two guys noodled around the Facility for about two hours with Rodriguez and me in tow. The main issues were macro: where would we put the control room? Who would staff it? What would we do with the prisoners while we were installing the microphones? After sizing up the Facility, our two guests stepped outside — I pictured them climbing into a Ford

Econoline van loaded with spools of wire and tiny electronic parts — and we never saw them again.

With our interrogation of 237 in shambles, I was coming under increasing pressure to change interrogators. The OGA, the FBI agents, the Joint Working Group, and even Davis had all, in one way or another, expressed their misgivings about allowing Anne-Marie to continue. Task Force Steve took me behind the curtain overlooking the prisoner cages and questioned my judgment in allowing two soldiers who were romantically involved to work together. He was right. Fraternization in a combat zone is strictly prohibited, and my decision to overlook that policy must have made me look like a politically correct patsy.

Steve wanted to put in Kampf, the interrogator he seemed most enamored of. I thanked him for his suggestions and told him that I wanted to think things through and would make a decision within an hour.

Fitzgerald said later that he knew exactly what I would do, and perhaps it was rather predictable. To set the effort back on course, I told Anne-Marie that I was going to go in to speak with 237 myself. I wondered whether it would be fair to use a switch-hitter. Would it violate the Geneva Conventions or somehow nudge us off the moral high ground to come in with a fresh interrogator after the prisoner had been exhausted by another? Rodriguez and I thought about this for a while before we came up with a way — some would say a preposterous way — to justify it. We tabulated the number of hours of sleep that I had had in the past few days versus the number of hours of sleep that Anne-Marie and the prisoner had had in the same time. By our count, I'd had just two or three hours more sleep than the prisoner since he'd arrived. That was close enough for me.

I sent Anne-Marie back into the booth with 237 to give me time to prepare an interrogation plan for myself. I went in at 0400 hours, planning to question him up to the 0930 meeting.

Prisoner 237 was being held in a room along the balcony several times larger than the other booths. The plywood on the windows had fallen down, and cool air was streaming in. He was young-looking and thin, with a slightly receding hairline and a black beard. He was sitting on a cot, his spine perfectly straight, one leg draped over the other, his hands clasped in his lap, a posture that betrays very little of a person's thoughts or emotions. It looks relaxed, but really it's locked down. The hands are held in place to refrain from making unnecessary gestures. Crossed legs keep feet from tapping or wrapping nervously around the legs of a chair. If the one dangling foot bounces a bit, well, that might be a sign of anxiety, or it might mean a person is enjoying the banter. And the combination of it all — the hands, the legs, the back — keeps a person from leaning forward or pulling back in reaction to a pointed question. The expression on his face was almost placid, and his eyes were bright. Prisoner 237 was ready.

My first impression was that this guy was a thinker, the first that I had encountered. He had the look of someone who wasn't at the top of the organization yet — whatever that organization was — but was making his way up; he was someone on whom senior figures would depend. And he was supremely confident. Before I could ask him a question, he asked one of me: "May I help you?"

When an interrogator faces a prisoner who tries to reverse roles that way, the tendency is to try to shut him down, the way Anne-Marie had. But a prisoner like 237 will see that as a sign of insecurity — the fact that the interrogator feels a need to assert control indicates a certain lack of control. I didn't respond to his question and, for the most part, ignored all of the questions that followed. And there were many. In the course of several hours, he asked about my religion, asked whether I had read T. E. Lawrence and *From Beirut to Jerusalem*. He was measuring me as much as I was measuring him, if not more. When we spoke about his time at the university in Arizona, he asked me where I had gone to school. This question I answered, hoping to draw him out on his experience in America, get him talking about his time out West. When I told him I had gone to Fordham, he replied that it was a "third-tier school."

If my personal pride was wounded by his dismissal, my professional side was pleased. Our personalities make us who we are, but in interrogation, they can also unmake us. The Fordham remark said a lot about 237, a prisoner, it now seemed to me, whose self-esteem depended on achieving a sense of superiority over others, whether it was an interrogator sitting across from him in the booth, a religious scholar in a madrassa, or, perhaps, the peers he measured himself against in Al Qaeda. I had gleaned some of this from Anne-Marie's interrogations before I even entered the booth, and it was on the basis of this analysis that I created my plan, essentially a Pride and Ego Down. I set out to convince him that we saw him as a small fish, which I thought might serve two purposes. In the best-case scenario, it might provoke him to disclose information to prove our underestimation of him wrong. Alternatively, smugness might make him so confident of our ineptitude that he would take a carefully prepared piece of bait.

The bait I had in mind was an updated version of a trick the Germans had used on the British in World War I. Reading old reports when I was assembling reserve exercises back home in Connecticut, I had encountered a case in which the Germans had gotten a British officer to betray the dispositions of the British line by convincing him that if he cooperated he would be eligible for a prisoner swap. The Germans were lying, but in both world wars and in the Civil War there were cartels by which prisoners would be exchanged, sometimes with the stipulation that they could not fight again. In my case, I told 237 that we would consider turning him over to Israel so that he could be part of an exchange of prisoners with the Palestinian authority. I described the mechanics of prisoner exchanges in great detail and named several prisoners from Hamas and Hezbollah who had been "turned over." The names were real — I had gotten them from real intelligence reports — and as I outlined this possibility, I could see that 237's wheels were suddenly turning. When he first arrived in our custody, I don't think he thought there was any way out of his situation, and so there was nothing to lose by shutting down. But now he was asking questions, and his inquisitiveness showed he was reconsidering his fate. He was also growing a little tired. As our conversation continued past dawn, his mind began to skip like a scratched CD. Twice I got him to give up names of people at a madrassa in Pakistan — he had refused to give such names to Anne-Marie.

At a few minutes past 0900, I instructed the guard to bring in a halal meal and told 237 that I was required in a meeting but would be back shortly. He asked if he could rest. I told him neither one of us was going to rest until we were able to figure out what his future would be. The morning meeting was more crowded than usual, with officials from our command, the Joint Working Group, Task Force Hatchet, the OGA station in Kabul, and the FBI all in attendance. Partly to punish them for second-guessing me, I made them sit through reports on all the other interrogations before getting to 237's story. When we finally got to that point, I described the progress with the prisoner, but attributed it to Anne-Marie, saying she had loosened the jar and I was just twisting it off.

As the meeting broke up, I sat down at a laptop to put together the second part of my plan for 237. There was something else I had picked up on during our five-hour chat: a seeming preoccupation with death. It was a subject he returned to, in glancing fashion, repeatedly. It first came up when he insisted that he describe for me the power of Islam to compel a man such as him, an Arab with every advantage and every ability and opportunity for success, to throw it all away for the good of his brothers. His monologue contained several references to final judgment, mortality. Then, at another point, he said he hoped "Allah would take me quickly." This was something I thought we could prey upon, but would have to do so delicately. The trick would be to get him thinking that he might be facing his demise in captivity without, as they had said at Huachuca, putting a dagger on the table.

Pecking away at the crusty keyboard, I typed a phony, four-page newspaper article about a batch of prisoners at Guantánamo Bay going on trial, being convicted by the military courts-martial, and getting sentences of death. The tone of the article was leftish, *against* the court decision, a touch I thought added to its verisimilitude. There were names of Al Qaeda prisoners at Guantánamo who I was certain 237 would recognize. I plucked several icons and menus off the *Los Angeles Times* Web site and pasted them around my text. When the article was finished, I passed it around to several people in the office, all of whom said it was convincingly authentic. I had Anne-Marie deliver the article to 237 — I thought he would be less suspicious if it came from her. When Anne-Marie came out of the booth a short while later, she told me 237 had grabbed the article — a collection of pages stapled together — and read it immediately.

FORT LEAVENWORTH, KS — Defying the small but vocal number of protestors who had waited until the sun began to appear over the horizon of the flat, midwestern landscape, three convicted members of Osama bin Laden's global network of terror were executed for their role in the 9/11 attacks on New York and Washington, D.C.

The protestors, a mixed group of Americans of Arab descent, death penalty opponents, and antiwar activists, passed the last minutes before the scheduled execution in a frenzy of shouts through anguished tears. When six o'clock, the appointed hour of death, passed, the protestors fell silent. They boarded two government-provided buses to the heckles and jeers of more than five thousand angry supporters of the execution of Amed Salim Swedan, Mohamed Fadhil and Musa'ad al-Fatuh.

And therein lies the problem, says Richard Durham, president of the American Civil Liberties Union. "What happened at the federal prison at Leavenworth yesterday was a travesty of U.S. justice about which every American should be ashamed." Mr. Durham is quick to point out that the military tribunal, convened on April 30, could never possibly have heard enough evidence to support the execution of the Saudi, Egyptian, and Qatari nationals. "It is a case of a kangaroo court in the extreme, and actually hurts our hope of catching more of those responsible for the atrocities of last fall."

At a Justice Department press conference yesterday, chaired by Attorney General John Ashcroft, the navy admiral who rendered the verdict against the three had a distinctly different opinion: "I have heard the objections of the ACLU, and can tell you that nothing could be farther from the truth," said Vice Admiral Lewis Patch. "We have thirteen of twenty-eight Al Qaeda leaders who are still alive in custody. We executed three today, two others face execution, and the remainder will not face the death penalty because of their cooperation with our ongoing investigation."

The article went on to "quote" White House spokesman Ari Fleischer and the dean of the criminal justice department at Georgetown University. It alluded to the possibility that some cooperative prisoners would be spared and placed in a witness protection program. It ended with an anonymous source telling the *Times* that "very sensitive information" had been revealed by some in custody, including "names and positions of other Al Qaeda members, some of who are presently in U.S. custody but whose identities or true roles were unclear."

Of course, it wasn't flawless, but then again, I wasn't a newspaper reporter. The long-winded lead perhaps exaggerated that paper's reputation for indulging its writers. The liberal, ACLU slant could have been a bit more subtle. But it worked. Prisoner 237 plowed through the article, Anne-Marie said, his face turning a paler shade with each page. Finally, he put it down on the table in the booth, rolled his head to the side, and vomited on the floor.

Prisoner 237's physical reaction to my newspaper story was more than even I had hoped for. It gave me fresh confidence that he could be broken if we could keep the pressure up. I went in and right away told him that if he was unwilling to cooperate with us, he could assume he would face a trial and "all of the consequences of that." The lack of specifics meant no dagger on the table. Martyrdom is fine, I told him, "but you have to admit, it's a career-limiting move."

Then I expounded on the futility of Al Qaeda's situation and again dangled the prisoner swap deal. This time I also tossed out another little detail that had just turned up in the steady stream of reports now coming back from the States on Prisoner 237: he had a young daughter still in America.

"The Afghans are cooperating and ratting out all the Arabs anyway," I said. "There is no question about the outcome. We're talking about history lessons here. Your choice is either to have your family in America read an article like this one with your name in it or to say good-bye to all of this and carry on your fight for another day."

This again was carefully constructed to prey on his ego. His self-esteem was so tied into his sense of himself as a success in

Al Qaeda that if he thought that career were over he would shut down. Alternatively, if he thought there were a chance he might resume it, he had motivation to talk.

The question that came out of his mouth was exactly what I wanted to hear. He didn't protest his innocence. He didn't try to revert to his lame cover story. He was taking the bait.

"You are going to let me go just like that?"

"I am going to be honest with you in a way that I know you are not going to like but I think you have to understand," I said. *"We don't think you are that important."*

I watched him and got goose bumps at his reaction. He leaned back in his chair and smiled and laughed. "I think you had better hope that you are right if that's the decision you have reached," he said.

"Well, welcome to the world of international espionage," I said as condescendingly as possible. "You are a newcomer. We have been in this business for a long time. There are risks and there are rewards."

"And you will be satisfied with a history lesson as a reward?"

"I will be satisfied when you answer the questions that I pose to you."

Prisoner 237 thought about this for several moments. As he did so he closed his eyes and incurred the wrath of the guard, who shouted at him to stay awake. The prisoner was exhausted. His eyelids were falling because it took all his energy to think.

Suddenly, 237's story changed. He wasn't just an itinerant religious scholar but on the staff of an Islamic charity that had been placed on the U.S. State Department's terrorist list in January 2002. It was an offshoot of another "charity" that was set up by bin Laden. He didn't want to be truthful with us up until this point, he said, because he "did not want to endanger the organization" or its "important work." I regarded this as a positive triumph. I had shaken him from his initial story and now forced him to a second one. All that was left now was the patient peeling back of this onion.

Then a knock on the door interrupted us. Outside were Hartmann, Vaughn, Hasegawa, Kampf, Rodriguez, and Walker. In the last few hours, the FBI had filed another report on 237's studies in Arizona, but the most important information came from Kampf. He said he had just learned from Aier that 237 had taken the *Bayatt* — the blood oath of loyalty to bin Laden — in a ceremony in Afghanistan just a year earlier. The timing matched up with when 237 had, by his own admission, been in the country. I went back in the booth, gathered my things, and stopped the session with no explanation.

We went back to the ICE and huddled for about thirty minutes. Hasegawa and others were convinced this prisoner had been plotting harm to Americans, if not participating directly in the September 11 plan. I wasn't ready to leap to that conclusion but was sure by this point that 237 was at least a logistics person for Al Qaeda, perhaps a coordinator for sleeper cells.

When you're in the heat of an interrogation, and you get something as powerful as the information Kampf had gotten from Aier, it's almost impossible to resist the overwhelming urge to use it. Everyone in the room agreed that we had to confront 237 immediately, inform him in forceful fashion that we now had him by the balls. And so that is what we did.

I went back into the booth with Anne-Marie — I wanted 237 to see us as a team — and we laid it all out for him. We told him that we had two prisoners (we fabricated the extra source) saying they'd witnessed him taking the *Bayatt*. And almost immediately I regretted it.

The prisoner looked back at us and said, with no change of expression, "I don't know what you're talking about."

As he said this, he took his right leg off of its resting position on the knee of the left. Instead, he tucked his right foot underneath his left thigh so that he was now sitting on the foot, causing the leg iron to go taut. Prisoner 237's reactions in the booth were powerfully physical. The best example was his gastric response to the *Times* article. This change of posture was extremely telling. He was retooling his defenses. He had processed our accusation, determined in seconds how he would reply, and was now physically realigning himself for this new direction in our dialogue.

For the next several hours, we came at 237 from every direction and could not get him to budge. If anything, he grew more resolute and retreated even from some of his previous admissions.

I had thought we had him on the ropes, that he was tired, still reeling from the phony newspaper clip, and that confronting him with our new find would be a tremendous kick to the groin. But we had miscalculated horribly, for two main reasons. First, confronting him with the fact that he had taken the *Bayatt* only reminded him of his blood oath and of how close he was coming to betraying it. Sometimes betrayal becomes a cycle for prisoners. They reveal more than they should, become disgusted with themselves for doing so, and in that wretched state of mind convince themselves that they were never capable of resistance in the first place, and they reveal more. I was hoping we might enter this cycle with Prisoner 237, but he cut it off before it started. The other reason was that confronting 237 had eliminated his incentive to talk. I had hoped that he would see the window for escape — the prisoner swap — closing. Instead, he saw it slam shut. Now, no matter what we said, he knew there was no way we were going to let him go.

We huddled in the ICE one more time but couldn't reach any conclusions about how to proceed. After arguing in circles for the better part of an hour, we agreed to take a break, to rest up for four hours and then come back. It was midnight, and I was on the verge of collapse. I wandered over to the command facility and took a shower, then made my way back to my cot. I woke up at about 3:30 in the morning to make a trip to the MP Porta-Johns. Walking down the balcony, I looked in to see 237. He should have been asleep — I had intentionally woken up about twenty-five minutes before our four-hour time limit on sleep expired. But instead he was sitting on the floor, Indian style, while a man in uniform sat in the chair looming over him. Colonel Foley, the top intelligence officer with the U.S. military command in Afghanistan, was interrogating 237 himself.

Enraged, I ran back to the ICE and entered the little cubby that served as Chief Rodriguez's office. He was asleep at his desk.

"Chief?"

"Mack?"

"Colonel Foley is in with one of the prisoners."

"What?"

"He's in the booth with 237."

Rodriguez pushed me aside, and I followed him as he walked down the balcony, knocked on the door, and, very politely, poked his head inside and said, "Sir, can I just see you one second please?"

Foley came out of the room smiling sheepishly and saying, "Good morning."

He claimed that he had just been on a visit to the Facility and saw 237 alone in the booth, a "target of opportunity," Foley said. He said he knew we were having trouble and put his hands up to make quotation marks around the word *trouble*. I have no doubt that he was acutely aware of the trouble we were having. Here was a prisoner positively identified as Al Qaeda who had spent time at an aviation school in the United States, and we hadn't come close to breaking him. This must have come up in every Joint Working Group briefing and been the subject of great consternation to every officer up and down the intelligence chain of command.

"Sir, we cannot allow anyone but interrogators in with the

prisoners," Rodriguez said, his loyalty to me probably making him take a bit harder line with Foley than he would have liked.

"Yeah, yeah, yeah, I know," Foley said dismissively. "From now on I'll leave it to the experts." He was walking down the balcony toward the stairs. I was as furious as I had been at any moment in my experience in the army. If Foley had been a captain or a lieutenant, I'm sure I would have pursued this with the command. But he was a colonel confronted by a chief warrant officer and a sergeant first class. There wasn't much we could do but watch him walk away.

I tried to exact a small measure of revenge by removing his name from the access roster. But that only caused a ruckus a few days later and earned me a lecture from Major Gibbs, a whirlwind of a woman who was in the process of replacing Hartmann and Vaughn as our liaison to the Joint Working Group.

At the 0930 meeting several hours later we got devastating news: 237 would be placed on the next plane to Guantánamo.

I went in with 237 one last time for a session that only punctuated our record of failure with this prisoner. As soon as I sat down, he told me he was certain that we had made up our minds about him and that he had now decided to remain silent and put his fate in the hands of Allah. In desperation, I told him that I thought that his was a very good game, that he could keep his defenses up longer than any prisoner I'd seen. But it was only a matter of time, I said, before he broke, whether that was at Bagram or at Guantánamo. He replied that after a while the truth would blur for him, and that he would say whatever we wanted to hear just to have the solitude that would come from the end of our questioning.

A few days later, 237 was off to GTMO. I knew that I had bungled the interrogation horribly and that my management of it had cost us dearly. Anne-Marie was the wrong choice. She showed me that interrogators' methods change even over relatively short amounts of time, and not always for the better.

The fake *Times* article had worked beautifully, but I didn't follow up quickly enough. Confronting him with the *Bayatt* was another blunder. We had also undermined ourselves by letting him see so many faces — first Anne-Marie's, then mine, then, inexplicably, Foley's. Even the FBI had managed to spend some time in the booth with him. Prisoners know they're winning when their interrogators keep getting swapped out. Finally, allowing ourselves to rest was a mistake because it let him get some rest too. That was enough to rejuvenate him, to give him new energy to resist our questions.

I made mental notes of all these shortcomings. We needed to learn from them because by this point the war in Afghanistan had devolved into an endless series of raids and manhunts for Al Qaeda and Taliban leaders and lieutenants. If we were going to break them, we would need to do a much better job than we'd done with 237.

Our civilian intelligence counterparts referred to themselves as "OGA." When in sympathetic company, our British intelligence friends preferred to refer to their American counterparts as "OTT," or Over the Top. It was a good summation. The agents from the FBI, on the other hand, were regular guys with real names, and wives and kids back home whose pictures they were eager to show you. They respected soldiers, it seemed to me, maybe because some of them had been servicemen before, maybe because they weren't and wished they had been. They talked about home and offered to take mail back for you or give you access to their e-mail system if the line got long in our tent.

John and Eamon were the first FBI types I managed to get friendly with, though not the first I had worked with. The first time I saw them, John, the bigger of the two, was wearing a T-shirt with a "Never Forget — NYPD Emerald Society Mourns Their Own 9/11/2001" emblem. Eamon was only marginally more discreet, wearing a navy-blue golf shirt emblazoned with a stitched logo of a Long Island public golf course. Both had crew cuts and salt-and-pepper hair, Claddagh rings, and khaki shorts with holsters holding Glock pistols. These two guys were the older brothers of practically every kid I had ever gone to school with. Meeting them actually made me a little homesick.

Once or twice a week during their seven- or eight-week stay, the two New Yorkers would show up for the "roundup" meetings Rodriguez and I had at the end of each day, usually at 2100 hours, to swap notes on the day gone by and talk about the agenda for the next morning meeting. John and Eamon used the roundups as their chance to get little tidbits of news, which they loved sending back to the bureau in New York before the information came out in official channels. They'd listen to Rodriguez and me rattle on about the direction of the interrogations and collection priorities and offer whatever help they could to resolve any questions we had. They also kicked around the Facility for a few hours after the "roundup" to see if tired interrogators taking smoke breaks had any other insights. Then, about an hour before midnight, they'd pop in and let me know by wink and nod that they were going to retire to their own "Facility." If I were able, I'd excuse myself — ostensibly for my evening shower — and stroll behind the massive hangar that housed the Puzzled Palace, over to the VIP tent where the FBI agents and other intelligence types lived.

It was a long tent — actually several connected end to end — with a wooden floor covered in red industrial carpet. The tent was divided into two-man "rooms" by flannel drapes that formed walls around each two-cot section. The rooms were a mess, with individual equipment and coolers and newspapers lying around. There was no mistaking this area as one occupied by short-termers. It was the kind of mess officers make when they are not forced to set the example.

Whenever I was in this tent I felt as if I were sneaking into the first-class cabin on an airplane. At the end of the tent there was a kind of kitchenette on the left and a computer set up for unclassified e-mail on the right. My civilian clothes shielding me from the suspicious looks of the occupants, I would make my way to the far back to where John and Eamon had staked out the most prime real estate of all: a back bedroom that opened out onto a patio. Outside were chairs and little coffee tables made from pallets by local Afghan carpenters hired privately for the work. There was a halved fifty-gallon drum on a platform for barbecuing. Just off the wooden deck that formed the floor were hulks of Russian MIGs and rusting HIND helicopters, all resting at acute angles, with cockpits slung open. In the moonlight, you could just make out the snow on the highest peaks in the distance.

The beer was some Uzbek commercial variety with blue labels and silver writing. The bottles were big, and two was plenty for me if I was going to maintain my balance. They liked to throw the empties into the darkness toward the MIGs, placing the incriminating evidence into the surrounding minefields. John and Eamon had cigars, and I quietly hoped that the red embers at the ends of our stogies weren't helping some sniper find us in his scope. They also had a satellite phone, which they insisted I use to call home or my girlfriend in England. I did, several times.

Sometimes the cavernous tent would yield up some curious officer serving in Bagram on a temporary basis, like some consultant in town for a project. John and Eamon would keep their company, but the beer was strictly for friends. With Bronx-Irish moxie, they would deny interlopers' requests for brew — "Nah, we're all out" — then pull another bottle for themselves from the ice chest minutes later. Nobody ever made a second request: they got the idea.

THE KID

Every now and then, we would walk down to in-processing and find a smooth-faced teenager standing among the lined-up bearded men. When teens were brought in, it was generally because the Special Forces or Rangers didn't think they had any choice: the kid's father or uncle was being taken into custody, and there was no other relative to leave the teen with at the raid site. The MPs in our facility never put bags over the boys' heads and never put their hands or feet in shackles. I saw only a dozen or so teens taken into custody while I was in Afghanistan, and they truly were handled with kid gloves.

Major Gibbs, our new liaison to the Joint Working Group with the departure of Hartmann and Vaughn, practically adopted every youth that came into custody, hovering over them, raiding the mess hall for every container of chocolate milk she could find, and generally mothering them. Doctors gave the kids full checkups, and we arranged to have the army dentists examine their teeth. The MPs were extremely gentle with underage prisoners, and the interpreters absolutely doted on the kids, checking in on them every half hour, reading books to them at night. We tried not to put kids in the general-population cages; we didn't want them around the other adult prisoners. Instead, we put them in an empty booth or a VIP room with an MP — usually a female — stationed outside twenty-four hours a day. If the boy had a relative that had been taken

into custody with him, we put the two of them in the room together.

We questioned the kids but didn't *interrogate* them. I usually
sent in Anne-Marie or Pearson, females I could trust to take a
softer approach. If the teen had a relative in custody, we usually
let the relative sit in on the questioning, although always behind
the young detainee so the two couldn't interact. With underage
prisoners, we were trying to get basic information about their
families and home villages. Don't get me wrong — we gave
them ample opportunity to give us information on the men
they were captured with. But it was never confrontational, and
more of our energy was spent trying to figure out where and to
whom they should be released. The general rule was that we
didn't keep anyone under sixteen, and our goal was always to
get children out of the Facility and back home within ten days.
(That may not sound fast, but by army standards it's practically
the speed of light.) The only Arab boy I recall being sent on to
Cuba was the younger of the Syrian father-and-son team that I
had interrogated at Kandahar. All the other teens I saw were
Afghans or Pakistanis.

For all the care we took with these underage prisoners, we
didn't delude ourselves into thinking that their time with us was
pleasant. As Fitzgerald said, we were running a dungeon, and I
often wondered what sort of psychological scars the kids would
take from the experience. One teen we took into custody at
Bagram cried for the better part of two days. His uncle, with
whom he was captured during a raid in the south, didn't want
to be taken out of the general-population cages because he considered it preferential treatment that would cause him to lose
face with the other prisoners, so we put the boy in with Papa
Smurf, where the kid continued sobbing and wouldn't stop. He
looked about thirteen and must have been about four and a half
feet tall. Smurf did everything he could to console the kid and
kept scolding us for taking him into custody. "Why? Why do

you take him? Why do you bring him? What could he know?"
We tried bringing the uncle up for visits every few hours, which
drove the MPs crazy and only gave Smurf a temporary respite
from his roommate's tears. Finally the uncle gave in and agreed
to take one of the VIP rooms with the kid. Not long after, they
were released.

The most unusual prisoner we ever encountered was a teenager named Hadi. Even the circumstances of his arrival were
strange — he was delivered to us alone, in the middle of the
day. I remember seeing him for the first time as he stood erect
while his picture was snapped for our mug shot book. His features were neither Afghan nor Arab; his face was smooth and
round, and his hands and feet were already full-grown, waiting
for the rest of his body to grow into proportion. His straight
hair was parted in the center, giving him the look of an urban
skater. He was wearing baggy white pants and a white top over
a T-shirt with blue ribbing around the collar.

Most prisoners arrived at the Facility in states of supreme
agitation. Indeed, most young prisoners were crying. But Hadi
was remarkably composed, even capable of offering a tentative
smile to a soldier arriving to witness his in-processing. Heaney
conducted a toned-down screening, in which the kid said he
was Indonesian and that he was seventeen. Few prisoners we
saw spoke more than one language, and if they did, they tended
not to admit it. But when Heaney asked Hadi what languages
he spoke, he freely offered that he spoke Indonesian, some Arabic, and even a bit of broken English.

The first question I had about this prisoner was what were
we supposed to do with him. And that proved to be difficult
to answer. Kampf questioned him, and so did Walker. Both
came away saying they believed the essence of his story was
true. He said he grew up in Indonesia and had run away from
home after a falling-out with his parents. He was only the third

prisoner we had from that country, and his unfamiliar features had the other prisoners in the cage squinting at him. He admitted that he had become a small-time player in a criminal syndicate selling everything from drugs to forged passports but had never been in "serious" trouble. He was in our custody now, he said, because he had stumbled into some sort of sting operation. Indeed he had. A check of classified reports showed that he was one of three prisoners captured in a choreographed U.S.-Indonesian snatch near Surabaya, a city about four hundred miles southeast of Jakarta. The other two prisoners were Arabs that the OGA had apparently decided to keep. Only Hadi was discarded by OGA and sent to us. After his first interrogation, he changed his age as he had given it to Heaney; he now claimed to be fifteen.

His story was plausible but problematic. Kampf and Anne-Marie both thought he was clearly older than fifteen and that he had probably tried to shave two years off his age after spending a night in the cages with other prisoners who no doubt told him underage detainees were released. He certainly didn't leave anybody with the sense that he was a foreign fighter, or somehow connected to the Taliban or Al Qaeda despite the unexpected emphasis on Indonesia and the Philippines in our Washington-dictated collection emphasis. But aspects of his story were disconcerting. How did a runaway teen from Indonesia know so many languages? What was he doing with those Arabs near Surabaya? Why was he so unfazed by being in a U.S. prison in the middle of a war zone? Why had the OGA pawned only him off on us?

Since I was going to have to make the call on what to do with this prisoner, I went in to question him myself. I walked him through the time line he had given Walker, and he didn't miss a step. Toward the end, he started to ask a couple questions of me. He said he could hear planes nearby and wondered whether he was being held at an American air base — he didn't know he was in Afghanistan. In particular, he wondered whether there were fighter planes on the base. When I told him that was possible, he smiled and said, "Just like *Top Gun!*"

It wasn't until my second session with him that a tiny crack opened. I was trying to get him to talk about his background in more detail, and so we started comparing what it was like to grow up in America versus where he had grown up. I'd start many of my sentences by saying, "Back home in the States . . . ," and he'd think for a minute and come back with observations about his homeland, saying, "In Indonesia . . ." Then he slipped. At a fairly meaningless moment in our conversation, under no pressure whatsoever, he started to tell me about another piece of his childhood, but instead of placing the events in Indonesia, he said, "In Sudan . . ."

The sentence skidded to a stop right there, and Hadi froze for a moment. He realized he'd just told me where he was originally from, and he must have known that Arabs immediately fell under greater suspicion than Afghans or Pakistanis or even baffling cases from Indonesia. He looked at me for a second, and then started laughing. He laughed and laughed as though he had been caught on camera doing something silly. I smiled back and pushed a can of Coke toward him across the table. It was a tiny gesture, but I think he was both surprised and reassured that he didn't get in trouble for having lied. It broke the ice, probably provided the first indication that we Americans could be trusted, and over the next several hours, he told a much more detailed story that was almost Dickensian in its character. No doubt some of it was embroidered for effect, exaggerated to elicit sympathy from his interrogator. But at the same time, I often got the sense that there were more disturbing aspects of his story that he was skipping over. There were sudden turns in his life that seemed sharper than the circumstances required, and a string of severed relationships that bespoke deeper problems than he disclosed, starting with his decision to leave home.

Hadi said his father was a Sudanese "import-export" man and his mother Indonesian. He was born in Sudan but had moved with his family to Indonesia when he was very small. His father was a much more devout and strict Muslim than Hadi wanted to be. By the time he was a teenager, he was skipping Friday prayers to carouse with his friends in the more affluent, expatriate neighborhoods of Jakarta. He was also always very curious about the West, drawn to its movies, music, clothes, and culture. He seemed to spend much of his money on American sneakers. His father so disapproved of this fascination that he would fly off into fits of anger if Hadi so much as came home wearing a T-shirt with a Nike logo. Over time, the friction with his father became so severe that the father gave him an ultimatum: abide by Muslim strictures or leave. Hadi told me he left — about six months before he came into our custody.

He tried to stick with school for a while but gave up and got by stringing together odd jobs and assignments as a spotter or runner for drug peddlers and crooks — a far cry from what sounded like a fairly middle-class background. He crashed at older friends' houses at first but later scraped together enough money to stay in a cheap hotel.

Not long after he began staying there, three men with the Indonesian intelligence service approached him and questioned him. This part of the story seemed plausible to me because we were aware that Indonesian intelligence had hotels, markets, bazaars, and other public facilities under surveillance as part of their search for suspicious Arabs living in Indonesia as well as other unsavory foreigners. Like their subcontinental equivalents along the mountainous eastern borders of Afghanistan, Indonesian intelligence agents were said to be collecting U.S.

bounties for any Arab they turned in. They probably had as much trouble figuring out what to do with Hadi as we did — he looked like he could be from practically anywhere, and his language skills would have served him well in over half the world. The leader of this trio offered to take Hadi from the hotel and set him up in a nearby safe house. Hadi said the man, whom he called Harjantee, simply wanted to help the troubled teen. I'm sure there was more to it than that, but I didn't start to piece it together until later. Hadi, low on money and happy to be offered a free place to stay, went along. He was taken to a nearby factory warehouse, empty and on the edge of Jakarta, where there was a back room equipped with some beds and a kitchen. Harjantee left him for the night and came back the next day with some fresh clothes. He was accompanied by two Indonesians who also became short-term residents of the safe house.

Despite pressure from Harjantee, Hadi didn't want to go back to his parents and was beginning to think that his best option would be to get to Oman or the United Arab Emirates, where he thought some distant members of his father's family would take him in. Harjantee said he would help Hadi get there, but as the weeks went by, it became clear Harjantee didn't intend to fulfill that promise. Hadi was becoming increasingly valuable to Harjantee's operation, working as a talented snitch, scouting Jakarta's small but concentrated Arab community for anyone suspicious, and pocketing money when his information led to arrests. Hadi's ambiguous features enabled him to blend in with different crowds, and his language skills allowed him to listen in on almost any conversation. He learned to walk past sites he thought might be safe houses without drawing so much as a suspicious glance from posted lookouts. He learned to spot telltale signs of Arabs in hiding, like purchases of ethnic food at local markets in quantities that suggested something other than innocent culinary experiments by locals.

But Harjantee also seemed to be growing personally attached to Hadi, increasingly adamant that the boy not leave. Hadi tried once, after a feud with one of his Indonesian roommates, only to have one of Harjantee's men pick him up on the street hours later and persuade him to return. Back inside the safe house, Hadi said he found Harjantee sitting on his bed, sobbing and begging him to stay. When Harjantee heard about the spat between Hadi and the roommate, the Indonesian intelligence officer became enraged, telling the offender that if he so much as looked cross-eyed at the boy he would kill him.

Hadi stayed in the house only a short while longer before he decided to leave again, this time for good, and with the "help" of his vagrant roommates. One of the two, a man named Surya, offered to introduce Hadi to a man who might help him get to Oman. They traveled to a bustling market area in Jakarta and waded through thick crowds to an out-of-the-way shop. Out front were brass pots and cookware. In back was a man named Kusuma who, by Hadi's account, was a player in a sort of transnational underground railroad. He could line up passports and airplane tickets or other transport out of the country. The reason for his roommates' kindness soon became apparent. They wanted payment of 930,000 rupiah (about $110 U.S.) for delivering Hadi. This fit with what we knew about Islamic "charities" offering cash rewards to those who helped Arabs get out of Indonesia and to less dangerous climes now that the Americans had made even this distant land too dangerous a place for militant expatriates. Kusuma was tied into Muslim Aid Fund, one of the conduits of those rewards for safely harboring Arabs. Kusuma was working both sides of the rewards game, though, sometimes taking the fund's money to hide an Arab while alternately turning other Arabs in to the authorities, depending on which side was offering the highest bounty.

Kusuma pulled a fast one on these Indonesians, too. The two of them spoke only Indonesian. After haggling with them

for a few moments, Kusuma turned to the boy. Speaking rapidly in Arabic, he told Hadi to listen and not say a word. He
said that the men were trying to sell the teen, that he was going
to refuse to pay the bounty, but that he nevertheless intended to
help Hadi. He told the boy to meet him at another location
later. Kusuma said all of this as if he were straining to see some
sign that the boy understood what he was saying, trying to confirm he understood the Arabic being spoken. Kusuma then
turned back to the two hopeful (if greedy) men with a look of
indignation. "This boy is no Arab!" he announced. "He doesn't
understand a word I'm saying." His refusal to pay the men triggered a shouting match. The two Indonesians were incredulous
and angry. They couldn't decide whether they were being had
by Kusuma or had been duped by Hadi into believing he was
Arab. Either way they weren't going to get their 930,000 rupiah, so they left with the boy, probably intending to search out
another potential buyer. But before they could do so, Hadi
slipped away from them in the market and, following instructions, hooked up with Kusuma a short while later.

Again Hadi found himself something of a kept boy. Kusuma
was essentially running a franchise operation with passport and
currency forgers of varying degrees of quality all over the place.
His brass shop in the market was his headquarters, and Arabs
snuck in practically every day trying to purchase a ticket home
and a suitable identity to foil post-9/11 security measures. Others wanted to go still farther east, to the Philippines. Hadi was
able to tell me terrific details about price fluctuations in the Indonesian market for hiding Arabs. It was almost like a stock
market, with numbers rising and falling based on the size of the
bounties the United States was paying for cooperation in the
war on terror and whether Islamic charities were willing to ex-
ceed those prices toward keeping the Arabs hidden. Saudis and
some other Gulf Arabs generally had little trouble raising the
cash for their care and continued anonymity. The minority

North Africans were usually too poor and were sometimes given up to the police for the reward. No one was in a position to trust anyone else. Arabs mistrusted the Indonesians, who were ostensibly helping them but with greater frequency were giving up their erstwhile dependents when the price was right. Indonesians mistrusted the Arabs, whom they perceived as possible agents of the police sent to root out the underground network. In addition, Indonesians sometimes became victims of Arabs who coerced and blackmailed their hosts into continued assistance.

Hadi stayed at Kusuma's house and served as a lookout for his growing operation, often perching up on a roof at the bazaar. But again, Hadi had placed his fate in the hands of someone who didn't seem eager for him to leave. Kusuma was able to arrange elaborate covers for some hiding Arabs — some of whom were very dangerous Al Qaeda types. For others he managed to produce documents of such high quality that it was increasingly possible for Al Qaeda personnel on the lam to get back to their home countries undetected. (Hadi told me one story about how Kusuma had helped a small group of Arabs leave through the port city of Java by hiding in shipping containers.) But Kusuma never seemed able to arrange Hadi's exit. Sometimes he claimed he couldn't get the correct paperwork. Other times he said Indonesian intelligence had suddenly blocked the route he had hoped Hadi could take.

After months of waiting, Hadi got what he thought was going to be his ticket home, not from Kusuma but from his old roommates from the warehouse. They returned to the brass shop one day and saw Hadi in the crowd before he saw them. After hearing his account of his frustrations with Kusuma, they again offered to help, this time by introducing Hadi to another group of Indonesian Islamic militants who were helping two Arabs escape. The plan was for the Arabs to make their way, with forged documents, into Singapore, where they would board a commercial plane at the airport and make a series of connecting flights that would take them through Moscow and eventually back to the Middle East. The scheme was preposterous, starting with the plan to get to Singapore, where security was sophisticated and the chances of duping the authorities was small. But for all his street savvy, Hadi was still a teenage kid, and he somehow failed to see all the holes in this idea. Nor did the Arabs he was traveling with. All three of them stepped right into a trap. As their vehicle approached the airport in Jakarta, the pair of Indonesian escorts in the front seat pulled over, saying they needed to take a leak. They stepped to the side of the road and kept walking. Hadi and his two Arab traveling companions knew they were had. Indonesian intelligence agents swooped in seconds later, and the three were taken away at gunpoint.

Hadi said they were driven to a sort of police substation where Hadi was separated from the Arabs and questioned by the police. At one point, Hadi said, two Americans, a man and a woman, came to question him. They were primarily interested in the Arabs with whom he had been caught and rejected his claim that he'd never seen them before that day. The Americans told Hadi that he had been caught in a sting designed to catch the people "responsible for the attacks on the Twin Towers." It was a classic Establish Your Identity approach, and it worked. Desperate to distance himself from his captured companions, he provided an account, of varying precision, concerning the passport and currency forging ring he had been a part of in Jakarta. The Americans questioned him for something like five hours and returned a second time and questioned him for another two hours. He stayed in a stockade until Indonesian police took him from his overcrowded cell and put him on an airplane. When it landed, he was transferred to a cell, where he stayed overnight and was questioned by another American in civilian clothes. He thought that he was in the United States.

He was actually in Kabul, and within hours, he would be delivered to our front door.

My interrogation notes went on for twelve pages, and his tale was so captivating I hated for the session to end. "I want you to know that I am going to ask you to tell this story again, and it had better be the same. Is there anything that you would like to change, alter, or delete before we close out this discussion?" I watched to see if he betrayed any deceit, any sign of insecurity. But he seemed completely unfazed by the admonishment or, in fact, by his entire circumstance. He smiled and told me that there was nothing he wished to change but asked if I would tell him where he was. Thinking about if for a moment, I said, "You are in the custody of the U.S. government; we are trying to ascertain who are the good guys and who are the bad guys. Which one are you?"

He looked up at me and shrugged his shoulders.

I raised my eyebrows to signal how serious I was.

"I am a good guy," he said in Arabic, with a grin. "You just don't know it yet."

Until May, the prisoners got to keep their hair and beards as long as they liked. Then an order tumbled down the chain of command — maybe it came from the provost marshal, perhaps from Cuba, we never knew — to start giving the prisoners trims. In a policy quirk that no one ever explained, all the prisoners had their hair shorn, but only the Arabs were required to have their beards shaved. The MPs called it "Operation Chop Bob."

The prisoners didn't want anything to do with this grooming. It took four MPs, all wearing rubber surgical gloves and Hefty-bag smocks over their fatigues, to hold each prisoner in place. (Three would keep the prisoner's limbs from flailing, and the fourth would stand behind and hold his head still with two hands cupped under his chin.) The barber was a tiny female MP from the deep woods of North Carolina. She'd shove a big plug of tobacco in her cheek and approach the prisoner warily, holding her implements up and out at her sides.

"All right, I'm gonna shave you," she'd say in English they couldn't understand. "And I expect you to be a good boy."

The prisoner would start jerking and screeching and flailing and yelping like a dog being held down on the examining table at the vet.

"We got a wiggler here!" she'd yell as she lunged toward the prisoner's scalp and started buzzing through thick, black, coarse hair. The bloodcurdling cries echoed across the shop floor. The other prisoners would leap from the floor and poke their heads through the wire wearing looks of bewilderment and terror. It was the most traumatic-sounding and -looking activity that ever took place in that cavernous prison. And once the rest of the prisoners caught on to what was happening, they bucked and dug in their heels as if they were being dragged to the electric chair.

I hated when it was time for the barber to go to work. It was a huge manpower drain, requiring so many MPs that it shut down interrogations for hours. I was constantly telling the female barber to "chop faster." And the interruption didn't end there. An Army Criminal Investigation Division warrant officer named Mike showed up and said all the prisoners needed to be rephotographed now that their hair and beards had been cut off. So the day after the snipping started, the snapping began too.

When the MPs brought the teenager to me the next time, I delivered dinner for two. Roast chicken, mashed potatoes, string beans, chocolate milk, and two cans of Dr Pepper. For dessert: army sheet cake with chocolate icing. The boy didn't even pause to look up at me as he answered questions between mouthfuls. When he was done, I offered him my piece of sheet cake, and he devoured that too. (I asked if he had not been fed in the cages, and he said he had actually just finished dinner before being brought before me.) Hadi was oddly upbeat under the circumstances, in captivity far away from his friends and estranged family. He peppered his Arabic with American colloquialisms. When he finished the chicken, he grinned and dubbed it "finger-lickin' good." At one point he told me about his fondness for football and made it clear he did not mean the American variety. "Football," he said, kicking out his foot. "Not *football*," he said, motioning as if he were throwing a pass.

My sessions with Hadi yielded a series of rich intelligence reports on passport and currency forgery rings; the clerics and mosques catering to Arabs seeking to get in or out of the country; the interlocking relationships between these underground networks and Islamic charities; and the swings in prices being paid by Arabs to secure their freedom. Clearly the scale of what was happening in Indonesia alarmed the community; the reports prompted a flurry of follow-up questions from every corner of it, and about a week after Hadi's arrival, there was an impromptu visit from the OGA's field station in Kabul.

Our visitors included an older OGA hand named Phil, who identified himself as the new chief of station; a younger officer named Eric, who carried a brand-new collapsible-stock Colt M-16; and a fortyish woman with a serious smoking habit and an accent straight out of Jacksonville, Florida. It was the woman from Jacksonville, sporting a terry-cloth halter top she declined to replace even when confronted with the reality of Muslim sensibilities, who wanted to see Hadi. She asked me for a rundown of the prisoner's case and didn't appreciate it when I expressed mock surprise that she didn't know Hadi's story already from his previous interrogations by the OGA in Indonesia. She was even more put off by my insistence that she share her interrogation plan with me before we entered the booth. She admitted that she had no such thing and said her visit was purely "exploratory." Guessing correctly that she spoke no Arabic, I insisted on serving as her translator, figuring that if things started to go sour I could prevent her from doing too much damage. To be sure, I called for Hadi ten minutes before she was scheduled to meet me in the booth and explained that he was going to be spoken to by "a Canadian who might be asking you some questions similar to the ones that I have already asked." I told him not to worry, and that we were offering her the opportunity to speak with him mainly because she was interested in Indonesia.

She showed up moments later in the terry-cloth top. I pulled off Hadi's knit hat, which the prisoners wore even in the early summer heat. She came in, sat down, and tried to get the conversation started with some strained small talk. "So I hear you like Tom Cruise movies?" She was surprisingly self-assured but then skipped through topics in no discernible order, prompting him for his observations of the Indonesian intelligence one minute and picking away at his relationship with the captured Arabs the next. Hadi answered the questions patiently, giving her the same answers he had given me. Then, without any segue, she pulled out her tough, TV-interrogator persona, apparently hoping to shake him. "We think that you are in Al Qaeda. What do you think about that?"

I looked at her for a moment, long enough that she turned toward me, waiting for the translation. I turned to Hadi and said, in Arabic, "We are looking for people who might be in Al Qaeda, do you know anyone who is?"

"I have never met anyone who is in Al Qaeda," he said. I converted his answer to: "Al Qaeda doesn't take fifteen-year-olds." Images of Fort Huachuca and the Vietnam video passed through my mind yet again.

The woman looked at me and jotted something down on her notepad. She took a cigarette in her mouth, held it for a minute, and touched her ears and nose. She put the cigarette out on the table before tossing the butt in a small pile on the floor. After an uncomfortably long silence, she looked at me and said, "Can I speak to you outside for a minute?" I called for an MP to look after Hadi while we stepped out of the room, and the woman and I went out onto the balcony. She wheeled around on me, her face red.

"This kid's only fifteen?'

"Yes."

"Why does it say he is seventeen on the report that y'all sent up?"

"He only told us yesterday."

"Is he lying? He could be lying."

I was tempted to be a smartass and say something about how we had never encountered any prisoners who lied. But I thought better of it. "I suppose he could be," I said. "But I am not taking any chances. The last thing I want is for the Red Cross to file a complaint that we are holding a fifteen-year-old and subjecting him to interrogation." I thought she would pull out another cigarette; you could see her thinking about it. She cocked her head and put her hand on her hip.

"Well how the fuck do you think I feel about going in to talk to a fifteen-year-old?"

"Lady, I have no idea. I figure you are with the OGA and you guys can do what you want. Didn't you guys question him already? Didn't you send him to us?"

"Oh, fuck me! Will you please go in there and tell him that we're finished talking or whatever it is you tell him?"

I sent Hadi back downstairs. He was completely bewildered by what had happened. I later told him that the lady was a crazy Canadian policewoman. Hadi never brought her up again, but the OGA did send a note that eventually reached the provost marshal's office about a "fifteen-year-old in army custody." We combed back through our records with the provost marshal standing over us and dutifully reported the youngest person that we had was seventeen. I never heard from the Jacksonville smoker again.

* * *

On the day that 237 was taken to Cuba, a new group of prisoners arrived from Pakistan. They had been captured as part of an expanding wave of cooperative sweeps by the authorities in that country's largest cities. The twenty-eight prisoners had already undergone extensive interrogations at a Pakistani prison before being turned over to us. This group came with a substantial set of notes that explained the circumstances of their capture and provided some background on what the prisoners had already revealed. In other words, they had already been exploited by the OGA and were now being turned over to us for processing so they could be sent on their way to Cuba. But for all their notes to us on these prisoners, the OGA managed to leave out one little detail: many of them had been captured with Abu Zubaydah.

Zubaydah was by far the biggest catch of the war on terrorism to that point. A thirty-one-year-old Saudi native, he was implicated in the September 11 plot and was maybe four of five on the depth chart after bin Laden. Some described him as a "choke point" in the organization: bin Laden and Aymen Zawahiri hatched the plans, but it was Zubaydah who oversaw their execution. He was grabbed in a March 28 raid on a compound in Faisalabad that erupted in a shoot-out. Zubaydah tried to escape but was shot three times, sustaining wounds to the stomach, groin, and leg. A related raid went down shortly thereafter in Lahore. We screened the new arrivals — during which some of them admitted they had ties to Zubaydah — then gathered in the ICE in the morning to go over what we'd learned. A sampling of my notes from that session — which list the prisoners' numbers, the assigned interrogators, and preliminary observations — provide a fairly typical snapshot of our guests.

T156 (Davis): 22 years old, Mauretanian.
    Arabic speaker; captured on the border of Pakistan and Iran. Lost his passport in Karachi; student; young,

cocky — nearly defiant; says he is trying to get back to Iran through Pakistan. Demands immediate release.

T157 (Hasegawa): 45 years old, from Sudan.
Arab, traveling to Iran through Peshawar.

T158 (Heaney): 31 years old, Sudan.
Caught with three other Arabs; had airline ticket and $2,000 to go to the Sudan, Syria, and Qatar. Lived in the United Kingdom, speaks English, is an accountant.

T159 (Kavalesk): 36 years old, Sudan Arab; trained in 1994 at Camp Al Farook.
Met Abdul Sheikh Al-Liby; met Abu Zubaydah in Pakistan; doesn't know how many people witnessed closing of camp outside Kandahar or who was in Zubaydah's house.

T160 (Kampf): 34 years old, Arab from Libya.
Fought with the Taliban; undoubtedly has exfiltration route information; needs to be spoken to again; called the Americans "heartless killers"; graduate of camp located outside Jalalabad; prob. involved with explosives.

T161 (Walker): British Libyan.
Desperately afraid of Libya; caught in Lahore; keeps talking about the "Sons of Khaddafi," a group of "spies" who later "found him." Weird guy.

T162 (Walker): 37 years old; Libyan; Arab.
Was a veteran of the Libyan army; entered into the fight against Russia in '94 with Chechnyan rebels; captured in Lahore; lived in guesthouses throughout Pakistan; clearly knows Zubaydah

T163 (Kampf): Sudanese; speaks Arabic and Persian Farsi.

Director of budgeting and accounting for Islamic Heritage Fund; married to a Pakistani.

T164 (Hasegawa): Knows about NGOs in Pakistan; for five years worked at Islamic Heritage Fund; gave names of heads of each IHF department; there are two guys who had come from Qatar — may know about USS *Cole* bombing. Hasegawa thinks is "too friendly."

T165 (Pearson): 32 years old; Sudanese.

Speaks Arabic and a little English; $15,000 in new U.S. bills; claims to be accountant of the Islamic Heritage Fund.

T166 (Davis and Kampf): 27 years old; Algerian.

Fought with Lashkar-e-Taiba (Pakistani militants fighting in the Kashmir); number one priority; prosthetic leg. Mines in Kashmir — W thinks is mine expert.

T167 (Kampf): 32 years old; Saudi of Yemeni descent.

Trained in Jalalabad in 2001; missing a leg; attendant at the Mecca stone in Saudi Arabia. Says leg missing from childhood accident??

T168 (Heaney): 28 years old; Egyptian.

Supposed to go to Pakistan for knee surgery; met unknown Afghani; he persuaded POW to go to Afghanistan for a "teaching"; definitely playing the language game — serious motherfucker.

T170 (Walker): 37 years old; a Sudanese.

Speaks Arabic and Pashtu, a little English; works for the Islamic Heritage Revival Society (translation mistake?); appears cooperative and helpful. Very shifty according to Walker.

T171 (Kavalesk): "Master's degree"; 49 years old; Palestinian (!?).

SSG Roberts says "guilty as sin"; shifty eyes, suspicious stories; unemployed; claims to be a former teacher.

T173 (Walker): 33 years old.

Married, one-year-old girl; captured in Lahore. Student in Peshawar and Afghanistan (Jalalabad). Crazy story about getting to Afghanistan to "save himself." The Tunisian government report says his brother is a terrorist.

T174 (Kampf): 31 years old; Lebanese; speaks Arabic well, English.

Was in the Syrian air force. Severe kidney problems. Think he is lying. Says he was a honey trader. Captured in Lahore. Doctor says good to go. Watch him.

By the time these prisoners had been turned over to us, the OGA and FBI were already acting on the information they were getting from Zubaydah, who became one of the first senior Al Qaeda figures to be taken not to Bagram or Guantánamo but to an "undisclosed location." Wherever he was, he appeared to be talking. Acting on information they said was provided by Zubaydah, the OGA and FBI arrested a former Chicago gangbanger who was accused of joining Al Qaeda and plotting to detonate a radioactive "dirty" bomb in the United States. Jose Padilla, who had changed his name to Abdullah al Muhajir, had met Zubaydah in 2001, and he been under surveillance for weeks before the thirty-one-year-old was arrested on May 8, 2002, at O'Hare International Airport after arriving on a flight from Pakistan. Padilla's plan didn't appear to be very far along, and he didn't appear to be in possession of the materials to make a dirty bomb — a device that uses conventional explosives to disperse radioactive material. But Attorney General John Ashcroft said the arrest "disrupted an unfolding terrorist plot," and Padilla, though a U.S. citizen, was designated an "enemy combatant" and transferred to a naval brig in South Carolina. Though his arrest had happened in early May, it wasn't disclosed in Washington until June 10.

I looked in on Davis one afternoon and found that he had his prisoner sitting in his chair with his arms extended on either side. He wasn't holding anything or staring into a bright light. He was just sitting there, as though he was going to flap his arms and try to fly. I told Davis he had a phone call, and he came out to the hallway.

"What's up with that guy?"

"Just your average Arab motherfucker," he said.

"Why are his arms up like that?"

"He hates Americans and feels it's necessary to keep telling me."

"Davis, you can't discipline prisoners for being glib."

"You make Carlson carry a pallet of water up to the break room because he rolls his eyes at you in the morning meeting," he said.

"I'm the asshole sergeant. I can do that. But being the interrogator does not — as you well know — make you the arbiter of justice for the detainees."

"They'll think we are total fucking pussies — we can't let them fuck us every time."

"Words are weapons. Use them," I responded, using my *Karate Kid*, Mr. Miyagi voice in an attempt to defuse the situation before Davis said something that required real discipline.

"Are we done?" he asked like a defiant teenager.

"We are done. Oh — dinner at 1645 hours. Why not be there?"

"I'll see if I'm done here," he said, pausing to see if that response would work.

"I'm sure you will be," I said.

Davis's behavior was just part of a rising trend. I was now roaming the hallway and increasingly finding prisoners in stress positions: standing, kneeling, holding their arms out in front of them, sometimes even doing push-ups. At Kandahar, I would have considered this a clear violation of the Conventions. But at Bagram, my thinking had changed. I never supported or allowed stress positions to be used as an instrument to coerce someone to talk. But I recognized that there was a need to punish prisoners for provocations in the booth. Punishing them for insulting America, as Davis had done, was not acceptable. But any sort of threatening or offensive action toward an interrogator — or a refusal to follow simple rules like staying in the chair — was fair game. I used stress positions on two prisoners myself — one for spitting at me and the other for launching into a prayer after being told to wait. (Prisoners could pray in the booth, but when I said so, not as a way to disrupt the interrogation.)

The basic rule was we couldn't punish prisoners for anything we wouldn't be punished for in our own army. We couldn't make them stay in a position any longer than a drill sergeant would require of a recruit. This sometimes meant fifteen to thirty minutes of "attitude adjustment," as they say in basic training. Of course, this had been Cavanaugh's argument at Kandahar — that he was just doing to prisoners what drill sergeants had done to us — and at the end of the day, I accepted it. Even so, I lived in fear that a prisoner would be injured while being punished, that some detainee would have a heart attack doing push-ups or something. Thus, after the first few weeks at Bagram, having prisoners kneel with their arms extended was the only stress position allowed. Having them do push-ups was silly anyway — most of them didn't even know what push-ups were, so before we could make them do a set, we first had to teach them how.

The most remarkable thing about our stress position regimen was that it was utterly unenforceable. If a prisoner had refused to adopt a stress position, there was nothing we could have done. We couldn't force them; there was no more severe punishment we could resort to. I was always worried that one prisoner would stand up to us, discover our bluff, and spread word through the cages. Amazingly, no prisoner ever so much as objected.

A few days after his marathon work on the Riverbed 32, Geoff approached me to announce that he was so exhausted that he didn't think he could continue in the booth. We talked outside the doorway to the ICE, on the balcony. The blankets that shielded the long hallway from the prisoners' view were behind us, as if we were standing on a stage in front of drawn curtains. He spoke slowly, without any of the wit or sarcasm that usually enlivened his words.

Fitzgerald was sorely disappointed that his enlistment expired but that he was still in country, and I knew he was also affected by fresh rumors that it might be months until we were relieved. He noted — again — that other agencies were rotating their interrogators out on a regular basis, an argument he cherished and articulated often.

"How can they leave us here for seven months to do this job?" he asked. "Look at your guys!" he said. "Do you see them? You are running a shop staffed by the living dead. They walk around here in dusty clothes they haven't washed in two weeks. They are the only ones on this entire base with pale skin. They are wigged out, and it's wigging me out to be around them."

I didn't have a very good answer for him. Surveying the morning meetings, I could see that the time in Bagram — about a month and a half — had been more debilitating than five months in Kandahar. And though Geoff and I were friends, he more than anyone chafed at the way I ran the place, which, he correctly assessed, was largely modeled on the work-every-one-to-the-bone world of public accounting. We had scrapped schedules in favor of minimum requirements that kept everyone in the Facility pretty much around the clock: two interrogations a day, every report finished within twenty-four hours. I kept statistics on the interrogators' productivity, tracking how many interrogations they completed, how many reports they stuffed into our records, and how many of those warranted dissemination to the intelligence community as IIRs. The numbers were all posted on a bulletin board in the ICE. If an interrogator's ratio of IIRs to interrogations fell below 33 percent, I was on his case until his numbers started climbing. It was our equivalent of a batting average. Even the morning meetings were structured to pressure interrogators to work harder. Each day, every echo had to recite what he or she had accomplished in the last twenty-four hours. If someone wasn't pulling his weight, he could expect hostile glares or worse from his peers. Just to keep up statistically, some interrogators had taken to catching up on rest in the booth. They wouldn't fall asleep, but they would pick a prisoner who required only a few bits of follow-up and stretch the session out for hours, letting the prisoner prattle on about the Koran while they stared back with glazed eyes hiding a mind that had been cycled down to sleep mode.

Though Geoff got along with the rest of the crew fairly well, they weren't exactly his crowd. They didn't get his humor or serve as an audience for his antics the way Talbot and Lawson had. In fact, he would schedule his interrogations late into the night to avoid "overexposure" to his colleagues, as he put it. While the other interrogators were getting dinner together or unwinding in the ICE after an afternoon rotation in the booths, Fitzgerald spent almost every evening in Viper City, taking din-

ner with the Afghan translators. Then he would go back to h
tent alone and shut out the world for several hours.

One purchase he made at Bagram said it all. In the midd
of this grueling period, Fitzgerald had Arnold Toynbee's
Study of History shipped to him — all twelve unabridged v
umes. Fitzgerald had a friend locate the set for him in the stac
of a rare book dealer in Fribourg, Switzerland. The friend p
chased the set for $650, had it shipped to his home on Long
land, then sent it to Afghanistan for Geoff. Each book wa
good seven hundred to eight hundred pages of dense text.
the time he left Afghanistan, Geoff had finished the first eigh

Tuning out his rant long enough to make a decision, I t
Fitzgerald that I would give him three days off. This was
heard of, and I knew that I didn't necessarily have the autho y
to do it, so I told him just to come to the morning meetings d
then go back to rest at Viper City. I knew that this would c se
some dissent once the interrogators realized what was hap n-
ing, but I hoped that three days would strike the right bala e,
short enough to fall within their tolerance, long enough to ve
Fitzgerald a second wind. I told Geoff to lay low.

THE ARAB COLONEL

———■———

One of the few reliably effective levers we had with the prisoners was convincing them that where they ended up next depended on us — which was only partially true. In Afghanistan, we only had three options: releasing prisoners, turning prisoners over to the Afghan interim authority, or sending them off to Guantánamo. I can't speak for the OGA, but no prisoner in our custody was ever turned over to another nation. Of course, that didn't mean we couldn't use fear of repatriation. We had started off with ordinary rumors about shipments to this country or that to unsettle the prisoners. Our little lie about paying countries to take these charges off our hands had sent ripples of anxiety through the cages, and the success we had with our rumor mill got me thinking about raising the stakes. I wanted to plant a series of rumors that would build toward some staged event in the cages. At one point I wrote down fifteen or sixteen ideas, then settled on five or six that seemed likeliest to work. At the next morning meeting, we spent some time discussing them in the ICE, refining the list further and settling on a plan. Then, exactly six days before the next scheduled shipment to Guantánamo, we set it in motion.

The first thing we did was select one of the English-speaking prisoners that we knew liked to gab in the cages. He had been interrogated by Davis and had given up all the information he had, but Davis cooked up some new questions as a pretext for returning him to the booth. We told Davis to use Booth 4, a cavernous space with a powerful echo. Interrogators who used the booth always came out commenting on how easy it was to hear other peoples' conversations outside on the balcony. In the middle of Davis's phony interrogation, Rodriguez knocked on the door and asked the Cape Codder to step outside for a moment. Out on the balcony, Rodriguez spoke just loud enough for the sensitive acoustics of Booth 4 to pick up his words.

"How well do you speak the Gulf dialect of Arabic?" Rodriguez asked.

"Not perfect, but well enough," Davis replied.

"Good," Rodriguez said. "He's going to be here soon."

The next day, we summoned a prisoner from the Gulf region up to one of the booths. Kampf went in and asked him about the kinds of foods and drinks Gulf Arabs liked.

"*Y'anni,* why are you asking me?" the prisoner said.

"We just need to know."

"Is it for me?"

"No, it is not for you."

The next day, we interrupted a few carefully selected ongoing interrogations with deliveries of envelopes. The echoes would split open the envelopes and pull out letters with a conspicuous copy of one of the Gulf region's state seals, as well as some official-looking Arabic text. Of course the interrogators would set the letters on the tables in plain view of the eagle-eyed prisoners.

The MPs also played an important role in this elaborate production. Throughout our five-day buildup, as the MPs were escorting hooded prisoners up the staircase to the booths, they would whisper into the sacks vaguely unsettling things like, "You're going places, pal."

By the fourth day, the cages were buzzing. Prisoners were whispering to one another, with English-speaking detainees pressing the guards for information and asking interrogators in the booths what was going on. Some of their questions echoed previous rounds of rumors. A couple of the detainees asked us again whether it was true we were selling prisoners. We knew our plan was really working that fourth night, when Heaney was walking past the cages on the shop floor and was summoned over to the wire by Aier. In an urgent whisper, Aier asked whether one of the Gulf states had sent any of its intelligence service personnel to work with the Americans at Bagram. Instead of answering Aier one way or another, Heaney was brilliantly noncommittal. Within hours, you could practically see the ripples of anxiety. These prisoners knew all too well what happened to detainees in the Gulf states: those countries' reputation for cruelty and torture was a source of fear across the Arab world. Perhaps some in our custody had even experienced it firsthand. We could only hope.

The day before a shipment to Guantánamo was usually traumatic enough for the prisoners. The MPs started making preparations midday, laying out new jumpsuits, manacles, leg chains, and spray-painted goggles (more comfortable than hoods) on the shop floor, in plain view of the cages. When they weren't in use, the hand and leg chains hung on pegs on a wall on the main shop floor. As the MPs pulled them down and laid them out, they would yank on the chains and move the manacles through their cycles, locking and unlocking them, making sure everything was in working order. For much of the afternoon, you couldn't escape the sound of chains rattling as the shiny chrome pieces were picked up, twisted around, and tossed back onto the concrete floor.

That evening, while the MPs were still making their preparations, the rest of us were taking care of our last-minute details, too. The interrogators arranged their dossiers and summary reports in stacks on tables in the ICE. I went down to see Aier, who was situated, as usual, in the far-right cage. Through the wire I asked him in English to translate for me a few words I would need that evening.

Manifest.

Travel duration.

Extradite.

Remand.

He gave me the Arabic for each. All of those knitted-cap heads were turned toward me. Some were sitting with their knees pulled up to their chest, others Indian style, some with their legs stretched out before them. But nobody was lying down on his sleeping mat. No one was reading the Koran or praying.

Finally, it was showtime, and the only thing we were waiting for was the star.

Before our plan had been put in motion, I had gone to visit Roberts at his tent in Viper City and asked if he would be willing to play a Gulf state Arab colonel. I didn't look forward to doing it. His attitude had become so malignant that we almost never bothered to summon him to the Facility anymore. When it came to getting him to do any actual work, Roberts was, as Hasegawa liked to say, "just another Arab who had to be exploited." And yet, Roberts was perfect for the role. He spoke native Arabic and could effect a flawless imitation of that region's accent and dialect. And because we hardly ever used him in the booth there were only three Arab prisoners in the cages who might recognize him. (We moved these three into the cage of Pashtuns from the Riverbed 32.) I told Roberts about our idea and said I thought he'd be great for the role. He had been cordial to me when I arrived, and as I laid out the plan, describing how he would be on center stage, how we couldn't pull it off without his unique abilities, he became quite enthusiastic. I had checked in with him several times during the week to make sure he was still on board. But now he was half an hour late for our scheduled 1630 curtain call. As the time ticked away, I sent Turner to go find him.

Ten minutes went by, then twenty, with no Roberts. Finally, he showed up in the ICE looking like Johnny Cash in black jeans, a black T-shirt, and a black leather belt with a silver buckle. Since nobody but MPs wore uniforms in the prison, we didn't think it would matter that we didn't have him in a real Arab military uniform. The only flaw in his costume was that he was still wearing his tan, suede U.S. Army boots. I prayed the prisoners wouldn't notice this.

Having already been briefed on his role, Roberts grabbed a roll of army "hundred-mile-per-hour tape" — which is the same as duct tape, except it's olive drab green instead of silver — and we went down to the shop floor. The MPs were all assembled, fully geared up with helmets and flak vests and even their MP armbands. Weikmann, the North Carolina national guardsman and senior MP sergeant, had them turn out sharply dressed, as if they were expecting a visit from a big-shot general or a foreign dignitary.

The MPs saluted and the bearded Roberts responded with a suitably affected bow and a foppish, full-palmed salute rendered at an acute angle. Truly, he was born for this.

The MPs showed us to the cage where the prisoners scheduled for transport had been segregated and ordered to line up. The MPs were moving with such precision that I almost thought Weikmann had told them Roberts *was* a visiting colonel. Roberts and I stepped across the sally port, which had red industrial carpet, and into the cage with the prisoners. We were accompanied by two MPs. One was carrying a stick, the other a clipboard with prisoners' names. Neither they nor we had any weapons. Earlier that afternoon I had confirmed with the guards up on the balcony their standing orders to have their rifles ready and to shoot into the cages if we came under attack.

One of the MPs called out a prisoner's name, and the detainee stepped toward us nervously, holding his arms tight across his abdomen.

Roberts leaned forward.

"You are so fucked," he said in the unmistakable, perfect diction of the Gulf.

The first prisoner looked at him with a visage of terror. Handing my clipboard to an MP for a moment, I took the roll of tape from Roberts and tore off a piece. Roberts moved to take the dangling strip from me, but I stopped him.

"No, no," I said in Arabic. "Don't forget, you can't touch anyone. You really shouldn't even be here, brother."

I grabbed the tape strip and slapped it on the prisoner's chest. Then, with a marker, I wrote the Arabic word "transport" across the green surface.

One by one, we summoned all twenty prisoners in the cage. Thirteen were marked for transport and seven had the word "remain" taped to their chests. To the latter, Roberts expressed his regret he wouldn't be seeing them . . . yet.

We repeated the same formula in the next cage. In this group were two prisoners I had interrogated, two Arabs of no intelligence value. Just days earlier, I had calmed their fears by telling them that they would be treated very well in Cuba. When the first was called, I pasted the strip of tape across his chest and he burst out in tears.

"No . . . NO, MIKE! You *promised!* You *promised* if I helped I would go to the good place! You PROMISED!" He was on his knees, sobbing and begging for mercy. The MPs were aghast and handled him as one would the mother of an accident victim in the throes of a soul-crushing loss, gently moving him aside. Somehow, I felt nothing for him, absolutely nothing. To one of his pleading shouts of "WHY?" I said coldly, "We have new information."

I was worried that this highly emotional display might incite the other prisoners to violence, an act of revenge for reducing a fellow Arab to that deplorable state. But the other prisoners did nothing.

Speaking in Arabic loud enough for the front row of detainees to hear, Roberts asked me whether we would "sedate the prisoners" before transport. This was a departure from the script and I didn't know the word "sedate." He tried three alternatives but couldn't get me to understand. In an act of brilliant improvisation, he walked back toward the cage, to Aier, and asked him in Arabic for the English translation. Aier told him, and Roberts, grinning, asked the question in broken English, using his "newly learned" word. The prisoners' eyes were popping out of their heads, and they appeared unrelieved even after the MPs answered Roberts by shaking their heads no.

When the tape parade was over, Roberts and I parted company with the MPs, who affected their own little nervous bows in response to the tall foreign officer's unfamiliar display of courtesy. We walked toward the back door and left the Facility talking in Arabic. Out of sight from the prisoners, we hurried the whole way around the back of the building to the front door and snuck up the stairs to the ICE like a couple of youthful hooligans making a getaway after unleashing a barrage of water balloons. The balcony was lined with interrogators and other members of our staff peeking at the cages through narrow gaps in the curtain of blankets.

Papa Smurf was also looking down at the cages. "Damn," he said, trying out a new bit of slang he'd picked up from the MPs, "you really dissed them good!"

Below, it was as if we had shaken a bees' nest. The prisoners were lying on their stomachs and pretending to sleep, except that their heads were swiveling back and forth. The usual, absolute quiet was replaced with a barely perceptible murmur. Some were consoling one another, telling themselves it would be all right. Others were beyond consolation. Then the praying started. One by one the prisoners got onto their knees and leaned forward to kiss the floor, bobbing up and down in fits of spiritual desperation so powerful that the MPs couldn't enforce the three-prayers-at-a-time rule.

Half an hour later, there was a call up to the balcony from the prison floor.

"Hey, MI-KEY!" one of the MPs said in his southern drawl. "MI-KEY! Seyend dowen an A-rab spey-ker. We gotta sick one here."

I parted the blanket carefully. Larry Hallard, one of the MPs, was staring back up.

"Hold on — I'll see if I can find someone," I said.

Back behind the cover I looked down the balcony at the interrogators who, like me, were peeking through the blankets at the cages.

"Chris, why don't you go down?" Heaney said. "Maybe it's a very simple Arabic word." The spectators buried their faces in their arms to muffle their laughter.

"Gare-bear," I said, "I think this is a job for you."

He muttered some slur on my Arabic skills, then the bald Marylander moseyed downstairs, eating an apple.

The "sick" detainee wanted to be allowed into the sally port — the space between the two gates into the cage — so he could get close enough to Heaney to whisper. He kept motioning to Heaney to undo the latch, but Heaney just taunted him, pretending not to understand. "WHAT?! Speak louder — I can't hear you."

Finally, he let the prisoner into the sally port and there was a short exchange. Heaney did an about-face and told the MPs the prisoner should be brought to the dispensary. Then he walked toward the back staircase, hollering up to the blankets that he was "going to get the doctor, 210 is sick." He was such a good actor, I half expected him to do it.

A moment later, the MPs were bellowing at us again. "Hey up thayer! We got ourselves an epidemic!" There were two more prisoners at the wire wall, holding their stomachs. It was working. Goddamn, it was working.

Heaney went back down, to keep up the appearance that the rest of us were asleep or busy. He wandered over toward the standing prisoners but was diverted when two others in the first cage also came forward to the edge of the wire, clutching their stomachs. They weren't even in a cage where prisoners had been taped. This threw us into interrogation triage mode. We were ready for last-minute appeals from prisoners bound for Cuba; I had even numbered them in intelligence priority precisely for this situation. But we never considered the possibility that prisoners from other cages would come forward, too. And some of these were Afghans. How they had picked up any of Roberts's Gulf Arab colonel act was anybody's guess. I sent Turner on a bike to get the Afghan interpreters.

An hour after the incident there were four booths occupied with sick prisoners and two more who needed to be pulled as soon as those damn interpreters got up to the Facility to tackle them. The first prisoners to come forward were the most frightened. The next wave approached us out of fear that the first batch to "fall ill" might be giving away their cell mates' secrets to escape the Gulf-bound plane. Even Roberts got into the excitement: he put the smelly Iraqi in with Papa Smurf (who was none too pleased to have such a guest) so he could use the VIP cell room for another interrogation himself, still posing as the colonel.

While all these interrogations were under way, I took another peek through the blankets out onto the prison floor. Prisoners were consoling one another, some were crying, and all the prisoners, in all the cages, were praying. It was as if we were witnessing the hajj.

The huge effort concluded about 0200 the next morning, when Weikmann put his head into the ICE and told me to get the prisoners scheduled for transport to Guantánamo

back downstairs. It was like somebody canceling Christmas. I
went into the booths and told the echoes to close things out. As
they did, they told the prisoners that if their new information
checked out, "We will consider changing your destination."
Even so, there was more crying from prisoners who couldn't
deal with the uncertainty.

The information we had extracted was good. Some prisoners had ratted on one another. Another batch sought to "clarify" their original stories. There was one who retracted his
previous story altogether and spent hours telling us new details
about Kashmir and the struggle to assist the Pakistani Islamists
in their fight against the Indian army. Kampf and Hasegawa,
who were questioning this prisoner, produced the longest report that had ever been filed at Bagram. Davis's interrogation
of a Syrian man showed up in the Department of the Army's
brief the next day: "Human intelligence confirms other sources
which indicate Arabs and Afghans loyal to the deposed Taliban
regime are attempting to escape into Iran." Davis's report also
provided some fascinating stories about Iranian towns near the
border with huge communities of Afghans. Many of these had
been living there since the Soviet invasion.

The interrogators were at their laptops by 0230, when the
transport process began in earnest. The MPs had a terrible
time getting some of the prisoners out of the cages. One or two
who implored me to have mercy clung to the concertina wire
and had to be pried loose. Others appeared quite philosophical,
remarkably resigned to their fate.

There was a downside to our little operation. When these
prisoners stepped off the plane in Cuba, they would know
they'd been had. I had broken an important rule: never make it
harder on the next interrogator. My only rationalization was that
I was concerned that many of these prisoners we were sending — most of whom had been captured in raids in Pakistan
that had netted Abu Zubaydah — probably had information

that might affect operations in the border badlands. I hoped the
ruse would flush out some piece of intelligence that JTF 180
could use — information on a planned ambush, an escape
route, something. But we didn't score any tactical intelligence
or any information that couldn't have waited until they had arrived at GTMO. We put notes in the prisoners' files to tell the
interrogators at GTMO what we had done. I never heard any
more about it.

I tried at one point to turn Hadi back over to Kampf, who had
questioned him before he met me. I had initially gone in only
to get a read on him to help us make a call on what to do with
him. I thought it was largely accidental that I had been in the
booth with him when he made his "In the Sudan . . ." slip and
then volunteered new information. I certainly didn't think I
had any magic touch with him, and now that we were over the
hump with him, I thought I should go back to my senior E job.
But when Kampf tried to resume questioning the kid, the detainee very cheekily reverted to his old story. I was peeved by
this but also somewhat impressed that a teen would be savvy
enough to work the system that way, to get the interrogator he
wanted back in the booth. For some reason, he felt a connection with me.

      In preparation for our fourth session, I asked Bill Ellis if I
could use one of his translators. His guys were older, more mature, and I thought that would help set the right tone for what I
hoped to cover and also assist me in communicating the finer
points of my message. I needed Alan, the trooper Billy sent over
to help me, only to communicate my words; I could understand
Hadi's Arabic even through his Indonesian accent. Hadi
seemed relieved to have someone to help move the conversation along and asked me over dinner if I could explain Chris-
tianity to him. The question caught me off guard and I asked
why he was interested. He told me that he was just interested in

all things Western. He asked if I had a copy of the Bible in either Indonesian or Arabic. There's no doubt that he was genuinely curious, but he was probably also trying to play me, exaggerating his interest in his captor's faith to curry better treatment. I thought about his request but turned him down. I was worried about how it would go down if anyone ever found out we were giving Bibles to prisoners. It wasn't a religious mission we were running here.

Hadi fleshed out some of his original story, providing more people's names and drawing a detailed map of a neighborhood in a Jakarta suburb where an Arab arms-and-forged-passports dealer lived. He provided e-mail addresses for some of the thugs he met while working for Kusuma, including the address of the guy who was running Arabs out of Java in shipping containers. The kid's memory was amazing.

Before we took our midinterrogation break, I confronted him with a suspicion that had been nagging at me since our first encounter. There were no explicit indications of sexual abuse in the story he told, but there were many suggestive aspects. Maybe the Indonesian intelligence officer saw a valuable teenage operative in Hadi. Or maybe there was another reason he took in this underage runaway, setting him up in a secret house and sobbing like a jilted lover when he left. Maybe the Pakistanis were trying to sell Hadi to the forgery kingpin in Jakarta because there was reward money for helping Middle East Arabs. Or maybe they were trying to sell Hadi to the man for some other purpose. Either way, he again ended up living with and dependent on an older male who seemed disinclined to let him leave. And then there was Hadi's break with his father. Maybe the old man did throw his son out because of his lax faith. Or maybe there was something else going on. Perhaps Hadi's father was abusing him. Or perhaps he saw homosexual tendencies in his son that he couldn't tolerate.

"Did anyone ever touch you wrongly sexually?" I said.

Alan, who had been beautifully and simultaneously translating my English to Arabic, suddenly hesitated. He was in the green fatigue uniform of his country's army, leaning back on his chair enough to lift its front legs slightly off the ground. He turned and looked over at me, as if he weren't sure it was appropriate to pose this question. He waited so long that I took in a breath of air to say the words myself in Arabic. But before I could utter them, Hadi answered the question without benefit of translation.

"No."

"Hadi, I want you to know that we are concerned about you and that if this happened — if someone touched you — we want to help." This time Alan translated without pause.

"No, Mike," Hadi said. "Nobody tried to touch me." As he said it, he closed his eyes and shook his head. In strategic debriefer school, we were taught that when people close their eyes that way, it can be a significant clue. Sometimes they just don't want to look at you while they're sharing a painful, or perhaps untruthful, piece of information. Sometimes it's as if they can't bear to look at whatever images are flashing across their mind's eye. I never brought it up again, but I remained suspicious until the day he left. I remain suspicious even now.

From the beginning, I thought Hadi could be a valuable snitch for us. He was very smart, constantly anticipating where I was headed with a line of questioning. His perfect Arabic meant he could vacuum up information from the most important corners of the cages. His youth made him less threatening to detainees who might otherwise be reticent to share their secrets in whispers when the MPs weren't looking. He was eager to cooperate with us, to show us he was a good guy. But before I began down that path, I needed to test him, to see if we could trust him to tell the truth, and I had given a good deal of thought to how we could do that.

When the MPs had taken Hadi away after our last interrogation, I walked into the booth next door, where we kept the smelly Iraqi with the pockmarked skin. He had been moved up into the booth on a permanent basis at the request of the OGA. We tended not to see much of them these days, but they came calling whenever we had an Iraqi in custody, so desperate were they for intelligence on Saddam Hussein's regime. I don't know how they were able to take it day after day, subjecting themselves to the Iraqi's fumes. The MPs washed him two or even three times a week as opposed to the single weekly bath afforded general-population prisoners, but to no avail. The heat at Bagram seemed to ignite something so sour in this man's sweat glands that at one point we called a doctor to look at him. The doctor couldn't find anything wrong and was pissed at us for taking him away from more serious duties to examine a patient with BO.

The Iraqi was desperate for attention and any kind of contact. He would sit in his room and listen for the sound of approaching footsteps, then scamper to the doorway and paw at people as they walked by, begging them to come inside. I chewed him out once and told him he needed to quit his "Mr. Grabby Hands" routine because the MPs might mistake his behavior for something more menacing. He reformed himself — sort of — and turned to trying to catch people's attention with conspiratorial whispers and a wide-eyed look that said he had some secret. Once the person was inside, he'd let on that he hadn't told his entire story, that he had some big revelation to share. But he never had anything authentic left to tell and was merely gilding his prior information with thick, obnoxious coats of faux significance. The only ones who didn't seem to figure this out were the folks from OGA. They were so keen for news on Iraq that they refused to believe this guy didn't have something valuable to say.

I had long since figured out that the best way to escape the

Iraqi's clutches was to stride past his cell swiftly and, if necessary, mutter an apology over the shoulder. But now I had a special assignment for him. I told Al-Iraqi (as we called him; his real name, we had discovered, was Hamid) that I wanted him to pretend he was an Iraqi captain who had fled Iraq after the first Gulf War and that he was hiding from us the fact that he had a brother who was a member of Saddam Hussein's personal bodyguard detail. Al-Iraqi's eyes brightened and he quickly offered a better idea, suggesting that we describe his brother as a physician assigned to the Saddam family retinue. I agreed with this modification but stopped him before he could create an even more elaborate background for himself. I explained that we would have a prisoner join him for a short time, during which this overnight guest would have the assignment to question Al-Iraqi about his personal life. Al-Iraqi was to share the information about his brother as if it were a big secret he was keeping hidden from the Americans. I parted with a final warning: "We will be monitoring everything from the microphones in the ceiling, so be careful you don't give your *real* story away." He laughed nervously and tried to stop me as I walked out of the room to explain that he *had* been telling the real story. I gave him a knowing wink and left the room with him hounding me — "Mike, Mike, Mike, wait! Come sit with me!" — as I walked down the hallway.

We had to be careful about keeping Hadi upstairs for an entire night. The rest of the prisoners would surely notice that — killing our chances of transforming him into our mole within the cages. To camouflage things, we took three other prisoners up for the night as well, just sticking them in booths with no one to talk to. Turner had converted the reception room and an annex to the screening room into new booth space so that we would not want for it — at least temporarily.

After the morning meeting, the MPs took Hadi back downstairs along with the decoy prisoners. I avoided going past Al-

Iraqi's room, but some of the other interrogators told me he had stopped them to say the "mission is complete." I waited another night before I spoke to Hadi and brought him an enormous bowl of vanilla pudding. He was a bit bored with my follow-up questions about the phone numbers and e-mail accounts he'd previously given us. But he answered them patiently, knowing that when that business was over I would answer more questions about America. He wanted to know what school was like in the United States and particularly whether high schools were really the way they appeared in Hollywood films. I had the impression he saw one too many episodes of *Saved by the Bell.*

Realizing I had to be careful not to give away any details that might trip me up later, I kept my response simple and changed topics as soon as I could. I had been planning a Columbo-like maneuver of walking out of the room and turning around with "just one more question" to probe him about his night with the Iraqi. Instead he turned the tables on me.

"Why did you put me upstairs last night?" he asked.

"We move prisoners around and put them upstairs and don't ever talk to them. This way no one knows who is being helpful and who is not. This way no one is suspicious."

"I thought you put me in so that I would speak with Hamid," he said.

"Sometimes we do that; we put you in with another prisoner and listen in to what is being said," I told him, carrying on the lie that the interrogation rooms were bugged.

"You don't trust me?"

"Not yet, Hadi. Not yet."

"But I want you to trust me," he said, resting his chin on interlaced fingers, his shackled arms resting on the table.

"That comes in time. We want to trust you, too. Everyone is very fond of you, and we are trying to figure out how we can help each other."

"I would like to show you that I am trustworthy," he said.

"We'll see. Sometimes it takes time to build trust. We'll see," I said, gathering up my papers.

"The Iraqi told me a secret," he said. "But you already know."

This was Hadi's equivalent of a finger poke in the eye. Hadi was smart. He knew I was trying to get information out of him, had by now surmised that I'd put him through a test and so thought he would make me work for the results. He was referring to the "bugs" that we had planted in his mind, if not in the room.

"Maybe we don't know. What's the secret?" I asked, my Columbo maneuver pretty much ruined.

"He told me that his brother has a job working for somebody very important in Iraq."

"Did he say who?"

"No. But I think I might get him to tell me. Can you put me back in with him?"

"*How* did he suggest that he had a brother with an important job? *What* did he say *exactly?*" I asked.

"I don't remember what he said *exactly*. But that's how the conversation went; that's what he was saying to me. But I think he will say more."

I began to wonder whether Al-Iraqi had been playing it straight with me. Maybe he had decided to string out this assignment just for the company in the room.

"What do you think he meant? What do you think his brother does?"

Hadi blinked deliberately a few times, then proceeded to call my bluff about the bugs.

"If you record what you hear on the microphones, you can play it back. He speaks Arabic with the Iraqi dialect. I might have missed something."

"Hadi, maybe we should put you back upstairs with Al-Iraqi. But that would defeat the purpose of rotating prisoners in and out of the cages. If you went upstairs twice the other prisoners would be suspicious."

"Maybe just put me up with him for a little while tomorrow. Maybe around dinnertime. He likes to talk while he eats."

"Maybe," I said, packing up my papers and closing my notebook. "I will talk to you again soon." I stood up and patted him on the shoulder patronizingly and called for the MP to take him downstairs. Just as I had reached the door, I turned around and executed my Columbo motion after all, though with a different purpose than I had originally envisioned.

"You know, Hadi, we didn't bug the room you and the Iraqi shared last night."

"I know that," he said with a tiny smile.

"How's that?"

"Because you guys always write everything we say," he said, pointing to the thick file of handwritten notes I had in my hands.

About 0200, three hours after I had finished speaking with Hadi, Kampf came into the ICE fresh from having deposited one of his prisoners back down in general population. He was a few seconds into his Yahoo in-box when he remembered he had something to tell me: "Sergeant Mackey, 219 had a message he told me to give to you. He said, '*Huah kana taubeeb.*'"

The Iraqi's brother "was a doctor."

By late June 2002 we had about eighty prisoners in custody and were screening new shipments two or three times a week. Papa Smurf and Al-Iraqi were taking up two upstairs booths permanently, leaving us with only four more for interrogations. And at least one of these was always occupied by someone from the FBI, OGA, or one of our allies' intelligence services. The chronic shortage of space seemed crazy in such a cavernous facility. Interrogators were fighting for booth space and often were forced to wait their turn until the rest of Bagram was asleep. But Bagram rarely slept.

One of the cool things about the army is that when you need something done, the manpower is generally close at hand. In our case, there was a huge consignment of Louisiana national guardsmen engineers. All I had to do was sketch out a plan for a VIP cellblock on the second floor, and they took the blueprint, marked in some improvements of their own, and made it a reality in three days. They took an echo chamber of a room that nobody ever used and built six ten-foot by twelve-foot cells with locking doors. The walls were ten feet tall but came nowhere near the ceiling of the building. There were no roofs on the cells, just chicken wire nailed neatly across the tops. They also pulled the plywood down from the windows and replaced it with more chicken wire, creating the best-ventilated, coolest spot in the Facility. I kept four of the cells stark, unadorned but for a wooden platform on which prisoners could place their blankets and sleep. These were for no-frills isolation. The remaining two cells were outfitted with cots, Afghan prayer rugs, and Afghan pillows. These were VIP cells for rewarding prisoners or for approaches that required a gentle touch. There's a school of thought in interrogation that you want the relationship between interrogator and detainee to become like that between parent and child. The CIA's Kubark manual describes in detail how a prisoner's defenses degrade as he "regresses" toward this childlike state, how the adult ability to process complex problems crumbles as a prisoner spends time in captivity. The idea is for prisoners to look to you for interaction and approval, to become dependent on you for their every need. Isolating prisoners helps feed that dynamic, as does doling out special treatment. Often we used the VIP cells for prisoners who we were working to convince that cooperation could lead to a special deal — perhaps a future at those farms in Virginia I was always talking about. Anyone in a VIP cell got hot food, either from the chow tent or the Afghan vendors outside the gate, courtesy of the echoes, who took up a daily collection for this purpose after the morning meeting. No one would confuse the VIP cells with rooms at the Ritz-Carlton, but they were better quarters than we soldiers had.

One of the first to be relocated was Al-Iraqi, who was moved into one of the VIP rooms. He didn't like it, despite the creature comforts, because he preferred being able to loiter in his doorway and harass passersby on the balcony. He cried about being forced to relocate and promised to share new "recollections of great value" if I would reconsider. I told him the only alternative was general population, and he was terrified to go back down there, believing that his cover was blown and that his "brothers" knew he was a snitch. Hasegawa hated the Iraqi with such passion that he wanted to send him down to "general pop" anyway and give the rest of the prisoners sharpened spoons. I wondered if Hamid's odor might have been enough to protect him.

John and Eamon were replaced by two new FBI agents, Ron and Robert (or "Robie," as he liked to be called). They were also from New York but were polar opposites of their predecessors. These were sophisticates, with mirrored, wraparound sunglasses and futuristic-looking pistols held in expensive holsters. They wore safari gear and surfer T-shirts and appeared almost disappointed it wasn't winter, when they might have shown off a still more impressive wardrobe. They were nice enough but patronizing, constantly marveling at our capacity for "suffering" and noting each time they arrived that everyone was wearing the same clothes as last time. They also called me "tough guy" and "buddy," which I loathed. The good news was they weren't around much because they gravitated to the OGA field station in Kabul. There were few if any prisoners there, but keeping company with the OGA was cooler to them than the day-to-day grind at the Facility.

One afternoon they appeared and asked to speak with Ghul Aga, one of Hasegawa's prisoners and an excellent source on Hekmatyar. Who knows why a couple of FBI guys would be interested in Hekmatyar, but there they were, in full, stylish regalia. After a brief discussion, they went down to one of the booths to wait. I assigned Turner to go in with them as a minder, and as he left to join them in the booth we were all startled by a loud crack, as if someone had dropped a pallet from a great height. I thought one of the walls in the new VIP complex had collapsed.

I stepped into the hallway and overtook a very cautious Turner. Then I smelled the distinct sulphur odor of a spent cartridge. One of Weikmann's MPs stepped into view at the other end of the hallway with his rifle, helmet, and flak vest. FBI agent Ron stepped out of his interrogation room with his hands up, as if he were surrendering. He said his pistol had gone off. Although no one but MPs and interrogators were allowed to be armed in the Facility, our FBI guests had managed to get their weapons past the MPs.

Back in the ICE, Ron explained that he had decided to "clean" his pistol while they were waiting for Turner, and the thing "accidentally discharged." Thank God there was no prisoner in the room to get hit by the ricochet. Ron and Robie begged Weikmann and me not to tell anyone what happened. We agreed and didn't see them again until they came to say good-bye a week or two later. They gave us a six-pack of beer, and I noticed a touch of contrition about them; they even seemed to be dressed less flamboyantly. Although I'd take the FBI every day and twice on Sunday over the OGA, I hoped we would have no more of Hoover's men for a while.

I did not put Hadi back into the room with the Iraqi as he had requested — no doubt hoping for another local Afghan meal. Instead, I left him to think about our chat and his reluctance to come forward with the full information. As much as this irritated me, I also thought it showed some positive, self-serving instincts. For a teenager, he was remarkably clever. Al-Iraqi never doubted there was a microphone somewhere over his head, but Hadi had our ruse figured out from the start and basically manipulated me into admitting it.

I received two sheets of follow-up questions on Hadi during our break. As always, the community wanted more details of everything. But most of all, they wanted to know a lot more about some of the people he'd encountered when he was on the run. Where did they hide? How did they communicate and move around? As I was wrapping up my questions, Hadi asked if he could speak for a moment and offered a bit of unsolicited information from the cages. A Russian from the Pakistani Family Pack, a group of eighteen-odd prisoners shipped to us from that country and named by us (as were all groups) for ease of reference, he said, could speak very good Arabic, which was news to us. Hadi couldn't hear much of what was being said by the man since they were in separate cages. But he could hear the burly Russian's exchanges with the other Arabs. After I thanked him for the information, he volunteered to be transferred into that cage so he could hear more. He made this offer with an adult assuredness that made it clear he was completely comfortable with such an assignment, that it was the sort of thing he had done for his previous guardians a hundred times before.

It was dawning on me that Hadi might be put to an assignment more important and far-reaching than camp snitch, that perhaps he might be someone we could turn to our side and send back into the world to work for us. He had passed every test in our interrogations and had certain valuable qualities. For one, he was so remarkably composed, almost imperturbable. A few months on the streets didn't account for the instincts he showed, his ability to size people up so quickly, to use his wits and words to win sympathy and get what he wanted. He knew that the information he gathered was his currency with us, and he used it for food and preferential treatment. But the information he provided was accurate, and that was the most important thing. His neutral appearance, neither Afghan nor Arab, gave him enviable flexibility. His youth also worked to our advantage, because for all his savvy there was an abiding immaturity, a still-malleable view of the world and his place in it that we could shape.

The sadder aspects of his story also made him a promising candidate for turning. He was estranged from his family, making it unlikely he would long for his former life. It's an unpleasant admission, but the possibility that he had been abused worked to our advantage, too. People emerging from such experiences, especially at such a young age, are like mistreated puppies. They pine away to be treated well, and when they are, they're more loyal than a person who hasn't had any experience with the crueler possibilities in life. It was a terribly exploitive thing to consider, and risky. If it worked, we would be consigning him to a future from which there really was no easy means to sever the connection. But I thought that if we could get him into the right hands, he would be better off than if he were to remain in our prison, or be released back onto the streets.

He was already highly sympathetic to the West, practically captivated by it. After it occurred to me he might be turned, I started taking steps to reinforce his affection for us, for the West. I let him eat dinner in the interrogator lounge with Kampf, Heaney, Pearson, and myself. Another time, I let him try some macaroni and cheese my parents had sent from the States. God, he loved that stuff.

We also let him watch some of our DVD movies in the lounge. We'd never done that before and never would again. But this was a special case, and I wanted to reward him for the information he'd already provided, the snitch work he'd already performed. I also hoped to heighten his curiosity about America. He was always asking me about American schools, American movies, American girls. At one of our morning meetings, I told everyone that I needed to use the lounge from 1:30 to 3:30 the next morning. Afterward I approached Dawn, a new analyst from the 500th MI Battalion who arrived to reinforce Carlson's one-man show, and told her that I wanted her to join us and that she could wear civilian clothes (I generally required the analysts to be in uniform). She was eager to help. I also asked Kampf to come and to bring his pistol for security. We situated him in close proximity to Hadi but far enough away so that he could draw his weapon if there was a problem. An MP was assigned to sit outside the room. The final ingredients were popcorn, a large wedge of army sheet cake, and a Pakistani-pirated copy of *American Pie*.

The lounge was a well-appointed space by then. There was a tiny DVD player, about the size of a Walkman, plugged into a big-screen television. There were "couches" we'd constructed by taking two cots and connecting them so that you sat on the seat of one and used the seat of the other as a back. There was a refrigerator and a microwave on a shelf, and the engineers had put in floor-to-ceiling shelving that was stocked with trashy novels and magazines.

That night I led Hadi out of the booth and along the balcony without handcuffs or leg irons or a bag over his head. The door to the ICE was shut so that he couldn't see any of our maps, mug shots, or equipment inside as he passed by. He was almost giddy as we stepped into the lounge. Dawn and Kampf were already there. Dawn, who was about nineteen, had even dolled herself up for the occasion, letting her long, blond hair down and rolling her sleeves up to her shoulders as if she were seeking the sun. Like the goofy teen he was, Hadi didn't sit next to her and instead planted himself right next to me. He ate the cake, then poured ketchup over his popcorn and ate that, then devoured some of our chocolate stash and washed it down with Coca-Cola. He laughed uproariously at the movie and seemed to get even the jokes that spoofed esoteric aspects of American pop culture. Every time there was a sexual innuendo on-screen he would cover his eyes with his hands and say, "Oh my god, Oh My God, OH MY GOD!"

At one point he got up without asking me and wandered over to fetch some more food. I made him sit back down and told him he wasn't to move, that we would get whatever he wanted for him. A couple times he tried to strike up a conversation with Dawn. After a particularly racy scene, he looked over with a wide grin and said, "Would you do that?"

But Dawn, a sweet Florida girl from a modest background, didn't speak any Arabic, and Hadi's English was weak. "Ah cain't under-stayand yew!" she kept saying to him with her own silly smile.

Kampf and I got him to repeat his question in Arabic and laughed hard. That made Dawn really squirm. "Whut's he saaaying? Whut's he saaaying?"

At the end of the evening, I told Hadi it was time to go back to the cages, and he extended his wrists for me to apply the cuffs. I was about to pull the sack over his head when he pulled his neck back and started to speak.

"I want to help you," he said. Thinking he meant with the hood, I told him to lean forward.

"No, I want to help you — the Americans."

"Why?"

"You are better friends for me; you *are* movies and cake and girls," he said.

"We can look into that," I said noncommittally. The bag over his head and his hands in the cuffs, we turned the corner onto the main shop floor. An MP took him from me. As Hadi was being put back in the cage with the Pashtuns, Weikmann and I discussed the next round of prisoner moves, and I asked him to place Hadi in the middle of the "Family Pack." Hadi's awe at American movies and cake and girls wasn't exactly an expression of a noble yearning for liberty, but it was genuine. It might be enough to propel him into a new life.

Interrogators don't exactly have a history of heroic depictions in American cinema. In cop dramas like *L.A. Confidential*, the Fear Up is the ubiquitous approach and is usually executed with the barrel of a gun in the prisoner's mouth. War movies have understandably focused on the drama of the front lines or the war room — not the lowly intelligence troops questioning prisoners a safe distance from the flying bullets.

When interrogators or linguists do find their way into the frame in these epics, it's often when they are accompanying infantry into a village or onto a battlefield. For a long time, the only interrogator role anyone could even remember seeing was Johnny Depp's turn as a Vietnamese-speaking linguist in *Platoon*. He wasn't central to the plot, but at least he came across as principled. Then Steven Spielberg went and made *Saving Private Ryan*, a film in which even the Nazis come off better than the echo who accompanies Tom Hanks's unit on its Pan-European search for the sibling-deprived private. Jeremy Davies's German-speaking intelligence trooper looks like the consummate wuss, talks his unit out of executing a captured soldier, then — in one of the most cowardly acts ever captured on celluloid — saves his own skin by pointing the Germans to the position of his Jewish American comrade. Needless to say, when the interrogators at Bagram got the chance to go out into the field with fighting troops, many of us called them "Depp missions."

For most of the war the only interrogators who got to go out on such missions were those who were assigned full-time to one of the mobile interrogation teams. Chief Tyler, my old boss on the night shift in Kandahar, had gone out with Special Forces troops once looking for a possible bin Laden grave site. A couple others, including a contract linguist, had deployed with Tenth Mountain Division troops for Operation Anaconda, the massive March assault on Taliban and Al Qaeda positions in the Shah-I-Kot mountains of eastern Afghanistan. Few of the regular interrogators had a chance to go out into the field until shortly after we got to Bagram. Again, Steve from Task Force Hatchet was the instigator. The idea was not to do detailed interrogations in the field but to have at least one person there trained to do quick questioning of prisoners in the moments after capture and assess their intelligence value. After watching dozens of prisoners brought back from raids only to be released later, Steve thought he could improve the kept-to-captured ratio by having an interrogator on hand to do on-the-spot screenings.

The interrogators were eager to go. The chance to see some action offset any concern about the danger, which wasn't great. When interrogators deployed, they did so in the "third wave," meaning they only moved in after the Rangers controlled the wider perimeter and teams of special operations troops had secured the target. The echoes would help decide which Afghans to load on the chopper and which to release.

There were obvious candidates. Hasegawa and Kampf were both active-duty airborne troopers from Fort Bragg. They were fit and excellent soldiers. They could keep up with all but the best Rangers. Heaney and Davis also made sense, even if they looked odd in combat gear after so long in civilian clothes, their beards an incongruent sight under their Kevlar helmets.

Hasegawa had just two days to prepare for his first mission. The target was a compound in Deh Rawood, a village near Kandahar that had been a bastion of support for the Taliban and was also rooted in the poppy (that is, opium) trade. The compound was described as a safe house or meeting place for Taliban loyalists and militants, and the raid was part of a series of takedowns planned to subdue groups thought likely to launch attacks to disrupt the *Loya Jirga,* the national elections taking place mid-June in Kabul. Hasegawa spent much of a day researching information on the classified computer databases, reading intelligence reports filed over the last three months on activity in Deh Rawood. Then he started packing. The list was pretty short: three MREs, one pair of socks, one brown army T-shirt, one army poncho with quilted liner, ballistic helmet, Kevlar body armor, and two weapons: an M-16 with 210 rounds and an M9 pistol with 45 rounds. No laptop or satellite phone — just a digital camera, extra zip ties, a small green notebook, and a pen.

The plan was for the whole operation to take less than twenty-four hours and for the raiders to be on the ground for just a fraction of that. Rangers would set up a perimeter, special operators would punch into the compound, and a third group of intelligence and medical personnel — Hasegawa's group — would be brought in when the compound was secure. The raiders were divided up into subunits called "chalks," which were numbered according to their order of arrival on the scene. Each chalk would be on its own CH-47 Chinook helicopter, the big bird with twin propellers on top. There were seven chalks total, and Hasegawa was in Chalk 6.

The night of the raid, the task force assembled on the tarmac at 0100 hours, and waited there for several hours. Hasegawa spent much of that time settling down his Afghan translator, who had never been on such a mission either, and giving the civilian last-minute instructions on how to stay out of trouble. "My gun is on my right side. I need you to stay behind me, on my left," Hasegawa said. "If you trip or anything happens I can reach back and grab you. If we have to run I want you to grab the handle on the top of my backpack and keep up. Keep tugging on it so I'll know you're there."

A loud, "Let's go!" cued everyone in Chalk 6 to climb on board. There were a dozen or so people in the copter, including another interrogator who worked missions for Task Force Hatchet full-time, a couple of medics, and some assorted intelligence and Special Forces types. Hasegawa slept through much of the two-hour flight and didn't wake up until the helicopter was in a flight pattern, awaiting permission to land. The operators had burst into the compound while Chalk 6 was still airborne.

Finally, the helicopter touched down in the middle of a field and the tail dropped. Wearing night-vision goggles, Hasegawa guided the translator off the helicopter and they made their way to the edge of the field, their faces pelted by bits of dirt and hay whipped up by the prop wash. The chalk leader led them toward the compound, along a towering wall, through a doorway, and into a courtyard. On the right was a manger for some goats and on the left were a series of rooms. Hasegawa caught up with the ground commander, who informed him that eight detainees had been taken with no resistance. No one had escaped. The prisoners, all Afghans in their twenties and thirties, were lined up in the courtyard with zip ties on their hands and hoods over their heads.

One by one, the prisoners were led by Hasegawa and the other interrogator into one of the empty mud-walled rooms for quick screenings. Echoes always start out by looking for little telltale signs: is one prisoner cleaner than the others, better dressed, better spoken? But none of these detainees stood out, and there wasn't much to glean from their pocket litter. The next step was to get each detainee to identify himself and all the others in custody, get him to talk about how long each of the others had been at the compound, what they were doing there, where they were from, what their jobs were. You're basically looking for two things: discrepancies in their answers and signs of deception. The latter can include evasive or vague answers and defensive body language — fidgeting, limbs pulled tight to the body, excessive sweating, lack of eye contact.

Within forty-five minutes, the echoes had divided the prisoners into two groups: four who were definitely going to Bagram and four who got to stay home. But during the screenings, the echoes got a tip — the name of another villager who was said to have contacts with Berader or other high-value targets. It was possible the detainees were just trying to use the Americans for some tribal score settling, but three prisoners had offered up the same name independently, and his residence was less than a mile away. Within an hour, the raiders had a fifth suspect to take back to Bagram.

It was daylight when the task force started regrouping at the helicopter landing and loading prisoners on one of the Chinooks. The raid had netted a pile of AK-47s and at least one rocket-propelled grenade. Hasegawa arrived back at Bagram just as the prisoners were lining up for in-processing. One was later released, but the others were all sent to Guantánamo, including the Afghan who had been identified by the other detainees.

I also gave Geoff Fitzgerald the chance to go on a Depp mission. I pulled him aside after a meeting in the ICE and took him into the "office" behind the blankets, overlooking the cages below.

"I have a mission for you if you will take it," I said, just wishing that I could have grabbed the assignment myself.

"What is it?" Fitzgerald replied warily.

"How would you like to go out on one of the raids — a five-day mission with the Royal Marine commandos?" I asked.

"Hell, no," Fitzgerald said, without so much as pausing to consider the matter. "I've got a desk job."

I was stunned. I figured he'd jump at the chance to get out in the field, to see a little piece of history before it was digested by some future Toynbee. "Geoff, everyone else would jump at this opportunity," I said.

"Well, you should have asked them then." He shrugged.

A classic Fitzgerald-Mackey argument ensued. He resented the "Do you know how lucky you are" tone that accompanied my offer. To him, it was symptomatic of a broader inferiority complex — a "penis envy," as he put it — that he considered pathetically pervasive among MI types. It cropped up from time to time, and his argument went like this: Why should we, the brains of the military, have so much anxiety about our contribution to the war that we feel we have to ape Special Forces guys? To Fitzgerald, commandos were just glorified jocks — pitchers and quarterbacks from suburban high schools who traded baseballs for bullets. There's no doubt they had skills. They could slither right up to the enemy on their stomachs, survive on worms for days, and plunk a target with a piece of lead from a mile away. All very impressive. But they couldn't speak Arabic or juggle a million intelligence requirements and 703 follow-up questions from the community while sitting three feet away from some Islamic firebrand who has no reason to talk.

"Do you think those Special Forces guys are wracked with interrogator envy?" Fitzgerald would say. "You think they're over there in their special sunglasses, polishing their special weapons, saying, 'Man, if only I could do some hot-shit interrogations and write some hot-shit reports?'"

Needless to say, I was disappointed. I have tremendous admiration for active-duty soldiers — particularly combat-arms soldiers — and desperately wanted to go out on one of the missions myself but couldn't because of my position. It remains one of my biggest regrets of the war. So to have this offer thrown back in my face this way irked me, and I wanted to sting him a little bit for his attitude. "You're a good PR man, Fitzgerald," I said, "but I wouldn't say so as a soldier." Fitzgerald just stared back at me with his arms crossed.

Eventually, Fitzgerald did go on a mission, albeit of another sort. We received a request for an Arabic interpreter for the

Loya Jirga. I had visions of Fitzgerald translating for diplomats and attending receptions at the U.S. embassy. Once Fitzgerald's name was a definite for the mission, I even washed and stretched into a mildly unwrinkled form a few of my Brooks Brothers shirts for him — all of which proved to be a total waste of time. Fitzgerald's actual mission involved wearing full "battle rattle" and working with a Task Force 500 counterintelligence team in Kabul, going from place to place in the city, speaking with their informal contacts, getting a read on the streets for the mood of the people. There were risks, but none so severe as that faced by the other troops on the mission who for some reason made Fitzgerald their driver, putting him behind the wheel of a Humvee through the streets of the decrepit capital for ten days. He probably would have had more fun had he taken me up on my original offer.

Unlike Fitzgerald, Paul Harper was sorely disappointed to be permanently assigned to Bagram. The "real" CI work, he thought, was in Kabul. But he grew to appreciate certain aspects of his assignment, not the least of which was his proximity to Anne-Marie Walker, now his fiancée. He worked mainly as an analyst, poring over reports to root out connections and patterns that helped us understand Al Qaeda's structure and operations in Afghanistan. But he also did a fair amount of "force protection" work, meaning anytime something came up that looked like a threat to security, the task of investigating went to him.

One of his cases involved an enemy who was shot in the back of the leg. The man was treated and released to our custody at the Facility, where he was placed in a room on the bottom floor that was set up as a makeshift medical clinic. Heaney, who was our designated sickbed interrogator, questioned the prisoner and discovered that he wasn't even a soldier. The detainee said he was captured in a raid on his village and was lying down on the ground, his hands zip tied behind his back, when he was approached by an Afghan interpreter working for the U.S. troops. The prisoner recognized the interpreter as Ishmail Khan, a notorious thug from the Paktika province who was an "ally of the Taliban and a friend to the Arabs." When the translator saw he had been recognized, he took an AK-47 that had been seized from the Afghans and tried to kill the shackled prisoner as he lay helpless on his stomach. He only got off one shot into the prisoner's thigh before a coalition soldier tackled him and pried away the weapon.

Harper went in to question the prisoner and emerged two hours later saying he was convinced the "fucker was lying" and that he needed to go do some research on his top secret databases. The next day, the shooter arrived — though nobody *told* us he was the shooter. He was just dropped off with no tags, no note, no indication of who he was or why he was in custody. Compiling some reports, Turner noticed that the two men were brought in by the same Army Aviation squadron, from the same location in Paktika province, from an operation conducted by the same army outfit. Heaney took a book of mug shots in to show the wounded prisoner, and he picked out the new arrival instantly. Bingo.

Harper went in to question the shooter but quickly showed his limitations as an interrogator. He was good at volume and cadence but awful at planning and questioning. He tried to regress from a Fear Up Harsh only to get frustrated and start screaming again. After Harper failed to break the prisoner on the fourth try, I asked Heaney to take over the interrogation.

Right away, Heaney thought the detainee was hard-core Taliban and proposed monstering him. The two grappled for about ten hours before Heaney took his first break, leaving the prisoner with one of our civilian translators, Mr. Hami. Hami was one of the best in the crew, not only because he followed protocol perfectly in the booth but because he understood the

Afghan tribal scene so well that he was constantly giving us valuable insights into prisoners' backgrounds, motivations, and loyalties. A few minutes after Heaney emerged, Hami stepped out of the booth, too, saying the former translator was ready to talk. In a span of minutes, Hami had convinced him to admit that he had been recruited by Taliban sympathizers to spy on Americans. There was such a need for speakers of Pashtu and other Afghan dialects that the troops who went out on missions had lower standards than we had in the prison. All of our linguists were U.S. citizens, recruited back home, subjected to security checks, and then shipped over to work for us. But the army was willing to hire local Afghans for operations in the field, and performing security checks on natives wasn't easy. It's not like they had reliable employment records, neighbors you could interview, credit ratings to inspect. They were guys with one name who don't know how old they are. Our prisoner had been getting two paychecks: one from his Taliban sponsors and the other from the U.S. Army. He'd work with the Americans for a week at a stretch, then fill in his pro-Taliban masters on U.S. methods and operations.

After Hami had shaken this admission loose, Heaney went back at the prisoner even harder and got him to admit that there were other Taliban sympathizers who had taken similar assignments with the Americans. And this is where Harper's skills really came into play. He and Peter Papadopolous, another counterintelligence agent who had recently arrived from Fort Bragg, now had a clear-cut espionage case, the kind they had been trained to tackle. The prisoner said he had only met one other "spy" and had no details on what sort of position he had taken with the Americans. So Harper and Papadopolous scoured the provost marshal's employment records and narrowed the list to a handful of suspects. They then showed the work-permit photographs to our prisoner, who identified his acquaintance.

The second Afghan, it turned out, had been out on a sweep with a 101st Airborne infantry company just days earlier. When Harper and Papadopolous questioned the airborne troops who had worked with the guy, they started talking about how unusually inquisitive he was — always asking why soldiers lined up the way they did when they closed in on a compound or how many troops were at the base at Bagram or when the next rotation of soldiers was due to arrive. One of the soldiers said he'd seen the Afghan pacing off distances between buildings on the base at Bagram. Harper and Papadopolous came away livid that these airborne troops hadn't reported any of this suspicious activity.

Rodriguez was the only one I told about my plan for Hadi. I thought he would be against it, but he showed only a positive reaction when I explained that I thought the boy should be turned over to the intelligence service of one of our European allies rather than to OGA. I thought Chief would go for the safer answer, the more conventional route of giving the OGA a chance. But he was as unimpressed as I was with our encounters with the boys and girls from Virginia. Rodriguez agreed Hadi had a number of things going for him — uncanny brains and calmness under pressure. He had been with us only a short while, and that was important. That meant there would only be a short gap in his time line to have to account for with people who knew him before he was taken into custody, people he no doubt would be collecting on now.

I wasn't without reservations. I thought he might be damaged goods, that he might be playing us (Let's face it, I'm a tax adviser), and that turning him over to Simon might be more trouble than it was worth. I also had a nagging concern, entirely illogical, that Hadi may have been some sort of plant sent in to collect on us. Two men from his gang had set him up, ditched him with the Arabs near the airport. Were they acting in cooperation with the OGA? Were they on the take in their own right? It might be the near side of a flight of fantasy, but could they possibly have sent Hadi with the Arabs intentionally to spy on us, assuming he would be released because of his age and could then report back?

I needed to see Simon. I walked the long way down Disney Drive, past Motel 6. The garrison was changing incredibly fast as the new task force, JTF 180, reinforced itself. Now there were MP speed traps for people going too fast on their four-wheel ATVs. Uniformed soldiers were obliged to salute officers encountered on what were now dirt-pack sidewalks. The little PX had expanded, and, though the lines were still long, there were no more shortages. They even had chairs, of which we bought many at no small expense to throw into the chair-eating Facility.

Simon and his colleagues were in a hangar, surrounded by junk fighter jets and aviation debris. The dust was so fine at Bagram that it would have done no good to plow berms — they would have just blown away. So the troops had to fill enormous, reinforced cardboard boxes with dirt and stack them on top of one another to make walls that surrounded minigarrisons like those of our allies. Two Royal Marine guards stood at the entrance twenty-four hours a day. After a radio consultation, Simon came out in a resort t-shirt that said BAHAMAS on it. I had to leave my pistol at the gate. I had traded in my M-16 for a Beretta pistol some time earlier. But since I'd never fired a Beretta — the reserve unit back in Connecticut had only old .45s — I never put a bullet in the chamber. I did keep a loaded magazine with me, however. And a piece of black electrical tape over the hole in the bottom of the pistol's handle to keep the dust out. As I handed over the pistol, the guard noticed that it wasn't loaded and, in a not-so-veiled reference to a spate of friendly fire incidents in the previous weeks, said that was probably the only way Americans were likely to avoid killing their allies.

I told Simon that I wanted to introduce him to a prisoner who I thought could be of value to his people "outside the Facility." I told him the whole story and I was very blunt. I didn't want it to come off as any sort of a sales pitch, in case he didn't agree with my assessment of Hadi. He immediately agreed there could be potential and asked why I didn't make this offer to the OGA. I responded with a short recitation of names of prisoners whose interrogations had been undermined, flubbed, or otherwise complicated by them — cases with which he was familiar — and he just nodded. He was a true diplomat, a good spy.

The next day, I prepared Hadi for his first meeting with Simon. "There's a man coming to see you. His name is Paul. He's not an American. He works for some of our friends. He wants to ask you some questions."

"Why?"

"Because he needs to know the answers. That's the reason we ask questions."

I didn't make any mention of the true reason "Paul" was coming to see Hadi. There would be time for that later, if this interview went all right. I did go out of my way to give Hadi the impression that "Paul" was senior to me, had more power than me. I wanted to lay the groundwork for Hadi transferring his allegiance to my friend.

Simon arrived armed with chocolate, just as I had advised, and after introducing the two I stepped out of the booth. When he emerged from the interrogation — the interview — he only wanted to know when the transfer could be arranged.

The next step was to put the plan to the Joint Working Group through Major Gibbs. I found her one afternoon near the Puzzled Palace inside the massive Soviet hangar that loomed over our Facility. She was hanging out in the shade near a stack of dozens of crates of bottled water, petting one of the many cats she'd adopted at the base. (She was so army that she'd given her cats names like Apache and Comanche.) I made a sales pitch to her and told her that we couldn't turn the kid over to the OGA. If we turned Hadi over to them, I said, they would treat him like a wet wipe, just use him up and throw him away. I was expecting resistance from her, but she immediately grasped the plan and supported it in full. She took the case to Colonel Foley at JTF 180's intelligence command and in two days persuaded him that the prisoner could be turned over to Simon and his gang.

A couple days later, Simon came back from one of his frequent trips to Kabul. He brought back more Bombay Sapphire gin, India Tonic, and another real lemon. We took this touch of civilization up to the rooftop of the Facility. The rooftop was broad and flat enough that some of the troops had even taken to playing Frisbee up there. There were also some beach chairs, too decrepit for use in the booths. It was approaching dusk as Simon and I lifted ourselves up over the lip of the roofline, and the effect of the sun dipping toward the distant mountains and diffusing its red light through the fine Afghan dust was spectacular. Sipping that nectar and staring into the sunset, we plotted out Hadi's transfer to Simon's custody. He wanted to be the one to tell Hadi, and I agreed, but secretly planned to tell him first myself. I wanted to make sure that if Hadi reacted adversely, he would have a legitimate chance to object or back out.

In some ways, the transition had already begun. After their first meeting, Simon had essentially replaced me as Hadi's mealtime visitor each day. Food is important in both the Arabic and Indonesian cultures. Sitting down and eating with somebody is crucial. I yielded that dinnertime slot to Simon because I wanted Hadi to stop seeing me as his sugar daddy and start seeing Simon as his provider, his benefactor.

I went to see Hadi the next night, alone, and spoke to him in Arabic with no translator. It was too sensitive.

"You're going to go and work for Paul."

"What does that mean? How will I work for him?"

"You're going to go about your own life. It could be weeks, a month, or a whole year. At some point, someone is going to come up to you and say, 'Hi,' and you're going to sit down with that person, who will say to you, 'I need you to help me,' and you will help him."

"For how long will that happen?"

"Forever. That happens forever."

"Will I ever get to go to America?"

"I don't think so."

"Will I go to where Simon is from?"

In my mind's eye I thought Hadi might finish his "work" — whatever that might be — and go to Europe for school or some government job. Maybe he could teach language. I had asked Simon whether Hadi might ever go back with him and he said yes, it was possible. He talked about how they gave residence visas to people all the time. But I was skeptical, and I didn't want to raise Hadi's expectations.

"I don't know. Probably not, but it's not out of the question."

"Will they give me lots of money?"

"No. They'll give you something, but you're not going to get rich."

"Where could I go? Could I go to Oman?"

"I don't know. You should certainly make it known that's where you want to go."

Lastly, I told Hadi to make sure he acted surprised when "Paul" came in to inform him of the plan, an instruction he executed to perfection.

It was several days later when I took the paperwork to the provost marshal, walking down Disney in the darkness and wondering where the moon had gone. The forms for releasing Hadi were no different than those you would use for the transfer of any other piece of property, whether a shovel or a tank.

Description of property: male, seventeen years old, no scars.

Is it aviation fuel? No.

Is it combustible? No.

Quantity? One.

I got the signature I needed and carried the papers back to the MPs' cantonment, just outside the doors to the Facility. I woke up Weikmann, who fumbled for his glasses as I gave him a highly altered account of what was going to happen. In particular, I told him that this prisoner was being turned over to the OGA; telling Weikmann the truth would only complicate things, give him a reason to start questioning the transfer, gum it up. He got up and gave instructions to night-shift guards. Everything was ready for the early morning.

Of course, Davis, Kampf, and Hasegawa were all interrogating at 0400 local time when I hoped to pull Hadi and tell him my good-byes. The MPs had issued him new clothes — gray Afghan pantaloons and a matching gray top. He was waiting in the medical in-processing room, and he was a wreck. When I saw him he grabbed my shirt, one hand on the front of the collar and the other cupped around the back of my neck. He said he wanted to stay with me and said he would rather stick around Bagram as long as he could, even if it meant in the end he would have to be shipped to Cuba.

"Mike, I want to stay with you."

"That's not possible, Hadi. It's time for you to start thinking like an adult. You've got adult chores ahead of you."

Hadi was sinking into despair, and I became nervous that the whole deal might unravel. "You don't want Paul to see you like this, do you? He'll think twice if you're all tears. He's offering you the most unbelievable opportunity," I said.

He collected himself and went with me into the MP vestibule. I signed him out and we stepped outside. There was a silver Land Rover waiting at the end of the pathway to the Facility. I walked Hadi to the passenger-side door and let him climb in. I walked around to the driver's side — the right side in this vehicle — and started the engine. I had asked that no one else be in the vehicle because I didn't want the MPs at the gate to have anything more complicated to consider than a single U.S. soldier with appropriate property forms and a single prisoner. The MPs opened the door on Hadi's side of the vehicle and looked at him and checked to see that there wasn't anything else — or anyone else — hidden in the Land Rover.

We drove up Disney Drive and then down a rutted roadway to the airfield and there was Simon, getting out of an identical vehicle. I jumped out and closed my door and walked around to the passenger side and opened Hadi's. I handed him an envelope with $100 of my own money and told him everything was going to be okay. He leaned his head against me and sobbed quietly. I was wearing a blue Brooks Brothers shirt, and when he finally pulled his head back my shirt was wet on the chest.

"*Al mustakbal sah'takoon jyiad jud'an. Ma'ah salama, ya' achi,*" I said. (The future will be good. Peace, brother.) They took him out of the Rover and walked him, without chains or a bag, through the hatch of a British C-141.

The schoolhouse definition of "prepping" is getting the maps you'll need, preparing a questioning plan, looking up key words in a dictionary, picking your cover story, and organizing the booth space. But at Bagram, we began to use "prepping" in the same sense that the infantry preps a battlefield with artillery or air bombardment. For us it came to mean "reducing" the prisoner, softening him up.

For example, we were still making sure the prisoner got no more sleep than the interrogator he would face — and less, if possible. Prisoners were frequently brought into the booth the night before they were to be interrogated — or during the day if they were on a night interrogation schedule. They wouldn't be questioned but kept in the room with an MP for two, three, four hours, and then returned. Part of the reason for doing this was to ensure that all the prisoners appeared as if they were being taken up to the booths regularly so that no one acquired the label of "collaborator" among the others in the cages. But the main advantage to us was that they were forced to stay up a few extra hours.

We also used a variation called the Red Cross letter trick. The night before a prisoner was scheduled for questioning, we would put him in a booth and give him a stack of forms for letters that the Red Cross would send to prisoners' families. We'd tell the prisoner that we'd send as many as he could fill out but that the writing had to be very, very neat. And of course no matter how they looked, the MPs always said they weren't neat enough. Sometimes the guards wouldn't even look at the notes (they couldn't read Arabic anyway) and just handed them back, saying, "Too messy. Write it again."

It wasn't a total scam. The letters were eventually translated and — if they met the security criteria — turned over to the Red Cross to be mailed. (Detractors said this was the only flaw in the tactic — it meant more work for us, too.) The Red Cross, which monitored those letters very carefully, always thought the prisoners with the most letters were the ones who had been cooperating. In fact, it was the ones who we were having the hardest time breaking, since they had been through the most interrogations and by extension the most pre-interrogation Red Cross letter tricks. Ironically, when the Red Cross selected the prisoners they wanted to interview each week, they often picked prisoners with the fewest letters in the stack, thinking they were the hard cases and therefore most likely to have been mistreated.

We also ensured our target prisoners were scheduled for light work details timed to wrap up shortly before they went into the booth. Plus, we often gave a prisoner due for a session in the booth special scrutiny in the cages, busting him for talking or some other petty infraction, any excuse to subject him to MP punishments like having to stand in the sally port for thirty minutes. Sometimes the MPs would even catch prisoners talking in their sleep and wake them up to make them stand in the sally port. With less than three months to go before the first anniversary of September 11 — and the fear that another attack might be planned — we were not about to relax.

By July the temperature at Bagram was reaching well into the nineties. It was always at least several degrees cooler inside our cavernous, concrete Facility than it was out in the hot sun, but even so, it became something of a competition to find the coolest spot inside the Facility and stake it out with your cot. I'm pretty sure I won. There was a corner on the second floor, above the front entrance to the building, that seemed to have its own microclimate. It wasn't on one of the four main corners of the structure, but a right angle formed where the facade of the building cut in several feet and then continued on. There were banks of windows that had been boarded up with plywood to ward off the icy blasts of winter. One piece of plywood had fallen off, allowing sunlight to stream in, and there were other holes and gaps in the plywood on the adjacent wall that allowed air to flow across the space. I not only positioned a cot in the path of this aerodynamic effect but set up a basic bedroom, with a little desk for my personal papers, outdated *Economist* magazines, a chair that I restored, and a supply of bottled water with a miniature cistern.

The MPs loved to mock my fastidious little display. Once, I arrived at my sanctuary to discover a couple of new prisoner blankets folded neatly, with chocolates arranged thereon; a bouquet of flowers in a rusty Soviet-era tin can; and a pair of new rubber prisoner sandals under the cot. There was a little folded note that said, "Welcome to the Ritz-Carlton, Bagram." I surveyed all of this effort until I heard behind me whooping laughter: Weikmann and some of his MP sergeants were standing on the main balcony-hallway, pointing and smiling and telling me they hoped it was "up to my standard."

My spot was a thousand times better than the dank echo lounge, where the only illumination came from an industrial floodlight the engineers had hung from a sidewall when the building was opened. The beam was so bright that a shade had been fashioned out of a piece of metal suspended in front of the light by a hook, giving the place the look of a permanent solar eclipse. There was always somebody sleeping in there, and protocol dictated that new entrants be as quiet as possible so as not to disturb those seeking an hour or two of rest. In fact, the air in the lounge was so stale that I was worried the room was a breeding ground for sickness, and I asked the engineers to put in windows. They cut two holes in the outside wall and even made two hinged sets of shutters to close when temperatures dropped.

The only one who had a setup rivaling, if not surpassing, mine was Papa Smurf. His apartment was like the inside of *I Dream of Jeannie*'s bottle. There were blankets and rugs and pillows and books and a full supply of water and food — and he didn't eat army food, only local dishes that the interpreters fetched for him from outside the compound. They got cigarettes and treats from the PX for him, too. It was such a comfortable space, and Papa Smurf was such distinguished company, that the interpreters spent a good deal of time hanging out in there. Indeed, until Chief Rodriguez laid down a rule against it, the Afghan interpreters would even sleep in there. (Even after that rule was imposed, the Afghans would slip in there for naps. I was generally disinclined to enforce Rodriguez's rule because Papa Smurf's lounge was the only thing that kept the interpreters close to the compound after their shifts were done. Otherwise they went back to Viper City, too far away for emergency screenings or sudden requests.)

Smurf was generally happy in his role as camp mascot. It was certainly better than the alternative — being in the cages. Every once in a while he would belie his concern about his fate and ask me if I knew what would become of him. Of course I couldn't offer anything. That decision would be made echelons above my head and controlled by people with no incentive to share their deliberations with me. After one of these talks, I took a look at our file on Papa Smurf and was alarmed to find it almost empty. Here was a senior official who had been in custody for at least seven months, and all we had on him were three thin reports. I had just assumed that our predecessors at Bagram had fully interrogated him, and even though it was their job to do so, we'd be the ones to catch flack for it if the chain of command ever got curious about this guy. We had to do a complete interrogation and I had to assign someone to do it, even though losing any of our interrogators to a VIP prisoner whose information was now at least seven months out of date was quite unappealing.

I was about to give the job to Anne-Marie Walker when she got into an altercation with Smurf. The ex-Taliban had been loitering outside his room — technically a no-no — and Anne-Marie told him to go back in. Papa refused and Anne-Marie pulled rank on him, rank in the sense that she was a soldier and he was a prisoner. Well, Smurf had a fit about this and demanded to see Roberts, the last of the old Bagram team and a staunch Smurf ally. Roberts went in and listened to Smurf whine about the unspeakable insult he'd endured, a (supposedly) respected offical from a (formerly) sovereign state being ordered around by a lowly (female) specialist in the U.S. Army. Roberts did a decent job talking Smurf down and explaining that he had to respect Anne-Marie's authority in such a situation. But Roberts also went a little too far, essentially agreeing with Papa that Anne-Marie was a bitch and ought to have been more deferential to a prisoner of such standing.

Then Roberts really went too far and chastised Anne-Marie. She was the first one in my door, complaining about the outrageous defiance she had to endure from Papa Smurf and the unfair upbraiding she had taken from Roberts. I told her to collect herself and go to lunch. Then the second wave hit. Roberts came into the ICE and gave me one of those "Come Here!" motions that I don't react to very well. We ducked behind the curtain on the balcony, and he went on for twenty minutes about how these "fucking children" interrogators thought they were lesser gods. I told him I would take care of it, but Roberts wouldn't let it go and showed up at the morning meeting the next day and hijacked the thing to continue his rant.

"All of you guys are really an embarrassment!" he said. "You're nothing but a bunch of kids with a license to be assholes. And now you're turning on people whose importance and position you can't *possibly* even understand." Then he started dissing the other interrogators' skills. "Most of you should be ashamed of yourselves. The army has spent thousands of dollars to teach you Arabic, and the majority of you can't speak a fucking word of it."

As Roberts poured it on, Fitzgerald stood up and walked toward the door. It was his way of saying he'd heard enough. That's a move you might be able to get away with when you're a hotshot account manager in a staff meeting at a public relations firm. But in the army, if you're a lowly E-5 sergeant, you don't get to walk out on a staff sergeant in midsentence, no matter the circumstance. Rodriguez glared at Fitzgerald and told him to "Sit down!" Then he wheeled back toward Roberts and cut off his diatribe. "That's enough, thank you."

Roberts foolishly tried to press on, but when Rodriguez stood up and took one menacing step in the staff sergeant's direction, Roberts's rant quickly faded to a mumble. That's when I stood up and said, "OKAY, that's a wrap. I'll discuss this matter with the parties involved separately. FITZGERALD — you have water and ration duty today. Scheduled arrival time is 1100 hours local. Be there, please."

The meeting broke up and Roberts tried to leave, but Rodriguez and I caught him. Roberts was such a terrible example of a sergeant — so selfish, so myopic — that I found myself taking Anne-Marie's side. But she wasn't totally without blame either. Smurf was Roberts's prisoner, even if that was true only by default, because no other interrogator had been assigned to the ex-Talib. If she had a problem with Smurf, she should have taken it up with Roberts or with me, unless there was a real security risk. And, perhaps just as importantly, the sanctity of rank was at stake. When a specialist tangles with a staff sergeant, it's just a fact of life that the specialist can't get off scot-free. So Anne-Marie got a reprimand and she didn't like it. What she didn't know was that in the end, she came out ahead. By poisoning her relationship with a prisoner I was about to send her in to debrief, she got out of a thankless assignment. Instead, the job of debriefing Smurf went to Roberts.

RICIN

The only trouble with the interrogators taking part in Special Forces missions with Task Force Hatchet was that it seriously upset the interrogation schedule. When Hasegawa, Kampf, or Davis was on a mission, he could be out of the Facility for up to a week. And they took one of the precious Pashtu translators every time they deployed. The "terps," as we called them, went out with no weapons, no training, and no idea where they were going or what to expect. Trying to cut down on the toll on our roster, I sent Harper, the counterintelligence agent, out on one of the raids.

Harper had in fact been begging me for a chance to go out with the Special Forces, and when I told him he was getting a turn, he was so excited I thought he was going to wet his pants. He ran off and returned to the Facility decked out like he was going to lead the assault. He had borrowed Davis's Colt M-16 and Rodriguez's pistol and was carrying enough ammunition to supply a fortress. He was also wearing a battle dress jacket with cargo pockets — which had been taken from a pair of pants — stitched to his sleeves. To top it off, he had wrapped all his gear in layers of tape. It was my job as his sergeant to perform the precombat check. I made him hop up and down to prove that all the ammo and armor he was packing wouldn't clang like cowbells when he moved. To my amazement, nothing so much as pinged. *Must be all that tape,* I thought.

The mission was an urgent one. A Taliban figure using his satellite phone was overheard by one of our eavesdropping planes earlier the same day. According to a hurried briefing we got from Task Force Hatchet, the target had served as a liaison between the Taliban and Al Qaeda and had been on the phone long enough for spy planes to pinpoint his location, in the far northeast corner of Afghanistan. Whether he would still be there when the operators arrived was another question.

By this point in the war, the novelty of getting preraid briefings by Task Force Hatchet had worn off. The battles of the winter and early spring had given way to an endless series of small raids targeting remnants of the Taliban. Most ended in disappointment, either because the targets slipped away or because those who were caught were such minor figures that their capture seemed only to reinforce the growing sense that the highest echelon leaders — Omar, Berader, bin Laden, Zawahiri — would not be captured while we were in the country. The interrogators still appreciated the access to Task Force Hatchet, and their adrenaline still flowed as they came out of these briefings and went to work preparing for a new delivery of detainees. But where once the interrogators emerged from these sessions amazed at what they were told, now they were just as likely to grumble about how much was left out. The latest briefing was a case in point. Task Force Hatchet outlined the operation and provided some basic information on the ex-Taliban figure who was its principal target. But they didn't provide any details on what the spy planes had heard.

Embodying this divide between the haves and have-nots was a new face at this particular briefing, a twenty-eight-year-old counterterrorism analyst named Becky. She had once been an army interrogator herself — in my reserve unit in Connecticut. Now she was working for the Pentagon's spooks as some sort of analyst. She had recently sent us an e-mail from Washington with a list of boneheaded questions for a certain prisoner: "Be sure to ask if he ever had contact with any Al Qaeda" — that sort of thing. In a sarcastic reply that inadvertently went out to others in the intelligence community, I said that her list of questions was so penetrating it ought to be incorporated into the curriculum at Huachuca. Needless to say, she didn't appreciate that. Now she was here at Bagram, attending our morning meetings and our Task Force Hatchet briefings and, with her top secret clearances, holding cards the echoes could never see.

At the conclusion of the latest briefing, Fitzgerald, Hasegawa, and Davis surrounded her, cajoling her to give them some information they could use in the booth, something learned from the intercepts. Becky relented, a bit. "Okay," she said. "The man's *cunya* is Abu Rafiq." That was it.

Harper, back almost as quickly as he had gone, showed up in the ICE around 0300, still buzzing from his first mission with the Special Forces but disappointed at the outcome. There had been no Taliban minister, he said, only three men, all related to one another, who appeared to be caretakers for a local elder. The Americans had discovered some intriguing evidence, including a satellite phone charger and a fax machine that had been thrown down a well. But the target of the raid, and the phone he used, were nowhere to be found. Harper was called forward once the area was secured, and he advised the Special Forces to take all three males into custody. There were also women at the compound, but Harper followed procedure and ignored them altogether. Americans were loath to so much as approach anyone in a burka because to many Afghan males there was no such thing as innocent contact with their women. Violating this cultural taboo risked turning villagers against us at a time when we desperately needed their help locating the Al Qaeda or Taliban among them.

A group of us got up to go downstairs for what was shaping up to be another underwhelming in-processing. As we got to the stairwell, we could hear a commotion. At the bottom of the steps, we found ourselves in the middle of a small mob at the main entrance. There were at least ten people trying to push their way into the building, including at least one representative from each of the U.S. civilian intelligence agencies who had raced up from Kabul. A cordon of irate MPs was blocking their path because the OGA officers were refusing to hand over their weapons. Finally, one of the OGA officers solved the crisis by turning over her pistol, giving her companions an honorable way to back down. But once inside, the crowd was even more unruly, demanding to be in on the screenings of the new prisoners.

The reason for all the excitement soon became clear. Harper was right that the Special Forces had forced their way into the compound and taken three Afghans into custody. What Harper didn't know was that while he was questioning those prisoners, another piece of Task Force Hatchet was searching other buildings at the site. In a small, barnlike structure, they discovered some pots with a strange substance in them, a white powder in plastic bags. At first, the operators thought they'd stumbled into a stash of drugs. But a test indicated it was anthrax.

It was a preliminary result obtained by nonexperts using relatively crude field equipment. But it was, without a doubt, the single most alarming piece of news we'd gotten since we'd arrived in Afghanistan. There had been discoveries of equipment and recipes for various chemical and biological compounds discovered in crude laboratories in Al Qaeda training camps and safe houses. We'd seen reports that search teams had found residue of certain poisons in makeshift laboratories. We had even seen a videotape — which would be shown months later on television news — of Al Qaeda experiments on dogs with sarin or cyanide gas. But in this case the Special Forces had found a significant quantity of poison, perhaps ten pounds of it, and had captured the men holding it.

I huddled with the interrogators while the prisoners posed for mug shots, got their quickie medical exams, and changed into prison garb. "It looks like they found some poison at the raid site," I said, wary enough of the field test to avoid being more specific. The interrogators were all over me, asking what it was, how much was found. "We're not sure," I said. "This is a field test. But you can see the crowd here. Somebody thinks it's a big deal."

Hasegawa wanted me to approve monstering right from the start and I agreed — the first time I had done so. If these people had chemical or biological weapons, there was no point holding anything back. All three went into the booth — prepared not to come back out until the prisoners were broken.

The next hour was one of the most bizarre of our tour. As I went back upstairs and into the ICE, all of our illustrious guests were headed out. Eric from the OGA said a fresh report had come in from the JTF 180 chemical/biological weapons lab at Bagram. The powder in the pots was insecticide, not anthrax. I stopped to absorb this blow as our visitors filed past me, out of the ICE, along the balcony, and down the stairs. As they retrieved their precious guns, an MP fetched a shiny Colt for one of the FBI agents, paused to inspect it, and handed it over with a parting jab. "Here you go," he said. "It looks like it's never been fired."

I pulled Fitzgerald, Davis, and Hasegawa from their booths and told them to take it easy. False alarm. There were no chemical weapons. Shaking their heads in disgust, they shuffled back into the booths to wrap up what were now run-of-the-mill screenings with prisoners who would likely be candidates for release. It was 0330. A Facility that had been buzzing was now almost silent. I went back to the ICE and slumped down at my desk, wondering what kind of war this was, what kind of enemy this was, that a trio of lowly Afghans could give whiplash to the most powerful intelligence apparatus in the world.

And then, it happened again. Thirty minutes later, the same runner from the JTF 180 lab showed up. Another test had been done. It was anthrax after all. Not only that, it was "weapons grade." I didn't know whether to laugh or grab my gas mask. I reinterrupted Davis, Hasegawa, and Fitzgerald and explained that we were on again and that I wanted a quick huddle in the ICE.

Once more I sent a weary Turner to fetch the rest of the translators from Viper City. The meeting began with the three interrogators telling us the results of their abortive first sessions. They all complained they had lost their momentum when the first stand-down was ordered. All they could tell us was that there were two brothers and a cousin. All three denied anything to do with chemical weapons. And Fitzgerald's prisoner, the oldest of the group, insisted the substance was insecticide.

Everyone agreed that Fitzgerald's prisoner was the one to watch. Fitzgerald said he was smart, pressing buttons he thought would play to American vanity, talking about his admiration for American technology. Fitzgerald called this prisoner "the sycophant," but the other interrogators just called him "the cousin," probably because they didn't know what "sycophant" meant. Hasegawa and Kampf were working in tandem against the older of the two brothers, who seemed scared and bewildered. Davis said his prisoner, the younger brother, seemed mildly retarded. His speech was slurred and his mind wandered so badly that he was incapable of answering any but the most elementary questions. There wasn't much Davis could do with him but probe that feeble mind and hope he might blurt out something — a name, an item they'd hidden at the compound — that we could use to make the others think their slow-witted relative was giving up the game.

We had to work out an approach, one that would be coordinated and ironclad. I proposed a Hate of Comrades approach —

tell them they're in deep trouble because they allowed themselves to be used by Arabs. For an incentive, we would tell them
that if they cooperated they would be treated as prisoners of
war rather than terrorists caught with a barn full of chemical
weapons.

"What does that mean?" another interrogator said. "What
does 'incentive to be treated as a prisoner of war' mean?"

"It means we will not put him on trial," I said. "We won't
hang him for trying to kill us with his 'weapons-grade anthrax.'
He's to be treated like an enemy combatant, the kind we release
when the war is over. We're trying to get them to accept a window here. There has to be a plausible escape route for them or
they aren't going to talk. They have no reason to talk!"

Somebody raised the issue of the "dagger on the table" because of the hanging reference. But there was a distinction here.
He was right that we couldn't tell the prisoner he was going to
hang if he didn't talk. But we could certainly point out to him
that he might face trial as a terrorist — and let him draw his own
conclusions about how post-September 11 America was treating
convicts in that category. "No issue," I said. "We say we believe
the anthrax was for use in the United States. That would make
them terrorists. We execute terrorists. We're trying to scare the
shit out of them so we can get the goddamn information."

But my proposals weren't picking up many votes. Somebody else objected that my idea was "too complex a scenario. It
sounds like you're offering a couple of Afghan farmers a choice
between 'murder two with intent' and 'vehicular wrongful
death.' They're not going to get that."

An MP interrupted our meeting to tell us a "mass of brass"
was assembling at the Facility entrance. The field phone in the
ICE was ringing constantly with calls from officers in the Puzzled
Palace — just a few dozen yards away in the giant hangar on
base. Rodriguez had even gotten a "What do you know so far?"

e-mail from U.S. Central Command headquarters in Tampa, Florida. To all these inquiries, we had to make the uncomfortable admission that we didn't have anything yet.

Santos, the reports editor, proposed a Fear Up approach. Focus on the simpleton brother and get him to give up something, then take it to the others, convince them they're being sold out. But I worried that a Fear Up could get out of hand with the interrogators under so much pressure. I also thought it was too early to try an approach that left you stranded if it didn't work — close relatives are the hardest to get to rat on one another anyway.

Hasegawa chimed in with some ill-timed sarcasm: "We could kick the shit out of one of them while the others watched. We could tell him we'll stop when he's ready to talk. That'd be incentive to cooperate with us." There was too much tension in the room, and the wisecrack cut too close to what we were all thinking. No one laughed, and Rodriguez and I shot "not funny" glares at Hasegawa, who sheepishly retreated. "Okay, you can kick the shit out of me for a lame joke," he said.

Our debate had dragged on for half an hour, and still there was no consensus. Then Santos tossed out another idea. "Why don't we tell them the poison contaminated the area around the compound?" he said. He was proposing a Love of Comrades — convince the prisoners that their decision to harbor this stuff had put their relatives back at the compound in serious jeopardy. The only way we could get U.S. chemical teams out to neutralize the stuff was if they told us everything there was to know about it.

Everyone thought this was a stroke of genius. Someone even suggested we go into the booths wearing white surgical masks as props to convince the prisoners that we thought our lives were in danger just being near them. Major Gibbs joked that we ought to give the prisoners atropine injections to seal the ruse. I saw nothing but problems with this plan. We were going to convince some guys who had probably been sitting on this stash for months with no ill effects that suddenly their families' lives were in danger? But we were running out of time, so I settled things by saying we'd run a hybrid strategy, combining my Hate of Comrades approach with Santos's contamination scenario. The interrogators grabbed carpenters' dust masks from the engineers' tent and latex gloves from the medical station and went back into the booths. It was 0400. It had already been a long night.

Fitzgerald dutifully strapped on the mask and gloves before he reentered the booth, but right away he felt ridiculous and took them off. His prisoner, who appeared to be in his thirties, had light-olive skin, green eyes, black hair parted on the side, and a neatly trimmed beard. He said his name was Ghul Mahmud.

"So, Mahmud, why do you think American soldiers came to your house?"

"I have no idea."

"Maybe you ought to *think* of some suggestions," Fitzgerald said. "Why do you *think* it might have happened?"

"I don't know," Mahmud said.

"Well, you're going to have to make something up," Fitzgerald said.

Fitzgerald loved this opening. It was so unsettling for prisoners, put them right on their heels. For starters, it eliminated the "I don't know" answer that prisoners loved to hide behind. *Make something up.* Now the detainee has to start talking, which is the last thing he wants to do and is the first objective for any interrogator. But there's also a mind game at work here. Asking the prisoner to explain why he *thinks* the Americans came to his house sounds like a safe question to answer, as if Fitzgerald were just waiting for the prisoner to disabuse him of whatever erroneous suspicions the Americans had. But really, it was a question that cut right to the chase, the uncomfortable territory that the prisoner would much rather tiptoe around — the reason for the raid. He knows the Americans must have some information on him or they wouldn't have knocked down his door. The trouble is, he doesn't know how good the Americans' information is; he doesn't know exactly what they know. So now his mind is racing. How can he try to come across as cooperative without casting suspicion on himself? What kind of answer is going to satisfy this interrogator who's practically inviting him to lie? *Make something up.* So Mahmud does what a lot of prisoners do under the circumstances — he starts with a lie, but he tries to mix in just enough fact for his fiction to be credible. And that's a tough strategy to sustain.

"I have a friend," Mahmud said. "He comes to the house sometimes."

"Why would we be interested in him, Mahmud?"

"My friend knows some people who tried to do bad things to Americans. I told him not to visit me anymore, but still he comes."

"What's your friend's name?"

"Saleh."

"Who does Saleh know?"

"Saleh knows a lot of people in Afghanistan. A lot of guys who are with the Taliban and who are hiding."

"Who else does he know?"

"I don't know."

"Maybe you should think a little harder here."

"Well I think he goes to Pakistan sometimes."

For the next two hours, Fitzgerald bored into the detainee's story. He had Mahmud plot the route from his house to Saleh's on a map. He got Mahmud to admit that he had worked for the Taliban in Kabul, although the prisoner insisted he was only a low-level functionary. The prisoner said he had returned to

Afghanistan in 1994 once the Taliban rose to power, after fleeing to Pakistan in 1979 when the Soviets invaded. He said he
had spent his adolescence in a refugee camp in Pakistan. When
Fitzgerald asked how he learned to speak both Dari and Pashtu
so well, Ghul Mahmud said he had attended a school run by a
Saudi charity.

"What else did you learn?" Fitzgerald asked.

"I learned Arabic."

"How well do you speak the Arab language?" Fitzgerald
asked, now bypassing the translator and speaking in Arabic
himself. Ghul Mahmud's eyes widened, as if he suddenly regretted mentioning the Arabic. But Fitzgerald drew him out,
and Ghul Mahmud spoke in classical Arabic that was better
than most Arabs'.

As the three-hour mark ticked by, Fitzgerald asked Ghul
Mahmud if he went by any other names. The prisoner said no.
Then Fitzgerald proposed a break. "You've got to get something to eat. I'm going to leave you here for an hour and then
we're going to keep talking."

When Fitzgerald stepped into the ICE, he told me that he
had one report to write, on this character Saleh and the location of his house.

"Is he telling you the truth yet, Geoff?" I asked.

"No, not a chance," Fitzgerald said.

Someone else asked Fitzgerald if his prisoner was Abu Rafiq.

"I don't know."

A gaggle of officers from the Puzzled Palace and folks from intelligence services had gathered in the ICE, too impatient to get
their bulletins by e-mail or phone. One of the colonels was
reading my *Economist* and complaining about what a "liberal
rag" it was.

At 0930, Hasegawa, Davis, and Kampf emerged from their
booths for a status report. Davis declared his prisoner a complete

waste of time. I asked him if he thought the prisoner could be bluffing, whether his apparent disability could be an act. Davis said again that he thought the prisoner was "worthless," but he would go back in to be sure.

Kampf and Hasegawa's prisoner was concerned for his addled brother and asked about him repeatedly. As critics of my proposal anticipated, the prisoner didn't understand the distinction between prisoner-of-war status and captured terrorist, but it was clear he did not want to face the consequences of the latter. When the scenario was outlined for him, he let loose a stream of prayers and pleas: "I swear on the life of my mother. . . . I swear that if I lie may I die and go to hell. . . . On the life of my wife and daughter, I tell you this is the truth, . . . May I gouge out my own eyes if one word of what I've told you isn't the perfect truth." Early in the war we were swayed by such displays. Now, if anything, such pleas told us we were on the right track.

All of the interrogators had asked about the poison. Davis's prisoner didn't seem to comprehend the question. The other two insisted it was just insecticide, "Some serious redneck home remedy," as Fitzgerald put it, a substance they put on cows to get rid of fleas or something. And until a more definitive test came back on the substance, a sample of which had been sent back to a lab in the states, it was entirely possible the prisoners were telling the truth.

Back in the booth, Fitzgerald continued his circuitous approach. This time he started out talking about September 11. You could never anticipate how a detainee would react to the broaching of that topic. Some might be unnerved, but others, particularly the loyal Taliban and Al Qaeda, might actually be hardened by it. It could remind them of their organization's might, refocus them on the sacrifices made by others in the pursuit of their cause. Fitzgerald rarely raised the subject with

Arabs but often brought it up with Afghans, many of whom were dismayed by the civilian toll of the September 11 attacks.

"Do you know why we're here in your country, Mahmud?"

"No."

"Why do you think?"

"You're here to get the Arabs."

"Right. Why are we here to get the Arabs?"

"Because of bin Laden?"

"No. Not because of bin Laden. What did they do to us?"

Fitzgerald and Mahmud danced around this topic for a while. Mahmud mentioned targets Al Qaeda had hit over the years, the USS *Cole,* the embassies in Africa, the Pentagon.

"What else?"

"I don't know what else."

"There was something else hit that was not like the things you mentioned," Fitzgerald said. But Mahmud wouldn't say it, wouldn't speak of the towers.

"What do you think of all these attacks?" Fitzgerald asked.

"It's none of my business," Mahmud said. "I'm just an Afghan trying to live my life."

Fitzgerald backed away and again turned the subject to the reason for the raid. "How did we know to come to your house?" Fitzgerald asked.

"Well, Saleh was there during the night before you guys came and got us. He was talking on his cell phone. And I told him, 'Don't use that. The Americans can hear you. They're going to know where you are.'"

"Where is the phone?"

"Saleh has it."

If there really was a Saleh, and he had really used a satellite phone at Mahmud's compound, it seemed to Fitzgerald unlikely that he would have left with it. It was too risky to travel around with those things at this point in the war. There were a growing number of American checkpoints and American patrols, and the first things they looked for when they stopped Afghans in vehicles were weapons and satellite phones. If you were caught with either, you would be taken straight into custody. And if the Americans got your phone, they would have access to any numbers recorded in its circuitry.

"Who else lives in the compound, Mahmud?"

He mentioned his two cousins already in custody, and Fitzgerald asked about the women who had been left behind. Mahmud shifted uncomfortably at the question and said his wife, sister-in-law, and mother were there.

"Maybe we should bring *them* to this place," Fitzgerald said, entirely for effect. Women were never taken into custody. "Maybe *they* can tell me where the phone is."

Mahmud had been growing increasingly agitated with Fitzgerald's questions, like a patient in a dentist's chair bracing for the drill to strike a nerve. But there had been nothing in his behavior to suggest the paroxysm prompted by the mere mention of the women he had left behind. Mahmud leaped up out of his chair as if he were going to lunge at Fitzgerald. But instead of charging, he flailed his arms wildly and screamed — as if trying to demonstrate the sort of fury he could summon — but stopped carefully short of anything that might invite a blow from the MP. After his brief standing tirade, Mahmud fell back into his chair as if he were going into some sort of seizure. The MP gripped his rifle and shouted at the prisoner, then called for backup from the other MPs down the balcony. As the MP moved into restrain the prisoner, Fitzgerald rose from his chair slowly.

"Don't worry," Fitzgerald said to the MP as he walked out of the booth. "This guy's a big faker."

It was midafternoon. I was inside the ICE, surrounded by a group of colonels and other officers waiting for news, when Heaney entered and whispered that Fitzgerald wanted to see me in the hallway. Fitzgerald didn't want to get anywhere near these visitors lest they corner him — the star of the show — and demand a detailed brief.

I knew from the moment he opened his mouth that he had something interesting. "This could be leading anywhere," he said, "but I think the phone is hidden in the house."

"What phone?" I asked. "The satellite phone?"

"Yes. He said someone was walking in the orchard with it at night — the night of the raid."

Fitzgerald went back to the booth, feeling his pockets as he left. "Hey, have you got a pen?" he asked.

"What?"

"I can't find my pen."

"Jesus, Fitzie, did you leave it with the prisoner?"

"No, I forgot it in the ICE from this morning." He had been in there ten hours without a pen, hadn't taken any notes. In the schoolhouse, he would have failed planning and prep for that.

I threw him one of my pens and he went back in.

By now, Davis was actually making some headway with his semiretarded prisoner, a tribute to his resoluteness and skill if ever there was one. He came out to say the detainee remembered going to Pakistan to buy the "pesticide" and confirmed the name "Ghani" as the owner of the place. But even getting small pieces of information from this prisoner seemed to place enormous strain on his recollective capacity. It was as if removing even minor facts from that damaged gray matter involved so much rummaging around that it threw everything else into disarray. The prisoner was becoming emotionally unhinged. His tics became full-blown twitches. His misaligned features became further contorted. His whimpers turned to sobs so loud that they unnerved his brother next door (which was fine with us).

At one point, Davis went to the latrine and Santos took his place. The idea was just to keep the prisoner talking. We thought if he stopped for too long he might just shut down. But the interrogator switch had an unexpected effect. Instead of shutting down, the prisoner suddenly couldn't shut up. He started babbling so profusely and incoherently that Santos didn't know what to do, until, exasperated, he started yelling back, spewing a stream of nonsense on his own. Santos started out reciting the words to the Eagles song "Hotel California" at the top of his lungs, in semisentence bursts. And when he finished that he started belting out the Our Father in similar fashion.

> Our
> Father who ART!
> In heaven: hallowed BE THY NAME!
> thy kingdom come thy will be done
> ON EARTH — you heard me; don't sit there looking like you didn't hear me — ON EARTH as it is IN HEAVEN!
> Oh yes. HEAVEN YOU LITTLE CHEMICAL-WIELDING FUCKER!

The prisoner sat on the cot looking up at Santos. He was like a colicky baby distracted by a rattle. Suddenly realizing that he was the only one shouting, Santos paused. The two just looked at each other for a moment, frozen. This mind meld unnerved Santos, and he bugged out his eyes, contorted his mouth, and arranged his features into the universal expression for "Duh." The hypnotic eye contact broken, the prisoner started to cry.

After Fitzgerald's update, I took Rodriguez and Gibbs and a new liaison officer to JTF-180, a marine major called Kane, into the "office" behind the blankets to tell them Fitzgerald thought the satellite phone was likely still at the compound. "We should go back there and find the phone," Kane said. Indeed, he went straight to Task Force Hatchet to propose a repeat raid not only to search for the phone but to speak with the women left behind. Task Force Hatchet agreed and asked to have Harper go back out with them. However, everyone knew it would be problematic for a male soldier to question the women. Then Major Gibbs suggested an alternative.

"We'll send the lovebirds!" she said, her face beaming with inspiration, referring to Harper and his girlfriend, Anne-Marie Walker.

Women are precluded from the combat arms in the army and had never taken part in any of the Task Force Hatchet missions in Afghanistan. Walker and Pearson had asked to do so plenty of times, but I never let it happen. I didn't doubt they had the courage, I just worried they couldn't handle the physical requirements. You had to carry all your gear, including food, water, and weaponry, on your back. You had to be able to keep up with the fittest soldiers in the army. And depending on the mission, you might have to do it for days across some of the most rugged terrain in Central Asia. I didn't want to try to be an enlightened NCO only to find out that some part of a mission had to be scrapped because one of our soldiers couldn't keep up. Indeed, there were some men in our unit that I wouldn't let go. But now there was a good reason to ignore my no-female policy.

Walker was sitting in the echo lounge eating popcorn when I told her the news. "You've got to get ready really, really fast," I said. "They're going to take you out on a mission."

She leaped to her feet, and a satisfied grin spread across her face.

Walker immediately began packing and assembling her gear, with help from Pearson. When they emerged at 1630, it was as if the two of them had been primping for some *Mad Max* prom. Walker was wearing her Kevlar helmet, flak vest, LBE, protective mask, and rucksack. She looked so tiny. I wondered what the Afghan women would make of her. I also wondered what the special operators would make of her.

But Anne-Marie was bursting with excitement — not a trace of apprehension. Rodriguez asked her if she was ready to use the Colt M-16 she had borrowed for the mission. "I hope not," she replied with reassuring maturity. "But I'm ready to if it comes to that."

We went into the room next door to the ICE. Harper was in there finishing up his last-minute preparations. The chemistry was really weird. Major Gibbs thought everything was soooo cute, and Major Kane wanted to gag. I performed the precombat checks and snapped at Pearson when I discovered a few shortcomings. "Sergeant Pearson! Why isn't this water bottle full?" She was too good a soldier to answer the rhetorical question, but I could almost hear her thinking, *Because I've never been out in combat myself and don't know how to do a precombat check.* I thought, *Me neither, sister.*

The combat inspection finished, Walker and Harper left the Facility to get their briefings. Major Gibbs crowed about "what an army it was nowadays." Kane, a USMC reservist but one of the most professional officers we worked with in our tour, was chaffing at this double-dare mission, no doubt thanking his lucky stars his uniform said MARINE CORPS.

Shortly after Task Force Hatchet went back out, we were alerted to new prisoners on the airstrip — Afghans and Arabs taken in operations along the Pakistani frontier. My worst fears were being realized: my varsity interrogators — and translators — were tied up with the anthrax cousins. Walker was headed out with Task Force Hatchet, accompanied by another interpreter. And still another "terp" was on loan to General McNeil, the commander of ground forces in Afghanistan. Our cupboard wasn't bare, but it was close. I still had Pearson, Santos, Turner, Kavalesk (another late-comer reinforcement from the 500th MI Battalion at Fort Gordon, Georgia), and Heaney all ready to go. I called Bill Ellis over at his empty facility and begged for some of his linguists. There was only one left, he said. The others were out on Royal Marine operations. The remaining translators agreed to double up and support both the ongoing monstering and the in-processing. Weikmann sounded reveille for his sleeping night shift and promised to maintain enough troops to support this two-front operation. Even Papa Smurf was willing to help translate, he said, "as long as I don't know any of them." Everyone was pitching in.

The only exception was Roberts. He did not see himself as being required to have anything to do with Afghan prisoners and was so singed by the Papa Smurf-Walker affair that he had confined his workload to debriefing Smurf and doing some translation work for the OGA on an Iraqi prisoner we took into custody a few days earlier. Trembling with anger, I took him aside and explained that we needed him — Heaney and Pearson were the only Arabic speakers I had left, and Heaney would be needed for in-processing. The request rendered in a suitably supplicant fashion, he assented. I was glad it worked out, but I also decided that this was the last time I was going to have to appeal for his participation. Keeping him at a distance had made our lives easier, but we could no longer afford it. His long leash needed a serious yank.

Meanwhile, Fitzgerald was back in, his prisoner strapped down to a cot the way a seizure-prone patient might be tied to a gurney. Mahmud was sedate now but still in his "spell." Fitzgerald asked questions for a while but got no answers, only blank stares and senseless ramblings. Another interrogator would have been driven to distraction by this prisoner's antics. But Fitzgerald pulled his chair over to the prisoner's cot as if he were a psychiatrist settling in for a session with a troubled patient.

Over the months in Afghanistan, Fitzgerald had sat through hundreds of hours of interrogations, listening as his English words were translated into Pashtu. The language didn't mean anything to Fitzgerald, but he had heard certain syllables and snippets so many times that they were permanently planted in his brain. It became another one of his comic performance pieces to recite these disembodied Pashtu phrases. He used to do it in the ICE, babbling away and gesturing like he knew what the hell he was saying.

Hovering over Mahmud, Fitzgerald started in with his routine, *"Ho Maktab Aliday Andada Achindaday?"* They were words, or at least fragments of words, that Mahmud might understand, but they were all jumbled. The prisoner squinted up at him from the cot. So Fitzgerald repeated it, this time waving his arms as if he were imploring Mahmud to take his nonsensical question seriously and considered it impolite that he had not yet replied. *"Ho Maktab Aliday Andada Achindaday?"*

Mahmud seemed like he was starting to catch on but wasn't sure. So Fitzgerald rattled off some more gibberish. *"Hodon Misti?"*

A smile slowly spread across Mahmud's face. Then the smile gave way to laughter. Fitzgerald smiled back, partly at the joke but also at what he had accomplished: Mahmud's "spell" was broken. Fitzgerald told the MP to untie the prisoner and put him back in his chair.

It was dusk as Fitzgerald wandered into the ICE looking for some coffee, and I remember standing by and feeling guilty, as if I had drunk the last cup.

"How's it going, Geoff?" I said, making another pot.

"Not bad, not bad."

"Getting anywhere on the poison?"

"Says it's definitely insecticide or something. He says the owner of the compound is some sort of religious figure — a deputy Imam or semiofficial sacrament distributor, or something like that. Like a cross between a Long Island alderman and a Greek catholicos."

Once again, Fitzgerald got what he wanted: I dug in the

mental hard drive for the historical-sociological reference and
came up with nothing.

"How *you* doing?" I asked.

"I can no longer blink my eyes without thinking to do it
first, but I'm finding it an exercise in self-discipline, so —
pretty good overall, thank you."

The new Arab prisoners arrived just as Heaney was wrapping
up the first seven Afghans' in-processing. The doctor said two
of them — again, brothers — probably had tuberculosis. To
quarantine them, we had to empty the entire VIP wing. Trying
to find a spot to put the displaced VIPs would be impossible.
But at least we finally had a legitimate reason to wear the surgical masks.

The two prisoners with TB were not only brothers but also
twins. For some reason, they had dyed their hair and beards
bright, cherry red. Quite a few Afghans dyed their beards red or
jet-black, but these two, with their red hair and orange jumpsuits, took the cake. The MPs took one look at them and broke
out in a minirevue of the *Wizard of Oz:* "We represent the Lollypop Guild. And in the name of the Lollypop Guild, we wish
to welcome you to Taliban Land."

Walker and Harper returned around 0300, ten hours after
they had departed. Thankfully, they didn't bring any new prisoners back with them.

I pulled the varsity interrogators out of the booths to debrief Harper and Walker. The raid revisited had gone well.
They didn't find the phone, but Walker's questioning of the
women was successful. She had struck the perfect tone, pre-
senting herself as a woman who understood their plight and
wanted to help them reunite their families. She told the women
that the longer it took for the Americans to sort out the facts of
the case, the longer their men would remain in custody.

Afghan women had no reason to be particularly fond of

American soldiers. All we did was show up at their homes, take their men, and leave them stranded. But neither did they have much reason to be loyal to the legions of Arabs who had brought so much trouble on their households and on their country. Maybe Anne-Marie had the magic touch, or maybe these women were just tired of being married to the mob. Either way, these females in shawls were won over by this blond American in combat gear. Mahmud's mother acknowledged that her son was not merely a caretaker at the compound but was actually its owner. She admitted that he had done bad things, but like many an indulgent mother, she attributed his misdeeds to the unsavory company he kept, meaning Arabs. She gave us names and descriptions and information on when and how many had visited her home in recent months. Finally, she acknowledged that her son used a satellite phone, that it was he who made calls in the orchard, and that his *cunya* was Abu Rafiq.

It was creeping toward dawn when the interrogators emerged from their booths to get this update. They had been at it for more than twenty-four hours, stopping only for brief meetings and meals. The monstering was starting to take its toll on the prisoners. The smarter brother had buckled and was now describing Arabs that frequented the compound, including Mullah Berader, who had been spotted on his red motorcycle. Davis's man suddenly remembered more detail about the trip to buy the insecticide and admitted they went with an Arab to get it. The Cape Codder had no faith that the dumber of the two would ever be able to give precise directions, but the prisoner did say it took all day to get there. He also started to talk about expensive-sounding Toyota SUVs, a detail we kept under wraps. Bin Laden was said to have favored 4Runners. If that leaked out, we would have been trampled by every colonel, FBI agent, and OGA officer in Central Asia.

So the information was good. But the monstering was taking an equally heavy toll on the interrogators. Hasegawa, Kampf, and Davis were done. I could see it. Hasegawa had brought his chair in from the booth, dragging it behind him, and it made a *dunk, dunk, dunk* sound as it hit his heels. He sat down, tipped his head as far back as his neck would let it fall, and rubbed his temples with his fingers while he answered questions. Davis was also reclined, and his eyes were closed. Kampf refused to even let himself sit down and spent the meeting leaning against the doorframe of the ICE. All three looked in better shape than Geoff, who nevertheless insisted he could go back in.

"Fitzgerald, are you sure you can do it?" I asked.

"Yeah. I got some juice left. The prisoner's going a little batty, though."

"What do you mean?"

"He said he wouldn't discuss anything further until I get the '*shar-than*' off the walls."

Kampf and Davis, whose Arabic was strong enough to get this reference, laughed. Hasegawa and I sat there squinting.

"What's a *shar-than?*" I finally asked.

"A lobster," Fitzgerald said. "Trouble is, I think I see it too."

Hasegawa, Kampf, and Davis called it quits. We put the prisoners to sleep on cots in their booths but not before offering each a can of Coca-Cola. The three finished echoes fell asleep in the ICE, their limbs splayed out at odd angles. Hasegawa had a burning cigarette dangling in his mouth.

Fitzgerald had another cup of strong coffee, turned gray by the irradiated milk he used, and went back into the fight. It was 0400 hours. I put my head on my arm. Rodriguez's clacking on the laptop was like a lullaby, and I drifted off thinking about the raid, the prisoner in with Geoff, and the twenty-four hours that had passed.

* * *

"One of our women soldiers spoke with your wife and mother," Fitzgerald said. "You're Abu Rafiq, aren't you?"

The prisoner still had enough of his wits about him to try to play this off. "Yes," he said. "I thought I told you that."

"Your wife also said you're involved with bad people."

"Yes, I am," Mahmud said.

"Do you want to talk about this?" Fitzgerald asked.

Mahmud said he wasn't sure.

And then Fitzgerald used my favorite line.

"Mahmud, for you the war is over. These Arabs ran your country. You couldn't do anything about it. Maybe you've got a nice little life because they're giving you some money. But it's no longer worth it."

Fitzgerald pulled out a digital camera — a large, clunky, thick-cased model — and flipped it around to allow Mahmud to see the pictures on the tiny flat-screen monitor. They were shots of his wife and sister-in-law that Walker and Harper had taken at the compound. At Huachuca, we'd been taught to take photos found in a prisoner's pocket litter and put them on the table in the booth at a moment when the prisoner seems particularly vulnerable. We were supposed to point to little Ivan sitting in his apartment in Grozny and talk about how much he must miss his father. In this case Fitzgerald was showing pictures of women with shawls pulled over their heads — one shawl was black, one was red.

"What happens if you don't get to go home?" Fitzgerald said. "What happens to your family?"

At 0900, I went to get breakfast. I sat at the command tent picnic table, my hair matted and my face unshaven, eating eggs and French toast sticks. It was only when I caught sight of Davis in the chow line that my mind returned to the work at hand. As he sat down, he looked drunk, with red eyes and scraggly beard, clothes he had been wearing for three days, and a cigarette bouncing from his lip.

"Fitzgerald broke his dude," he said with all the enthusiasm of a corpse.

I ran back to the ICE, practically colliding with Majors Kane and Gibbs as I darted up the stairs. They had also heard the news. We found Fitzgerald on the Internet in the ICE. He didn't even bother being coy.

"He was the guy we were looking for. He owns the compound. He's been a translator for bin Laden and helped organize his dealings with the Pakistani arms makers, including a dealer who sells poisons. It's not anthrax, it's ricin," he said in one long breath.

Fitzgerald answered the barrage of questions calmly, clearly, resolutely. There was no specific plan for the poison. There was a chemical "expert" who was supposed to figure out how to deploy it, but he hadn't been seen since December. Al Qaeda wanted anthrax but could only lay their hands on ricin, a potent but basic poison made from castor bean plants. (Recipes for ricin had been found in Al Qaeda safe houses in Kabul in November 2001.) The supplier was indeed a one-eyed man in Pakistan. What was in their barn was their entire stock of the stuff.

Major Kane ordered Fitzgerald to file a CRITIC, an intelligence report of such high priority that it is immediately disseminated to the highest levels of the Pentagon and even the White House. It makes SPOT reports look like smoke signals in terms of speed and coverage. None of us interrogators had ever heard of a CRITIC, and Kane had to coach Fitzgerald through the process. Fitzgerald was operating on sheer adrenaline now, and even that gave signs of running out. As he pecked away at the keyboard, his eyes appeared to be swollen shut. He looked mildly annoyed at all the attention. When he finished typing, he stood up and ambled off toward Viper City.

After he was gone, I saw Mr. Dasi — the interpreter who was with Fitzgerald for the "breaking" point — who was now headed down to Viper City himself. I stopped him to ask why the prisoner had finally broke. I thought I knew the answer: monstering. We had never interrogated a prisoner that long — twenty-nine hours straight. Mahmud was seeing crustaceans on the walls by the time he was done. He had simply been worn down by Fitzgerald's will to keep going.

"What was it, Mr. Dasi? Did the prisoner say why he finally gave in?"

"Yes," he replied. "He said once he realized this was the worst the Americans were going to do, he decided it was time to reconsider which side he was on."

Fitzgerald's interrogation reminded us of something else, too: the truth can be what you think it is. My memories of this story are so vivid and clear that I can still see these scenes unfolding before my eyes. I remember the conflicting reports on the poison, the argument in the ICE, the follow-on raid by Walker and Harper, the increasingly exhausted looks on Fitzgerald's face as he slipped into the ICE to give us updates. Most of all, I remember Major Kane leaning over Fitzgerald's shoulder as he typed up the CRITIC — a type of intelligence report I had never encountered before and never would again during my time in Afghanistan.

Kane, Heaney, Rodriguez, and most of all Fitzgerald remember it differently. There is significant overlap in all of our accounts but also some significant differences. We all agree on the basic outlines of the story — the raid, the suspicious drums of poison, the follow-on raid, and Fitzgerald's grueling interrogation. But none of them remember Fitzgerald filing a CRITIC, or even having heard of that sort of report. According to a spokeswoman for the National Security Agency, a CRITIC is "intelligence and other information concerning possible foreign threats to U.S. national security that are so significant that they require the immediate attention of the president and the National Security Council." Given that definition, I have to admit that it's hard to imagine the disclosure by a prisoner in Afghanistan that he possessed ricin but had no specific plans for it would warrant CRITIC distribution.

According to Kane, Heaney, Rodriguez, and Fitzgerald, there was a report immediately filed, but it was simply a SPOT report, not a CRITIC. The next question is what was in it. Heaney has a specific recollection of Fitzgerald emerging from the booth, walking nonchalantly down the balcony, and saying, "It was ricin." After Fitzgerald wrote up his report, Heaney went back in with the prisoner to do mop-up work, getting details that Fitzgerald was too exhausted to collect. Kane and Rodriguez also share my recollection that the main thrust of the report Fitzgerald filed was that his prisoner had admitted the substance was ricin. But Fitzgerald, admittedly the most important witness in this account, insist that was not the case.

"The detainee never told me that he was in possession of ricin or any other poison other than insecticide," Fitzgerald recently wrote to me. "The detainee never told me that there were any Arabs ever in his compound; the detainee never told me he worked for Osama bin Laden. He worked for another Al Qaeda commander whose name I cannot disclose. The detainee never told me that he purchased poisons in Pakistan or shipped poisons into Afghanistan. Instead, the detainee brought money — lots of money — from his Al Qaeda handlers in Pakistan. This money was then used to finance anti-Western, Taliban-commanded operations inside Afghanistan; the detainee never revealed to me any knowledge of any plan to deploy chemical weapons. The plans the detainee revealed to me were all guerrilla operations using conventional weapons."

Asked what went into his SPOT report, Fitzgerald said he doesn't remember, that perhaps it was simply the confirmation of the prisoner's identity. I suppose that is possible, but that would be unusual, because SPOT reports are ordinarily reserved for the dissemination of intelligence requiring immediate attention, such as an imminent threat to troops. A prisoner admitting his name wouldn't ordinarily qualify.

Interrogators are supposed to get to the truth, to be concerned above all with clarity and accuracy. We were always so exasperated by how messy, inconsistent, and incomplete prisoners' accounts were. But in this case, it is our own account that bears some of those characteristics. It's a reminder of just how elusive truth can be when you are a collector of what the army likes to call "human intelligence." Everything we gathered came through a long, thick prism of prisoners' perspectives, cultural biases, skewed self-interest, fragmented memories, complex motivations, and partial access to the critical information we sought. It would be naive to think that the information wasn't then refracted again as we processed it and passed it on. When it comes to our own roles, and the way each of us saw his own contributions to this war, distortion is unavoidable, and as the ricin story demonstrates, sometimes irreconcilable. Some details have a way of dissolving when you have bags under your eyes.

It is no doubt less surprising, but perhaps more telling, that Fitzgerald and I also have very different feelings as we look back on this episode. To me, his breaking of the prisoner was inspiring, an amazing show of resolve and, most importantly, a major triumph. This was a battle of wits we had clearly and finally won. But Fitzgerald, who tends to downplay his contributions and take a darker view of events in Afghanistan, doesn't see his interrogation of Abu Rafiq in that light. "The mood was not triumph," he wrote in his e-mail. "The mood was trudging on through hardship and bullshit, sustained by a deep but non-bombastic sense of duty and the importance of the mission." Interrogators interrogating interrogators.

*   *   *

Whatever Fitzgerald's mood, we received a lot of praise for breaking the ricin prisoners. Colonel Foley, the head of Joint Task Force 180's intelligence command, congratulated me at a bit of an awkward moment — while we were taking a leak into the piss tubes (so-called desert daisies), eight-foot-long pieces of plastic piping jammed into the earth so only about three feet stuck out. It was about eight inches wide and the idea was to relieve yourself into the aperture. The colonel's words were very nice, but I must say I felt a little uncomfortable; I wasn't exactly sure what the protocol was for rendering proper military courtesy when confronted by a field-grade officer in a field of desert daisies while in civilian clothes. In the end, he resolved the matter by extending his hand to shake. We then spent a couple of uncomfortable minutes in front of the hand-washing stand without much more to say to each other.

Maybe it was as a result of Geoff's big win, or maybe because they were winding down their operation, but we had a very important guest in the person of Brig. Roger Lane, the head of the British Expeditionary Force in Afghanistan. He was an impressive man who, Bill Ellis explained, was a veteran of Northern Ireland, the Falklands, Operation Granby, and every other scrape the British were in over the last thirty years. He'd been in Norway for something like ten winters of hard Arctic training.

The brigadier appeared impressed with our operation and asked many good questions, including how long it took the average prisoner to break (anywhere between five hours and never) and which ethnicity was the toughest to crack (the Wahabi Saudis and the Yemenis). He was keen to know about the repatriation process and pressed me for details on how we vetted prisoners before they were released. This intrigued me, and I asked some questions of my own. The brigadier proceeded to suggest that some American officers thought we were a little too fast to label people "farmers" and let them go, only for them to resume guerrilla activities once the chopper cleared the horizon. I couldn't tell whether he was challenging me to elicit a response or whether there was some real concern behind his smile.

Later I brought up the matter to Major Kane, who confirmed that there were some complaints coming out of the Ranger troops and Special Forces that they were "reprocessing" detainees. I couldn't believe this and asked for details — but none were offered. He dismissed it as the idle chatter of combat arms (himself being originally an infantry officer) and advised I drop it. Of course I didn't. The interrogators gasped when I mentioned the rumors at the next morning meeting. This was a serious charge: we were now releasing too many people and had come full circle from the accusations months earlier that we were sending too many low-value detainees on to Cuba. Rodriguez and I agreed that from now on we would require two interrogations by separate echoes and another interrogation by me before recommending any prisoner for release.

When the interrogators were in the booth late at night, and all of my e-mail had been sent and the letters to the little kids written, I took up a little hobby. On squares of wood about eight inches by eight inches, I drew the unit crests for all the intelligence battalions represented at Bagram. The designation "task force" means a unit comprised of pieces drawn from other disparate units, if not from other branches of the armed services or other agencies or foreign militaries. Task Force 500, for example, was a real hodgepodge, with national guardsmen, active duty, reserves, and sister-service troops represented, even with the paring down of the interrogator presence. Each unit's crest was carefully stenciled in ink and made complete with that unit's motto. The last block was completed in July when Evan Cassidy, the interrogator from New Orleans from whom I took over the interrogation of the Beatles, arrived from Kandahar, the last member of our MI team to be recovered from that garrison.

The Fourth of July was declared a "Safety Stand-Down" day. All nonessential operations were suspended. There were posters in the chow hall touting a ten-kilometer road race, an interservice soccer match culminating in an international play-off, a speech by the commander of the XVIII Airborne Corps, Maj. Gen. Dan McNeill — the same general who had been informed by me that London was in England — and other activities designed to cheer the troops and help us forget how far from home we were.

In addition to the "mandatory fun," each military organization scheduled its own observances, and the tiny remnant of Task Force 500 left in Afghanistan was no exception. Captain Bournworth and our first sergeant, Guilford, planned a company picnic replete with a barbecue of local food. The NCOs and Captain Bournworth and his executive officer all chipped in, and Mr. Dasi, the interpreter, went to the local market and returned with a live, white lamb in tow. I think the Afghan native made everyone who shared his tent a little nervous when he shortly thereafter showed his talent with a sharp blade. The lamb was rotating on a spit above amazingly hot coals in just minutes from its last conscious moment on its hind legs. I sized up the spread after returning from my morning run, Dasi warning me to back away lest any of my sweat contaminate the food. In one giant Tupperware bowl, cleaned and borrowed from the Facility the day before, was enough rice for half of China, while in a second lettuce and tomatoes were piled high above the rim. "Afghanistan is a verdant country, *ya Wasim*," he said, using the Arabic name my teachers gave me at the DLI. "Now don't tell anyone we use human waste as fertilizer." I decided when the time came, I'd have an MRE.

Weikmann and the MPs had put up a giant American flag in the Facility, complementing the three-by-five flag already hanging above the cage. The MPs played "The Star-Spangled Banner" and "God Bless the USA" on a boom box. The prisoners appeared utterly unfazed by the whole affair, but whatever the ones in the jumpsuits thought of it, I was overcome with a moment of national pride. By God, we were in Afghanistan. On the Fourth of July. What a magnificent army.

At 1330 I got back to the Facility, having set the example in physical presence, if not consumption of local food. Back in the ICE, I noticed Roberts sitting there clicking away at a laptop.

"Have you been to the company area yet, Edward?" I asked, knowing the answer.

"I'm not going," the staff sergeant replied.

"Did you understand this morning that my requirement for each soldier to visit the company area included you?" The other soldiers in the ICE could feel the electricity in the office.

"Fuck the company, mahn," he said. "I'm not going anywhere near there." He had been furious with the army for what he perceived as his abandonment in Afghanistan after so many others had redeployed. He indicated that various agencies had approached him with an eye toward getting him to work for them. Given his imposing size, native Arabic, and sheer presence, that was no doubt true. But the battalion had blocked his way, and now he was disobeying a direct order and doing so in earshot of other soldiers.

I should have been calmer, but I wasn't. "Sergeant Roberts," I said, "go to the company area *now.*"

"I told you, fuck the company area, mahn. I'm not going down there to celebrate anything to do with the Five-oh-oh," he said.

"You are NOT behaving in a manner consistent with your rank, Staff Sergeant Roberts. You will go down to the company area as I have instructed." He didn't move, just stared into the computer screen.

"Okay — then get the fuck out of this Facility — MOVE

IT! YOU ARE FINSHED HERE." With unbelievable restraint, he simply got up, collected his notebook, and walked out. He got down to the MP vestibule and withdrew his weapon. While he signed it back into his possession, I opened the Facility access roster. Weikmann stood by, aware of the intensity of the moment but unable to piece together what was happening. I struck Roberts's name from the roster while he holstered his Beretta. As I escorted him the few steps to the main door, Weikmann opened the roster to see what I had done.

Roberts said something to me as he left, and I replied, "Good fucking riddance." I closed the door and was sun blind for a moment but could hear the MPs in front of me singing, "Ding-Dong! The Witch is Dead" I asked whether there was a single event for which they didn't have a ready jingle. Dixon broke out into the Beatles:

> You say yes, I say no.
> You say stop, and I say go go go . . .

I had to feel my way up the pitch-black staircase. My hand hit one of the wooden unit plaques I nailed into the concrete and I got the worst splinter of my life from it. Everyone on the echo floor was still staring down the hall. "What happened to Safir?" asked Papa Smurf, using Roberts's stage name. I passed by without answering. Hasegawa was there smoking in the doorway to his booth, shaking his head side to side and saying, "Duuude." Evan Cassidy and two MPs were also wide-eyed.

"Corporal — you watch the prisoners; that's your job. Sergeant Cassidy, go interrogate somebody — and NOT me."

The last man in the hallway could not be dismissed. It was Rodriguez. He had been at the company picnic himself but had come through the back entrance to the Facility and was already aware there had been a blowup. We walked right past the ICE and out the Facility back door, where I explained events to him.

As always, Chief supported me without so much as a single hint of dissent. We agreed to let the commander call us when Roberts finished his complaint. We would stand together.

The phone eventually did ring, but it wasn't the commander. It was First Sergeant Guilford, who was the top non-commissioned officer for Task Force 500. "Did you tell Roberts he could go *home?*" she asked.

"What?!"

"Roberts put his name on the departure log at the terminal. He says you told him he could leave. What the hell is going on?"

"I threw him out of the Facility for insubordination," I said. "I sure as hell didn't tell him to leave the post, First Sergeant."

Moments later the phone rang and Rodriguez and I were summoned to see Captain Bournworth down at Motel 6, the Soviet-built office buildings on the other side of the base. The buildings no longer served as army headquarters, which had moved into one of the new structures popping up all over the base. Now Motel 6 was largely empty, with plenty of space for our little episode of army *People's Court*. Bournworth couldn't help but smile when I explained what happened. "Sergeant Mackey, I am sure you were right, but you cannot dismiss a soldier from his place of duty. Hell, I don't know if *I* can do that."

I challenged him. There was no way I was going to let Roberts get away with gross insubordination in the field, in a combat zone, to a top-three-grade NCO. My army may be one that disappeared before I even joined, but there was still some sense of decorum, some accountability for behavior. "Jesus Christ, sir, I wouldn't let a detainee talk to me like that. And *my* actions are under scrutiny?"

He said I had it all wrong. He agreed Roberts's behavior was insubordinate, and agreed that an example would have to be made, but said that my reaction, throwing him out of the Facility, was wrong. The first sergeant chimed in: "Sar'ent

Mackey, I sympathize with you, but this is not the corporate world. This is the army. We can't go around just firing people."

In other words, the army was not as tough as public accounting when it came to disciplining employees whose actions undermined the organization. Bournworth must have read my mind because he added swiftly, "I can't say I'd have done it differently. I'm just saying we'd both be wrong."

There was some delay before a decision was reached. In the end, Roberts was sent to the medical authorities for "psych eval." I am not sure what they determined, but after some delay he was sent home. He got what he wanted and had his first real shower and real dinner many weeks before any of us who were left behind. I did hear a couple of rumors that he faced some sort of disciplinary action back at Fort Gordon. Knowing the way these things work, he's probably been promoted since then.

THE BEARDED LADIES

The next group of prisoners to arrive had been captured try-ing to cross the Iran-Afghanistan border wearing burkas. There were four of them, and we called them the "Bearded Ladies." Several days after their arrival, the MPs called up and said one of the "ladies" wanted to speak with me, had asked for me by name, "Mike." We generally made prisoners wait twenty-four hours or so before responding to such requests — we didn't want them to think they could summon us whenever they felt like it. And I didn't intend to respond to this prisoner's request at all. He was Anne-Marie Walker's prisoner, so the next morn-ing I told her about his request. She thought perhaps it meant he was ready to break, but when she went in with him, she dis-covered he was insistent on talking to me. I thought about wait-ing another twenty-four hours but was too curious.

Around 0400 I had him pulled from the cages. We sat in Heaney's in-processing room on the bottom floor. Two prison-ers had been brought in that night, and one of them smelled so bad the MP in the room puked. The vomit scent lingered de-spite my efforts to clean it. We sat down in two plastic chairs, our knees almost touching. He was a black African from Dji-bouti but had grown up in London and spoke fairly good English. He said he had observed me on the shop floor and had asked another prisoner for my name.

Instantly, I remembered a scene on the shop floor from the day before. I had attended Mass and was walking past the cages whistling a hymn, I think it was "Come, Holy Ghost." Suddenly I realized what I was whistling, who my audience was, and stopped myself. But the whistling kept going. A prisoner carried on my hymn as I kept walking, trying to ignore this little mind game. That whistling prisoner, it now occurred to me, must have been the same one sitting in front of me now.

"You are a Christian?" he asked, ignoring the "Where the hell are you going with this?" look on my face. "You are an American Christian?"

"You have ten seconds to say something useful or I'll send you back to the cage," I barked.

"I am Abdullah. I am from Africa, but I used to be a Christian. I broke my mother's heart when I found the truth."

"That's not doing it for me, Abdullah. Try harder. Try the truth about why you came to Afghanistan. About the school you attended in the Sudan. About all the money you had when you were caught. Tell me why you had all that money, or the satellite telephone numbers for known Al Qaeda personalities. Tell me those things, Abdullah, and then I will discuss your conversion to Islam."

"You are a very intelligent man," he said. "You have that look about you. But I am trying to speak to the 'faithful' you. I am trying to make you understand something more important than the things you have just asked me."

This little fucker was trying to run an approach on me.

"If I'm right, and you are a Christian, well, you are nearly there. You nearly have the truth. I will do you the greatest assistance ever if I introduce you to the truth." He said this while his hands were clasped in front of him, as a child prays. The tips of his fingers were up against his mouth. The wrist irons hung down on his forearms.

"Why do you believe in three gods?" he asked.

"Why did you have thirty thousand Omani dinars when you were captured?" I replied, leaning forward to within a few inches of his face.

"Your religion says Jesus is the Son of God. And that as His son, He is also God. But this makes two gods. And then you have the Ghost, who is also God. So you have three gods, like the Romans or Greeks."

"Why were you trying to cross the border into Iran?" I asked.

"It does not say anywhere in the Bible that Jesus is the actual Son of God. That is a fiction made by man. Jesus was a prophet. But Jesus is not Allah. We worship the same God, but you have him confused. You obscure him with the lie about the Trinity." He spoke in a kind, almost pleasant tone, his African accent lending a singsong quality to his words.

"I will convert to Islam if you tell me what you were doing with the other three, trying to cross into Iran," I said with a smile.

"Ah," he said, with his hands back at his lips, "you have nothing to fear from us if you are a Muslim. We are like cousins, you and me. If you accept the wisdom and the Word of Islam, then you will be my brother."

"I would convert to Islam, and accept Mohammed as the Prophet, if you would tell me the truth about what you were trying to do."

"If only I could believe you," he said, an odd role reversal. "There is the chance you would say this only for me to tell you everything what [sic] has happened to us. Then your Christian brothers would pull you back. They would influence your heart and have you turn against me."

He really thought there was some kind of a Christian conspiracy and that if I converted to Islam, I would convert to his cause as well. These Muslim firebrands were so wrapped up in this stuff, they lost all touch with reality. I told him that I was trying to save lives, like a policeman. I just wanted to prevent violence. If I could do that as a Muslim, then I would. He countered that once a person turned to Islam, he could not turn against his Muslim brothers. He suggested that if I truly converted, I would not be able to use the information on his capture against him. That would endanger a fellow Muslim. That would violate Islam.

The discussion followed this path for a while, and I angled for a way to turn this man's possible dementia to my advantage. But after a little more than an hour, I broke it off. I told him that Islam was a powerful force but that I could only be turned to a religion whose adherents loved peace so much that they placed the pursuit of it above their concern for themselves. He could demonstrate this, I said, only by telling me his whole story.

His last words that night were, "You are very intelligent."

The next morning, I asked Fitzgerald — my former colleague in Catholicism — whether it actually said anywhere in the Bible that Jesus was the "Son of God." He shook his head and bellowed, "*That's* why I became a Presbyterian!"

Once Hasegawa, Kampf, and Davis had recovered from their efforts against the ricin prisoners, I gathered them in the ICE and told them they would be pulled out of the rotation for as long as it took them to break the Bearded Ladies. "Please provide me with a detailed interrogation plan by dinnertime. I'll need you to get replacements up to speed on your outstanding cases. Include that in your plans."

Major Gibbs, Major Kane, and even Chief Rodriguez expressed reservations with my plan. Kane, who was given to speaking in infantry terms, told me that perhaps I should "conduct a reconnaissance in force" before I led an "all-out frontal assault" on these four. He was worried that forcing our top interrogators to go flat out again, on minimal rest, might wipe them out.

He, Rodriguez, and Gibbs were increasingly approaching me with warnings that the troops were exhausted, which I knew was true. The interrogators were generally getting four or five hours of sleep in a twenty-four-hour period, and even those few hours of rest weren't necessarily consecutive. By this point, we were so stretched that Turner and Santos were in the booth regularly, and I had told Pearson to prepare to give up much of her document-exploitation work to do the same. We had just been advised that Anne-Marie Walker was next to go home and would be on her way back to Fort Gordon, Georgia, within a week. When that news broke, even Rodriguez was readying himself to serve as a pinch hitter.

But despite these pressures, I didn't think we could afford to let up and wasn't all that sure it was necessary. I felt bad for the translators but not the troops. We were safe indoors while the infantry was out fighting. "All we lose is sleep," I would say. "They lose lives."

I also thought the Bearded Ladies were worth the allocation of precious resources. There was so much about their story that was suspicious. They were from disparate countries — one from Mauritius, one from Djibouti, and two from Yemen — and it was uncommon for Arabs from the Gulf to mix with Arabs from North and Eastern Africa. They were between twenty and twenty-five, the age bracket in which we found almost all of the firebrands. They had been captured with a lot of money — Omani reals, Pakistani rupees, and Iranian reals. (I took that to mean they had been to Iran before, though of course it wasn't the only way they might have come to have Iranian currency.) They had not bothered to take with them any travel documents, but the money suggested they were probably planning on bribing border guards or paying "coyotes" to help them get over the frontier. The telephone num-

bers they carried were for handheld Thuraya satellite phones —
there was evidence the phones belonged to Al Qaeda types. So
we were going forward.

While the interrogators were planning their attacks on the
Bearded Ladies, I went to the afternoon meeting. Captain
Bournworth announced Hasegawa and Kampf's airborne battalion was planning to deploy as our relief and was expected to
arrive within two weeks. This was a complete surprise. Until
that announcement, we had been told to make ready for a long
siege and that our best hope for relief was sometime in September. Suddenly, we would see our replacements by the end of
July! I never walked a happier walk than I did heading back to
the Facility that evening. I whispered the news to Rodriguez,
the only one I was permitted to tell, and the two of us wore
drunk grins the rest of the night.

When I did return to the Facility, it was to a considerable
amount of good news. Gary Heaney, with Victor Kavalesk —
the native Russian who joined us late in our operations — had
made substantial progress on the Russian prisoner that Hadi
had told us could speak some Arabic. Rodriguez had managed
to delay that prisoner's departure, enabling Kavalesk and
Heaney to get some very good information. Now they were
writing excellent reports about radical Islamic groups in the
former Soviet republics — the "Stans" — and even Russian
drug gangs in places as far afield as Minsk. Little mosaic tiles,
to be sure, but tiles nonetheless.

The interrogators kicked off their efforts against the
Bearded Ladies at midnight, partly for dramatic flair but also
because the temperature was cooler at that hour and the timing
fit the schedules of the interpreters, whose internal clocks were
so messed up by this point from the unpredictable work schedule that it was as if they were in separate time zones. They also
hoped the expected "breaking hour" would come in time for

them to write their first reports before our higher headquarters would see our daily schedule and barrage us with questions about why we were putting so many of our top players on these four prisoners. Hasegawa, Kampf, and Davis were thinking politically now as well as tactically. They understood the game.

My days were now filled with so many administrative tasks related to the impending arrival of our replacements that I seemed to make my way down to the shop floor only when there were guests that needed showing around. Usually these were representatives of the Red Cross or some random members of Congress visiting this work in progress of a country. One morning I was showing two officers from a coalition country a corner of the shop floor where we were going to erect a small holding cell for prisoners in their custody. As we passed the main cages, one of the detainees motioned for me to come over. I gave him a stern "not now" look, but this guy was adamant and started hollering my name: "MIKE!"

I thought there might be a medical problem, so I wandered over. It was one of the Arab holdovers from the Pakistani Family Pack, a twenty-three-year-old prisoner from Sudan. He looked very nervous and I feared he was hurt somehow. He motioned for me to lean into the wire, to get closer to him, as if he wanted to tell me a secret. When I refused, he made a peculiar motion with his hand, like a catcher sending signs to a pitcher on the mound. He formed a fist against his chest and then flicked out the fingers in a pulsing motion — three quick bursts. As he did so, he glanced from side to side to make sure none of the other prisoners could steal his signs.

I asked him what this little gesture was supposed to mean, but he wouldn't say. After a moment of back and forth, I turned to rejoin the two tall soldiers from the outback. When I looked back over my shoulder, the prisoner whimpered and wore a look of despair. As we walked away the two asked me what was up. I recounted my exchange with the prisoner and demonstrated the odd hand signal and said I didn't have a clue what it meant. Larry, an MP positioned nearby, started laughing.

"Sergeant Mackey, don't you know what he was trying to tell you?" he asked, the other MPs now grinning too.

"No," I said.

"How long have you been in Afghanistan, Sergeant Mackey?" he said, making it clear I was about to become the butt of a Bagram joke. "That ole boy had a wet dream and was trying to tell you he needs a new jumpsuit. Their religion says they can't sit around in clothing with their seed all staining it!"

Even the two guests were a little repulsed.

"Damn, was that 250?" asked an MP. "We must give that boy two jumpsuits a week."

Somehow I had managed to remain ignorant of this phenomenon. Back in the ICE everyone had heard of it and made the finger motion exactly as the prisoner had done. Heaney remembered this and the next time we saw Stacy, a cute OGA officer, he made that motion behind her back, causing the whole staff to erupt in laughter. Stacy wore a look of bewilderment.

With the varsity squad on the Bearded Ladies and the rest of the staff heavily engaged on other assignments, the task of screening a group of Arabs captured after a firefight in Khost fell to me. I hadn't been interrogating much lately, so I didn't mind, until Kavalesk told me the prisoners were not in the cages — they were at the hospital. "You bedder geht dowin dher qvickly," he said in his thick Russian accent, "becuz zey are nearly dead."

We had interrogated dozens of prisoners in the hospital, both in Kandahar and Bagram. This responsibility usually fell to Heaney, whose exploits in the hospital were the stuff of team legend. He interrogated prisoners who could barely drool, let alone talk. Once, the Marylander had a badly wounded, delusional prisoner convinced that Heaney was his father and got him to spill all kinds of good information. Now, with Heaney tied up on another interrogation, I had to fill in for him.

The hospital was about three-quarters of a mile away, down Disney Drive and past Motel 6. Mr. Jodsi, an interpreter, and I walked rapidly down the dusty road in the hot sun. The hospital was run by a reserve surgical unit from Pennsylvania. The place smelled like the inside of a balloon, with white tent insulation buttoned onto the green canvas shell. The insulation helped humming air conditioners keep the interior remarkably cold. If it weren't for the signs declaring MASS CASUALTY WARD and COMBAT BURN UNIT, it could have passed for a hospital back home. The nurses, taken right out of their regular jobs at hospitals in Pittsburgh and Harrisburg, wore medical shirts and smocks with rainbows and teddy bears on them.

Four detainees from the Khost raid had been delivered to the hospital, and by the time I got there, two were dead. Body bags had been rolled out over their corpses, but the bags were too stiff to drape down over the sides, and I could see limbs and blood. A slight depression, a lip, on the edges of the gurneys prevented the blood from running down onto the thick rubber floor.

The surgeon was explaining to me that a third prisoner was in the operating theater and a fourth was being stabilized in the trauma ward. As he did so I watched a handful of other doctors and nurses looking after a Special Forces soldier. He had been shot in the hand, and I could see the muscle and bone as the doctors examined it to see whether they could save one of the fingers. The soldier was almost expressionless and was wearing a T-shirt that said WALTER MONDALE FOR PRESIDENT.

The doctors said I could speak to the prisoner in the trauma ward. There were six or seven hospital beds in there, surrounded by a jumble of medical machines and life-saving equipment. There were mats on the floor with specially designed channels for the wires and cords that snaked their way to the generators outside. Down the right wall of the tent were three private rooms, walled off with the hanging insulation, each with a section of material pinned back, exposing the hospital bed and associated medical equipment therein. Only one "room" was occupied, and outside it an MP sat reading a Tom Clancy novel.

Just then another MP entered the room. It was Kimbal, one of the MPs from our Facility. He was sipping on a juice box, and the straw poked under the surgical mask he wore. I realized I was the only one not wearing a mask, but nobody told me I had to, so I started pulling my screening papers out of my knapsack.

"Kimbal, who's the prisoner in that private room?" I asked.

"That ain't no prisoner, Mike. That's General Hagenbeck." Hagenbeck had been the top ground commander throughout the first half of the war. "He's come down with something."

At least I wouldn't have to worry about the general's clearance as I interrogated the enemy fifteen feet from his sickbed.

The prisoner's bed was propped up so high that he was practically sitting upright. There were tubes going into his nose and mouth, and he was filthy, with gobs of dried blood and mud spattered on the stark-white bed linen. He had been hit inside a safe house with a shotgun blast at close range. The wounded Special Forces soldier told me that his unit had only recently begun using the safe house where the action took place. Perhaps the Arabs were going to use the safe house themselves, only to discover the U.S. troops were there first. Big mistake.

The hole in the prisoner's abdomen was hidden under layers of bandages. The most evident wounds were dark dots all over his face and limbs from the peppering of pellets. One had hit his left eye, and a yellow fluid seeped through the white mesh of his eye bandage. His wrists were zip tied to the frame of the bed. Kimbal told me it was because the prisoner had tried to rip his tubes out.

There was no name on the incoming patient registry for the prisoner, only the MPs' scribbling of the number 280, which they had crossed out and revised as the other prisoners had died. He was now 278, the number he would die with.

I examined the four Ziploc bags containing all the prisoners' possessions, but nobody had bothered to mark whose possessions were whose. I sat on the edge of one of the empty beds and pulled out all the trash and money. I gathered from the contents that these men were Arabs and not Afghans. There were notes on the backs of photographs of children and currency from various Arab countries. There was an ID card with a photo matching the man lying down in front of me. It had the look of a work pass or university ID, with a birth date, an address, and the name Layth (an Arabic first name that means "lion cub").

I looked up from the piles of possessions and saw the prisoner's head was turned in my direction, his one eye partly open and focused on me. Standing up, I walked toward him and he closed his eye and turned his face toward the ceiling.

"I'm Mike, from the U.S. government. The doctors said you were well enough to speak with me. I want to notify your family that you are in detention here. Tell me how to reach them."

No reaction.

"Tell me about your family, Layth. Is that your name? Are you Layth?"

Nothing.

We carried on for five or ten minutes, me asking questions and getting nothing but silence. At one point he said his name was Abdullah Surya but was quiet again for perhaps five more minutes. Then suddenly, he just began talking. It was as if he knew he was going to die and didn't want to leave the earth without telling someone how he had spent the last months of his life. He didn't give me any particularly valuable intelligence, didn't sell out any of his Arab colleagues, but he did trace his recent travels. He said he came to Afghanistan in 2001, before the attacks in New York, and trained at Khalden Camp, not far from Kandahar. After the U.S. invasion he fled to Pakistan and hid in Rawalpindi for months. He had only recently returned to Afghanistan. That was pretty much all he would say.

I was anxious to get more information from the man, but it was like speaking over a bad telephone line. I had to repeat everything over and over again. The patient was drifting in and out of consciousness, at one point claiming that he had shot down a helicopter at Bagram Air Base two or three days before (there had been no such incident to my knowledge) but then denying he said it a few moments later. At last the "line" went silent as he slipped off into an unconsciousness from which I later learned he did not recover. I filled out a file on the information he provided. Where the form prompted the writer to indicate whether the prisoner was available for recontact, I wrote, "No."

Bagram was quickly becoming a series of good-byes. The next to leave was Sergeant Major Ellis. After he got the word to start packing, he invited the whole gang to his facility, situated in a cantonment that now resembled a ghost town, for one big fling before he left. I told only the NCOs in the unit — excluding everyone below the rank of sergeant, partly because of my belief in the privilege of rank, partly because we needed some troops on hand in case prisoners came in, but mainly because Heaney, Fitzgerald, Santos, Hasegawa, and Davis were the troops I knew best and felt I could trust to have a few beers, tell a few stories, and avoid trouble.

The party had a real Austin Powers vibe, with an enormous bonfire, a barbecue, beers on ice, and a raucous crowd of thirty or so people. I'd never seen anything like it take place in an American compound. Billy had even persuaded a group of

Spanish nurses to attend, although they quickly fled the persistent advances of some Royal Marines.

As a preventative measure, I had told the MPs at the Facility that no echoes were to be allowed back into the prison that night. I characterized this edict as enforced rest for the interrogators, although the real reason was that I didn't want anyone to go into the booth with beer on his breath. The thought that one of them might commit some inebriated excess was not appealing.

I exempted myself from this prohibition and left the others at the Viper City gate, now manned permanently by 82nd Airborne troops. They went to their tents to sleep and I went back to the Facility to find Davis — who had been at the party — sitting at a laptop.

Davis's beard was in its full, Robinson Crusoe bloom. His body had become slightly pudgy, with walks to the chow hall or the shitters constituting his only exercise. His smoking was out of control, to the point where he was bumming cigarettes off even high-ranking strangers who came to visit us. Looking at him now, I thought I could even detect the beginnings of a hunch. Before I could say anything, Davis started asking some question about my interaction with the Sudanese kid who tried to convert me to Islam. I asked why he was up here after I told everybody to stay down in Viper City. He said he had left the party hours ago and didn't drink anything. He was doing research on the computers, preparing to go back into the booth for more. The only other person in the office was Rodriguez, who was too good an officer to join us for the drinks, and too good a man to keep us from going. I caught him — the only time in my Bagram memories — sound asleep on a cot he pulled into his little office from the echo lounge.

It was a strange night. There were no interrogations going, only two prisoners who had been pulled up to sit alone in the booths to maintain the charade of ongoing business for the others in the cages. Both prisoners were sleeping with their heads down, MPs sitting beside them rereading magazines they had read a hundred times before. Outside of Davis and the semiconscious MPs, the only other person who was awake was Papa Smurf at the end of the hallway. He was standing there, also smoking, holding his cigarette in that Euro way: the embers upright, the filter between his thumb and forefinger. He was leaning over the railing, getting a good look at the jumpsuited prisoners below.

"Do you hate them?" he asked me.

"The Arabs?"

"The Arabs and the Afghans. Us. Do you hate *us?*"

"I hate *those* guys," I said, pointing down below. "Not even all of them, really. But most of 'em aren't very good people."

"In your interrogations, do you think they hate *you?*" he asked.

"I dunno. Sometimes I think so. Sometimes I think I can almost see how much they hate me. I talked to a guy in the hospital a couple of days ago. All shot to shit. I think *he* hated me. A few of those guys really hate us. Most of them do, I guess."

"They are afraid for [*sic*] you. Where they come from, the army, the police, the intelligence, they torture people. They are afraid what will happen to them." He was wearing flip-flops and he kept clinching his toes together, making the sagging sole slap the bottom of his foot rhythmically. "Do you fear for them?" he asked, again confusing his prepositions.

"Sometimes I do. Not as individuals. But sometimes I get worried about the global conspiracy of what's happening. You see how widespread this shit is and you get to thinking it's really pretty damn huge and pretty much everywhere. But then you get to talking to some of these fuckers and you figure — this is as good as you got?"

He laughed. "Don't forget, these are just the ones who got caught."

It seemed very weird to be talking to him like this, but I was giving in to the growing sense of freedom that comes with being a short-timer, of knowing that soon I would be no longer involved. And in a way, I felt as if I owed him an explanation.

"You know we don't hate Islam," I said. "We're not trying to fight Islam. That is such a lie, and so many of these poor idiots think we are trying to put the kibosh on you guys. It isn't true."

"You guys don't even know your own religion," Smurf said.

I wondered if he had this conversation with others of us. Hasegawa had no personal connection to the September 11 attacks, but he seemed to take them very personally, and to him every suspicious prisoner was part of that conspiracy. Hasegawa was smart enough to know we had a highly prejudicial sample in the cages below, but he didn't admire the piety of the Arabs and Afghans as Heaney, Pearson, and I did. I can't imagine he ever looked over the balcony at night with any sympathy, let alone admiration, for the praying men below.

I looked at Papa Smurf, who kept his eyes trained on the prison floor. "I appreciate Islam," I said. "I respect it. And I don't think these guys represent it. These jokers are criminals, not soldiers or emissaries of your religion."

Smurf nodded, and a long silence followed. Then, just as suddenly as he had opened this conversation, he ended it.

"Good night, Wassim," he said, and flip-flopped into his room.

The exchange left me profoundly unfulfilled. I felt like I had failed to convince him of my honestly favorable opinions of Arabs and the Arab world, of Islam and the countries that embraced it. Maybe he thought I was trying to put one over on him, or run an approach. Anyway, I didn't expect him to so suddenly check out of the conversation, and now I felt stupid. As I climbed into my cot, I thought about whether our efforts in Afghanistan had been hindered by our barely passable understanding of the enemy's culture. Of Afghan clans and Saudi tribes we knew nothing until we had started to pick up a rudimentary knowledge in Bagram. We were only beginning to see how cultural differences and ethnic divisions could be manipulated toward our ends. All of that was only just dawning on us, and we were getting ready to leave.

PART

IV

FOR ME, THE WAR IS OVER

I couldn't believe I had slept past sunrise. I stood up, stretched, and took two hobbled steps on the creaking ankle I had developed in Afghanistan. (It bothers me still, but only for my first few steps each morning.) I was looking for my running shoes when I noticed over the railing that the prisoners were all awake down on the shop floor. They had already had at least one set of prayers. It was late.

I couldn't wait to go home, but I had the sense a pretty momentous part of my life was finishing up. As I jogged down Disney Drive, I tried to memorize the details of the place so I could remember them as an old man. The dust, the old Russian offices and officers' barracks slowly being transformed into a U.S. military garrison — I wanted to make a mental documentary of it all to replay in my mind when I was back at my desk at work navigating European tax regulations.

On the way back to the Facility, I saw Captain Bournworth stretching for his own run. He beckoned me over and we talked for a moment about the handover. Rodriguez and I were to work out a transition that would let the newcomers observe for a few days, then perform the work for a few days under our supervision, and then take over entirely. Bournworth knew both Rodriguez and I opposed the method of handover: we thought removing all our experienced interrogators at one time was the height of folly. No matter how good the replacements were, they could not possibly take over this job effectively with four days right-seat, four days left-seat driving. It was a recipe for sending interrogation technique back to that of the dark days of Kandahar in December. But while Bournworth sympathized, his hands were tied. Army says, army does.

I had taken to walking off my runs inside the Facility — the prisoners stared at me oddly, but the cool, relatively dust-free air was a relief. Walking up the stairs to my little hovel, I caught sight of a blue, six-pointed star painted on the far wall about eight feet up. It was as big as a serving platter and visible from the shop floor, with two blue bars, top and bottom. Someone had painted a large Israeli flag on the prison wall! Then I saw two others, on other sections of the wall, also in view of the prisoners.

Weikmann didn't seem to understand the magnitude of this provocation and reacted as if it were merely a case of vandalism. Kavalesk, Heaney, Pearson, and Turner were in the ICE getting ready for the morning meeting, but none knew anything about the Zionist graffiti. Rodriguez and I duct taped some newspaper over the offending symbols, which, it turned out, were the creations of a couple of MPs who were surprised their "humor" was such a big deal. To them it was a simple "in your face" to the prisoners. The MPs were made to clean the markings off the wall with stiff-bristle brushes but were not punished beyond that.

We next said good-bye to Anne-Marie Walker, whose contributions to the effort were many. I was sad to see her go, not because of any personal affinity toward her — she wasn't a big fan of me either — but because she was a solid performer in the booth and her expertise would be missed. I am sure she wasn't too disappointed to get back to the real army and out from under the leadership of two reservists with their own way of doing things. Of course she was sad to be temporarily leaving her fiancé, Harper, but she had been deployed for more than a year — having spent months in Kuwait before arriving at Kandahar in December — and was ready to go home.

She left a few days after the advance party for our replacements from Hasegawa and Kampf's airborne unit began to arrive. The contingent was led by a Major Holmes, who quickly made it clear he wasn't thrilled with the way we were running things at Bagram, the "circuslike atmosphere" of the place. And though his troops weren't due to arrive for another week or two, he began pushing for some changes. The first thing he tried to do was ban smoking in the Facility. (He regarded the icon of an interrogator offering a cigarette to a prisoner as passé.) Our policy, he declared, was encouraging smoking among the troops, dangerous from a fire-safety standpoint, and a hazard to nonsmokers. Fortunately, Major Gibbs intervened and brokered a compromise whereby troops could smoke, but only in the booth.

On the day that Walker left, Holmes took me to a quiet corner and lit into me, furious that I would allow soldiers to conduct themselves in such an "unprofessional manner." He had apparently seen Harper and Walker saying their good-byes. And he said it wasn't the first time in his two weeks at the Facility that he picked up on these "vibes." There had been other people "sitting too close" or "making eyes at one another." He declined to elaborate.

But the thing that made Holmes angriest was our appearance. He didn't buy our theory that civilian clothes were an advantage in the booth. I tried to tell him that these detainees came from countries in which only rogues and criminals and conscripts — the lowest of the low — were in the army. If we were in uniform they would assume the same of us. In addition, wearing civilian clothes also enabled us to pass ourselves off as officers from the OGA or other agencies — akin to the security and intelligence services these detainees feared in their homelands. None of these arguments made an impact.

I agreed with Holmes on one point — that the ICE was trashed and too cramped. A few weeks earlier I had selected a location for a new one but was reluctant to get the project under way until the last minute, partly because I was worried the move would be a distraction but more because the proposed location would force me out of my little ventilated bedroom. Now, a few weeks before our replacements arrived, I decided the time was right to get the project rolling. The space was probably used by the Soviets as a planning room or engineering-design room. It was on the second floor, the same floor as the ICE, but at the front of the building. It had plenty of room and a spectacular view over the shop floor. It would be easy to heat in the winter and would benefit from those cooling breezes during the summer. Rodriguez and I called those brilliant engineers again, and they started making their racket.

Other than the odd Arab prisoner from Pakistan or transfers from other U.S. facilities, our stock and trade had become Afghans. The highest of the high-value targets — bin Laden, Zawahiri, Mullah Omar, Mullah Berader — remained at large. But the increasingly homogenous demographic in our cages told us that a major phase of the war — the capturing, killing, or at least displacing of the thousands of Arabs who had descended on the country to fight jihad or train for terrorist assignments — had all but ended.

At the beginning of the war, we had held on to everybody. In the middle, we were releasing about half the Afghans we took into custody. By the end, we were releasing eight out of ten. Indeed, by late July, just one of the Riverbed 32 was still in custody. All of the others from that raid, the first of our tour in Bagram, the one on which we were introduced to Task Force Hatchet, had been repatriated. The one remaining prisoner was, of course, 141, Fitzgerald's man. We picked up tiny scraps of information on him from time to time. A snitch in the cages told us he overheard 141 saying he was being untruthful; an Afghan caught in a raid near 141's point of capture identified him in the mug book as a "war hero." Two other Riverbed detainees told us, as they were being led to the helicopter pad, that 141 was a "scoundrel" and a "thief." Our hunt for the truth continued.

I had tried to do what I could. In June I added a new routine to my daily life at Bagram. After I brushed my teeth in the morning (which I did at 0430 and 2200 regardless of when I got up or went to sleep), I met Mr. Jodsi, our jolly, older civilian translator, inside the MP vestibule. Accompanied by the sergeant of the guard, we would approach the cages. There 141 would be ready, like a pet waiting to be let out of the house. The four of us would proceed to the in-processing room, where the prisoner would sit Indian style on the floor.

"What is the connection between Abdul Fawaz and Mullah Berader?" I would ask.

"I tell you everyday, I do not know this man."

"Where did you meet Mullah Berader?"

"I tell you on my life and on the lives of my family and on my eyes that I do not know this man."

"Where is Mullah Berader now?"

"I swear to you on my eyes and ears and on my mother's life I do not know; may Allah heap blessings upon you and give you everything that is good. I promise you I do not know a thing."

"Why are you protecting Mullah Berader?"

"I swear to you again and on the lives of my children and on my eyes that I do not know this Mullah."

"You are lying, but you do not need to. When you answer me truthfully, I will put you on the next helicopter home. All of the people with whom you were captured have been released because they were truthful. You can go the instant you eliminate our suspicion by cooperating and supporting justice."

Mr. Jodsi had been translating the whole thing so long now he knew it by heart. When the prisoner gave his replies to the standard questions, he would just say, "Blah blah blah," to the intense annoyance of 141, who always wanted his whole, impassioned appeal translated verbatim, regardless of how often we heard it. I was annoyed, too — try as I might, I hadn't broken 141.

Over time, others began to doubt that 141 had anything to tell. Near the end of July, Rodriguez and I sat in the ICE preparing our Friday report, which included repatriations recommendations. We came to our favorite prisoner, 141.

"What do you think, Mackey?" Rodriguez asked. "Time to give up?"

"I think he's on the ropes, Chief, I think he's on the ropes," I said.

"You gonna hand him off to your replacement?" he asked in a tone that made it clear he thought that was unnecessary.

"You suppose I shouldn't, Chief?"

"Weeell, I'm just sayin' . . ."

After a few minutes of his double-talk and conversational contortions, I surrendered. We put little 141 on the "repat" list. Major Gibbs chuckled at the appearance of the name when she arrived to review the compilation. "Given up, eh?" she crowed with a smile. She was great for this job: good humored, detail oriented, but not a micromanager. But it was times like this my eye began to twitch.

"ONE MORE DAY! Gimme just one more day with 'im!" I said. "I'll show you who's given up!" The handful of interrogators in the ICE just laughed.

Not more than twelve hours later, Hasegawa showed up in the ICE with bloodshot eyes and a huge smile: "Ladies, we broke the Bearded Ladies!" The half dozen of us in the office cheered. It had been three and a half days. There had been constant interrogations but no monstering in this case, meaning the interrogators always had at least one prisoner in the booth but didn't question any of them around the clock.

Their work was textbook. The interrogators had mapped out detailed translator schedules and questioning plans. They used other detainees in the cages to spread rumors that unsettled the prisoners, planting information that Iranians and Afghans along their countries' common border were selling out the Arabs. Finally, one of them broke, the Mauritius man with the fair skin and funny lips. Using the information garnered from that interrogation, Davis broke a second prisoner with a We Know All approach. A third surrendered upon learning that two of his comrades had capitulated.

The last of the Bearded Ladies was stubborn. Kampf dueled with him for hours with no break before the interrogators improvised. Under heavy MP guard, they brought two of the broken prisoners into the holdout's booth. The two were acutely uncomfortable as Kampf ticked off their disclosures. "Didn't you tell us . . . I believe it was you who told us . . ." The unbroken prisoner at first erupted in anger at his friends but quickly began weeping and moaning that they had all been duped.

We separated the prisoners again and told the one who hadn't given up that he now had a choice: Cuba or take your chances with which Arab government we sell your ass to. Kampf rolled out the picture of the Cuba facility that I once used as a prop in my Kandahar shift-change brief. He pointed to the facilities for "cooperative detainees," where prisoners were speaking "leisurely" with U.S. intelligence personnel prior to being repatriated to Afghanistan on "special visas."

Within minutes, the prisoner provided information on Arab escape routes to Iran that even the others hadn't disclosed. A short while later, the Ladies were sent to GTMO.

* * *

The day finally arrived. A telephone call from Motel 6 announced the arrival of our relief. I went down to greet them — five members of my reserve unit and thirty or so more from the airborne intelligence battalion. Among the troops from my unit were Kelleher and McGovern, buddies from Fordham who were practically unhinged with excitement to be, at last, in the war. Our little group of ten would give way to a unit more than triple in size.

When the replacements arrived at the Facility the next morning, they were all in uniform, as per Holmes's obscenely shortsighted orders. Immediately, the prisoners were abuzz, asking us who these *army* people were. After several protests on our part, the new command agreed to allow our replacements to wear civilian clothes in the booth, but only in the booth. The poor bastards had to come to the Facility in uniform, change into civilian clothes for interrogations, and then change right back when their booth time was up. Once the transition was over, it would be all uniforms all the time.

Heaney and I had arranged lectures on Afghan tribal structures and Arab ethnicities to help the newcomers get up to speed. We also set up a system where groups of new arrivals shadowed veterans as they went about their daily duties. But Heaney and I both knew that none of this was a substitute for real booth experience, so we hatched a plan to make that happen, too — by recruiting some of our existing detainees to do a little role-playing.

We went through the list of the ninety or so prisoners in custody and picked the eight who were the most cooperative. Seven were Afghans scheduled for repatriation within days. The other was an Arab — a low-level fighter — bound for Cuba. We gathered them in Heaney's screening room early one morning and explained that there were new U.S. intelligence personnel at the Facility, and that we wanted them to help show the newcomers how to deal with prisoners in an "effective and humanitarian" manner.

"We want you to pretend you are here for the first time," Heaney said, "so we can give the new guys an opportunity to practice on you."

The wide-eyed looks on these prisoners' faces said it all. Some were confused by the idea — or at least how it came across in translation — and feared they were going to be sent to a new prison. A few fretted that this would nullify all the interrogations we had already conducted with them and jeopardize their imminent release. Others, probably the most sensible of the bunch, just thought it was a harebrained scheme and asked over and over, "Why would you do this to me?" After half an hour of discussion, four wanted to go back to the cages, but four agreed to help us with our plan. The instructors at Huachuca would have been horrified: here we were in the middle of a war getting real prisoners to pretend to be role-players.

Early the next day I woke up Sgt. Paul Hedder, my replacement, and told him new prisoners had arrived. He gathered up his troops and rushed to the Facility, where a handful of my guys were already standing around (aware of the ruse). There were a few clues that this wasn't a real in-processing. We had to have one of the MPs play the doctor because we didn't think it was right to drag a real physician over for this stunt. And the fact that we assigned these detainees existing prisoner numbers — lower than new arrivals truly would have warranted — had a couple of the new interrogators scratching their heads. But I just explained this inconsistency away by saying it was yet another prisoner-processing glitch.

The interrogators asked clunky questions that reminded me of our ineptitude at Kandahar, and they burned through those questions in just a few hours, leaving them to stare at the prisoners for long stretches trying to think of something to say.

The replacements hadn't anticipated what a toll this would take on our already overworked translators, who protested and peeled off as the futile exercise wore on. Some of the prisoners, confused by the sudden change in treatment, demanded to speak with their original interrogators. After twenty-four hours (although with no one prisoner in the booth for more than three hours or so), the replacement interrogators emerged exhausted, having collected scant new information, but pleased with themselves for having stayed up the whole time.

The morning of that long-awaited changeover, I began the meeting as I always did, recapping some statistics and taking care of housekeeping. I announced that the remainder of the morning meeting would be handled by Hedder and invited him to come up to the front of the room. I told the outgoing interrogators what a pleasure it was to serve with such great, honorable soldiers. I advised the incoming interrogators to have patience and remember their training, in particular the Conventions. "Above all, remember this: no man can do much wrong if he remembers — always and everywhere — to put New England first!"

There was a nervous, polite cheer from the members of my reserve unit, who immediately recognized the motto. The active-duty guys didn't know what to make of what I said. Hedder came up and replaced me without much ado.

There was a great effort at packing all of Task Force 500's equipment into containers that had to be checked by military customs people. This was hard work, and I was surprised when Hasegawa and Kampf didn't show up for duty one morning. I went to the first sergeant and asked if she had seen them. "Sergeant Mackey, they've decided to stay on," she told me. Those two interrogators and Rodriguez had volunteered to stick around for a few more weeks to coach the newcomers. I was shocked and tried to persuade them to reconsider, but they were adamant that they should stay. I felt bad that they were making this sacrifice while I was headed home. The guilt increased as the days wore on and our departure drew nearer.

When we weren't packing, most of us were trying to make ourselves available for whatever the replacements might need from us. Fitzgerald, on the other hand, could be found smoking cigars and wrapping up his Toynbee reading or playing cards with the interpreters. When one of the new arrivals, McGovern, asked Fitzgerald about a report he had written on some prisoner back in June, Fitzgerald replied, "Sorry, Sean. I'm deleting all the mental files I've created since December, and I'm already up to July."

Our departure was delayed several times. Finally, in a terrible windstorm, we wandered out to the edge of the airfield, blasted by the tiny specs of sand. We were there for five hours before it was clear which plane was going to take us to Germany and then home. While we waited, huddled in some flapping tents, I watched the MPs drive slowly up to the runway in a caravan. Another plane had landed a few minutes earlier and waited there with its cargo door up, lowering it only when the MPs were in position. It was hard to see what was going on — the MPs were clustered around the hatch and their vehicles obscured most of the scene unfolding just two hundred yards in the distance. But of course we were accustomed to the drill and knew what was happening. For those guys coming off the plane in chains, the war was over. And it was over for me, too.

EPILOGUE

In the middle of June, as yet another batch of prisoners was being herded into the reception area downstairs, Major Vaughn from the fusion cell pulled me aside to tell me that he thought I was driving the interrogators too hard. We were working too many hours and it was beginning to take a toll on the echoes, he said. I nodded deferentially and said something about how I valued his opinion but respectfully disagreed. Why should we interrogators cut back on our workload? We were just questioning prisoners in the safety of an old Soviet hangar. We didn't need to be particularly well rested. We weren't the infantry, and we were a long way from the front.

"Sergeant Mackey," he said, "you *are* the new infantry, and this is the new front."

It's been nearly two years since I left Afghanistan, and though the war is long over for me, it doesn't look as if it will end anytime soon for the United States and the interrogators who continue to serve in the military and the civilian agencies. I didn't realize it at the time, but that dusty assemblage of tents and concertina wire that greeted us at Kandahar was just the first installation in what would become a network of U.S. prison facilities around the world. Kandahar gave way to Bagram, which operates still as part of an archipelago of facilities that includes the increasingly permanent structures at Guantánamo Bay, vast prison compounds in Iraq, and secret lockdowns where the CIA has held senior members of Al Qaeda. As this book went to press, the United States was said to be holding as many as ten thousand people at these facilities, and the scandal at Abu Ghraib, the notorious prison on the outskirts of Baghdad, was still growing.

The truth is, concern about what was happening inside this network of U.S. prisons had been growing for some time.

Over the past year, dozens of prisoners have been released from Guantánamo Bay — mostly Afghans, although there have also been Pakistanis, Brits, and others. Many have been interviewed by human rights organizations and the press and have been asked to describe the conditions of their detention. I recognize some of the names I have seen in the papers and remember their faces and their stories. Some have made allegations that they were tortured and beaten, others have had surprisingly positive things to say about their time in captivity, but most have offered accounts that fall somewhere in between.

Amnesty International interviewed a number of Afghans released from American custody and included some of their accounts in an August 2003 report that criticized the United States for its treatment of prisoners. "Abdullah" told his Amnesty interviewers that he was taken into custody in March 2002 and that upon his arrival at Kandahar he and others were ordered to the ground, kicked in the ribs, and searched by dogs. "Alif Khan" told Amnesty that during his detention at Bagram and Kandahar he was "subjected to sleep deprivation, denied water for prayer and ablution," and forced to undergo "intimate" body searches every day. "Sayed Abassin," described by Amnesty as a twenty-eight-year-old Afghan taxi driver, was stopped at a checkpoint in April 2002 and taken to Bagram. There, he says, he was handcuffed and shackled for the first week, "kept in twenty-four-hour lighting and woken by guards when trying to sleep," and forced to stand or kneel for hours on end. He was then transferred to Kandahar, where, he said, detainees were placed in stress positions if they so much as looked at a soldier's face.

When I read such accounts, I have a mixed reaction. There are almost always kernels of truth in what they say. Prisoners were strip-searched, though not every day. They certainly were "kept in twenty-four-hour lighting," not because they were being bombarded with light in some high-tech interrogation chamber but because the cages on the ground floor at Bagram were kept lit around the clock. And there is no doubt that prisoners were stripped and doused with water — for their baths.

The more extreme claims strike me as exaggeration, if not as patently untrue. We dealt with the enemy justly and humanely. We practiced methods of interrogation that were long on trickery and deceit, but we never touched anyone. The MPs could not do their jobs without touching prisoners — as guards, they escorted prisoners to and from the cages, clothed them, bathed them, fed them, and put them in and out of their shackles. We relied on guards to help prepare prisoners for interrogation by doing such things as assigning them menial chores, putting them in isolation, or mixing up their meal schedules. We never directed or encouraged MPs to abuse prisoners, and we would not have tolerated such treatment if it had occurred. But I realize that mine is not the most impartial position from which to comment and that, unfortunately, the credibility of such protests has been undercut by the serious cases of abuse that have come to light.

The first disturbing report came in March 2003, when the *New York Times* reported that two prisoners had died in custody at Bagram in December 2002. Mullah Habibullah, approximately thirty years old, died on December 3. And a twenty-two-year-old Afghan taxi driver named Dilawar died exactly one week later, on December 10. American autopsy reports found "blunt force injuries" in both cases and deemed both deaths "homicides." These deaths happened well after I had left. In private, interrogators who were there at the time have told me the cases involved MPs, but I don't know for sure. The military has been investigating the matter for well over a year now but to date has brought no charges against anyone involved and has provided no information on what its investigation uncovered.

The war in Iraq has been marred by numerous stories of abuse. In December 2003 an officer with the Fourth Infantry Division, Lt. Col. Allen B. West, was fined and forced to retire after he fired his pistol near a prisoner's head to scare the detainee and get him to talk. In January 2004 three MPs were discharged from the army after beating and kicking prisoners at Camp Bucca, a detention camp in southern Iraq. In February the International Committee of the Red Cross submitted a scathing report to the command in Iraq, documenting widespread abuses. It said physical and psychological coercion "appeared to be part of the standard operating procedures" and provided a litany of alleged abuses during interrogation, such as "beatings with hard objects (including pistols and rifles)" and prisoners having their faces pressed into the ground with boots, being stripped naked for days, being forced to wear women's underwear over their faces and being photographed by the guards, and being forced to remain in stress positions for long periods.

Then, in May 2004, the world was shown photographic evidence of the sadistic abuses at Abu Ghraib — pictures of prisoners being sexually humiliated, stacked up in pyramids of naked flesh. One iconographic image was that of a hooded prisoner being forced to stand on a cardboard box with wires attached to his hands. An MP trying to keep him awake apparently told the prisoner that if he fell from the box, he would be electrocuted. Despite the MPs' claims that they were doing the bidding of interrogators who wanted guards to help soften up prisoners for questioning, there was evidence that these abuses had little to do with interrogation. Some of the MPs themselves testified in military court hearings that the prisoners subjected to abuse that night were brought into the cellblock after being involved in a fight or riot in one of the main outdoor cages. The cruel treatment meted out by the MPs was their version of punishment. At least two of the prisoners identified in the photographs were also subsequently interviewed by the media in Iraq and said that they were never even questioned at Abu Ghraib.

In his investigation of the abuses, U.S. Army Maj. Gen. Antonio Taguba found no evidence, "written or otherwise," that the MPs had been ordered by interrogators to engage in such acts. At the time this book went to print, no interrogators had been charged in connection with the torture at Abu Ghraib or the earlier abuses involving Lieutenant Colonel West or the MPs at Camp Bucca. But that is meager consolation, and Taguba's report singled out two interrogators for serious criticism. One was a young female echo who was put on administrative duty after she sought to humiliate an uncooperative detainee by having him strip naked and walk back to his cell in front of other prisoners. The other was a civilian contractor interrogator (I had never heard of such a thing) who was accused in the Taguba report of directing MPs to assist in "setting conditions" for questioning. "He clearly knew his instructions equated to physical abuse," the report said. As the book went to print, a follow-up investigation of the conduct of military intelligence troops and officers at U.S.-run prisons overseas was just getting under way.

To me, one of the most interesting documents to surface amid the Abu Ghraib investigations is a one-page sheet outlining the "interrogation rules of engagement" in effect at the prison at the time of the abuses. On the left side of the page is a list of the standard sixteen interrogation approaches that echoes were free to use in questioning prisoners. On the right side of the page is a list of nine additional techniques that required prior approval from the commanding officer. When I saw it, I was stunned. It allowed for the use of military dogs in the booth, allowed prisoners to be put on sleep deprivation for up to seventy-two hours, allowed sensory deprivation (which, as I understand it, meant keeping prisoners hooded) for an equal period, and authorized the use of stress positions for as long as forty-five minutes at a time. Each of these methods went well beyond anything we allowed at Bagram, where we were not technically bound by the Geneva Conventions (because of the Bush administration's ruling that our prisoners were "unlawful combatants") but understood from the beginning that were to behave as if we were. We had agonized over how far we could go, constructing elaborate rules and rationales and coming up with the most menacing name we could think of — monstering — for a sleep-deprivation technique that looks meek by comparison to the methods interrogators were authorized to use in Iraq. In Afghanistan we had been left largely on our own to sort out the ethical boundaries of our job. But in Iraq harsh methods were approved at the highest levels, by Lt. Gen. Ricardo Sanchez and other senior officers. It made all of our hand-wringing seem either silly or, in retrospect, unintentionally enlightened.

The rules of engagement at Abu Ghraib may have had nothing to do with the sadistic behavior that took place in the high-security cellblock known as Tier 1A. But both represented the gravitational laws that govern human behavior when one group of people is given complete control over another in a prison. Every impulse tugs downward. We had seen it in our unit in Afghanistan. The prohibition on the use of stress positions early in the war gave way to policies allowing their use to punish prisoners for disrespectful behavior. The rules were relaxed further by those who followed us at Bagram, and within a year stress positions were a formally authorized interrogation technique by the command in Iraq. Rules regarding sleep deprivation, isolation, meal manipulation, and sensory deprivation followed similar trajectories.

I'm not sure that we struck the right balance at Bagram or that the rules of engagement at Abu Ghraib were unreasonable. The question of how far to go doesn't have an easy answer, and in the wake of September 11, the calculation is more complicated. The price for erring too far in either direction may be paid in blood. We saw firsthand in Afghanistan how ineffective schoolhouse methods were in getting prisoners to talk. We failed to break prisoners who I have no doubt knew of terrorist plots or at least of terrorist cells that may one day do us harm. Perhaps they would have talked if faced with harsher interrogation methods. On the other hand, one of the most profound tragedies of Abu Ghraib is that the images of depravity will inflame anti-American sentiment in the Muslim world for a generation, driving who knows how many would-be jihadists into the ranks of Al Qaeda and other terrorist organizations. In the middle of the scandal, the U.S. military revised its rules of engagement for Iraq, banning most of the harsher techniques, including sleep deprivation, the use of dogs, and the practice of keeping detainees in hoods for days on end. The only option remaining was extended isolation. But in the wake of Abu Ghraib, even if the United States commits itself to the highest ethical standards in its treatment of prisoners, the questions are *How long will it last?* and *Who would believe it?*

In the last days of our deployment I wrote letters to the mothers and fathers of the interrogators serving under me. In each letter I tried to capture a moment of their son's or daughter's experience and achievements. While I wrote, I thought of the parents of these soldiers I'd spent a war with, those who had raised children who grew up to become interrogators. People regard ours as a ghoulish profession — so much so that when civilians ask what they do, most echoes simply say, "I'm an interpreter," to make it easier. (Indeed, the army stopped calling us "interrogators" several years ago, changing the name to "human intelligence collectors," to the ire of traditionalists like me.) Before we left Afghanistan, there were already criticisms of the detention of Al Qaeda and Taliban prisoners and questions about the methods we were applying to interrogate them. It occurred to me that some parents might like to be reassured that their children had not taken part in anything sinister. I was tempted to address it outright but decided not to. They knew their kids.

Hasegawa and Kampf served in Afghanistan for two more debilitating months. I saw them briefly at Fort Bragg, not long before my unit made its way back to Connecticut. They took some time off and no doubt recovered their accustomed energy, but the extension of their tour had all but done them in. Hasegawa was considering getting out of the service and seemed to be committed to that path when quite suddenly he reversed course, announced his intention to re-up, and headed back to DLI for a year to study Japanese.

Kampf had made some connections with Task Force 11's Steve while he was in Afghanistan. The young Texan with the near-perfect Saudi accent had so impressed Steve that they decided to make the relationship legal. Kampf transferred into that elite unit and served with them in combat operations in Iraq.

Davis and Pearson were members of the Third Infantry Division. We parted company with them at Fort Gordon's airfield. Pearson was beside herself with the chance to see her kid. I said good-bye and thanked her. She wasn't showy and wasn't a varsity player in the same league as Hasegawa or Kampf, but she was tireless and reliable. She later went to Fort Irwin, in California, where she put all those talents to use in helping to train other troops. Her job was to portray captured enemy soldiers so that intelligence troops rotating through Fort Irwin could practice their interrogation skills.

Davis had a tough trip home. We were delayed in Germany

on the way back and he spent a good deal of time in the old town of Frankfurt getting to know the local beers (as we had all done). He was hungover on the flight back and got off the plane in the damp of dawn in Georgia with one thing in mind: more sleep. The result was that I never really got to pass on a final thank-you for his contributions. I thought the mute Cape Codder could find work at the OGA — his Arabic and obvious commitment to keeping everything hush-hush would probably conspire to open up whatever doors he encountered. In fact, he still had a fight ahead of him — he deployed to Iraq with the Third Division. He is now applying his skills for civilian agencies.

Heaney, our master screener, also found himself in Iraq. He was injured in a noncombat accident while away and ended up getting back to the States on a medical discharge. He moved to the Midwest with his new wife and is now applying his IT skills more than his questioning techniques.

Anne-Marie Walker was reunited with her fiancé, Harper, and the two married shortly after we redeployed. Their unique circumstances, on account of their similar lines of work for the same employer, mean that they will probably sacrifice a lot and be separated often for the sake of the service. Walker always wanted to be a schoolteacher, but after she returned from duty in Iraq, she was considering continuing her interrogator career with civilian agencies or private contractors. As far as I know, Harper is still assigned to the 202nd MI Battalion.

Turner approached me toward the end of our tour in Bagram. We had walked to Viper City from the Facility and were parting company to make our way back to our respective tents. He suddenly announced that he wanted to become an officer in the unit when we got back to Connecticut. I looked at him as if he were insane and laid into him about his capacity to lead men when he himself had performed so marginally in Afghanistan. He seemed taken aback by this, no doubt because he had found so many good and practical outlets for the talents he did have, and he had been rightly praised for these. But there was no escaping his shortcomings, and I wasn't about to lie to him about them. I hope I evaluated prisoners more effectively than I did my own men. Turner also served in Iraq and was awarded the Bronze Star.

When my reserve unit returned from Iraq, it was once more without Rodriguez, who volunteered to stick around yet again. Rodriguez was one of several members of my Connecticut reserve unit who spent months working at Abu Ghraib. One young analyst, Sgt. David Travis Friedrich, twenty-six, was killed in a mortar attack at the prison in September 2003. Many members of the unit had left Abu Ghraib by the time the abuses occurred, but Rodriguez was there, and his voice appears in the transcript of the investigative hearings into the matter. He describes himself as the "old operations expert" in the prison whom young interrogators would come to for advice. In his testimony, he says he knew nothing of the abuses until investigators converged on the facility months later. He insists that interrogators were repeatedly reminded of their obligation to adhere to the Geneva Conventions and that they knew right from wrong. "Detainees being piled in a pyramid naked, or being forced to masturbate, has no MI or military purpose," Rodriguez says at one point in his testimony. "All of these acts would be criminal offenses. If I were ordered to do these acts, I would not carry them out. Embarrassment as a technique would be contradictory to achieving results."

Documents surrounding the case also contain the words of some of the accused MPs. They talk of staging contests to see how quickly a prisoner could be brought to tears or made to urinate on himself. The MP who placed the prisoner on the cardboard box and attached wires to his hands says at one point that she did it just to mess with his mind. There is no intelligence-gathering pretense, no claim to have been acting on orders from MI. And yet the MPs do cite words of vague encouragement from interrogators. They say they were given such instructions as "Loosen this guy up for us" or "Make sure he has a bad night." They claim they were complimented on their handling of prisoners and were told such things as "Good job. They're breaking down real fast."

I don't believe for a moment that our embrace of "monstering" in any way presaged the behavior by those MPs at Abu Ghraib. Those soldiers truly were monsters. But the comments they claim to have heard from interrogators ring true to me and reflect a hardening of attitudes that is not difficult to trace. By the time we left Afghanistan, we had come to embrace methods we would not have countenanced at the beginning of the war. And while those who followed us at Bagram dismissed much of the so-called wisdom we sought to pass on, they took to monstering with alacrity. Indeed, as we left, it was clear they did not regard this as a method of last resort but as a primary option in the interrogation playbook. What was an ending point for us was a starting point for them. And during their stint in Afghanistan, they undoubtedly added their own plays, many of which were probably exported to Iraq. As the battle against Al Qaeda shifted to a battle against Saddam Hussein and the Iraqi insurgency, pressure to adopt more aggressive methods must have only intensified, and the trend line we established was reinforced.

Perhaps the only positive aspect of the Abu Ghraib scandal is that it has prompted a serious probe of America's network of overseas prisons and a public examination of the methods U.S. interrogators use to get prisoners to talk. It's a debate America needs to have, given the work that will be required to win the war in Iraq and the war on terrorism. The public's view of what is right and wrong is not fixed in place; rather, it swings back and forth over time like a pendulum. What the nation would have sanctioned in the immediate aftermath of September 11, when the appetite for revenge was palpable, is undoubtedly more than it would tolerate now, particularly in the aftermath of Abu Ghraib. Interrogation policies shouldn't reflect either extreme.

In all of the soul-searching over the scandal and the effort to understand what interrogators do, there has been a familiar refrain — the adage that harsh treatment of prisoners only produces bad intelligence, that a tortured prisoner will say anything to stop the pain. That line has been recited for years by schoolhouse instructors and has gained new currency among those rightly condemning the abuses at Abu Ghraib. I know many experienced and fine interrogators who believe that tenet of interrogation doctrine wholeheartedly. But I don't find it particularly persuasive. If a prisoner will say anything to stop the pain, my guess is he will start with the truth. Our experience in Afghanistan showed that the harsher the methods we used — though they never contravened the Conventions, let alone crossed over into torture — the better the information we got and the sooner we got it. Other agencies seem to have learned the same lesson. In its interrogation of high-ranking Al Qaeda figures, the CIA has obtained secret legal rulings from the Justice Department to use certain coercive methods, including one called water-boarding in which a prisoner is strapped to a board and submerged in water until he is sure he will drown. If coercion doesn't work, why would the agency go to the trouble?

The reason the United States should not torture prisoners is not because it doesn't work. It is simply because it is wrong. It dehumanizes us, undermines our cause, and, over the long term, breeds more enemies of the United States than coercive interrogation methods will ever allow us to capture.

How the scandals over prisoner treatment will change the way American interrogators work is not yet clear. But one thing is certain: the work of the interrogators is not done. Fitzgerald came to Florida around Easter of 2003. I was back from Europe to visit my parents who winter there, and Fitzgerald's presence meant there'd be a chance to get out and have a few beers. We didn't talk much about our time in Afghanistan. Fitzgerald had clearly "downloaded and deleted" all those files. And my term with the army reserves was about to expire. While sitting at a bar not far from the sea, he turned to me and said, "I don't think the army's done with us yet" — the same damn thing he'd said in London before we got called up. So far, he's been wrong.

When I think of my time away, it seems like a distant childhood memory. It was very cold. That I remember. Then it was very hot. I remember that, too. Only my journal allows me any clarity, the spark to key in on certain events and certain people on both sides of the interrogation table. My war wasn't one of death-defying feats in the face of the enemy, but I came to know that face nevertheless.

APPENDIX: INTERROGATING APPROACHES

1. Direct Approach. In our schoolhouse training, if we didn't ask a pertinent question first (before trying to orchestrate an approach), we were immediately knocked down on our evaluations. The direct approach, we were told, would work on more than 95 percent of all POWs — the rest would require something more elaborate. But that statistic was based on forecasts for Soviet Russian soldiers and those impressed into their service from satellite states. To our surprise, the ratio was completely reversed when fighting Al Qaeda in Afghanistan.

2. Love of Comrades. If an enemy prisoner can be convinced that providing information to his captors means a better chance for his fellow soldiers to survive, an interrogator will run Love of Comrades. Sometimes this is supposed to be localized, for instance, "The wounded taken prisoner with you are in the camp hospital; would you like to see them?" Other times it calls for a different application: "If you help us understand where your unit's defensive positions are, we can surround them and offer terms — otherwise, we must carpet bomb the entire area." Because prisoners we encountered were not from any organized unit per se, this approach

was not easy to manipulate into something practical for our situation.

3. Hate of Comrades. The textbook example of a Hate of Comrades approach is when a prisoner has been abandoned — or can be convinced that he was abandoned — during the action in which he was captured. But any prisoner who perceives real or imagined neglect, prejudice ("They left you behind because you're a Ukrainian, you know"), or betrayal is ripe for this approach.

4. Love of Family. A tip-off — say, a photograph of a loved one in a wallet or a love letter in a confiscated knapsack — can be a clue that a sense of distance, loneliness, and the uncertainty of the future is already at work on the interrogator's side. Preying on this, and persuasively converting it into a reason to talk, is the challenge.

5. Establish Your Identity. This technique is popular with some student interrogators because it's confrontational and dramatic. The interrogator dreams up a set of circumstances and challenges the prisoner to refute the charges. A downed enemy pilot who, in a vain attempt to evade capture, donned civilian clothes could be accused of being a spy. "And spies, as you know, are shot." Since all our opponents in Afghanistan were nonuniformed irregulars, this approach had many variants and possibilities.

6. Silent. This approach — to my knowledge, only ever practiced in the schoolhouse — calls for the interrogator to simply stare at the prisoner in an attempt to unnerve him into submission. It usually devolves into the interrogator's breaking out into fits of uncontrollable laughter.

7. Mutt & Jeff (Good Cop, Bad Cop). Classic technique whereby one interrogator plays the irate tough guy and his partner moves in as a sympathetic soul there to "help." We got a surprising amount of mileage out of this method by getting quite sophisticated with the roles and cover stories.

8. We Know All. There's a limited scope to this approach, which demands a large reservoir of knowledge beforehand. Inspired by the impressive record of achievement amassed by Hans Scharff, the Luftwaffe's master interrogator in World War II, we used this tack with surprising effectiveness once the team was sufficiently familiar with the training, personalities, and organization of our enemies.

9. Rapid Fire. Another method limited largely to Huachuca classrooms, the Rapid Fire approach calls for an interrogator to belt out questions with such speed and disregard for interrupting the prisoner that a pertinent question slipped in at an opportune moment of confusion may elicit a valuable answer. If the principle isn't dubious enough, it also requires a tremendous effort to assemble enough questions to last the duration of the interrogation.

10. Befuddled Interrogator. An arrogant enemy officer with illusions of superiority is the target of this ruse, whereby the interrogator feigns complete incompetence in hopes of learning something valuable from a prisoner who either thinks there is no harm in telling a buffoon something he will never understand or, alternatively, attempts to impress the interrogator with tales of dupe and daring. On the surface a rather suspect approach, when modified so that the enemy is confronted by a youngish, "naive" female interrogator, the opportunity to boast is not infrequently taken.

11. Pride and Ego Up. Schoolhouse scripts call for this approach to be leveraged when a prisoner is devastated by the feelings of failure that sometimes attend a battlefield capture. High praise for a well-fought fight, or acknowledgment of the universality or inevitability of those feelings, can sometimes generate a sense of fellowship or gratitude on the part of a prisoner, which can be exploited to the interrogator's ends.

12. Pride and Ego Down. Again something to be plied against a haughty or proud prisoner, Pride and Ego Down attacks a prisoner's sense of positive self-image. A difficult approach to convert into a "break," Pride and Ego Down is nevertheless an often used — or really, misused — tactic, since taking someone down a peg seems to come so naturally when you're in a position of authority. Oftentimes it aggravates the contentiousness of the moment to no purpose.

13. Fear Up. Hands down, the most popular approach, not to say the most useful. Cop shows and war movies glamorize this "straight down the middle" method. But loud, accusatory, and pounding-fist-on-table sessions are difficult to back away from if you need to do so later in your interaction with a prisoner. And very few interrogators have the experience and skill to convert such a dramatic confrontation into a plausible reason for the prisoner to start talking. Junior interrogators frequently resort to a Fear Up approach out of desperation when confronted by a Sergeant Rock–type opponent. My experience has shown that those cases require more finesse, while prisoners who arrive in custody in a state of terror can sometimes have their fears exacerbated, getting them to a state of high anxiety. Occasionally this state is a positive one for persuading someone to give up the goods.

14. Fear Down. A cigarette, a can of Coke, or a kind word can sometimes work to allay fears. When appropriate, helping a prisoner regain his composure can cast the interrogator in a compassionate light — sometimes with the effect that a prisoner feels compelled to reciprocate with assistance for the source of the compassion, or at least be convinced that his would-be opponents aren't that bad after all. I always found it a challenge to run this approach and harder still to turn it into grounds for cooperation. Not surpris-

ingly, female interrogators were excellent with Fear Down approaches and used it to remarkable effect.

15. Futility. This approach and the next one, Incentive, are the basic building blocks of all interrogations. Futility calls for the interrogator to persuasively argue that the prisoner is without options and without hope. His cause is lost. His comrades are doomed. His only chance is to survive, and looking after his own self-interest is paramount. Run properly, carefully, and with sophisitcation, Futility is almost always a winner. By the time we left Afghanistan, we could run a Futility approach on another soldier ahead of us in a chow line and then move ahead to take his place when he ran off to commit suicide.

16. Incentive. None of these approaches works in isolation except the direct approach. I constantly reminded interrogators of the imperativeness of a good incentive — a hook — to seal the deal for cooperation. Establish Your Identity? Useless with out offering the way out of being an accused spy or rapist. Hate of Comrades? Going nowhere without suggesting the means of revenge. Even the silent approach has to be converted — incentive to end the maddening quietude and penetrating stare — before anything of value can be collected.

ACKNOWLEDGMENTS

The authors wish to honor the soldiers and marines who served with Task Force 500. This story could not have been told without the generous cooperation of: Geoff Fitzgerald; Henry Ritso Hasegawa; Gary Heaney; Ben Davis; Ethan Kampf; Chief Rodriguez, BSM, PH; and those who made major contributions.

The authors are also deeply grateful to the experts and academics who provided valuable insights, shared the benefits of their years of research, and account for the historical material woven into this story. Special thanks to: Lt. Col. Michael Bigelow, executive officer, U.S. Army Center of Military History at Fort McNair in Washington, D.C.; Conrad McCormick, the volunteer archivist at the U.S. Army Intelligence Museum at Fort Huachuca, Arizona; Brian McAllister Linn, director of the Military Studies Institute at Texas A&M University; Peter Maslowski, professor, Department of History, University of Nebraska at Lincoln; Frank Russell, assistant professor, Department of History, Transylvania University, Lexington, Kentucky; Col. Rose Mary Sheldon, professor of history, Virginia Military Institute, Lexington, Virginia; Carol Kerr, public affairs, U.S. Army War College, Carlisle, Pennsylvania.

ABOUT THE AUTHORS

Chris Mackey joined the army at seventeen and was assigned to the intelligence corps as an interrogator. After 9/11, he was recalled to the United States, assigned to Task Force 500, and subsequently sent to Kandahar, Afghanistan. He ultimately supervised all military interrogations conducted at the theater-wide detention facility at Bagram Airfield.

Greg Miller is a national security correspondent for the *Los Angeles Times* in the paper's Washington, D.C., bureau. He was the only American reporter granted access to U.S. interrogators and document exploitation teams.